Destroyers, Greyhounds of the Fleet

Destroyers, Greyhounds of the Fleet

Memoirs of a Naval Gunner in the Second World War

Peter Saxton

Pen & Sword
MARITIME

First published in Great Britain in 2025 by
Pen & Sword Maritime
An imprint of Pen & Sword Books Limited
Yorkshire – Philadelphia

Copyright © Peter Saxton 2025

ISBN 978 1 03611 229 5

The right of Peter Saxton to be identified as
Author of this Work has been asserted by him in accordance
with the Copyright, Designs and Patents Act 1988.

A CIP catalogue record for this book is
available from the British Library.

All rights reserved. No part of this book may be reproduced or
transmitted in any form or by any means, electronic or mechanical
including photocopying, recording or by any information storage and
retrieval system, without permission from the Publisher in writing.

Typeset by Mac Style
Printed in the UK by CPI Group (UK) Ltd, Croydon, CR0 4YY.

Pen & Sword Books Limited incorporates the imprints of After
the Battle, Atlas, Archaeology, Aviation, Discovery, Family History,
Fiction, History, Maritime, Military, Military Classics, Politics,
Select, Transport, True Crime, Air World, Frontline Publishing, Leo
Cooper, Remember When, Seaforth Publishing, The Praetorian Press,
Wharncliffe Local History, Wharncliffe Transport, Wharncliffe True
Crime and White Owl.

For a complete list of Pen & Sword titles please contact

PEN & SWORD BOOKS LIMITED
47 Church Street, Barnsley, South Yorkshire, S70 2AS, England
E-mail: enquiries@pen-and-sword.co.uk
Website: www.pen-and-sword.co.uk
or
PEN AND SWORD BOOKS
1950 Lawrence Road, Havertown, PA 19083, USA
E-mail: uspen-and-sword@casematepublishers.com
Website: www.penandswordbooks.com

To the Ship's Company of HMS *Hambledon*, all of whom came home, and in memory of David Saxton, George Kenchington and Fred Silver, who died at sea,

'If blood be the price of Admiralty,
Lord God we ha' paid in full.'

Kipling

Contents

Foreword		viii
Foreword by Vice-Admiral Sir Adrian Johns		x
Preface		xii
Chapter 1	Admiralty	1
Chapter 2	HMS *Collingwood*	6
Chapter 3	HMS *Pembroke*	19
Chapter 4	HMS *Excellent*	27
Chapter 5	Hunt Class Destroyers	34
Chapter 6	Commissioning	41
Chapter 7	Scapa Flow	49
Chapter 8	East Coast Convoys	62
Chapter 9	North Sea	76
Chapter 10	Salmon and Gluckstein	88
Chapter 11	Life Onboard	97
Chapter 12	Accolades and Bottles	110
Chapter 13	Invasion of Sicily	120
Chapter 14	Surrender of the Italian Fleet	135
Chapter 15	SALERNO: A Near Disaster	146
Chapter 16	A Lull Between Landings	158
Chapter 17	ANZIO: A Stranded Whale	169
Chapter 18	An Eye for a Tooth	177
Chapter 19	Hambledonians Afloat	186
Chapter 20	Normandy	191

Foreword

Six months after being demobilised in 1946, I began to write my war memoirs. After filling two, large exercise books, I had not progressed beyond my initial training! My problem was that the events I was portraying were too fresh in my mind. I had almost total recall and could not see the wood for the trees. Eventually I abandoned the project and, twenty years later, the exercise books were consigned to the coke-fired domestic boiler.

Throughout the following twenty years the urge to record my wartime experiences never abated; indeed, it became almost imperative that I get it out of my system. Now, after over forty years, my original, almost-total recall has deteriorated to the point where my failing memory has become its own editor. It has discarded the irrelevancies and retained only those incidents worth remembering and recording. Another aspect is that, had my first attempt borne fruit, I would have been describing the contemporary scene, whereas now I am writing about historical events. I should be very surprised if there are any wartime-serving personnel left in today's navy.

I am also very aware that, by virtue of far-reaching advances in technology, especially with regard to ship armaments, the navy in which I served no longer exists. Steam propulsion has gone and gunnery (the premier profession in my day) has been toppled and has had to give pride of place to more sophisticated weapons. Doubtless, today's Royal Navy sailor would view the last war's men-o'-war as being as antiquated as we saw the First World War's coal-fired dreadnoughts to be. Only one commodity remains unaltered; that is the quality of today's serving sailor – the descendants of Raleigh, Drake and Nelson. I trust, therefore, that they will forgive me where I have lapsed into the 'historical present'.

During our initial training we were told that diary-keeping in wartime was forbidden. Initially I obeyed the rule, until the temptation to keep one became too great to resist. That was when we went to the Mediterranean in 1943, and I knew I would be present where history was being made. The record I kept was quite brief. It was merely a recording of our movements and other ships involved with us. Daily entries amounted to not more than a couple of sentences, largely because I was too busy to enjoy the luxury of leisurely penmanship. But brief as these were, they have served as memory-rousers and have given the narrative a chronology it would not have had without them.

Bearing upon that, I confess that I am an inveterate reader of war memoirs – particularly naval ones. Any visit to a library, for whatever purpose, sees me drawn almost irresistibly to the war section. The result is that, over the years, I have read innumerable books about the Royal Navy in both world wars, mostly written by naval officers. With few exceptions, it has been plain that the authors had kept diaries, so, unless the prohibition against diary-keeping was only operative on the lower deck but not in the wardroom, in breaking the rule I have obviously been in excellent company.

Addingham
August 1989

Foreword

By Vice-Admiral Sir Adrian Johns

The term destroyer first appeared in the late 19th century. There was an emerging need to develop a counter to small, fast torpedo armed boats that were becoming an increasing threat at sea. So-called torpedo boat catchers soon became known as torpedo boat destroyers and, by WW1, had become simply destroyers. They were fast, unarmoured vessels, maids of all work and greyhounds of the fleet.

By the late 1930s, the Royal Navy was crucially short of small ships and a building programme was put in hand. Out of this arose the Hunt Clas destroyer. It was a new class, based on an escort sloop design and is comprehensively described later in the book. There had been a small window of opportunity to start the build in the 1938, but in fact the first keel was not laid down until the following year. As war was looming, the hard-pressed Admiralty design team was having to cope with many urgent demands and the first Hunts came off the production line with some serious design defects. Most notably, excessive top-weight necessitated removal of one of the 4-inch guns and the insertion of some 50 tons of extra ballast. In addition, it was realised that these ships were too narrow in the beam, a shortcoming which was rectified as the build programme continued.

HMS *Hambledon* was one of these early, imperfect builds, the so-called Type 1 Hunt, and this was the ship to which Ordinary Seaman Fred Saxton found himself drafted as a 19-year-old gunner in May of 1941. This was the ship that would become his home and life for the next 3 years and 2 months, in fact, his entire war afloat. These memoirs tell the story of Fred's war. From Scapa to Salerno, from the North Sea to Normandy, it is a wonderful glimpse of life in the navy and the war at sea from the lower deck of a wartime destroyer. The trials and tribulations of simply living in a small ship, and the hardship and the horrors of the war at sea are all vividly described. Fred's adventures take him from the bone-wearying screening of the east coast convoys to the landings in the Mediterranean and to D-Day itself. Most unlikely of all, he found himself a witness to history in the surrender of the Italian fleet in the presence of Cunningham and Eisenhower.

Life onboard *Hambledon* was always hard and often dangerous. The ship would have been lively in any sort of seaway and was often wet as well. Fred describes being on the upper deck manning his gun for 18 hours at a stetch, chilled to the bone and wet through. The men often didn't bother slinging their hammocks but just turned in where they could on deck, either in the messdeck or at their upper deck action station. Without any form of armour protection, the ship was inherently vulnerable, and the seamen had to live with the less-than-comforting thought that immediately below their messdecks were the magazines and fuel tanks.

But, of course, what this actually engendered was a unique sense of camaraderie, humour, teamwork and pride. Destroyer crews have always considered themselves a cut above the rest. I was struck by Fred's assertion that "There were no mediocre destroyer captains". They may not have always been popular, but they inspired confidence and respect. Today's modern destroyer, the Royal Navy's Type 45 Daring Class, is a world away from the Hunts of WW2. Yet there remains the same sense of dash and pride in being a member of the destroyer club. Today's sailor owes this to those who have gone before, men like Fred Saxton.

Able Seaman Fred Saxton, aged 22, left HMS *Hambledon* in July 1944. Despite all the difficulties and danger that he faced throughout his more than 3 years onboard, he claims "there was nothing really outstanding in this" – a wonderful understatement of modesty!

I commend his story to you.

Vice-Admiral Sir Adrian Johns KCB CBE DL

Preface

By Peter Saxton

My father, Fred Saxton, was born on 19 September 1921 in the village of Grimethorpe near Barnsley in the north of England. He was the second eldest son of Charles Burgin Saxton and his Mother, born Sarah Fellows in the potteries of Stoke-on-Trent. He had an elder brother Edgar, a younger brother, Harold, and two elder sisters, Maud and Elsie. His father was a colliery deputy, a manager who discharged his duties deep below the still-beautiful, rolling countryside of south Yorkshire. The family was close knit, and because of Charles' rank, was well respected in the community.

They were strict Methodists; Charles was permitted one gill of beer on Saturdays only, fetched from the local pub by Fred in an empty Tizer bottle. Sarah used to shave him on Saturday evening ready for chapel on the following day and Charles used to say that there was no better demonstration of marital trust than when your wife has a cut-throat razor held to your throat. And each weekend Charles, still black with pit dirt (no pit-head baths in those days) would proudly give his pay packet, unopened, to his wife.

Fred dreamed of going to sea, even as a child. He applied to join the Royal Navy and after a delay caused by mounting hostilities he finally joined on 14th November 1940.

He served with distinction throughout the war entirely in a Hunt class destroyer. These vessels were not referred to as ships, but boats. They were the largest unarmoured warships in the fleet with big, powerful engines and consequently they were very fast. He referred to them as 'greyhounds of the fleet'. They were constantly at sea in the North Atlantic, the North Sea and later in the Mediterranean. Their task was escorting the vital convoys plying to and from North America, protecting them against U-Boat and air attack. In the North Sea and the Mediterranean, they added E-Boats to their list of adversaries. His admiration for Hunt class destroyers was intense, particularly his own boat, HMS *Hambledon*. He had volunteered to join the Gunnery Branch, then the premier branch in the Royal Navy. It was a brave option – Gunnery Ratings and NCOs prided themselves on being tough and the most disciplined sailors in the Navy.

Hambledon was part of the Harwich Flotilla, and on a brief period of shore-leave he met my mother, who was a Petty Officer in the Women's Royal Naval Service (WRNS). Their courtship must have been a tense affair, with Mother watching the destroyers going out to sea and anxiously counting them back in when they recovered to harbour. She admired his staunch Methodism and his strict teetotalism. In yesterday's Navy, the sailors were issued with a daily tot of rum. He refused his tot and got an extra few pence a day in pay for doing so. He was tall – his shipmates called him 'Lofty'. He was handsome and with a Roman nose and raven-black hair he cut a dash in his sailor's uniform. My mother once admitted with a wink, 'He was a lovely looking fella!'

They were married towards the end of the war. As he remarked to her phlegmatically, 'If anything happens, at least you'll get a pension.' It is chilling to be reminded that armed servicemen had to think in those terms, and unromantic as it sounded it was, nevertheless, born of love and caring.

The war won, he was demobilised in 1946. After five years' fighting, constantly at sea, he couldn't settle down. He confessed to me that he once took a train to Hull and enquired about signing on again. With his record he was accepted subject to a medical. Shortly after that my mother announced she was 'expecting' as they used to say. That changed his mind.

His future life was shaped by study to get the education he had been denied by the war. His qualifications mounted and with them came advancement. He discovered he was a good writer and wrote prolifically. His first book was the story of three generations of the Saxtons – a mining and engineering family – written after careful genealogical research carried out before the internet – it was all public and parish records and gravestones in those days. The book was published by the Council as a work of important, social significance, alas posthumously.

He retired to Polperro in Cornwall to a house predictably overlooking the harbour. By this time, he was a Methodist lay preacher at the local chapel and read for a degree at Exeter University in his sixties. He spent his leisure hours sailing in a lobster-boat with a friend, who used to go to great lengths to explain how a boat worked. My Father bore it with patient good humour and remained reticent about his naval experience, although he once smiled at me and remarked 'I've wrung more salt water out of my socks than he's sailed on.' I once asked him that, of all the things he had been in his life, what he really considered himself to be. Without hesitation, he replied, 'A sailor!'

This is his account – Fred Saxton's war.

Peter Saxton
Mursley
6 October 2023

Chapter 1

Admiralty

The books I read as a schoolboy seemed to be mostly sea stories. *Westward Ho, Masterman Ready, Coral Island, Peter the Whaler* and (the best boys' book ever written), *Treasure Island*, were just a few of them. Sea poetry also played a part in giving me a fascination with seafaring, as I imbibed large chunks of Masefield and Newbolt. Finally, in our school singing, sea shanties seemed to predominate. Naturally, it was all to do with sailing ships – 'The tall ship with the star to steer her by' – but the spell had been cast and I imagined the ships of the Royal Navy as having inherited all the glamour and mystique of their forerunners.

The sheer size of Britain's Navy from 1850 to 1950 made it impressive, and I have often wondered how today's schoolboy views our present minuscule fleet. The Navy, of course, went with the Empire, when Britannia ruled the waves, and the two facts were undoubtedly deeply embedded in the national psyche of Victorian, Edwardian and Georgian Britishers. It had not been put there by indoctrination in its true sense. Such indoctrination as I got at school had automatically grown from Admiralty reaching back to Alfred the Great, then forward again through the Tudors and Stuarts, and culminating in Nelson. Admiralty was an integral part of British history, with a thousand years of continuity, and it is not an exaggeration to say that all foreign navies were modelled on the British – not least their uniforms.

It is impossible for a Britisher to appreciate what it feels like to live in a landmass, where the land miles roll interminably from every point of the compass. No one in these islands lives much more than sixty miles from the sea as the crow flies, so everyone is a potential sailor and the sea can be 'felt', even if it cannot be seen. The British have always looked to their Navy as their first line of defence, and every child's history books abound with true, sea-faring stories. I once spent some time in a naval establishment which had eight barrack blocks named after famous Admirals in alphabetical order: Anson, Blake, Collingwood, Drake, Effingham, Frobisher, Grenville,

Hawke. Discounting Q, X and Z, one could continue through the alphabet, and it would yield at least another twelve famous Admirals, with most of the letters producing several names.

The word Admiral (or Sea Viceroy) first came into use in England at the end of the thirteenth century. Surviving records show the first holder of the office to be William de Laybourne, who was created Admiral of the Seas in 1286. The office later became Lord High Admiral of England. But, of course, there can be only one such office-holder, and the name did not come into general use, with its ascending four ranks, until after the Restoration. In fact, to refer to all our famous seamen as Admirals before the Restoration is something of a misnomer. Francis Drake, for instance, was dubbed General, as was Robert Blake and it is plain to see why. Early fighting ships had fore castles and main castles (the former term still persists) to accommodate soldiers. In short, they were not the men-o'-war they later became, but rather, armed troop transports.

It was Charles II who brought the rank of Admiral into general use when he drew up a legal code for the Navy in the form of 'Articles of War'. Articles of War were certainly read to ships' companies at their commissioning during the last war, although they would be a modified version of Charles II's, which contained an impressive preamble:

'It is upon the Navy, under the good Providence of God that the safety, honour and welfare of this Realm do chiefly depend.'

Ships at sea (or fleets) were out of reach of England's common law, and the Articles of War enabled a Commander-in-Chief, while afloat, to act as the King's Vice-Regent or Sea Viceroy. Thus, he was empowered to summon a court-martial and to administer justice on all miscreants. An Admiral still acts in this capacity, indeed, the Commanding Officer of any Royal Navy ship – whatever his rank – has magisterial powers.

Certainly, long before Trafalgar, the British considered their navy to be superior to any other and, after Trafalgar, they were never in any doubt. There was never despair at the loss of the first battle; the final score would be settled in the second. Hence, a Falklands retribution followed Coronel and *Bismarck* paid the price of *Hood*. This does not mean to say that the first battle was always lost. The River Plate was a first battle which was won, and Jutland was a first battle which the enemy were reluctant to repeat. However, its fleet did terminate in Scapa Flow!

All enemy ships attacking or being attacked by Royal Navy ships were at a psychological disadvantage right from the start, not only because of the Navy's formidable pedigree, but also because they knew it would have to be a fight to the finish. The Admiralty has never taken kindly to ships declining action in face of a superior enemy, and only the commander of a grievously battered ship would be forgiven for doing so. Even then, he would be considered to have let the side down somewhat in face of the shades of Sir Richard Grenville.

It is difficult to imagine today how much the navy impinged upon our lives between the wars. I have mentioned the sea stories, poems and shanties and, in addition, every school had a portrait of the monarch in the full-dress uniform of an Admiral of the Fleet in its assembly hall. Indeed, in one of my classrooms, we had a framed print of Nelson's *Victory*. All my toy ships had funnels and, at a tender age I could only see the *Victory* as an unattractive hulk. If I whisper it very softly that is exactly what she is, but I hasten to add that one has only to step aboard her for history to come alive from the soles of the feet upwards.

My early ambition was to join the navy as a boy entrant in the boys' training ship *Ganges*. Parental consent was required under seventeen years of age, however, and this was not forthcoming. While I was impatiently awaiting my seventeenth birthday, my cousin, David Saxton, went to *Ganges* at fifteen years of age and, after training, was drafted to the battleship *Barham* in which he subsequently lost his life.

When my seventeenth birthday came, opposition to my joining the Navy had in no way slackened and, being wishful to leave home with my parents' consent rather than without it, I hoped persistent importuning might eventually pay off. All I succeeded in doing was to let it be seen that I was not to be deterred and, while no outright consent was ever given, at least the blank refusals dried up.

In August 1939, one month short of my eighteenth birthday, I wrote to the recruiting office in Sheffield and was granted an interview on 4 September. When I wrote, the country was at peace; unfortunately, war was declared before the date of the interview. This was, in any case, countermanded

24 hours later by a letter dated 1 September 1939 (the day German troops marched into Poland) which read,

> 'In view of the present situation, I do not propose to interview you on Monday. As soon as things straighten out, I will drop you a line making a fresh appointment.'

It was all very chummy – and very disappointing – and was signed by a Quartermaster Sergeant, Royal Marines named D. Brown-King, who had actually addressed me as 'Dear Sir!' The letter-writer must have been a supreme optimist. Things did not straighten out again for over six years, and I have often wondered if he would have fulfilled his promise, and when.

From then on, up to the Allied Landings in Norway in April 1940, the war on land was stalemate and was dubbed 'the Phony War'. The RAF was flying sorties over German cities, but was dropping nothing more lethal than leaflets, which exhorted the Germans to end the war if they knew what was good for them.

The Navy, however, was at full-stretch from day one, blockading Germany, patrolling the sea lanes and protecting the convoys. Meanwhile, people groped around in the blackout, wondering when the shooting war was going to start.

The first real excitement came in December 1939, when the German pocket battleship *Graf Spee* was sunk by three lesser-gunned adversaries; an exploit which, coming in the middle of a dark, cold winter, had, to quote Churchill, 'warmed the cockles of the British heart.' And so it did; it was also timely, since we had lost the battleship *Royal Oak* two months earlier and the aircraft carrier *Courageous* two weeks after declaration of war.

The Phony war came to an abrupt end when the Germans made their move into Holland and Belgium in May 1940 and from then on it was blitzkrieg, to which the Allies had no answer. France eventually conceded defeat and the British – after the withdrawal at Dunkirk, which was called a miracle – withdrew into their island fortress to await invasion. In March, 1940, before the war had hotted up, I wrote once again to Sheffield, offering my services as a shipwright. My letter was answered by Chief Petty Officer Harrad, who politely informed me that the Royal Navy had no vacancies in that branch. He also added the gratuitous information that the Royal Navy was no longer issuing travel warrants to would-be entrants, and ending, '... if one wishes to join, they must find their own passage here and back.' The whole construction of the letter left one hoping that Chief Petty Officer Harrad was a better seaman than grammarian.

It was obvious that I was not going to get into the Navy through correspondence channels so, on 2 July 1940, I went in person to Sheffield and volunteered my services. I had two fears: firstly, that I might be rejected on the grounds of doing essential war work, and, secondly, that I might fail the medical. In the event, I passed the medical as A1 and no questions were raised as to the work I was doing. I duly added my signature to the enlistment document which informed me that my services would be required while ever the present hostilities lasted.

I went home fully expecting to be called up within a month, but it was not to be. Another four and a half months were to pass (during which the Battle of Britain was fought and won) before the summons came. There were two pro formas, with information added in thick blue crayon. One was headed, 'Dear Sir' and informed me I was 'for entry HMS *Collingwood* on 14.11.40.' The other, which was headed, 'Sir', gave me instructions on how to exchange the enclosed railway warrant for a single ticket. The only way to exchange a warrant for a ticket was to hand it in to my nearest railway booking office. This I would have done automatically. However, the Navy had kindly set it out for me. It also set me wondering as to the standard of intelligence of naval recruits!

So, after two rejections and after what had seemed an interminable wait, I was, at last, in the Royal Navy. During the summer the Navy had taken possession of fifty lease-lend destroyers from America. To man these, something in the order of 7,500 men would be needed. It was probably this that drained whatever reserves of men the Navy had, and made room for a large intake of recruits in late 1940.

Chapter 2

HMS *Collingwood*

Admiral Collingwood was, of course, Lord Nelson's long-suffering second in command at Trafalgar. It was Collingwood who, on receiving the most famous battle signal ever sent to the fleet by a Commanding Officer – 'England expects …' said testily, 'I wish Nelson would stop signalling. We know well enough what to do.'

I was told that the Training Ship *Collingwood* – like its sister ship *Raleigh* at Torpoint – had been built with all speed after Munich. The Admiralty, assured that war was inevitable, had instigated the construction of both, to meet the demands of an influx of recruits, who would eventually meet the requirements of an expanded ship-building programme that had been set in train.

Collingwood is in Fareham, Hampshire, and when I left to join on 14 November 1940, I had never been further from home than about eighty miles to various seaside resorts on holiday. Four other boys (that is what we were termed then, the age of majority being 21) joined *Collingwood* with me on the same date from my home village. We were all schoolmates. Two of them were eighteen and two others, myself included, were just turned nineteen.

We went first to the Naval Recruiting Office at Sheffield, where our party swelled to about a dozen, and where we were given further travel warrants and handed in our ration books and civilian identity cards. Then one member of the party was handed a large envelope which contained the paperwork regarding the group, and we were packed off to the railway station by a Royal Marine Sergeant. The lad with the documents assumed control of the party, and he was probably the only one amongst us who had ever seen London before. Without his expert guidance we would have floundered somewhat on the Underground between King's Cross and Waterloo.

The second lap of the journey between Waterloo and Fareham was typical of many subsequent, wartime, rail journeys. As we left Waterloo, darkness was descending and the journey took four hours, due to air-raid activity. We eventually arrived in Fareham at 2100 hours, after many stops on the way, with interminable waits in a hot blacked-out carriage. Having by then been on the go for twelve hours we were bored, tired and very hungry. Eventually we tumbled out onto a railway platform at Fareham, lit by a single blue lamp, into the arms of an awaiting Petty Officer. He ordered us into a half-circle around him and ticked off our names from a list lit by torchlight, then ushered us into the back of a lorry.

Collingwood at that time was on the outskirts of Fareham, in a country setting. We swept in through the main gate and disembarked at reception. The roll was again called. A duty seaman messenger was then detailed to take us to the divisional office, whereupon he led and we followed as a crowd. It was the first and last time we were to proceed in a naval establishment in such a free and easy manner. There was a bright moon and, as we skirted the parade ground, we noticed that the largest building had a gaping hole in its roof.

One of the party asked how it had come about and the messenger assured us it was bomb damage. I doubt whether it was, because a bomb exploding inside would have damaged the walls. The place was in use anyway, as we discovered next day. The roof had probably been damaged by falling shrapnel – if it was a bomb it had certainly not exploded. The messenger's whole demeanour was typical of the attitude of old hands to greenhorns – the showing off of new-found sagacity. He couldn't have joined the ship himself more than two or three weeks previously, and his aim was to impress by putting the wind up us.

A short joining routine was carried out at the divisional office, where we were issued with station cards, two blankets and a pillow. The messenger was then ordered to take us to Hut 17D in the fo'c'sle division, and from there to the mess deck for supper. The hut contained twenty double-bunk beds on which we deposited our bedding and took no second bidding to proceed to the mess deck. While we were having our meal the air-raid warning sounded and we were ordered by the Chief Petty Officer Cook to finish quickly, collect our blankets and go to the shelters.

We were to see a lot of the shelters in *Collingwood*. They were huge Anderson types, like Nissen huts, set about 3ft into the ground and covered with earth which was grassed. After descending a short flight of steps we found it occupied by half a dozen others and lit by two or three candles. The floor was concreted and there were three concrete benches running throughout its length. One of the occupants said, 'Make yourselves comfortable, lads, you'll be here all night.'

And so we were. I spent: my first night in the Navy in a very cold shelter, sleeping on a narrow, concrete bench, fully dressed – including my shoes. At around midnight I awoke for the first of several times in the night. The candles had either been put out or had burnt out, and the shelter was in Stygian blackness.

Throughout the night the anti-aircraft (AA) guns ringing Portsmouth barked intermittently. At 6am the 'all clear' sounded, and one of the early occupants shouted, 'Come and get your kye lads.'

He led us to the mess deck where we were served with hot, thick cocoa melted down and boiled from the block, sweetened with demerara sugar. During my whole time in the Navy, I never saw white sugar. It was then back to the hut, and just sufficient time to take stock of our living quarters before the bugle sounded, 'Hands to breakfast and clean.'

Our training amounted to less than eleven weeks. It should have been twelve but Christmas intervened and we were sent home on ten days' leave. It was, of course, impossible to transform civilians into seamen in eleven weeks, and some of the time was swallowed up in kitting out, undergoing medicals, eye-testing and having dental treatment. The Navy undoubtedly saved my teeth. I had only four missing, but had been careless about the rest, and several fillings were found to be necessary. A Lieutenant Commander dental surgeon took me in hand, and after admonishing me politely about my careless attitude towards otherwise excellent teeth, brought them back into good order.

One double molar was decayed to the point where, after drilling was completed, only the walls remained. Any less conscientious dentist would have extracted it. After filling it expertly he said, 'I have my doubts about it, but give it a try.' The filling in question lasted twenty-six years, and was admired by every dentist I attended during that period. On more than one occasion, a new dentist would ask who had done it. Some said, 'Were you in the Navy?' as soon as I opened my mouth. After twenty-five years, the *Collingwood* filling was removed and replaced with a gold crown. Next year, the tooth will have served fifty years since being treated at *Collingwood*. The Navy educated me into looking after my teeth in an age that was – to say the least – very slapdash about dental care.

Many of the recruits into all three forces had been reared in the hungry thirties. The situation was not as appalling as it had been in the First War and although the Navy – being the smallest service – could afford to reject the doubtful, many entrants were not exactly physically fit. Good food for three months, with plenty of PT, saw men far fitter when they left *Collingwood* than when they joined.

Air raid activity played havoc with the training programme. During the whole of the eleven weeks we did not spend more than a dozen full nights in our beds. Mostly, we spent all night in the shelters and, during our time there, Portsmouth suffered its first full-scale blitz. All this depleted our training time through lack of proper sleep. After a full night in the shelters we were given, next day, what was known as a long forenoon. This meant going to lunch an hour later than usual, and having the rest of the afternoon off for sleep. Without it we were falling asleep during afternoon lectures and little learning was being absorbed.

Fareham is not on the coast. There were boats' davits alongside the parade ground and we were taught how to lower and hoist the whalers and cutters. But when we manned them for boat-pulling practice, our oars only cleaved the air. Only on one occasion did we man a boat on salt water. We went with our instructor and manned a cutter at Gosport Hard, where we were able to get a glimpse of some warships. There was a flush-deck, four-stacker, ex-Yankee destroyer, looking very strange amongst its more modern British counterparts. There was also a very old French battleship – a relic of the First War. She was probably the old *Courbet*, who ended her life as a block ship in Mulberry Harbour off Arromanches shortly after D-day.

It is surprising how quickly drill instils discipline. There was no more ambling around during working hours. We fell-in as a squad and marched as a squad everywhere we went, while on the parade ground we were put through all the drill routines with and without arms. For the first week we were still in civilian clothes and must have looked a motley crowd, with our civilian gas masks in their cardboard boxes.

The only time I slept between linen sheets, courtesy of the Navy, was while in *Collingwood*, and it was while collecting our linen from the linen store on the morning after our arrival that we had our first experience of enemy action. There was a Red Alert (which meant enemy aircraft in the vicinity) as we marched to the linen store to draw two sheets and two pillow cases. Marching back to the hut to make up our beds, an aircraft began to dive down onto us, and 'action stations' was sounded by bugle over the Tannoy. An officer who was walking up the road shouted, 'Take cover!' There was no cover to be taken and our Chief Petty Officer Instructor shouted, 'On the ground! Everyone lie flat!'

It had been raining, and the concrete road was muddy, but no-one needed twice bidding. The road seemed to me to be too vulnerable, so I sprinted across the pavement and a grass verge to lie against a brick wall. As I did so, the aircraft began machine gunning. There were no bombs. It was a twin-engined, fighter-bomber which had probably dropped its bombs elsewhere. As it pulled out of its dive, the Officer shouted, 'Man the shelters!' whereupon we rose as one man and began haring down the road. One man picked up either a bullet or a spent cartridge and handed it to the Officer, who said tersely, 'Never mind that; take cover!'

A man ahead of me caught the pointed toe of his left shoe in the trouser bottom of his right leg and it tore up the seam from ankle to knee. He staggered, but managed to keep his balance, and ran on with his trouser leg flapping like a cowboy's chap. When we were all safely in the shelter, there was a babble of excitement and nervous reaction, together with much hilarity about the torn trousers. Then someone called attention to the fact that none of us had any linen. It lay where we had dropped it, covered in mud, and our civilian clothes had fared no better.

At the beginning of the second week, we were issued with our uniforms and the civilian clothes were sent home, still caked in mud. When we went to be kitted-out we were halted outside a large hut which we entered in batches of six. Spaced behind a counter were six Wrens, who immediately began piling up items of clothing from racks according to the height and size of the man in front of her. Then a curtain was lowered down the front of the counter while we tried on the trousers. Items too large or too small were exchanged. Any other minor alterations were made by civilian tailors working in a hut close by. Then every item of clothing and kit was marked in paint with our personal name stamp.

The sailor's uniform is referred to as being worn by 'men dressed as seamen'. The term is used to differentiate between seamen, and those who wear the seaman's uniform but who are not seamen, such as stokers, wireless telegraphists, and signalmen. The seaman refers to his uniform as 'square rig' and 'men in square rig' sounds much more nautical than the clumsy term 'men dressed as seamen', but that is merely an opinion.

The uniform itself is like a second skin, the trouser tops fitting as tight as a corset, and one has to perform something of a contortionist act to don the jumper. There is only one way into it or out of it and no other will do. Many years after I left the Navy, I learned with horror that a zip fastener had been introduced and, being a traditionalist, I hoped that the story was a fabrication. However, it would please me to know that men dressed as seamen had been given more pockets than the inadequate two (one in trousers and one in jumper) we had. Having said that, I always found the uniform pleasant to wear – tight-fitting and open necked. On a man with the right figure it always looked good.

Its evolution is also fascinating. The earliest uniform for naval Officers was introduced in 1748 – and for seamen after Trafalgar in 1857. Originally the sailor's dress was not a uniform as such; it was what they wore as utility clothing, and the present-day uniform has evolved from that. The bell-bottoms, for instance, enabled them to be rolled well up when decks were being swabbed, and they were easily kicked off if a man fell overboard. The jersey and jumper evolved from two similar garments which were close fitting and not likely to flap in the wind or get caught in the rigging when climbing aloft.

The blue jean collar evolved from the kerchief Jack Tar wore around his neck to prevent his jumper, or monkey jacket, becoming soiled from his tarred pigtail. The three white tapes around its border have nothing to do (as is supposed) with Nelson's three victorious sea battles. They are merely decorative. Another fallacy is that the black silk scarf was worn in mourning after Nelson's death. It is a nice thought, but its original use was as a sweat rag which gunners hung around their necks and sometimes wore around their foreheads.

The round cap has evolved from the round straw hat worn by many sailors in Nelson's day. It is, incidentally, very uncomfortable to wear and sailors wear it at the back of the head (flat-a-back) for that reason. It is against regulations to do so but, until the Admiralty introduces a softer cap (dare I say it – like the German?) sailors will continue to push an uncomfortable cap to the back of the head and look sloppy.

Foreign navies have copied the British sailor's uniform in almost all respects, although most of them have steered clear of the British cap and come up with something better – with two exceptions. No-one but a Frenchman could wear a French sailor's cap; and the soft, white, stitched, linen cap worn by American sailors should be relegated to the kindergarten. The so-called British sailor's cap is really a brimless hat. In fact, add a couple of inches to its height and it is the hat of an orthodox priest. It is hard of texture, and only fits comfortably on a perfectly round head. And since few human heads are perfectly round there is a measure of discomfort which can only be alleviated by wearing a cap slightly too large. Old sea-dogs did just that.

The younger ones viewed such a recourse as losing their air of jauntiness (which, after all, is a sailor's right) and, inevitably, when ashore, tended to wear their caps flat-a-back. The Wrens' headgear has undergone several modifications, each one an improvement on its predecessor, whereas Jack Tar's seems to be stuck in a Victorian time-warp. So, it is not traditional in the true sense. Tradition only decrees a round, brimless cap, and such a cap could just as well be soft of texture and easy to wear, as hard of texture and uncomfortable. Most sailors I served with were prepared to admit that the German cap was smarter than theirs.

Newly-issued sailors' collars are a dark navy blue, and a sailor with several years' service will wear one and think nothing of it. Not so the new entrant. The dark blue collar screamed 'rooky', so we spent considerable time scrubbing the dye out of them until they emerged a lighter shade of blue not arrived at normally until after years of normal washing.

Regulations regarding dress were often broken. Caps worn flat-a-back and the cap ribbon, which should have been worn with the bow over the left ear was mostly pulled round over the left eye. Lanyards were compulsory under training but afterwards were optional except for ceremonial parades, and no-one wore them. Sailors tend to see them as being part of the little boy's sailor suit and eschew them.

We were issued with two HMS *Collingwood* cap ribbons, but from then on they had to be bought. In peacetime, a man was issued with free cap ribbons on joining any ship, but this privilege was withdrawn when the war started. As far as I am aware, the Admiralty laid dawn no firm instructions about cap ribbons during the war, and the result was that a man could wear any ribbon he chose. If this was deliberate policy to spread confusion as to ship movements and whereabouts, it certainly worked, because any given ship could be sporting a whole range of different cap ribbons. Had the Admiralty wished to call a halt to it, it could have insisted an HMS or HM Battleship, Cruiser, Destroyer, Corvette or Minesweeper (these were all available) and banned names altogether.

As it did not do so, the names remained and many sailors still wore named cap ribbons of ships in which they were no longer serving. Here is a classic example. Three sailors, all serving in the destroyer *Javelin* are ashore in Portsmouth. One sports a *Rodney* cap ribbon, another *Ajax*, another *Lightning*, the ships they had previously served in. Consequently, no-one would connect them with *Javelin* at all. And the ships whose names they wore could be anywhere in the world!

The 1937 Manual of Seamanship, Volume 1, ran to over 400 pages. We could not possibly absorb all its lore in ten weeks, and our superiors were aware of the fact. The science of seamanship is so wide and varied that, in the short time available to us, the butter of learning had to be spread thinly. We tied knots and carried out simple splicing in hemp rope. We learnt same of the intricacies of anchors and cables; we made attempts at boxing the mariners' compass: we carried out look-out routine and ship recognition under simulated night conditions and, of course, boat work in our dry-land boats. We learnt rules of the sea roads, correct ship positioning at sea – some of it poetically:

> Green to green – or red to red,
> Perfect safety – go ahead.
> If to starboard red appear,
> It is your duty to keep clear.
> To act as judgement says is proper
> To starboard – or port – back – or stop her.

The above is only of value to peace-time sailors. During the war, all ships were blacked-out and showed no navigation lights. The siren signals we learned (that is, the hooting signals made by ships signifying their steering intentions) were, however, more useful. There were no swimming baths in *Collingwood* and none of us was given swimming instruction.

The final two weeks of training were spent in the gunnery section which meant a change of hut. Ratings who gravitated to the gunnery section were considered to have 'arrived' and looked upon new entrants with lofty superiority. We were issued with rifle and bayonet and full webbing equipment. Drill – including bayonet drill – was stepped up. Rifles in the country were in short supply and we were told that, in the event of enemy invasion in the Portsmouth area we would be expected to put them to use. We also wore the canvas gaiters, which were standard in every Royal Naval gunnery school.

After their initial training, seamen could specialise in gunnery, torpedoes, asdic or radar or not, as they chose. These were designated 'non-substantive' rates which had no bearing whatsoever on promotion, although they carried extra pay. Any non-specialising seaman could, however, expect to find himself as an ammunition number in a gun's crew, so the course was useful in introducing him to gunnery and gun drill. It was also an excellent method of further instilling discipline, because the Gunner's Mate Instructors were strict disciplinarians – the Navy's equivalent of the Army's Sergeant Major.

Much had been achieved in that first nine weeks. Although by no stretch of the imagination could we be called seamen in its full sense, we were certainly not the civilians who had ambled through the ship on that first night nine weeks ago. We were smarter, fitter and much more alert. In the training hierarchy we had progressed from looking from the bottom upwards, to looking downwards at all those beneath us in the training schedule. Our collars were a lighter shade of blue and the nap had rubbed off our working uniforms; but only the very foolish imagined we were yet seamen.

We were given classroom instruction in gunnery fire-control and initiated into the mysteries of how allowances were made for wind speed – speed of own and enemy ship and the projectile's trajectory and range. But the only guns we saw were obsolescent breech loaders, which we manned as guns' crews doing each different job in our turns. The dummy shells were of wood, weighted with a metal filling to the weight of actual shells, and the charges were fashioned in canvas to the size and weight of actual charges. Since the guns did not fire, dummy shell and charge stayed in the gun and were pushed up into the barrel as fresh shell and charge were rammed home,

Eventually, they plopped out of the muzzle and dropped on to a thick rope mat to be retrieved and rushed back to the breech for loading again. We began tentatively learning the drill and shouting responses to orders. Initially, there were repeated pauses for fault correction; but the gunnery instructor's patience was very limited, and his reasonable explanations soon evaporated, to be followed by dire admonishments for faults and dilatoriness. No allowances were made for the fact that some were physically more nimble than others and some more intelligent than others. The point came when the instructor deemed sufficient instruction had been given and, from then on, this homogenous mass of idiots had to be licked into shape until it was performing like a well-oiled machine.

It must have been at this juncture where most ratings made a decision that anything to do with gunnery was not for them. At the start of the drill the breech block is swung open to accept shell and charge. While ever it is open, the rammer places his ramrod in front of it to prevent it being closed until the shell is in the breech and the ammunition number's hands are clear. After he (the rammer) has rammed the shell home, his ramrod is once again placed in front of the breech block until the charge is loaded. He then removes it and the breech worker slams home the breech block. The gun is then ready for firing.

One luckless rating, acting as rammer, forgot the drill and stood with the ramrod in his hand, one end of it resting on the deck like a pole. There was an immediate cry of, 'Check! Check! Check!' whereupon everyone froze. This order (as against 'cease firing') intimates that firing will be resumed when the error has been corrected. The Gunner's Mate then advanced upon the wretched Rating and, in a moderate voice, and in an almost avuncular manner, said,

'Listen, son. See this bloke here?' (pointing to the breech worker). Well, like all good sailors, he's keen to get a VC in action, so he wants as many rounds off as he can get. Without that ramrod where it should be – and it isn't – he's going to slam that breech shut, and this poor bastard (pointing to the ammunition man) is going to lose four fingers. Is that quite clear?'

'Yes, Sir.' Then, with his voice rising several octaves, he screamed, 'Well get it in place then, you brainless idiot!'

There was a plus and a minus from this sort of treatment. It tended to push home learning in a minimum of time, and to reduce mistakes to a minimum. It also certainly ensured that guns' crews were on their toes, if only to obviate the embarrassment from tongue-lashing. The minus was that the timorous ones went to pieces under it, and continued making errors through fear. But the minus was only a minus in initial training; after that it reverted to a plus since the people concerned made their own decision that gunnery was not for them.

When we arrived in the gunnery section, bunks were being fitted in the shelters, so once there and turned in, we were assured of a decent sleep and the long forenoon routine was discontinued. They came rather too late for our contingent to benefit from them. The air raids continued, and the corrugated asbestos roofs of our huts were often holed by falling shrapnel, proving the wisdom of their inmates being ordered to the shelters.

Throughout our time in *Collingwood*, cities all over the country were being blitzed. We had stood at the entrance to our shelter seeing the fires raging in Portsmouth, and there was a naval anti-aircraft (AA) gun in the vicinity of the ship joining in the barrage. We had ratings in the hut from London, Hull and Sheffield, who were given three days' compassionate leave when each city was blitzed, to enable them to go home to bombed-out families.

During my first month in the ship, a notice appeared on the hut noticeboard asking for volunteers to be trained as Fleet Air Arm gunners. This took my fancy. I saw it as being an exciting venture, so handed in my name. Within three days I was called for a medical and, much to my disappointment, failed it. My respiratory system was not considered robust enough for flying. I was young, naive and, I suppose, somewhat swashbuckling, but the failed medical probably ensured my longevity. The air gunner manned twin Lewis guns in the rear, open cockpit of the 'Stringbag' Swordfish aircraft, whose loss rate was high. Of the squadron which flew to attack the *Scharnhorst* and *Gneisenau* when they made their dash through the Channel, for instance, none survived.

Eventually, our training time was up and we were to be transferred to barracks. The last items of kit to be issued to us were our hammocks. With bunks we had not needed them, but they were issued to us prior to leaving, and our instructor showed us how to string them by their clews, and how to lash them up for stowing away. The whole consisted of two hammocks, with one bed mattress, two bed covers and one blanket. There were no sheets and no pillow; we made our own pillows with the folded spare hammock and bed cover. When ashore in establishments where bunks were supplied, we spread our hammocks out flat on them.

At that time, ratings leaving training were given the choice of depot they wished to be sent to – Devonport, Portsmouth or Chatham. I chose Chatham because I wanted a destroyer, and felt I was more likely to get one there, since Chatham dockyard could not accept large capital ships. Shortly after, choice of depot was withdrawn. Our Divisional Officer had warned us that when we left *Collingwood* we should be prepared to find ourselves at sea within days of entering the barracks. He was not exaggerating. If a large capital ship was commissioning, it could gobble up 1,400 men, and, indeed, some of our hut members went to sea very quickly. The issue seemed to rest on how your name came up in the drafting office.

My four friends also opted for Chatham, and I feel sure that the companionship we enjoyed had helped us to overcome any trauma we might have suffered in our drastic change of lifestyles. When I returned from Christmas leave after a month in *Collingwood*, it suddenly struck me how irrevocably I had cut the umbilical cord that tied me to my family, and I was overcome with an acute attack of homesickness.

I had no idea how long the war would last, nor, indeed, when I should get home again. It was not regret; I had no regrets. I was where I wanted to be and, throughout the war, never wished to be other than where I was. Up to that point I had given no thought to how drastically my life had changed, until returning from Christmas leave. Fortunately, the feeling did not last, and it was never to return. Return from all subsequent leaves saw me fully acclimatised within twenty-four hours.

On 29 January 1941, a large contingent of us left *Collingwood* for Chatham. I was not sorry to leave. I had enjoyed the training, but a trainee is a trainee, and I was eager for something else. All of us were only a few stages on from 'men dressed as seamen' and knew we had much to learn before being transformed from Ordinary to Able Seamen. In peace time a seaman's training could last up to two years, and we had taken eleven weeks! However, within a few days of arrival in RN Barracks, Chatham, all our HMS *Collingwood* cap ribbons had disappeared. We were no longer trainees.

Chapter 3

HMS *Pembroke*

The Royal Naval Barracks with the adjoining dockyard at Chatham were closed in recent years. So ended a long history of the Navy's close connection with the Medway towns. Chatham was the smallest of the three naval dockyards. Its dry docks were only large enough to accommodate a warship of 10,000 tons, so generally, it catered for the smaller man-o'-war.

'Drake, he was a Devon man, an' ruled the Devon seas.' The barracks at Devonport were named HMS *Drake*. Nelson sailed from Portsmouth to Trafalgar and spent much of his time there. Portsmouth barracks were initially named HMS *Victory*. Then, after the battleship *Nelson* was scrapped, renamed HMS *Nelson*. Consequently, Chatham's *Pembroke* never had quite the same glamour attaching to it as Portsmouth's *Nelson* and Devonport's *Drake* did. The reason was that the historical events attaching to the name were to do with the Commonwealth, and the Navy is intrinsically Royal.

The first *Pembroke*, for instance, was a Cromwellian ship named after the Protector to commemorate his capture of Pembroke Castle. It is significant, too, that one of the three barrack blocks at Chatham was named after a Commonwealth Admiral – Robert Blake – who secured his first sea command at the start of the Commonwealth in 1649. Blake is often referred to as 'the forgotten admiral', and it is not appreciated that his exploits for England were every bit as great – if not as renowned – as those of Drake and Nelson. Chatham, therefore, has never been able to lay claim to a historical sailor quite so romantic as Drake and Nelson.

Nevertheless, it can proudly lay claim to have built Nelson's flagship *Victory*, despite her resting in Portsmouth dockyard. Had she been returned to her place of birth, therefore, Chatham, not Portsmouth, would have inherited her, and there are some who say that is how it should have been.

Chatham barracks and dockyard were cheek by jowl; you walked out of the barracks into the dockyard, and the sights and sounds of the dockyard could be seen and heard in the barracks. They were on the northern edge of the town, access being via the long Dock Road. I calculate that, at most periods during the last war, there would be up to 3,000 personnel in the barracks, under training, coming in from sea from paid-off ships, and going to sea in newly-commissioned ones. The aspect was unmistakably Victorian, the three barrack blocks and all the administration buildings having been built between 1889 and 1897. It was very much a brick jungle. The three, huge, three-storey blocks were named Anson, Blake and Duncan, and living conditions were spartan. Polished floorboards with brown linoleum walkways, long wooden mess tables and forms with overhead hammock racks. Heating was by an open coal fire and a coal stove. Shore leave was every other night and, as there was little comfort to be had in the mess, men were glad to stay ashore at the Sailors' Rest, the YMCA or the Salvation Army.

There were, of course, canteens in the barracks, but they were too crowded for comfort. The duty watch, and those who chose not to stay ashore all night, slept in the famous (or infamous) Chatham tunnel. This had been driven into a cliff on the perimeter, and there were two entrances whose galleries descended down slopes of about 1 in 4 for some thirty yards, then branched off into several other galleries. In size and construction, it was similar to the London Underground train tunnels, with concrete floors and arch girders. It was electrically lit and safe from bombing, but it was most unhealthy. There was no proper ventilation, and little is left to the imagination as to the state of the air after hundreds of men had spent the night there. Hammocks were slung from girders, as close as bats in a cave, and late-comers spread their hammocks on the concrete floor down both sides, leaving only a three-foot gangway. The only toilet facilities were large metal drums in alcoves. It certainly solved the problem of danger from air raids and it was safe from direct hits by bombs. Once down there, one could hear neither the drone of aircraft nor the banging of guns, so one could turn in and sleep soundly, drugged, after midnight, from lack of oxygen.

The North Road ran the full length of the barracks, from the main gate to the gunnery school. Below it was the parade ground, with the drill shed and its office buildings. There were two pavements along the Borth Road, one of them for Officers only. This was not class distinction; it saved Officers having to make interminable salutes to the milling sailors going about the barracks. Men who were not undergoing training had to be gainfully employed during the day, but it was sometimes difficult to find gainful employment for such a large number of men. In 1940–41, when the invasion scare was at its height, a naval battalion was formed and would have been used to repel the invader. Twice a day, after breakfast and dinner, working parties were formed for cleaning duties throughout the barracks. Little civilian labour was required for cleaning.

Some working parties went into the dockyard – to the victualling depot, or anywhere where the human pack-mule was required. Some of the work was futile. A man could be detailed to polish a section of floor in an office corridor in the forenoon and find himself polishing the same floor in the afternoon. There were some zinc dustbins in the gunnery office, used for wastepaper, which were polished twice every working day! There were many trees in the barracks, and the autumn saw dozens of road-sweeping contingents sweeping up leaves. This boring routine went on for several weeks, until the last leaf had fluttered to the ground. On a windy day the roads would be cleared of leaves before dinner and the job would need to be done again after dinner. So futile and boring did it become that the odd two or three evaded work detail, but that did not make life any easier, They then had to keep on the move, dodging the patrols who challenged and pounced on any malingerer.

My ex-school mates were still with me and, after a couple of weeks with no draft to sea in the offing, we all decided to apply for gunnery courses. We were all accepted, but only three of us had the high standard of eyesight required to be anti-aircraft gunners. The other two went into other branches of gunnery. Before the last war, a seaman who specialised in gunnery was known as a seaman-gunner. Eventually however, gunnery became so broad that no-one could be expected to master the whole technique. Consequently, gunnery was fragmented into five branches, the AA branch being one of them.

The Navy's smartest and most disciplined ratings were its gunnery ratings. Its Royal Marines are sea-going soldiers and are trained to a higher standard of military efficiency than sailors. The role of the seaman, however, is to do with the efficient running of the ship in all its aspects, and this is a naval, not a military, matter. Nevertheless, sailors are expected to be smart in a naval sense and the gunnery ratings considered themselves to be the crème de la crème. The reason they did so was that, not only had they to undergo far more drill than any other branch, but also because they were trained to a high standard of efficiency in their profession and an alertness in carrying out orders. A ship in action against enemy ships or aircraft depended largely on its gunnery, and the first ship to score a hit had a decided advantage.

There could be a leisureliness about splicing a rope or pulling a boat. There could be no leisureliness about gunnery. Immediately gunnery ratings crossed an imaginary line where the barracks ended and the gunnery school began, they began to double. Walking – or even marching – in the gunnery school grounds was not permitted. Two friends walking side by side would break into the double at the point of the imaginary line. They may continue their conversation, but it would be at the double. As soon as ratings entered gunnery school, discipline was heightened to a degree never experienced by non-gunnery ratings.

All gunnery ratings wore canvas gaiters, gunnery Officers black, patent leather ones. There were no flapping bellbottoms in the gunnery school, and a man in gaiters was a marked man. He could be picked up for slouching or for not giving the smart salute worthy of his profession. The gunnery rating's bearing and drill – with or without arms – is superior because it is part and parcel of his training. It is, of course, not up to Guardsman or Royal Marine standard; nevertheless, it can be very impressive. Whenever the Navy required a ceremonial guard, it was provided from the gunnery school. The gun carriage bearing the coffin of a monarch was crewed by gunnery ratings.

There comes a time in this form of training when resentment of the constant discipline gives place to pride of profession. It begins to feel good to be smart, and to know that other people acknowledge it. There is also a sense of pride in knowing that the ship, to a great degree, depends on your skills and alertness. When gunnery ratings were chosen for ceremonial guards, the gunnery Officers usually went for men of reasonable height, and, as I was rising six feet tall, there was no way I could avoid them. In summer I did not particularly mind. In winter – especially with snow on the ground – it was a gruelling experience undergoing several days of non-stop drill with snow on the ground. When we came to slope arms there would be a dollop of snow sticking to the butt plate of the rifle which went into the palm of the hand. And there was no way of getting rid of it.

I saw a naval passing-out parade on television recently, and all the ratings drilling with arms were wearing gloves! That was a luxury we were certainly not permitted. There was one occasion, three and a half years later, when all higher gunnery ratings were piped to fall in outside the gunnery school. It was bitterly cold and drizzling, and the rig of the day was oilskins. I did not relish a ceremonial guard, so hit on the idea of bending my knees underneath the oilskin, thus reducing my height by some four inches. The gunnery Officer came down the ranks picking out the tall ones and saying, 'Fall in on the left.' He paused directly in front of me and said with a wry smile, 'Straighten up to your full height and fall in on the left.' Fortunately he was a man with a sense of humour. But somehow, when the parade took place, it was always worth the travail that had preceded it. Number one suits, clean collars, freshly blancoed gaiters, the swish of bayonets as they cleaved the air, the single crack our hands made as they hit the rifles in the 'present arms', and the gunner's mate marching alongside saying, 'Come on, lads, give it bags of swank – the girls will love it!'

The band struck up, made it all worthwhile. The Lee-Enfield rifle with long bayonet has been relegated to the museum, and ceremonial drill with arms by Navy, Army or Air Force has never been the same with its passing. During my time in the Navy, gunnery was the premier branch. It seems now to have taken second place to ship-to-air weapons, and the destroyers and frigates only seem to mount one gun. Such is the advance of technology, but it was ever thus. In the grounds of the gunnery school there were several of the old muzzle-loading cannon – the brass ones, of course – highly polished. They were stamped with their year of casting – some of them long after Trafalgar in 1805. I marvelled then that gunnery technology had advanced in half a century or so from the muzzle-loader to the breech-loader, the cannon ball to the sixteen-inch shell, and from the block and tackle to hydraulics.

The course was to last eight weeks, the first four being classroom instruction. AA gunnery covered all the close-range weapons, the pom-pom 2-pounder, single, four, and eight-barreled; the Oerlikon 20mm; the Vickers .5 inch machine gun – twin and quadruple; and the Lewis .303 inch gun. When the war began, the pom-pom was already seen as obsolescent and was being gradually superseded by the Bofors twin 40mm, but these were in short supply. The pom-pom remained the Navy's principal close-range weapon throughout the war. It had passed through eight modifications and, in the Mark 8, was at its peak. The Oerlikon, of Swiss manufacture, had appeared just before the war, and was an accurate, reliable gun. The Vickers .5 inch had evolved from an earlier ancestor, firing smaller bullets. The Lewis was in all respects the same gun as used in the First World War.

There was a further AA weapon in use at the beginning of the war called the Holman Projector. I can only think it was dreamed up by Admiralty boffins as a stop-gap, and it was intended to combat the dive-bomber. It consisted of a steel tube set in a steel frame. The operator had handlebar control of the frame for lateral movement and elevation and depression. In principle, it was a steam-actuated mortar which discharged Mills grenades – the steam coming, of course, from the ship's boilers. The second crewman fed the tube with grenades. After removal of the safety pin, the grenade was dropped into the barrel, whose sides held the trigger at safe. The pressing of a foot pedal released a jet of steam, which sent the grenade towards the target, hopefully to burst in its path. Heath Robinson could not have dreamed up anything better. Nevertheless, the Admiralty – desperately short of close-range weapons – accepted it as a stop-gap, fitted it in ships, and gunnery ratings were trained in its use. Eventually, as the flow of close-range weapons increased, it was phased out and withdrawn.

Classroom instruction consisted of weapon stripping and assembly, so that we knew exactly how they operated and how to overcome stoppages; also, how to aim them by means of what was known as 'eye-shooting'. The third subject was ammunition, propellant charges, disruptive charges and ignitors. The course opened up a whole new area of knowledge, begun in *Collingwood* and completed at Chatham, until we became expert in a subject vouchsafed to so few that we automatically became specialists, especially in eye-shooting.

As boys, we had all thrown stones at moving cats and birds, and had automatically 'aimed off' in front of them without being taught or, indeed, even realizing what we were doing. This was the principle of eye-shooting; 'eye' because no prisms or gun telescopes were used as in surface gunnery. The sight we used was known as the forward-area cartwheel sight, As its name implies, it was like a cartwheel, with spokes radiating from a cross in its centre, through two rings to the outer ring. Each ring, from inner to outer, represented 100, 200 and 300 knots of aircraft speed. There was also a back sight which had a small wire cross in its centre, which was lined up with the cross in the forward sight. Aircraft, of course, attack at different speeds and different angles of approach, all of which required different amounts of aim-off. The whole principle of eye-shooting was to learn how to compute aim-off in the mind, and apply it to the sight in the twinkling of an eye. At the start it seemed as though the impossible was being asked, but, like swimming, or learning to ride a bicycle, there came a point when, after much floundering, everything fell into place. Eventually, after practice firings, we were able to do it through automatic brain computation, as we had done throwing stones at moving targets. Some, of course, cracked it more quickly than others.

The piece of apparatus used in the classroom was called 'the aiming teacher'. The instructor had a contraption which worked something like a sextant, and which he pointed at our hand-held cartwheel sights, as a navigator shoots the sun. He placed his eye to the back-sight of the aiming teacher and lined it up with the sight we were holding at eye level. He then swivelled a small aircraft attached to his sight to give it an angle of approach and said something like, 'Torpedo bomber, angle of approach 30 degrees, speed 200 knots.'

We would then place our finger on the cartwheel sight, as being where we would position the nose of the aircraft. Initially, none of us knew what we were really about and made wild guesses. During the forenoon sessions, patience was shown by our instructor. 'No, son, you're missing astern. Try again.'

It is indicative of how young we were when the Gunners' Mates – some of whom were themselves only in their thirties and early forties – were addressing us as 'son' and 'laddie.' We accepted these appellations quite naturally, since there was an avuncular air about them. I believe, also, that these men – some of whom had already seen much action – were well aware that we were going to be soon experiencing what they had experienced and, despite the air of discipline they exuded, were solicitous about our safety and general welfare. The more intelligent ones eventually reached a point where the only information they needed from the instructor was the type of attack. With the information 'High-level bomber,' they would automatically assess the speed, see briefly the angle of approach, and place their fingers correctly on the cartwheel sight to his. 'Nice shooting, you'd bring him down with that.'

The technique began as a mystery and evolved into a known science. Now, all that remained were the practice firings, which, with tracer shells, would prove to us that the technique worked if applied correctly. In the classroom it appeared crude; but it was the best that gunnery technology could devise of its time and, later, I was to find it pleasingly accurate, until superseded by the gyro gunsight. In between sessions of practice eye-shooting and gun stripping, we had sessions of aircraft recognition from wall charts and models. With a very retentive memory I managed to reach a point where I could recognize the majority of our own and German aircraft, and a few Italian. Psychologically, even at that early stage, the Italian aircraft never seemed to pose the threat the German did!

At that period of the war, Chatham did not have an AA practice range, and all embryo AA ratings had to go to Portsmouth to do their practice shooting. Accordingly, after our four-week classroom instruction, we were sent to Whale Island, Portsmouth.

Chapter 4

HMS *Excellent*

Although it was named *Excellent*, few ever referred to it as such. It was inevitably called 'Whale Island' or 'Whaley', and was acknowledged as the most 'pusser' (highly disciplined) of all naval establishments. Sailors spoke of it disparagingly as 'All gate and gaiters' (all shouting and marching), but the ones who did so were usually non-gunnery ratings. In his heart of hearts, the gunnery rating was proud of its reputation, even if he preferred not to be there!

'Whaley' is a small island in Portsmouth harbour off Portsea, accessible from the mainland by a short bridge. The crossing of the bridge took you into a different world – a world that was one hundred per cent Navy, and probably the Navy at its most efficient. Gunnery instruction was taking place there in the practice gun batteries, but it was heavy calibre stuff, a different branch of gunnery from ours. We used Whale Island as living quarters only and did our practice firings elsewhere. The routine was that we had breakfast in Whale Island, dinner (there is no such meal as lunch in the Navy) elsewhere and returned in the evening to sleep on the Island.

Nevertheless, while there, we had to conform to the routine of doubling where specified, and marching (not walking) where not. We stayed there three weeks and were transported to and from the range by lorry. The AA range was at Eastney, to the east of Portsmouth, where all the guns were sited on the shore overlooking the channel. Apart from their use for practice firings, they were also useful in air raids. Consequently, all the trainees worked two watches. At night, half returned to the island and could go ashore, while the other half took their hammocks and slept at Eastney alternately.

My ex-schoolmate (Fred Silver) and I were absolved from this routine. We were detailed for wireless operator duties. There was a small brick building in the grounds, housing a wireless sending-and-receiving set. It was a short-wave radio on which we could speak to other stations dotted around

Portsmouth. We were shown how to operate it by two Sub-Lieutenants and, every evening after tea, we closed-up and tested communications with all the other stations, each of which had its own call-sign, and which answered our call-sign of 'Swallow'. After contacting each station, we closed down and fell out, with instructions to return at the double if the air raid warning sounded.

During our time on Whale Island, there was no air raid on Portsmouth, and I never discovered exactly what our role was. When we asked the two young Sub-Lieutenants what it was all about, they were evasive, and said something to the effect that, in the event of an air raid, they would give us numbers to broadcast. I have since assumed that the numbers would possibly be shell-fuse settings, and that the stations we were contacting were gun sites. Perhaps it was the intention to put up an AA barrage of shells, all with the same fuse-setting – perhaps experimentally. That is conjecture; the fact is, we were given no explanation.

We arrived in Portsmouth on the Saturday and began practice-firing on the following Monday morning. While at Eastney, I crewed and fired an eight-barrelled, hydraulic-operated pom-pom, but thereafter, by virtue of not serving in a large ship, I was never to do so again. It was very impressive. The whole mounting, with its crew, turned like a carousel, under hydraulic power. The laying and training of the eight guns were also by hydraulics, and the guns fired in pairs through electrically-driven firing tappets. It was dubbed 'The Chicago Piano' but, for obvious reasons, could only be fitted in capital ships.

Smaller ships had quadruples and singles, although not power operated. The .5 inch machine gun was like a miniature pom-pom, except that it fired solid bullets instead of explosive shells at the rate of 600 rounds a minute. It was mounted as a twin or quadruply. While at Chatham, one rating came under censure from a Gunner's Mate for describing it disparagingly. He was told that, in good hands, it was an excellent weapon. 'Aim this at a Dornier 17 near the tail, Laddie, and, if you're on target, you'll saw it off as clean as a circular saw. On my oath, because I've done it.' The Dornier 17 had a very slim body, and was dubbed 'The Flying Pencil'.

The Oerlikon cannon needed only a two-man crew – the operator and the ammunition loader. Like the pom-pom, it fired explosive shells with graze-nose fuses (fuses armed by the shock of the shell firing) at a rate of 450 a minute. Once strapped into it, the gun moved in whichever direction the operator turned his body, so it was admirable in use against surprise attack, swift changes of target, and fast and formidable fighter-bombers. The range of the Lewis (single and twin) was limited, and few AA ratings fired them. They were mounted on the wings of ships' bridges and searchlight platforms, and were more or less there for anyone to have a go. The uninitiated who did so inevitably opened fire before the attacker was in range, assuming the gun's range to be greater than it was. Every other bullet was a tracer and we were taught in the gunnery school to practise 'hose pipe' shooting. Send out the tracer, like a jet of water, ahead of the aircraft, and let him fly into it. Many aircraft were brought down by this method. One Gunner's Mate gave us this splendid advice, 'They'll come at you out of the sun, Lads – especially the dive-bombers. Don't wait for something to aim at because you'll be blinded. Just point your gun into the sun and open fire. Don't forget – point your gun – in the sun – and get your Hun!'

For the first three days we carried out gun drill to get acclimatised to each weapon. Then, on the fourth day, a Fleet Air Arm aircraft arrived, towing a drogue, and firing practice began. When every gun was firing there was a tremendous racket, and the sky above our section of the Channel was dotted with the black smoke puffs of our explosive shells. Close-range weapons are not as hard on the ears as the bigger calibre guns. Nevertheless, after a couple of hours of continuous firing, the ears ring, and there is an acrid smell of cordite in the nostrils and at the back of the throat – something that was to become familiar at sea.

Another useful piece of equipment was CRRA (Close-Range Recording and Analysis). The gun-layer (student aimer) and his trainer sat in the seats of a gun mounting, minus its gun. They then carried out the aiming-off on an aircraft, as though operating an actual gun, and pressed a trigger at the point where they would have opened fire. All their movements were recorded on a paper graph in a building behind them, and when the shoot was over, it was analysed. The graph would show the aircraft path, and whether laying and training had been accurate, or where the faults lay. The moment of opening fire was also shown. CRRA was very good. There could be no arguments with it. The apparatus was also mounted on a rolling platform, which reproduced the movements of a ship at sea.

The Fleet Air Arm aircraft arrived promptly at 0930 each morning, and began making its runs, simulating different types of attack. I have often wondered how the pilots felt with a crowd of learner gunnery ratings beneath them. On the four and eight barrelled pom-poms the Instructor could, in case of emergency, cut out all the guns by throwing a small lever which disengaged the firing tappets. When manning other guns, a bang on the shoulder-blade meant 'Cease firing!' The simulated attacks helped us to get experience of attacking aircraft, and now we were able to use the cartwheel sight in conjunction with tracer shells, and get the feel of the various weapons. Eventually, we had fired every gun on the range, and been given marks for our performances. On one occasion I was the last of the group to fire the Oerlikon, and as I strapped myself to the gun I could see that the aircraft was not making his usual turn to come back. It was late in the afternoon, and perhaps he was low on fuel. There was a Lieutenant Commander with a clipboard behind me, waiting to watch my shooting and award marks. I fully expected he would tell me to stand down. Suddenly he pointed out to sea and said, 'There's your target – open fire!'

My 'target' was a seagull flying serenely along on a parallel course to the range about a quarter of a mile away. I was somewhat taken aback. Nevertheless, I swung up the gun, placed the seagull in my sight, and pressed the trigger. The tracer zipped just ahead of the bird and it nose-dived to sea level and began to skim out to sea. I was anxious to get in another burst and pressed the trigger again just as the clipboard came down on my shoulder. In my exuberance I carried on for several rounds after the signal, and was soundly admonished for doing so.

The course ended on 5 April, and the following day we left Whale Island and returned to Chatham. On our return, examinations began in eleven subjects, including field training, section leading and a session at the rifle butts. After eleven days of exam-taking only one remained (in Ammunition), and we were due to take it the following day to complete the course. I had developed a rash on my trunk and had reported to the Sick-Bay to get ointment. It was an irritation but in no way debilitating.

Fred Silver and I had gone into the mess for tea. As we arrived, an order was being piped over the loudspeakers: 'All AA ratings under training fall in outside the gunnery office at the double!' Immediately, we both left the mess and ran down the road to the gunnery school to fall in with about twenty others. A Chief Petty Officer Gunner's Mate came out of the Gunnery Office and addressed us. There were two destroyers in Portsmouth, one of which was *Kelly*, the other, *Kelvin*. *Kelly* needed two AA 3s urgently. He asked for two volunteers, and Silver and I each took a pace forward. When the Chief Petty Officer asked for our station cards and I produced a sick card, he naturally refused to accept it until I had clearance. He advised me to run to the sick bay and get permission for draft. I covered the ground very quickly, only to find there was no surgeon on duty until the following morning. When I returned to the gunnery office, another rating had volunteered in my place.

I returned to the mess just in time to bid farewell to Fred Silver, who was leaving for Portsmouth. My disappointment must have been evident, because an old sea dog asked me why I was looking so down in the mouth. I told him I had just missed a draft, and when I mentioned *Kelly* he said, 'Do you know who her skipper is?' I had no idea and said so. 'Well, I'll tell you. It's Lord Louis Mountbatten and some sailors who sail with him don't draw their pensions. Thank your lucky stars, son. There's plenty more where she came from, and you'll get another soon enough.'

Only later did I come to learn what he was trying to convey. *Kelly* had commissioned under Lord Louis Mountbatten just as war was declared, and a few weeks later she was mined. In April 1940, she was in collision with another destroyer. In May 1940, she was torpedoed by E-boats, and was towed back to the Tyne with her decks awash and on the point of foundering. From 3 September 1939 to May 1940, *Kelly* had only spent fifty-seven days at sea. Most of the remaining time she was undergoing repairs. While she was spending her third period in dock, Lord Louis Mountbatten took over command of the *Javelin* and she, too, was torpedoed. This was the message the old sea dog was at pains to convey, although it did not allay my disappointment.

In April 1941, *Kelly* was ready for sea again, with Lord Louis Mountbatten in command. I imagine she would sail the day after Fred Silver had joined her and, towards the end of April she arrived in Malta, which was being heavily bombed daily. She eventually sailed to cover the evacuation of Crete, where she was bombed and sunk on 23 May 1941, Fred would have been at sea just over one month, and he did not survive. *Kelly* survivors were machine-gunned by enemy aircraft, but how Fred died no-one knows. He had been a year behind me at school, so would still be eighteen years of age.

As boys generally tend to eschew their juniors, I knew little of him before we joined up together. Nevertheless, we had lived and trained together for five months and, such was his personality, I had grown very fond of him. He was tall and slim, with sandy hair and blue eyes, and was somewhat shy; but he had an attractive, equable temperament, never raised his voice or lost his temper. There was no evidence of malice in him; he was the type who would never seek to do harm to anyone.

It is indicative of how short of AA gunners the Navy was at that time, in that two of our number were pulled out of a course before the final examination had been taken. The incident had happened on a Friday evening; I took the final exam on the following Monday morning and my total marks were 73.6%. The following day, I sewed a gunnery badge on my right arm, and was eligible for three old pence a day extra pay.

At that time, after making an allotment home from my pay I was drawing thirty shillings a month. The Navy never paid odd shillings; one had to wait until the odd shillings made a ten-shilling note before receiving it. If it was two shillings a week over ten shillings or one pound, one had to wait five weeks before receiving it. No coins were ever issued at the pay table.

I knew that, after passing out, my time in *Excellent* would be brief, and I was impatient to get away. Life in barracks was far from pleasant. Two weeks later, while walking through the drill shed, a broadcast pipe pulled me up with a jerk – 'D'you hear there? Ordinary Seaman F. Saxton, JX 234886, report to the Drafting Master-at-Arms' Office, now!'

I was passing the office as the broadcast started, and was actually tapping on the window as the broadcaster – a Leading-Seaman – was switching off his microphone. When I announced who I was, it took him several seconds to collect himself. To him, I must have appeared like a genie out of a bottle. He told me I had been drafted, and to have my kit outside that office at 0900 the following morning. I asked what the draft was, and he said irritably, 'A destroyer. You'll get full details tomorrow morning.' whereupon he closed the window on me.

At 0850 the following day, I was waiting for the office to open, along with a Leading Seaman. When the window opened, we were each handed a draft chit, with the instruction, 'You'll find her in number three basin.' Both of us were for *Hambledon* and when I asked the Leading Seaman what she was, he looked at me with some disdain and said, almost with a sigh at having to answer a sprog's tiresome questions, 'She's a Hunt Class. Go and find a hand cart and let's get this gear into the dockyard.'

Chapter 5

Hunt Class Destroyers

The destroyer – the most powerful of the unarmoured warships – played a crucial role in the last war. It is well known that the Battle of Britain hinged on the number of fighter aircraft we could put into the air with pilots to fly them. The Battle of the Atlantic was equally crucial and would have been lost without sufficient convoy escorts. 'The Battle of the Atlantic was the dominating factor throughout the war. Never for a moment could we forget that everything happening elsewhere, on land, and sea, or in the air, depended ultimately on its outcome.' *Winston Churchill*

A full-scale, building programme of escort vessels of all types had been set in motion when war began but it would be late 1940 before many of these came into commission. In the meantime, the brunt of convoy and patrol work fell to destroyers and we were desperately short of them. Indeed, throughout the war new construction never sufficiently exceeded losses to the Admiralty's satisfaction. In April 1940 the First Sea Lord, Sir Dudley Pound, sent a lengthy communication to the Commander-in-Chief Mediterranean, Admiral Sir Andrew Cunningham, giving him a run-down of the naval situation. His letter ends, 'What I would not give for another hundred destroyers.'

In his correspondence with President Roosevelt from September 1939 to August 1940, Winston Churchill repeatedly begs for the destroyers which America had retained moth-balled for many years. These destroyers were built in 1918 – 1919. When Italy came into the war, he pointed out that her entry, 'makes it necessary for us to cope with much larger numbers of submarines …' and that the only counter was destroyers. At this point he is requesting thirty or forty. When France collapses, his entreaty becomes more urgent, 'We must ask, therefore, as a matter of life or death, to be reinforced with these destroyers.'

He outlines losses and damage since the outbreak of war, and continues, 'Destroyers are frightfully vulnerable to air-bombing, and yet they must be held in the air-bombing area to prevent sea-borne invasion. We cannot sustain the rate of casualties for long, and if we cannot get a substantial reinforcement, the whole fate of the war may be decided …'

At this point he has pitched-up his request to fifty or sixty. Eventually, Roosevelt persuades the U.S. Congress to release fifty and, in his telegram of thanks Churchill writes, 'The worth of every destroyer is measured in rubies.' The worth of these fifty, very old destroyers as fighting vessels fell far short of rubies. Nevertheless, they did bridge a vulnerable gap and Churchill's eloquent pleas paid off.

Destroyers were not crucial to U-Boat hunting. This could be carried out equally well by frigates and corvettes, even asdic-equipped trawlers, but the former were not available in sufficient numbers until later in the war, and every destroyer was pressed into service. In many ways a fast, well-armed destroyer was wasted on convoy work. The 'greyhounds of the fleet' were held back as though on a leash and restricted to the maddeningly slow speed of the slowest ship in the convoy. A U-Boat hunter was, in essence, a floating listening vessel, and frigates or corvettes were adequate for that purpose. They could not, however, switch roles as a destroyer could, to doing patrol work and escorting capital ships, simply because they did not have the armament or speed. Destroyers fully earned the soubriquet 'maids of all work', and destroyer sailors considered themselves a breed apart from sailors serving in any other class of ship.

Destroyers are known in the Navy as 'the boats', and every destroyer sailor – both officer and rating – is proud to be known as a boat sailor. Fast, well-armed fleet destroyers are expensive to build, and were not well used deployed in a role other than that for which they were intended, that is, escorting capital ships and fighting their own kind. What was needed was a war vessel which would be neither corvette nor fleet destroyer yet would have the characteristics of both. The Admiralty answer was the escort destroyer and in this it got the best of both worlds. It could be quantity produced to a standard design quickly and relatively cheaply. It could be armed to meet both air attack and attack from minor, enemy war vessels. It could be a U-Boat hunter. Above all it would have destroyer speed – the virtue which enabled it to switch roles.

The first twenty were laid down just before the Second War began, from an original design by Thornycroft. This original design was considered rather too resplendent, and it was modified to come off the drawing board as the Type 1 Hunt Class Destroyer. Ship designers had their ideals that were often thwarted through shortage of equipment – usually ship armament. The Hunt Class design main armament was three, twin, dual-purpose 4 inch guns, and from two to eight torpedoes; but few Hunts were given their full due. Only types 2 and 4 got their full quota of guns, and only types 3 and 4 their torpedoes. But at least the Hunts all mounted the guns specified for them; some later destroyers (the new S Class for instance) had to make do with obsolescent guns which could not be elevated beyond 45 degrees.

The architectural design of the Hunts varied only slightly with the first three types. With the Type 4, however, the Admiralty gave Thornycroft a free hand, and they designed a superior Hunt which was given all its design armament plus three torpedoes. Only two were built – HMS *Brecon* and HMS *Brissenden* and they bore no relation architecturally to the first three types. They were handsome ships, with long fo'c'sles, short sterns and cruiser-type double flared bows. The dimensions exceeded slightly the first three types, but they had no extra speed. They were in service long after all the other Hunts were sold or scrapped. *Brecon* lasted twenty years and *Brissenden* twenty-three.

Beginning as an experiment, the Hunt Class destroyer came to be seen as among the most successful of the Second War's warships, and the American destroyer escort was designed after its fashion. Admiral Sir Andrew Cunningham was always proud to be numbered among the boat sailors. It was he who advised the First Sea Lord in 1938 that a rapid increase in Britain's destroyer building programme could be met by putting in hand a warship similar to the old 'S' Class ship he had commanded in the First War. He writes in his memoirs, 'This, I think, was the genesis of the well-known Hunt Class destroyer.'

He saw them as being invaluable for general service in the North Sea, English Channel and the Mediterranean, although their limited range (he said) restricted their use in the Atlantic. What he does not mention is that they could be oiled at sea from a tanker and Hunts, in fact, were to be used in Russian convoys. Admiral Cunningham also extolled the Hunts' anti-submarine capabilities. 'They were,' he writes, 'in great demand. Every Commander-in-Chief wanted them, and all forty of these little ships that were built gave yeoman service.' His memoirs are punctuated with descriptions of their exploits in the Mediterranean and he obviously thought highly of them. He was, however, wrong in his estimate of their numbers. Eighty-six Hunts were built – not forty! Contracts went to twelve different yards and thirty-one had emerged by the end of 1940. A further thirty-one were launched in 1941; twenty-three in 1942 and one in 1943. *Atherstone* and *Hambledon* appeared first in December 1939, the former by Cammell Laird at Birkenhead, the latter by Swan Hunter at Wallsend-on-Tyne. The last of the eighty-six was *Talybont*.

Destroyer Captains with experience in other classes of destroyer extolled the Hunts' manoeuvrability. They answered the helm well and could turn on the proverbial sixpence. They averaged one thousand tons displacement and were driven by 2-shaft geared turbines producing 19,000 shaft horsepower, which gave them a design speed of 28 knots. In good sea conditions and with an efficient engine-room and boiler-room complement this was often exceeded. The Hunts were named after the Country's many fox hunts, and, as hunting destroyers, the naming was apt. *Hambledon*'s ship's crest was crossed fox brushes surmounted by a fox's head. The Hambledon fox hunt meets in the village of Hambledon in Hampshire, where, incidentally, the first rules of cricket were drawn up. There had been a Hunt class of minesweepers in the First War and there is a Hunt Class of minesweeper today. The class may be perpetuated since fox-hunting is so intrinsically English.

Hambledon went to war with only two twin 4 inch guns instead of her design three. Her quadruple pom-pom was mounted where the missing third twin 4 inch should have been. Had the latter been supplied, the pom-pom would have been mounted on an elevated platform immediately abaft the funnel, with some slight restriction of its arc of fire. Her design complement was 146, but, with the fitting of extra equipment, it gradually increased to 170. She had a searchlight, which was removed when the platform it occupied was needed for a radar set since searchlights were seldom used in wartime. She had four Lewis guns, two Oerlikons and a Holman projector – the latter also being removed two years after commissioning. She was fitted with Asdics and radar, although her first radar had a fixed aerial whose sweep was only operative on either side of the bows.

Her twin 4 inch dual-purpose guns could elevate to 90 degrees from the horizontal, and they were semi-automatic. After the first firing the breeches opened automatically on recoil, ejecting the spent shell casings, then closed automatically when the next shells were inserted. A good gun's crew could put twenty 4 inch shells a minute into the air, that is, forty rounds per twin mounting, eighty rounds with two twins and one hundred and twenty with three twins. The average rate of fire was one round per gun barrel every four seconds – enough to daunt any pilot who, if he survived it, had then to face the close-range weapons. All the main armament was director-controlled whereas the close-range weapons had freedom to choose their targets and open fire at will.

All Hunt Class destroyers operating on the east coast had an extra weapon no other destroyer had anywhere in the fleet. It was a single pom-pom mounted in the bows forward of the anchor hawser-pipes. It was a bow-chaser expressly for engaging E-Boats and wherever a Hunt showed up with the bow-chaser fitted she was immediately recognized as an East Coast Hunt. It spoilt the lines of the ship and looked out of place. Someone described East Coast Hunts as looking like dogs with biscuits on their noses and it was an accurate and amusing description. But they were there for a very good purpose, as will be described later.

When the war ended, the Admiralty found itself with a massive number of warships of all types, many of which were now surplus to requirement. It sought to sell as many as possible and the Hunts proved popular with countries with small navies. It is interesting to see who bought or leased them.

Ecuador	2
West Germany	3
Denmark	3
India	3
Greece	8
Norway	4

China bought one and sold it to Egypt. Egypt bought a second one and sold it to Israel. This was former HMS *Cottesmore*, and she flew the Egyptian flag under two different names. When she changed hands again, Israel renamed her *Haifa* and she took part in the action at Suez in 1956. There were two Hunts named *Oakley*. The first was sunk in 1942, and a Hunt built as *Tickam* was renamed *Oakley* after her. She was one of the three sold to West Germany, who named her *Gneisenau*, the same name as the

German battleship that had been attacked and harried by Hunts in the War! There can be no greater irony than that.

Churchill knew his ships. When he described destroyers as 'frightfully vulnerable' he was not exaggerating. They have, of course, no armour at all and are known as thin-skinned warships. From bow to stern they are vulnerable at most points. There is a shell magazine forward, and a shell and depth-charge magazine aft. Amid ships are the high-pressure steam boilers and built into any spaces left are the oil fuel tanks. Yet many survived mine, bomb and torpedo, and either got back under their own steam or were towed back, some of them with decks awash and so badly damaged they were hardly worth repairing. Bombs were known to drop into destroyers' funnels, explode in the boiler room, and still not sink the victim. Some were blown into two pieces and with the fore part gone but, still making steam in the after part, came home stern first. HMS *Porcupine*, blown in half, came back in two pieces dubbed Porc and Pine.

Any destroyer sailor would expect his captain to throw himself at a superior enemy, as HMS *Glow-worm* did when she rammed the German cruiser *Hipper* at full speed tearing a gash in *Hipper*'s side and letting in 500 tons of water before she, (*Glowworm*), turned turtle and sank. HMS *Ardent* and HMS *Acasta*, two destroyers, attacked two German battleships *Scharnhorst* and *Gneisenau*. *Ardent* went down fighting relatively early in the battle; but *Acasta* threw herself at the *Scharnhorst*, torpedoing her with her last torpedo. Both destroyers took a fearful hammering and there was only one survivor from each ship. *Worcester* also took a battering from the same two battleships in their dash through the Channel in February 1942; but *Worcester* hung on to them and delivered a torpedo attack.

It was incidents such as these that made 'boat sailors' proud of their profession but, despite miraculous escapes, there were many destroyer losses. Britain commenced the war with 168 destroyers. The British and Commonwealth Navies lost a combined total of 154. During the war our shipyards produced 212 destroyers.

Hambledon's first commission had lasted only five months. After her launching in December 1939 there were some five months fitting out and undergoing trials. She was commissioned in May 1940 and her first captain was Commander S.H.Carhill RN. The following October she struck a mine off South Foreland, which blew off both her screws and damaged her port shaft. The original ship's company was paid off and the only information I could glean about it was that she had been engaged in a nuisance raid against Boulogne.

Many years later I learned that the operation had been to send a fire ship into Boulogne harbour on 7 October 1940. The raid had to be abandoned when one of the two escorting destroyers struck a mine. That destroyer was the *Hambledon*. The other destroyer, the *Vesper*, took *Hambledon* in tow and got her into Sheerness. Her repairs in Chatham dockyard took seven months.

Chapter 6

Commissioning

Leading Seaman Pays and I loaded our kit onto the handcart and pushed it out of the barracks into the dockyard, where we found *Hambledon* in Number 3 fitting-out dock. She wasn't the first Hunt Class destroyer I'd seen, but she was certainly the dirtiest. Apart from all the grime made by the dockyard workmen, her upper works were oil-bespattered, and it was obvious that much washing and painting needed to be done. I was curious as to why she was so oil-streaked, and learnt later that an oil incendiary bomb had landed on the jetty alongside her the previous weekend. It had burst, but not ignited, and she had been showered with the oil content. Unlike Plymouth and Portsmouth, Chatham never suffered a full-scale blitz. Bombs were dropped on Chatham spasmodically, but they were probably from aircraft attacking London, and neither town nor dockyard suffered the devastating raids other ports and cities did.

A few dockyard workmen were still onboard, and the upper deck was strewn with compressed air hoses and welders' electric cables. Pays and I carried our kit onboard and dumped it amidships. We were the last two of the ship's company to join her. He was a Torpedo man. I was Guns. It was 12 May 1941.

Gunner's Mate approached me. He eyed my Gunnery badge and said, 'Follow me!' He took me down into the Petty Officer's mess aft. He scrutinized the watch bill, then made out a station card and briefed me, 'Your action and defence station will be the four-barrelled pom-pom. You'll work ship in harbour in the second part of port watch. Are you temp, grog or UA.?'

He was asking whether I drew my rum ration (grog), or had I declined to do so (temperance), or was I under age, that is, under twenty. I told l him I was underage – a teenager. Gunners' Mates never parade their emotions, but I detected he was pleased to have me onboard for a very good reason. Under ideal circumstances *Hambledon* should have had seven AA ratings.

Had the four Lewis guns been manned by AA ratings, the number would have been eleven, but that would have been beyond ideal to the point of perfection.

As it was, we commissioned the ship with only three. For the rest we had to make do with ratings trained in other branches of Gunnery, who had certainly not been trained in eye-shooting. Throughout at least the first three years of the war the Navy did not have the close-range weapons it needed, nor the trained ratings to man them. Lord Louis Mountbatten had said that to protect itself adequately, a warship should have a close-range AA weapon on every available piece of upper deck space. The US Navy came close to achieving that ideal, especially on their aircraft carriers. The Royal Navy, however, never matched the Americans in that respect.

The reason was that air attack at sea had not been a feature of the First War, and it was some time after 1918 before the threat began to be obvious. The Second War came too soon for the weapons to be produced, and the men trained, for the weakness to be remedied. The shortfall tended to impair the fighting efficiency of ships in air defence. Somehow, we muddled through. Non-AA gunnery ratings manning Lewis guns and Oerlikons became self-taught in eye-shooting. They could see the line of fire of their tracer, and quickly adapted to the technique, principally because they had body control of their weapons. But they were not eye-shooting by use of the forward area sight in the full sense, and would have fallen short on mechanically operated weapons such as the pom-poms and .5 machine guns.

It was dinner time when I lowered my kit onto the after-mess deck. I could hear a babble of voices coming up from below where the meal was being served out. I felt very much the new boy. The others had preceded me by two to four days, and were already acquainted with one another. The Leading Seaman of the mess showed me an empty locker and suggested I put the contents of my kit bag into it when I had eaten. I then sat down to my first meal onboard – corned beef and mashed potatoes.

The initial triggers towards the formation of later friendships are often accents. People feel kindly disposed towards someone with their own accent. There seems to be a sort of a clan connection with which they can identify and feel comfortable. It happened here. In conversing with the Leading Seaman, my Yorkshire accent was apparent to one rating, who was the first to introduce himself. 'My name's Gee, better known as 'Horse'. I'm from Doncaster. Where do you hail from?'

The Hunts were the first destroyers to be designed with two seamen's mess decks. Hitherto, all the seamen had messed forward in the bows, with the stokers one deck below them, The Wardroom and Officers' quarters had been aft where *Hambledon*'s after seamen's deck now was. It was said that the Officers had the broad end and the ratings the pointed end!

It was not an ideal arrangement. When action stations were sounded, and they did almost every day, the after guns' crews, mouths still full of corned beef, had to rush forward impeding the Officers trying to get aft to the bridge. Eventually, the bridge superstructure of destroyers was enlarged to house the Wardroom and Officers' cabins, and the space aft became a second seamen's mess deck. Destroyer seamen, so messed, considered themselves fortunate. They could spread out a little instead of sitting in each other's laps, and the after-mess deck was seen as something of a privilege. 'Jack' (the navy vernacular for a sailor) would never admit that the powers that-be had done this expressly for his benefit, even if it had been that way. His version was that the seamen had been split up to lessen the chances of mutiny. With men at each end of the ship, theycould not get their heads together and hatch plots!

But there was a mutiny at a future time. After weeks at sea the *Hambledon* crew, exhausted, returned to port expecting shore leave. The order was given to prepare ship for immediate return to sea. We refused the pipe to 'All hands on deck!' The cover was removed and the First Lieutenant ordered us to get on deck immediately. We shouted back at him and some of the things we shouted were extremely rude. We were at the end of our tethers. The hatch went back on over our heads and was locked. We were now imprisoned. An hour later the hatch was removed and we were confronted with Royal Marines leveling their rifles down at us. The First Lieutenant said, 'I am going to give the order to come on deck one more time. If you do not obey me I shall order the Marines to open fire. Now get up on deck!' We got up on deck.

On the following day the Captain paraded the ship's company. He said, 'If anyone wishes to speak to me on this matter he shall step forward now and be heard.' I stepped forward and said that I wished to speak on behalf of the forward lower deck. The Captain said, 'You will speak on behalf of yourself or you will not speak at all.' I stepped smartly back into line and snapped to attention. There was an agonising minute's silence broken only by the gulls. The Captain said, 'Dismiss them Number One!'

The First Lieutenant dismissed us to duty, we having made our protest. But it was a very dangerous thing to have done. The penalty for mutiny in the Royal Navy in time of war was, and always had been, death. But battle-hardened Jacks like us were too valuable. England would find more useful ways for us to die. The Captain looked drawn. None of this was his fault; he was obeying orders. Nevertheless, a mutiny had occurred on board a Royal Navy warship under his command. I do not know what happened to him.

Owing to the mine damage, the after-mess deck had been newly fitted out with lockers and mess tables. The lockers were about eighteen inches cubed, and into them went all one's gear except for the overcoat and oilskin. They also doubled as seats, so there was much shuffling around when men wanted something from their lockers. These were topped with well-padded cushions which, like everything else in the mess, were new. It was by no means luxury, but it was far better than I imagined a destroyer's mess deck would be. It was to be my home for over three years, but we saw so little of it at sea that it acquired a certain attraction simply by virtue of its being denied to us at deck stations for such long periods.

To give some idea of vulnerability. Underneath our feet in one half of the mess deck was the shell magazine; underneath the other half was an oil fuel tank. When the ship rolled, the oil fuel could be heard sloshing around underneath the feet. No hammocks were slung at sea on the East Coast. If we were fortunate to get some time below during the night, men off watch slept on the lockers or on the deck. Often I had laid asleep on the deck, hearing the oil sloshing around, and feeling its movement beneath me. On such occasions I tried not to dwell on what would happen if a striking torpedo caused the deck I was lying on to collapse!

We had nine days to get the ship cleaned up and ready for sea. All the upper works had to be washed clean of oil before painting, and no-one was excused 'paint ship'. No uniform clothing was worn; we were all in boiler suits, slapping on the 'battleship grey'. The last of the dockyard men had now departed, and we began to clean up the grime they had left behind. It took a week to get her looking like a ship, but she was not yet a ship until she had a head of steam in her boilers.

A sailing ship without sails is no more than a floating hulk. Its sails were the life force; the sight of them and all the sounds they made. Similarly, the life force of a steam-driven ship was its steam; without steam it was a cold dead metal shell. Since warships are no longer steam-driven, I am at a loss to know what constitutes that which I now describe.

With steam in her boilers the ship comes to life, and all the senses bear witness to the fact of her resurrection. She sucks air into her boiler rooms and breathes it out through her punkah louvres. The steady thud of her pumps reverberate like heart beats. Her bulkheads become warm to the touch and her decks to the soles of the feet. She exudes a smell – a mixture of warm oil, smoke and steam – which can almost be tasted. On deck the funnel emits smoke and a wisp of steam curls from her siren. Suddenly her screws start turning, but she is not going anywhere. They turn slowly and churn up the sludge in the basin while she pulls tentatively at her mooring wires as the engineers test her engines.

During the nine days of clean-up I was able to get to know my mess mates and acquire a nodding acquaintance with other members of the ship's company. There were ten Officers, including a Surgeon Lieutenant and the Lieutenant Engineer Officer. The Captain, John Richard Barnes, was a Lieutenant Commander. The First Lieutenant was Eric Ian Pilditch RN. The senior Sub-Lieutenant and Navigator was Nicholas Fitzherbert RN. All were experienced Officers, as was the RN Engineer Lieutenant. There was also a Gunner, a Mr Renouf RN. So HMS *Hambledon* began her second commission with all her Senior Officers time-serving veterans. As the war progressed, some of these men would get their own commands and be replaced by RNVR (Royal Navy Volunteer Reserve) Officers.

Although this chapter is headed 'Commissioning', since *Hambledon* had already been commissioned, the ceremony that was held before we left the dockyard was, in fact, re-commissioning. We were piped out of overalls into No 3 dress, and the whole ship's company was fallen-in on the dockside. John Barnes then gave us a run-down on our imminent movement and likely future role. He finished by telling us exactly what he expected from us. He then went back on board and we were called to attention as he appeared again, accompanied by an elderly Rear Admiral. If we were expecting a rip-roaring speech from the Admiral, we certainly did not get one. *Hambledon* was already wearing the White Ensign, so no running up was necessary. That flag told all who saw it that she was a warship of the Royal Navy.

The Admiral recounted the useful work the ship had done on the East Coast during her first commission and hoped we would continue in the best traditions of the service. He closed by wishing us good hunting. We were then called to attention and he returned to the Wardroom from whence he had come, with John Barnes in his wake, presumably for liquid refreshment. It would have included a choice of every spirit except rum. Rum was for Jack, not for Officers. Each sailor got his 'tot' ladelled into his tin cup under the gimlet eye of a Petty Officer. Rum was 'cut' with an equal amount of water, which was called 'grog'. Grog goes sour if you don't drink it more or less immediately. This was to prevent Jack from storing it up for a big binge and getting fighting drunk and in serious trouble. Destroyers were a powder keg in more ways than one!

On 19 May 1941, we left the dockyard and moved down river to Sheerness for trials, On the following day dockyard engineering staff and a Lieutenant-Commander Gunnery Officer came onboard, and we slipped down the estuary to test engines and guns. Engine testing amounted to bursts of speed ahead, stopping, going astern and testing the steering motors and rudder. The Base Gunnery Officer was an elderly man who had probably been called up from retirement, and, like all elderly gunnery officers, he was hard of hearing. It was on his orders that I fired *Hambledon*'s quadruple pom-pom for the first time.

Then came the big one. When the twin 4 inch guns, the main armament on the ship were being tested, I was quite shaken by their wicked crack. After the 4 inch test the Gunnery Officer came onto the pom-pom deck and, without any ceremony, said, 'Train to red nine 0, angle of sight six 0, and give me six bursts of six. Increase your elevation with each burst towards 90 degrees!' After the six bursts, and with seventy-two shells expended, he said, 'That's fine. Train fore and aft and secure!'

He disappeared down the ladder while we began replenishing the used ammunition. When all testing had been done, we returned to a buoy at Sheerness. Most men onboard had never experienced the firing of the destroyer's main armament, the twin 4 inch guns, because these guns were a new innovation. One rating, who had served in a cruiser with 8 inch guns, avowed that the twin 4 inchers were harder on the ears. When asked to explain, he said the report from the larger guns was more 'whoof' than 'crack', and he would settle for the larger. We were issued with rubber earplugs, but they were not very effective and most of us discarded them for cotton wool, which could be tamped tight in the ears. This did not prevent the increasing deafness that I endured in later years.

Hambledon did not have a green ship's company. About a quarter were time-serving ratings, and the other three quarters, although 'hostilities-only' ratings, had served for six months on one of the fifty lease-lend ex-American destroyers, so at least they had acquired their sea legs. I was one of a few who had never been to sea before. The ex-Yankee, as we called them, included the re-named HMS *Bath* and many were the tales they told about her. She was top-heavy, rolled alarmingly in the slightest swell, and was prone to machinery breakdown. Her armament was a grim joke given the life-or-death game we were in. When she was paid off for modifications we were glad to see the back of her.

All the lease-lend destroyers constituted not much more than a 'presence' until they could be taken in, fitted with Asdics, modified and brought up to reasonable standard. Most of our modern destroyers had only one funnel, until even the modern Tribal class with two (one large and one small) began to look out of date. The Yankees, with their four tall funnels (the Americans used the term 'smoke-stacks') looked hideous. It was these that gave them top weight and caused rolling, so, when some of them were modified, two funnels were removed and their four boilers trunked into the two remaining ones. When they exchanged the Stars and Stripes for the White Ensign, they were named after British towns and cities which had equivalent named towns and cities in the USA.

As new tonnage came into commission, some of the Yankees were passed on to other allied navies. Five went to Russia, nine to the Royal Canadian Navy, and five to the Royal Norwegian Navy – including the *Bath* which was sunk by a U-boat in 1941. But eleven U-boats were sunk by the ex-Yankees. Another of them, HMS *St Albans*, distinguished herself by sinking a U-boat, then severely blotted her escutcheon twice by sinking a British minesweeper and a Polish submarine! In all, eight of them were lost to enemy action, and *Campbeltown*, with her bows packed with explosives, covered herself and her crew in glory when, she rammed and blew up the lock gate at St. Nazaire. She was, of course, considered expendable, but her last exploit equalled the Zeebrugge raid of 1918, and was the most audacious naval expedition carried out in the entire war. It was a signal success. The enemy was denied use of the dry dock, crippling their naval threat in the area for the remainder of hostilities.

Chapter 7

Scapa Flow

We left Sheerness for Scapa Flow on 21 May 1941 for what sailors call rubbing-up trials. Scapa Flow is the best natural harbour in Britain. It nestles within the Orkney Islands, sheltered and usually safe from submarines. It was the last resting place and the last act of defiance of the German Navy at the end of the First World War. Ordered to sail there after the defeat of Germany, they sat at anchor while the British Admiralty prevaricated and delayed a decision as to what to do. Eventually, the German Admiral of the Fleet, his dignity tested to the limit, sent out a code word to all the warships under his command. Getting as many sailors off in boats as they could, the sea-cocks were opened and the German High Seas Fleet was scuttled. These fearsome, armoured battleships sank slowly down at anchor, eventually to settle intact on the sea bed, where they still rest, visible from the air, today. The Admiral's name was Ludwig von Reuter. He may have been the enemy, but he proved himself and his crews to be fighting sailors to the last. I admired him.

We had been given a month to get our act together. All the different branches had to familiarise themselves with the ship, their part in its efficient functioning and the whole to act in accord. From Sheerness to Orkney by sea is about 600 miles and at an economical cruising speed of twenty-two knots would take us twenty-seven hours. We left at 0900 hrs and went straight into defence stations – four hours on and four hours off. Cleaning and meal preparation were done by the watch below.

On a small ship the cooks only cook the meals. All preparation of it is done by two men in each mess on a daily rota, who prepare the vegetables, make pastry and mix gravies and custards. All have to do it in their turn and those who did not know how had to learn very quickly or suffer slings and arrows from their shipmates. We were assigned 'No Man-o'-War' duties throughout the trip.

We passed convoys en route, but all we were required to do was get from point A to point B. I had the middle watch (midnight to 0400 hrs) below deck and it was pleasant to fall asleep in a slightly swaying hammock listening to the whine of the propeller shafts spinning below the mess deck. That month, operating from Scapa was to be the last time we would use our hammocks at sea for over two years.

We arrived at Scapa on 22 May and found it denuded of capital ships. Later we discovered why – the German battleship *Bismarck* was on the loose! After oiling we went to a buoy in the destroyers' anchorage in the Lee of Hoy and looked around to see who our companions were. Destroyers carry their pennant letter and numerals on their bows and stern and from them you knew the name of the ship. The letter denoted the class of ship and the number her name. Thus, 'L' denoted Hunt class (or any escort destroyer) and 37 was *Hambledon*. Most writers who have spent time at Scapa Flow describe it as inhospitable. There are no trees on Orkney and the only amenity ashore at that time was a corrugated iron, wet canteen. In winter the nights are long, the daylight hours short and the wind blows across the Flow making the destroyers snatch at their bridles and swing around their buoys. For small ships sailors, coming in from sea, it had nothing to commend it.

In the summer, however, it is much more pleasant. The wind departs for other climes; all the heather is in bloom and the days are long. Even when darkness descends, there is never Stygian blackness because there is an ethereal glow from the Northern Lights. Scapa, then, was all Navy. There were no houses or shops, only shipping. Boats and drifters plied across the Flow all day long and the only sounds on the clear summer air were bugle calls from capital ships and the trilling of Bosun's pipes. With double British Summer Time it was still light at 2200 hrs and one could walk the deck watching the sea birds still wheeling in the sky. Granted, there were no amenities ashore, but nature compensated in other ways.

We went to sea every day during that month doing practice anti-aircraft and surface shoots. We had a drogue-towing aircraft and a target-towing tug at our disposal and we made mistakes. The twin 4 inch put one of their salvos dangerously close to the aircraft on one occasion and the following inquest revealed a rating in the gunnery transmitting station had not followed his pointers correctly and had thrown the guns off target.

During one of the night surface shoots we were using the searchlight, which was layed and trained from the bridge. All the searchlight operator had to do was open the venetian blind shutter. Came the order, 'On searchlight – open fire!' The shutter was opened, the powerful beam lit up the 'target' and all guns roared. We straddled what we were aiming at but it was the tug – not the target, There was frantic flashing by Aldis lamp from the tug informing us of something that was now only too plain. Once again, someone in the chain had made an error. Fortunately, we were using solid, non-explosive practice shells.

In between practices we went out into the western approaches on convoy duty. We would escort a westbound convoy for two days, then turn to escort an incoming eastbound convoy. During these trips we experienced the Atlantic in all its moods and it was an awesome experience. At sea we wore anything we chose. All seamen were issued with what was called a 'goon skin'. It was in two pieces – a kapok-lined, inner garment like a boiler suit over which went an oilskin of the same shape. They were never separated. You climbed into both at the same time and fastened the fronts with huge press studs. They were warm and guaranteed to keep you buoyant even though we had inflatable life belts. We had thick woollen seaboot stockings and leather or rubber seaboots; also fleece lined mittens.

All these were free on loan; anything else such as mufflers, balaclavas and extra jerseys had to be bought from the clothing allowance. If a red goalkeeper's jersey kept a man warm he could wear it, and there was no requirement to shave at sea in bad weather. Small ship sailors took on an aspect of ruffian pirates, until hands were piped to fall-in for entering harbour, when there was a reversion to uniform.

The number of times in the year when the Atlantic is reasonably calm are few. Its moods can change from choppy to storm-lashed and when the rough seas arrive you begin to feel it is never going to let up. It can persist for day after wearisome day until you are assured it is never going to be calm again and has decided to take it out on you forever. Sailors use the phrase, 'We were shipping it green.' When the huge waves stand erect thirty to forty feet high, they are translucent and, with the sun behind them, they shine emerald-green. They begin to gather strength some distance from the ship, growing ever taller as they draw nearer. Then the foaming crest begins to bend into a perfect curl like a parchment and you just know this one is yours.

It is like a mobile wall of water marching towards the ship until it becomes top-heavy, leans over and comes crashing down onto the upper deck showering all the upperworks in foaming swishing spume. The ship staggers under the impact and the weight of water drives her down below her normal displacement. When she reasserts herself she shakes the water from her deck like a wet dog shaking its coat. This is a beam sea and it makes her roll. Sometimes she rolls so far over her guardrails sweep the water and one begins to hold one's breath wondering whether she is going to come back on an even keel. At that point she is vulnerable if struck by another heavy wave. In a head sea she will pitch and toss. She will dig her bows in deep, take water over her fo'c'sle and kick her stern high until her barely submerged screws begin to throw off spray. If her bows miss the start of a wave, it will run-on under her gathering height until her midships become the point of balance. Her bows and stern will then sag and her guardrails will tauten, sometimes breaking under the strain. Alternatively, when her bows and stern are each on the crest of a wave she will sag amidships and her guardrails will slacken and hang loose. If she did not act this way, of course, she would break her back.

Merchant sailors in a convoy in prolonged heavy seas sometimes wondered how destroyers stood up to the battering. One minute they would see their escort in full view high in the air; the next, she had vanished as though swallowed up into a watery grave, the only thing visible being the top of her foremast waving around in the air, and sometimes even that vanished from sight. In such seas it is dangerous to traverse the upper deck. Lifelines are rigged permanently – port and starboard – from which hang short lengths of rope with a thimble eye at one end and Turk's Head knot at the other. It was like mobile strap-hanging. You waited for a lull, grabbed your rope and hoped to make it between breakers. Sometimes you were lucky. If you were not the breaker would knock you off your feet and take you from the vertical to the horizontal, leaving you clutching your rope with both hands for dear life. When it passed, your feet found the deck once again and you completed your journey in a soaking condition.

All small ship sailors suffer sea sickness. A few just could not stand the rigours and requested to be drafted to bigger ships. Some were sick to the point of regularly vomiting, but everyone suffered varying degrees of nausea which manifested itself in different ways. The first to succumb go off their food; then smoking goes by the board. Eventually, only the fortunate few are eating and only the old sea dogs are puffing their pipes. It has nothing to do with sea time. We had a Leading Seaman with years of service who used to take a bucket on watch with him when he did his trick at the wheel. Alternatively, a 'sprog' Ordinary Seaman might well be able to eat his food and keep it down. Some unfortunates turned a delicate shade of green round the gills, and it was to these that the cruel impervious would say, 'Feel like a nice greasy bacon sandwich, do you?'

After several days of rough seas, your head is spinning and your body bruised through collisions due to the pitching and tossing. You are mentally and physically weary from the strain of it all. You long for the storm to abate and leave you in peace. You scan the heavens hopefully for a break in the overcast; for that little patch of blue cloud 'no bigger than a man's hand' which might signal a lull. Below decks everything has, as far as possible, been made secure; but there is always something that manages to break loose. Usually it is boots and shoes and the caps no one is wearing. There were racks above the lockers for our round metal hat boxes and our cases. In a reasonable sea they sufficed; in an unreasonable sea they did not.

Destroyers not only pitch and toss – they also kick. They teeter on the crest of a wave in the toss then kick slightly before they begin the pitch. It was this motion which unseated the hat boxes and cases, sending them crashing onto the deck and spilling out their contents. Sometimes the mess deck is awash with water from leaky scuttles, spilled washing-up water or the father of all breakers. It swills around with each roll of the ship, leaving behind matchsticks, buttons, safety pins – even spilled dried peas and lentils – like the sand in a gold prospector's pan. During mealtimes, one was as much standing as sitting, chasing items of crockery along the table and trying – not always successfully – to prevent one's food being deposited in one's lap. Taking soup in a rough sea without spillage requires much practice, until you can keep the plate level against ship movement as a compass is kept level by its gimbal ring.

Eventually, though, every storm does abate. You can feel it begin to slacken, feel it begin to ease off from full fury and hope that tomorrow it will be possible to clear up and dry out the mess deck; to open up a few scuttles and let in some fresh air; above all, that the ship will cease acting like a demented bronco and let you regain your equilibrium.

With *Bismarck* on the loose and, for all we knew, likely to loom up over the horizon at any time, we were shattered to receive the news that the pride of the Navy, the battlecruiser HMS *Hood* had engaged the *Bismarck* and had been sent to the bottom. Prime Minister Winston Churchill, himself a former First Lord of the Admiralty, knew this was not to be tolerated. He sent to the Admiralty one of his most famously succinct orders, 'Sink the *Bismarck!*' This was as much dire threat to the Nazis as it was direct warfare.

It was on our return from an Atlantic trip that news came through on 27 May that *Bismarck* had been sunk and our sadness at the loss of *Hood* was mingled with jubilation. But we in the lower deck became angry when the details came through. The *Bismarck* had been crippled in rudder by Fleet Air Arm Swordfish torpedo bombers. She was doomed to steam in a circular dance of death, going nowhere until the battleships of the Royal Navy found her and finished her off, battering her to pieces with gunfire. She should have been finished quickly by torpedo attack, as, eventually, the cruiser HMS *Belfast* was ordered in to do. It looked to us that there had been an unnecessary and vengeful waste of life.

We in the lower deck were confused and angry. There was an offence in the Royal Navy at the time called 'Dumb Insolence'. You had to be very careful how you skirted around that one. We continued to salute and address the higher orders correctly. But our eyes were cold. There was no warmth in our greetings. We were giving a message. They may have been Germans; but they were Jacks – like us.

It was not often that Scapa Flow was denuded of capital ships. So voracious was their oil consumption, and so precious were they as a fleet in being, that they only went to sea when there was a need for them to do so. The oceans were scouted by cruisers who could call up heavier units, as indeed happened with *Bismarck*. Destroyer sailors were well aware of the role of capital ships, but that did not prevent their resenting capital ship inactivity. They found it galling to keep going to sea and returning for oil, then going out again after one night in harbour to return and find the capital ships immobile. Their resentment regularly came to a head in pubs in Portsmouth or Plymouth. It only needed one inebriated destroyer sailor to shout, 'Get some sea time in, you useless buggers!' for all hell to break loose.

It was more prone to happen at Scapa than anywhere else simply because of chronic lack of amenities. When men went ashore to the wet canteen, they were taken and brought back on a large drifter. On the return trip there would be a few drunken sailors and a lot of assorted cap ribbons. Eventually the boat sailors would begin to sing their ditty. At some time in the past someone had taken the hymn tune 'Lyndene' from the hymn 'Yield not to Temptation' and scurrilised the chorus. It had absolutely no pretension to rhyme.

The actual chorus goes:

> 'Ask the Saviour to help you,
> Comfort, strengthen and keep you,
> He is willing to aid you,
> He will carry you through.'

Everyone knew the actual chorus. Those who had not sung it in Sunday School must have heard the Salvation Army play and sing it many times in the streets. It needed only one destroyer sailor to begin singing the scurrilised version for others to join him until there was a swelling refrain of:

> 'Keep the big ships in harbour,
> Keep the big ships in harbour,
> Keep the big ships in harbour,
> The destroyers will carry you through.
>
> Rat-tat-tat go machine guns,
> Pom-pom-pom go the poms,
> Bang, bang, bang go the four inch,
> The destroyers will carry you through.'

Naturally, the big ship men wouldn't put up with this for long and fights would break out with caps being grabbed and thrown about. If there were Army soldiers there and they squared up to a sailor, there would be a rapid intervention by any Royal Marine present. 'Booties' (Royal Marines) regarded fighting Jack as their own prerogative, and the Army could find someone else to fight. Hard to believe the British Army was short of custom.

As the drifter approached the first ship, the Leading Seamen and Petty Officers would demand order. If this first call was an imposing battleship, its looming presence might be sufficient to quell the hot-heads. Sometimes it was not and it was not unknown for the battleship's Officer of the Day, standing at the head of the ship's ladder to order the drifter Cox'n to stand-off until conduct befitting the Senior Service had been restored. Once on board their respective ships, those who had lost their caps would be in trouble for returning improperly dressed. I was told that sometime later two drifters were to be laid on as a matter of course – one for big ships, the other for small!

Included in our trials was depth charge practice. When this was carried out we must have dropped our charges in the middle of a shoal of cod. After the underwater explosions the sea was dotted with dead and stunned codfish and the Captain ordered the whaler to be lowered. It returned with a sizeable catch and for supper that evening we had fried cod, literally straight out of the sea into the pan. There was sufficient left over for us to barter the fish with drifter crews for eggs and home-grown tomatoes.

One of our assignments had been to act as sole escort to a large troopship from Lerwick in the Shetlands to Aberdeen. We proceeded to Lerwick independently and spent the afternoon and all night there while the trooper was loading. We eyed Lerwick longingly from the upper deck but no leave was given. Next morning, we preceded the trooper out of the harbour and she emerged with her upper deck lined with khaki-clad figures. I suppose the objective was to get this precious cargo of soldiers off the high seas as soon as possible. There could be no question of risking the German E-boat gamut down the East coast, so the convoy went into Aberdeen to continue its journey by rail.

The trooper was a pre-war liner with a reasonable turn of speed. We did an anti-U-boat sweep around it and got it safely to Aberdeen at 2000 hrs the same day. On arrival, we hung back and let the trooper go in first. When we followed, with ship's company fallen in on the upper deck for entering harbour, one of the piers was lined with the famous, Aberdeen herring-fishing lassies who waved at us and began singing, 'All the nice girls love a sailor!' How we wished! We had no leave in Aberdeen either;

in fact, in that month at Scapa, I do not recall any shore leave being given. We left Aberdeen at 0830 hrs the following morning.

Whenever we were in harbour on Sunday, a church service was held on the aftermess deck. Usually, it was conducted by the Captain but, where there were big ships, we might be privileged to have one of their Chaplains. When the Captain conducted it there was, of course, no sermon. All hands would be piped to church and hymn cards were issued.

Only the officers were able to sit on chairs brought from the Wardroom; everyone else stood throughout. The Captain appeared last of all and took up his position behind a purpose-made lectern covered with the Negative signal – a white flag with black crosses. The first hymn was announced and the Officers would strike up the tune. On one occasion, the Captain began singing first and everyone was so surprised that no one joined in. After the second line he stopped and said testily, 'I'm not here to sing solos.'

There would then be a prayer by the Captain from the Naval Prayer book, a Bible reading from one of the Officers and a final hymn. It was usually uninspiring; but one day we had a Chaplain-conducted service while at Scapa and I remember it clearly because of the effect it had on me. The man was very young (early twenties) and very blond; in his white surplice he looked positively angelic. I remember nothing of his sermon. All I remember was the text he used from Psalm 24:

> 'The earth is the Lord's, and the fulness thereof;
> The world and they that dwell therein.
> For he hath founded it upon the seas,
> And established it upon the floods.'

When the service was over I stood alone on the upper deck. Around me lay a mighty fleet of warships. Practically the whole of Europe was under the Nazi jack boot. Britain stood alone and I wondered what the final outcome of it all would be. Thinking on the text, it suddenly struck me that nations tended to fight over pieces of the earth like dogs over a bone, fighting and quarrelling as though they had created it and could do as they pleased with it. It seemed so far removed from, 'The earth is the Lord's and the fulness thereof.' I was appalled at man's blind arrogance.

We were now due to leave Scapa and return south. As we were lashing up our hammocks on the morning of 22 June, the BBC news bulletin announced that Germany had attacked Russia. There was an immediate babble of excitement and Able Seaman Colin Calder (who was later commissioned as an Officer) said, 'I'll bet Stafford Cripps bounded up the Kremlin steps two at a time this morning, wagging his finger and shouting, "I told you so!" Sir Stafford Cripps was our special envoy in Moscow at the time. The laughter that followed the quip was as much from relief as amusement. Germany had presented Britain with her first ally.

We left Scapa at noon on 22 June acting as escort to the County Class cruiser *Cumberland* which was bound for refitting in Chatham. *Cumberland* at that time was reputed to have been longer at sea since the war began than any other ship in the Navy. She had been operating as the lead warship in the South Atlantic Cruiser Squadron, whose other members were the heavy cruiser *Exeter*, and cruisers *Ajax* and *Achilles*. These three ships had hunted down the 'pocket battleship' *Graf Spee*.

The *Graf Spee* was a feared surface raider and she had to be dealt with. She was a brilliant piece of German engineering. She was armoured to battleship standards with an anti-submarine skirt. Instead of the four twin-gun turrets that were standard on battleships of the day giving a fire-power of eight 15 inch guns, she reduced weight by mounting only two turrets of three guns each. That made her two guns short, but the reduction in weight enabled her to achieve a battle speed of a cruiser. Not only that – she was not steam driven. She was powered by enormous banks of diesel engines. Whereas our battleships took a day or more to get up steam in their boilers from cold, this was a capital ship that could cast off at the touch of a button. And, loath to admit it, Kriegsmarine gunners seemed able to hit targets somewhat better than we could achieve with our equipment. Ignoring the naval maxim that you had to be able to out-gun anything you couldn't out-run; and out-run anything you could not out-gun, the Royal Navy South Atlantic cruisers, under the command of Rear Admiral Henry Harwood, went for her.

In December 1939, *Cumberland* had gone to the Falklands for a refit, while her three sister-cruisers were engaged in a running gun-battle with the *Admiral Graf Spee* in the first major sea battle of the Second World War. Rear Admiral Harwood had raised his flag in HMS *Ajax*, commanded by Captain Charles Woodhouse. The cruisers had caught up with her off the mouth of the River Plate in Uruguay. It became known as the Battle of the River Plate.

Admiral Harwood was a lateral thinker who was, apparently, not afraid of being shot on his own Quarterdeck. He did not necessarily obey the rules – which was all right in the Royal Navy if it went all right. Not if it didn't. The commander of the *Graf Spee*, Capitan Hans Lansdorff, was astounded. Harwood's cruisers were not using cruiser tactics. Cruisers were supposed to engage from a distance, but these warships were using their speed to get in close, effectively increasing their fire power. Langsdorff complained, 'Those cruisers are attacking me like destroyers!'

Capitan Langsdorff correctly concentrated his fire on the most powerful enemy vessel, the heavy cruiser *Exeter*, but as the Royal Navy squadron harried him from different sides he made the tactical mistake of shifting his concentration of fire from one British cruiser to another, instead absorbing their punishment and sinking them individually. *Exeter* was badly damaged and pulled out of the fight. Discretion being the better part of valour, Langsdorff also pulled out and retreated up within the River Plate (Rio de la Plata) and docked in Montevideo. *Cumberland* was ordered to make all speed to the River Plate to relieve *Exeter* who had only one gun turret left in operation. *Cumberland* steamed one thousand miles, at full speed, in thirty-two hours; but the battle was never resumed.

Hans Langsdorff, the Captain of the *Graf Spee*, denied any extension to the 72 hours of respite in a neutral port, ordered the priming of explosive charges within his warship. He then got her ship's company ashore. With a skeleton crew, the *Graf Spee* cast off at the touch of a button, moved down river, and blew herself up. Scuttling, I believe, was acceptable in the Kriegsmarine as an honourable option. Not in my navy.

It was rumoured that Langsdorff's decision was the result of a dupe. Royal Navy signals' intelligence had been transmitting radio traffic that the battleship HMS *Warspite* was coming flat out across the South Atlantic to engage the *Graf Spee*. German intelligence was intercepting these messages and relaying them to Langsdorff. Everyone was in awe of *Warspite* no matter which side you were on. She had the finest fighting record of any battleship in two world wars. It was not true that she was steaming southwest – she was in the Mediterranean – but Langsdorff believed she was, shortly to confront him. He refused battle. He scuttled one of the finest modern warships in the world. He then went to his cabin ashore, loaded his pistol, and shot himself.

The following may be apocryphal, but I record it anyway as the word that went round. A wireless signal was received on HMS *Ajax*. Captain Woodward said, 'Congratulations Admiral – His Majesty has appointed you KCMG!'

Admiral Harwood was pallid and confused after days of battle and very little sleep. He said,

'Remind me Charlie – what does that stand for?'

Maintaining a perfectly straight face his Captain replied,

'It stands for "Kindly Call Me God!" Sir. Let's get you below. You need some rest.'

The long-suffering *Cumberland* had to stay on station at sea for another eighteen months without her refit. When she eventually returned home, we were deployed as her destroyer escort to bring her safely home. The objective was get her safely through the E-boat infested North Sea narrows in daylight, and the trip was timed to that end. We took up station ahead of her doing an Asdic sweep at 22 knots. Any speed faster than that rendered the Asdics inoperable due to the acoustics from the wash and from the screws. U-boats were unable to operate south of a certain point in the North Sea owing to our mine barrier.

Consequently, after that line was reached, our Asdic dome was housed and speed increased. Although a fleet destroyer was normally comfortably capable of out-pacing a cruiser, *Cumberland* was an exception and was two knots faster than we were. That was very fast for a cruiser. She began to overhaul us, just to annoy us, and eventually swept past. She was quite near, and I could see through binoculars that her upperworks were streaked with salt and her waterline barnacle-encrusted. She had been almost continuously at sea since before the war began and, from the weather-beaten state of her, this was evident. Goodness knows what mental and physical state her ship's company were in.

Our cruisers varied architecturally far more than our destroyers and I was never enamoured by the County Class. Good fighting ships – yes – but sailors like their ships to look good too. With their three, tall funnels and high freeboard (height from waterline to upper deck level) they seemed to me more like liners with gun turrets than warships. I always considered the Southampton Class a far better-looking cruiser. Nevertheless, with their eight 8 inch guns, the County Class, apart from our battle-cruisers, were our heaviest cruisers. *Exeter*, who also mounted 8 inch guns, had used hers to good effect against the *Graf Spee*.

After stretching her sea legs, *Cumberland* eventually settled for an economical cruising speed and the trip proved uneventful. Signals passed from time to time by Aldis lamp. It was all very 'pusser'. Apart from both ships being blacked out during the night, we could have been an a pre-war exercise.

Both of us were now Chatham bound, *Cumberland* to pay-off and refit; *Hambledon* for final adjustments after her trials. We were in Chatham two days, then left with a clean bill of health on 26 June to join the 16th Destroyer Flotilla based at Harwich. Back at Scapa we carried out useful exercises, acquired some more North Atlantic experience and the ship's company was licked into shape.

The final item of news to reach us before we left Scapa was the Admiralty's announcement of warships lost at the Battle of Crete. HMS *Kelly* was numbered amongst them.

Chapter 8

East Coast Convoys

After spending the night at a buoy in Sheerness, we left with a northbound convoy on 27 June and arrived in Harwich on 28 June. We were to be based there in the 16th Destroyer Flotilla as a unit of the North Sea Command for the next two years.

Harwich harbour lies in the outlet of the River Stour, with Harwich town on its south bank. The estuary of the Stour is shared with the River Orwell, both rivers flowing into the sea at the same point. Where the two rivers form this common estuary, there is a promontory on which stood the pre-war boys' training ship *Ganges*. There was also a signal station on the promontory from which we received our instructions to proceed to sea. Inside the harbour on the south bank of the Stour is Parkestone Quay from which peace-time liners sailed to the Hook of Holland. Trains disembarked passengers at Parkestone, then ran through to Dovercourt and Harwich.

Harwich played a different role in the Second War from the one that it played in the First. In the First there were both destroyers and submarines at Harwich, the destroyers under Commodore Reginald Tyrwhitt, the submarines under Commodore Roger Keyes. Germany, then, had a large High Seas Fleet, which looked upon the North Sea as the German Sea. In order to bring home to them that it was not so, Admiral of the Fleet John Jellicoe lay with his awesome fleet of capital ships at Scapa Flow. There was a secondary fleet based on Dover. Thus, it was intended to bottle up the German Navy and, if it strayed into the narrows off East Anglia, Commodore Tyrwhitt and his destroyers would be ready to attack any battle fleet in the flank.

Such a strategy in the Second War was not needed. Nevertheless, Harwich played an equally crucial role in other ways. Initially, destroyers were held there against the threat of invasion, but by mid-1941 the threat had considerably lessened. For the remainder of the war, Harwich-based destroyers played a vital part in getting the East Coast convoys through to

London and the south of England by carrying out independent patrol of the coast, or as convoy escort. It was the base for the 16th Destroyer Flotilla. This flotilla was comprised of patrol sloops, a flotilla of minesweepers and some ocean-going tugs.

From the Channel northwards to the coast of East Anglia, this sea was considered to be the most dangerous around the British Isles. It was in these narrow waters that enemy aircraft came from airfields in Holland, and from where enemy E-boats raced from the Hook of Holland to attack the East Coast convoys. The area became known as E-boat alley. Merchant sailors dreaded having to pass through it at night and from the fall of France in mid-1940 to mid-1941, the E-boats had it very much their own way. Every day, throughout the war, a convoy of loaded ships left Methil in the Firth of Forth for the south of England, and more ships would join it from the Tyne.

Simultaneously, a convoy of mostly empty ships left the Thames northbound. Not all were empty; the north also needed its material and some of it went by sea to relieve pressure on the railways. A lot of the ships travelling south were colliers taking coal from Scotland and the Tyne for London's power stations and for domestic use in the south. These, with some food ships, and ships carrying steel and building materials, were vital to the war effort.

An indication of the dangers attaching to these waters can be gathered from the following incident. In February 1941, a large merchant vessel, the *City of Calcutta*, was due from America to Loch Ewe on the west coast of Scotland. Its cargo consisted of 1,700 machine guns, 44 aircraft engines and 14 million cartridges – all of it precious, sorely-needed war material. It was proposed to route the ship from Loch Ewe to Hull, until Churchill got wind of it. When he did so, he immediately minuted the First Lord and the First Sea Lord of the Admiralty:

> 'This ship must on no account be sent to the East Coast … That it should be proposed to send such a ship to the East Coast with all the additional risks is abominable.'

The ship was accordingly re-routed through safer waters. East Coast convoys leaving Methil usually formed into two files until reaching East

Anglia, when they re-formed into single file to go through E-boat alley. Thus a convoy of one hundred ships could stretch twenty miles. In 1940, there would be only two destroyers to guard it. By 1941, the situation had improved, but owing to our mine barrier, there was little room for manoeuvre. E-boat-hunting destroyers such as *Hambledon* had to be careful in their exuberance not to stray into our own mine fields, whereas E-boats with their shallower draughts had no such problem. The trip from Methil to the Thames, and vice versa, took two and a half days with, as always, the convoy restricted to its slowest member. Average speed would be around 8 knots.

There were destroyer flotillas based at Rosyth, Tyne, Harwich and Sheerness. The 7th Flotilla, based earlier in the war at Immingham on the east coast against the invasion threat, had now been withdrawn. The Harwich and Sheerness flotillas drew the short straw with E-boat alley. There were nine ships in the Harwich flotilla. Four of them were Hunts: *Cotswold*, *Eglinton*, *Hambledon* and *Quorn*. Another four were the 'V and W' Class: *Windsor*, *Portishead*, *Worcester* and *Walpole*. Then there was the Scots Class Flotilla, the leader of which was HMS *MacKay*. Although the V and Ws were over twenty years old, they were still seaworthy and in far better shape than the lease-lend American destroyers of the same vintage. We were glad to see them.

Scots Class destroyers were superior in speed to the Hunts and, importantly, all of them carried torpedoes. That meant they could be utilised as fleet destroyers. Their drawback lay in their gun armament. They had no quadruple pom-pom and the two single pom-poms they did mount were of early vintage. Their main armament varied, but none of their guns was of the high-angle, semi-automatic type. Consequently, they were very inferior to the Hunts as anti-aircraft ships. We had to focus. It was our prime job to keep the Luftwaffe, the U-boats and the E-boats off our capital ships and our merchant marine. Occasionally, the Admiralty would make a mistake. Our battleships, lolling at anchor in Scapa Flow, were not available to stop the dash up the North Sea by the German battleships *Scharnhorst*, *Gneisenau* and the battle-cruiser *Prinz Eugen*. It was embarrassing.

The patrol sloops based at Harwich were named after sea birds: *Guillemot*, *Kittiwake*, *Puffin*, *Sheldrake* and *Widgeon*. They had a displacement of 550 tons, but with a speed of only 20 knots and mounting only one 4 inch gun, their role was limited, There was also a Free French Destroyer called *Melpomene*. She had a useful speed of 34 knots and mounted two torpedoes, but the remainder of its armament was uninspiring. It was withdrawn in 1942 for use as a target vessel.

During daylight hours on the east coast, we were at defence stations (four hours on and four off); during darkness, we went to all-night action stations. In the winter, this meant that one watch was at action stations for twenty-one hours out of twenty-four. It was such a punishing routine that only one night could be spent at sea in winter and two in summer. In winter, we escorted a north-bound convoy as far as the Humber and spent the following night at Immingham; the following day we escorted a south-bound back to Harwich and spent the night in Harwich. During the summer, with more daylight hours, we spent two nights out and it was not necessary to put into Immingham. Whenever we were in harbour, (unless we were guard destroyer, when no shore leave was given) one watch was allowed ashore from 1300 hrs to 2100 hrs in the winter and 2200 hrs in the summer. Occasionally we were given all-night leave. For the first year, we spent little time ashore in Harwich, and Immingham at that time was little more than a village. There was a single-track railway into Grimsby docks. I used it on several occasions but never once visited Grimsby other than in the blackout. It was many years after the war before I saw Grimsby in the daylight.

The Humber has a notoriously high tide. We could secure at Immingham with the upper deck level with the jetty. When the tide ebbed, however, the upper deck would be twelve feet lower, which necessitated the berthing wires being paid out at regular intervals. This was done by the harbour watchkeepers but, if they had not been vigilant enough during the night and were caught off-balance, there would be a panic call for both watches of the hands who had to tumble out of their hammocks at top speed.

We could expect air attacks at dusk regularly in 1941. These could be from high – or low-level by Junkers 88s, Heinkel 111s, Dornier 17s and Messerschmitt 110 fighter bombers. The bombers came unescorted by fighters, such was the paucity of our own fighters available for convoy protection at that time. Daylight bombing of convoys had taken place regularly in the summer of 1940, but the Germans now chose mostly to come at dawn and dusk – chiefly the latter, when they could attack ships silhouetted against the setting sun.

Air attacks followed a pattern, with the aircraft breaking formation and each pin-pointing a ship on which to make a bombing run. Immediately they were sighted, the guns of all ships would open fire and the sky would become filled with tracer and black puff balls. Sometimes, in a convoy twenty miles long, we would see tracer going up ahead or astern, while our section of the convoy would be unmolested. At other times we would be slap in the middle of the attack with all guns blazing. At dusk the attackers' time was limited before darkness closed. Our radar would tell us from which direction they were coming and all guns would be trained onto the bearing, waiting for engine sound. Immediately the target was visible through the height-finder lens, the 4 inch guns would be given a fuse setting and the barrage would begin.

In the meantime, the close-range weapons would be standing by, waiting to open fire when the aircraft came within range. When the attack was over, we would take stock to see if there were any casualties and any rescue work to be done. As the drone of the aircraft died away, dusk would be rapidly changing to darkness, which meant danger from attacking aircraft was over for that night.

Then came a different menace – that of attacking E-boats. I have never been able to fathom why the Germans did not produce and make use of more torpedo-carrying aircraft than they did. To have been attacked in strength by torpedo-carrying aircraft at dusk would have been devastating on close-packed ships in convoy, but the fact was their main air weapon was the twin-engined bomber. Dive-bombing Junkers 87s were also few in number after May 1941 and one can only assume they went east to the Russian front.

We came near to being hit on several occasions but the attackers preferred singling out fat merchantmen rather than slim, fire-spitting destroyers. Our closest scrape came in September 1941, when the attack came so late that it was almost dark. We had begun to think they had given us a miss when tracer fire began to go up just ahead. Then we heard the engines of a bomber which came in at just above mast height. It loomed into view so suddenly that no-one got in a shot at it, and as it passed overhead with a roar, I could see the flames coming from its engine exhausts.

He dropped his bombs perhaps two seconds too early. They exploded in the sea on our port side and the force of the underwater explosions lifted the ship and heeled her over to starboard. He had come down low looking for a target and, in his excitement at suddenly finding one, he had released his bombs just too soon. Or again, perhaps he assumed he was flying higher than he actually was but whoever the pilot was, he would never come as close to hitting a ship again. Fortunately, the only damage we sustained was the smashing of electric light bulbs and the cracking of lavatory porcelain. Hedley Woodruff, who had joined the ship the day previously and was making his first sea trip, asked with trepidation if that happened every night. I had to reassure him that it did not!

Toward the end of the 1941 summer, a Leading Seaman second-class AA gunnery rating joined the ship to augment the three, third-class ratings with which we had commissioned. He was made captain of the quadruple pom-pom and I was made captain of the three-man, forward pom-pom. It was a job above my qualification but, until we were allocated a qualified gunner, I would have to do it without getting the pay for it! The Gunner's Mate said it was an accolade, but a winter up above on the bows was an accolade I would have gladly foregone.

I acted as trainer, had the gun trigger and could choose my target, but I still had a non-AA-trained gunnery rating as gunlayer, and it resulted in one enemy aircraft getting home which should not have done so. On this particular trip, we had onboard a civilian, a newspaper correspondent. I could see him on the bridge, wearing a trilby hat, and if he was looking for action he certainly found it. At dusk the convoy was heavily attacked.

This time the bombers came early and it was still quite light as they thundered in, broke formation, and began their bombing-runs. The main attack was just ahead of us and the forward, twin 4 inch began firing over our heads, causing the bones of our skulls to expand and contract. The fire gong on the twin 4 inch main armament always sounded a second before the guns fired. Although it was called a gong, it was actually an electric hooter and, as it wailed its ominous note, the body tensed against the unnerving, wicked crack that was coming. We could feel, on the backs of our necks, the heat from shooting flames issuing from the gun barrels, and we were breathing in the sweet, acrid, cordite fumes,

Suddenly we were presented with a magnificent target. It was a Junkers 88 which had dropped its bombs and was making its getaway through the convoy, flying directly across our line of fire. As I trained onto it, I had about twelve seconds of firing time which, in close-range terms, was an eternity, As I positioned it for aim-off, I could see that the gunlayer was aiming too low and, sure enough, when I fired, our tracers passed underneath. The infernal racket rendered vocal communication impossible, so I thumped him on his back and made an upward movement with my arm. He took the cue and elevated, but my sight immediately informed me he had over-compensated, and I suffered agonies of frustration as I saw my well-placed tracer zipping over the fuselage. Suddenly it was all over and the aircraft was out of range.

Much to my surprise, no questions were asked, and I can only presume that in the melee the bridge personnel had not been observing our tracer. The incident remained with me in the form of sick-making disappointment for a long time. I knew that all that was required was for the gun layer to let the aircraft fly along the horizontal wire of his sight, but he had failed to put into practice a technique which a trained AA gunnery rating would have effected automatically. It was to be almost two years after commissioning before our pom-pom armament was fully manned with ratings trained in its use.

After darkness came the E-boat menace. The Royal Navy did not have the exact equivalent of the German E-boat. Our largest Motor Torpedo Boats (MTBs) were half the displacement of the E-boat. MTBs displaced only between 22 to 50 tons. Their main speed was from 22 to 33 knots, and they were propelled by either twin or triple shaft-driven screws. Their engines were petrol-driven and they carried two torpedoes. Their close-range weapons were .303 and .5 inch machine guns. E-Boats by comparison could weigh up to 100 tons. Their engines were diesels which made them less vulnerable to being set ablaze by gun-fire and they were very fast, being able to touch close to 40 knots. They were also heavily silenced, which reduced the engine power output slightly, but gave them a considerable tactical advantage – they were hard to hear. They carried up to four torpedoes and two 20mm cannon. With machine guns against cannon, the MTBs were a poor match against the E-boats, until the RN Motor Gun Boat (MGB), armed with cannon, came into service to protect the MTBs. Eventually the two types' designs were merged and later models were effectively torpedo-carrying motor gun boats.

The name E-boat was coined at Dunkirk and was an abbreviation of 'Enemy War Motor Boat'. They were consummate torpedo boats, capable of maintaining high speeds and, with their low silhouette and heavily silenced secondary engine, proved difficult to detect before radar came into its own. The Germans viewed them as small destroyers rather than hit-and-run MTBs. With their replacement torpedoes, they could make an initial attack, then retire to reload and attack again. Consequently slow-moving merchantmen were easy meat to them. A further menace was their ability to lay mines. E-boats first appeared on the east coast in September 1940, and 'E-boat Alley' quickly got its name.

In the late summer of that year, they began attacking Bristol coastal convoys and minelaying, and they quickly became a cheap but very serious menace. In late 1940, they sank fourteen ships of a twenty-five ship convoy between the Thames and Bristol. MTBs at the time were no match for them and the destroyers that were, after Dunkirk, in short supply. So, for almost a year, the E-boats had it much their own way. Some destroyers were still without radar and destroyers had to evolve anti-E-boat tactics. Until they did, they themselves suffered. The destroyer *Kelly*, under Lord Louis Mountbatten, was an early E-boat casualty in May 1940. HMS *Wakeful* was also torpedoed at Dunkirk with heavy troop losses, and other destroyers lost to E-boats included *Vortigern*, *Hasty* and the two Hunts *Exmoor* and *Penylan*.

During the Battle of Britain, with all attention focused on the sky in the south of England, East Coast convoys were being bombed by aircraft during the day and attacked by E-boats at night. Colliers in particular suffered heavy casualties. Each one carried 2,000 tons of vital coal and some thirty vessels a day were needed to meet London's solid-fuel requirements. Come what may, the ships had to be fought through and the battle for the East Coast convoys was taking place, largely unheralded, while the Spitfire and Hurricane pilots were capturing the headlines.

During *Hambledon*'s first commission, she would be in the thick of that grim period and, after it, the E-boats must have looked back on their first year (as the U-boats did) as the happy times. Originally, there would perhaps be two destroyers to protect a twenty-mile-long convoy, and the E-boats were like foxes in a hen coop. They came from their bases in Holland and, as they neared the English coast, switched to silent engines and glided in to lurk hidden in the gloom. They particularly liked high cliffs, or they would congregate near a buoy to fool the early radar. The Navy built several decoy ships and there was a decoy aircraft carrier off East Anglia. It served its purpose until the E-boats found it, then it became a menace. They lurked around it until a convoy appeared, then streamed out to attack, inevitably from landward, before making their escape through the convoy.

When *Hambledon* arrived back on the east coast for her second commission, the E-boat golden days were subsiding, principally because we had more destroyers, and because destroyers had evolved tactics to deal with them. Although their early radar sets were pretty basic, they did considerably augment normal vision. E-boats certainly did not want to be caught out by an East Coast Hunt Class destroyer with its single bow-chasing pom-pom right up on the prow. We preferred independent patrol to close escort because there was freedom of movement and choice of speed. A blip on the radar screen would give us bearing and range. There were two, star shell fuse settings (long and short). Star shells were fired with short fuse settings to illuminate a fairly close target. As they burst in mid-air they released a small parachute magnesium flare which lit up the sea over a wide area.

The destroyer then turned bows-on to the illuminated E-boats which began to scatter. In the event of their turning to attack, they were presented with a bows-on destroyer coming at full speed and using her bow-chaser pom-pom as a whaling ship uses its harpoon. Usually they chose to scatter, seeking the blessed relief of darkness and, as they were able to outpace us by 10 knots, time was of the essence. As they drew away, the ship turned broadside on to enable the forward twin 4 inch and the quadruple pom-poms to open fire. The after twin 4 inch put up more star shells. As the range opened, the star shell fuse was changed from short to long, to ensure illumination as long as possible.

In war, one side introduces a winning feature and the other side has to find an antidote. In the winter of 1941, it was suspected that the E-boats were communicating with each other orally over short-wave radio. No visual or wireless signals were, therefore, necessary. They could string out and when one spotted ships, he could bring the others together for an attack. Then the leader could issue orders regarding direction and method of attack. The answer was to fit short-wave radio receivers into destroyers with German-speaking operators. We accordingly had a French-Canadian rating onboard who was fluent in French and German. There is then a golden period when you know what the enemy is up to, and he does not know that you know until his intelligence tells him so.

After mid-1941, the E-boats no longer had it their own way. More destroyers, with better radar sets and well-trained guns crews, made life increasingly hazardous for them, and ship sinkings by E-boats fell appreciably. By the time we left the east coast in mid-1943, they had been mastered and were little more than sneak-thief nuisances, Naturally, we could never relax because of their speed and the lurking they did – hence our all-night action stations; but they were certainly no longer the threat they had been in the first two years of the war. However, the loss of the destroyer *Vortigern* proved to us that vigilance could never be relaxed where E-boats were concerned.

Destroyers without radar sets, or with the very early types, had to rely on lookouts and were at a severe disadvantage. It is possible that the destroyer *Vortigern* had only an early radar set installed when she was torpedoed by E-boats on 15 March 1942. She had been converted from a fleet to a short-range escort destroyer and was acting as close escort to a north-bound convoy off the East Anglian coast, while we were patrolling ahead of it. Whether *Vortigern* had actually engaged them, or whether they caught her unawares, I never discovered, but she must have been struck by two torpedoes. The following morning the sea was flat calm and, having reached the limit of our patrol, we turned to come south.

As we came abreast of the first ships in the convoy, we were given the bearing on which *Vartigern* had gone down and we made a bee line for it. When we reached it, we found two RNLI lifeboats which had been called out during the night. One was the Cromer lifeboat, commanded by the renowned Cox'n Blogg; the other was from Sheringham. As we neared the lifeboats we began to see wreckage – wooden boxes, small floats and sailors' clothing – floating on the surface, There were also traces of oil fuel. We came up alongside the Cromer boat and John Barnes enquired of Cox'n Blogg if there were any survivors. He came out of his wheelhouse shaking his head sadly and, pointing to the Sheringham boat, he said, 'Nor has she'.

Both boats had been pulling dead sailors out of the sea since dawn and it was now noon. The upper decks of both boats were covered with bodies lying head to foot, like sardines in a tin. All of them were covered in oil fuel, their hair matted with it, their faces yellow with it. It was obvious that if Blogg found any more he was going to be inundated, and he appealed to John Barnes to relieve him of some. John, however, had to decline since we had a further night to spend at sea; he suggested Blogg take what he had for burial ashore. It was a heart-rending experience which is as vivid in mind today as it was on 15 March 1942. I heard of no survivors and every Remembrance Day since 1945 at 11am, my mind has gone back to that scene and I have stood in silence for *Vortigern*.

It was incidents such as this which turned us from ordinary peace-loving young men into killers. Anything German which came across the North Sea, whether on the sea itself or in the skies over it, was seen as a pestilence. Aircraft invaded our air space and dropped bombs on our shipping. E-boats loosed torpedoes, causing death and mutilation in waters we considered to be ours. Both sought to hinder the war effort and starve us into submission. We viewed the enemy as standing for an obscene violation of everything we saw to be wholesome. I never met a man onboard who was not convinced of his cause, or doubted that what we were doing needed to be done.

In our captain, Lieutenant Commander John Barnes, we must have had one of the Navy's best destroyer captains. Seamen who handle the ship's berthing wires soon become knowledgeable about screw and rudder movements, and are quick to criticise indifferent ship handling. Whether we liked John Barnes as a CO or not, all admired his ship-handling skills. The following incident will illustrate his talent.

I would imagine him to be forty to forty-five years of age. He was short in stature, with light brown hair and pale blue eyes. He did not shave his cheek bones and had a tuft of hair on each cheek. When he walked he tended to stamp on his heels and the peak of his cap was more curved than normal through being squeezed under his arm. It was his little idiosyncrasy of dress. He could be somewhat temperamental and the fact that (unlike his successor) no funny stories about him circulated the mess decks, seems to point to his having had little or no sense of humour.

There were no mediocre destroyer captains. All were good; some were better than others; a few were outstanding. In ship handling, John Barnes came into the latter category. Although *Hambledon* was not John Barnes' first destroyer, she was new to him when we commissioned. But from the moment we left the dockyard, he handled her as though wedded to her for years. A good ship-handling captain is a boon to all the ship's company because of the confidence he instils; but to none more than to the seaman branch which is responsible for anchoring, mooring and sea boats. After coming in from sea in winter, seamen can be cold and tired, and the sooner a ship is secured, the better. Consequently they can be extremely irritated with a pussy-footer who takes ages to ring-off main engines. John's orders to wheelhouse and engine room were always crisp and clear. He could make the ship do exactly what he wanted it to do under all conditions of tide and weather.

Destroyers alongside the jetty tied up two and three abreast to conserve space. We came into Harwich on one occasion and received instructions to secure alongside Parkestone Quay. Two destroyers were already alongside there, both flotilla Leaders with four-ring captains. One was our own flotilla Leader, the other was visiting from Sheerness. John Barnes was bringing *Hambledon* in with his usual aplomb and he was coming in bow to stern, making the best use of the tide. The two, four-ring captains were standing together on the quarter-deck of the outer destroyer and *Hambledon* was drifting in perfectly. Suddenly the signalman on the outer destroyer began sending a semaphore signal using his arms. The Yeoman of Signals on *Hambledon*'s bridge read off the signal as it was made: 'Come – in – bow – to – bow!'

The heaving lines had already gone across and two wires had been thrown overboard ready to be hauled in by the outer destroyer. Why was the signal made? Did our flotilla captain wish to see three ships all neat and tidy bow to bow? Or did he wish to show his visitor from Sheerness how expertly a destroyer could be handled? The answer to that no-one knew, and some destroyer captains could have been thrown off balance – but not John Barnes. Crisp and cool came the orders, 'Let go for'ard, let go aft; half speed ahead port, half speed astern starboard, wheel starboard 30.'

He screwed the ship's head away from the jetty, stopped the starboard screw, let the port screw continue for a while, ordered the starboard screw ahead, and the ship slipped smoothly out into the river. He then turned in a complete circle and, in no time at all, was coming back in. This time the tide was not to his advantage but that in no way bothered him, and soon the heaving lines were snaking out again, preparatory to a perfect berthing evolution. When eventually the seamen arrived on the mess deck, they were burbling with delight.

'Tried to throw him, didn't they?'

'Yes, but he wasn't born yesterday. Good old Barnesy!'

And so on.

It was fortunate for destroyer sailors that their ships sometimes needed to undergo repairs and to have their boilers cleaned. During the war, a destroyer's boilers needed cleaning every three months or so, and, as the operation took five days, we could almost be guaranteed five days' leave every quarter. It was not necessarily a dockyard job. The ships of the 16th Flotilla had theirs cleaned alongside Parkestone Quay, together with any other small repairs.

When shore leave was given, we had the choice of Harwich or adjoining Dovercourt. Should we wish to go a little further afield when all-night leave was given, the liberty boat would land us at Shatley pier and we could catch a bus to Ipswich, where we could book a cabin at the YMCA or Salvation Army. Men living locally were, of course, able to spend the night at home and men who lived in London considered it near enough to Harwich to make the effort of the journey both ways for a few hours with their families. Only ratings over twenty years of age were permitted all-night leave, and when my twentieth birthday arrived I was, overnight, eligible for all-night leave and a rum ration.

In late November 1941, we went into Chatham dockyard for thirteen days for new equipment and some modifications. One of the modifications was our acoustic mine burster. The introduction of the acoustic mine by the Germans did not result in the large losses of shipping that the magnetic mine did. The magnetic mine had caught the Navy unawares, and it was not until one of them was washed ashore, dismantled and examined, that the antidote could be found. The acoustic mine had, to a large extent, been anticipated and the antidote was immediately put into effect. Our initial device was a steel boom which hinged on a cleat riveted to the stem of the bows. At the top of it was what looked like a steel bucket, inside which was the apparatus which emitted sound waves ahead of the ship. On entering harbour, it was hauled upright; once at sea it was lowered into the water. It served its purpose until a modified version was produced, when the sound-making apparatus went inside the bows and the boom was dismantled after a relatively short life.

Another modification was to the radar. The Navy originally used the term RDF (radio direction finding) until the entry of America into the war. We then assumed their term RADAR (radio detection and ranging) and so it has remained to this day. Our original set, which was only operative through a fixed aerial 30° on either side of the bows, was removed. In its place went the latest set with a revolving aerial. This could detect aircraft approaching from any direction and was far superior to the one it replaced. It was not quite so effective beamed at sea level, nevertheless it was used for that purpose when we were night patrolling and served us well until our turn came for separate surface radar. This was, of course, the problem.

Equipment was scarce and ships had to get in the queue. Ships went into dockyard and had some work completed and some half-completed. For instance, one would return from leave to find a new platform riveted to the upper deck. It would stand there for several months, denuded of equipment, until the next time in dock saw the intended equipment installed on it.

Many other less important jobs were done, such as the splinter mats on the quadruple pom-pom being replaced by a steel plate shield to protect our bodies from shrapnel. But the most startling transformation was that the dockyard painters had decked us out in camouflage. Gone was the battleship grey. We were now painted white with pale blue embellishments. There was an elongated blue triangle on either side of the bows, starting with its point at the stem and broadening as it spread aft along the fo'c'sle. The funnel had a diagonal line running up it, one side of the line being painted blue, the other white, while the after freeboard was saw-toothed in white and blue. The idea was to make the ship merge with the moonlight instead of appearing a black silhouette. We knew it was effective from seeing other destroyers so camouflaged, but apart from that, it enhanced the whole appearance of the ship. I had now been in the Navy a year, and was upgraded from Ordinary to Able Seaman. It was the only promotion I ever received in the Navy without passing an examination, On 7 December 1941, just before we left the dockyard, America declared war on Japan after the attack on Pearl Harbour. We returned to Harwich in high spirits; we knew the end of the war was still a long way off, but Russia and America were now ranged with us against the Axis and victory was a foregone conclusion.

Chapter 9

North Sea

There is no other sea quite like the North Sea anywhere in the world, and any sailor will testify that it can never be taken for granted. It does not have the long, rolling swells of the Atlantic and its breakers are not so massive but, nevertheless, it can be very unsettling in its capriciousness. When the wind comes roaring through the narrows at hurricane force, churning up the sea in its path, it can take hold of destroyers and toss them around like corks, until life on board is every bit as disconcerting as life on board in the Atlantic. The Atlantic has vast open spaces in which to vent itself, whereas the North Sea is pent-up by land masses on both its flanks. It is funnel shaped, the neck of the funnel being formed by the coast of East Anglia and the Dutch coast. In storm conditions, because of this restriction, it seems to acquire an angry fury even the Atlantic does not have, especially in its southern reaches, where it is seldom calm, even when ashore there are only light breezes.

The winter of 1941–42 was a severe one, and manning the forward pom-pom was gruelling to say the least. We went to action stations at dusk, which was usually 1600 hrs. After dark, each watch went to supper in turn and we were all back at action stations again by 2000 hrs, there to remain all night. At 0700 hrs, one watch fell out for one hour for breakfast, returning to relieve the other watch, which went below to clean up and prepare dinner at 0800 hrs. Thus, from leaving Harwich at noon one day to arriving at Immingham at noon the next, one watch had spent fourteen hours on deck, the other twenty-one hours. On the return trip, the watch that had done twenty-one hours did the same again, since we had spent twenty-four hours in harbour, thereby putting them back where they were on leaving Harwich two days previously. Only two nights in Harwich on return would see them with the reduced hours, and sometimes that was a long time coming. By any reckoning it was savage and it stretched those who kept watch on deck to the limit – both officers and men. The Atlantic routine was four hours on and four off around the clock, but on the east coast that was out of the question.

The gun mounting was forward of the anchor hawse-pipes, so that when the ship buried her bows in the sea, the water came full bore up the pipes. Although we wore our waterproof goon-skins, the sea found its way down our necks and into our seaboots. Our balaclavas and mufflers quickly became saturated until our necks were sore from the salt water. In a really rough sea, there was the danger of being swept overboard, and we would seek permission to come down the fo'c'sle and take shelter in the twin 4 inch gunshield. It was never refused unless we were in danger of air attack. However, the weather could be reasonable at nightfall, then blow up after dark when the bridge personnel were not aware of the state of things up forward. And since we could not request to fall out until conditions warranted our doing so, when we did eventually get permission we were inevitably soaked. It was a Catch 22 situation.

It is difficult to describe the extent of the cold because similar conditions do not appertain on land. We came on watch with full stomachs so, until midnight, it was bearable, But as the food became digested, so the body heat began to fall and the cold struck deeper and deeper until it seemed to reach the marrow of our bones. The only sustenance after that, until breakfast, was the thick cocoa made at midnight, when one rating from each gun was permitted to slip away to the galley to collect the life-restoring liquid. Having nothing to do but stand around the gun, or sit on the mounting, the time dragged and hour followed weary hour, until one fell into an almost paralysing stupor which only an alarm was capable of dispelling. To be chilled to the bone and dry is agony enough; to be chilled to the bone and wet is infinitely worse.

At around noon, we would be off the mouth of the Humber and, having seen the convoy safely through E-boat alley, we would proceed up the Humber to Immingham, there to spend the night. By noon the following day we would rendezvous with a southbound convoy to repeat the operation. In summer, with more daylight hours, we spent the second night at sea, always returning to Harwich. There were times when, after getting a soaking from a head sea, I would, on receiving permission to fall out, run down to sit on the hot deck at the base of the funnel under cover of darkness, to try and dry my inner clothing. It never proved successful;

all I succeeded in doing was to fill my goon-skin with steam! But at least I had the blessed relief of a little warmth for a few minutes.

The gun was very reliable and the only stoppage we were likely to get was due to faulty ammunition. We always tested close-range weapons outside the estuary and on one occasion that winter, the gun stopped firing, I knew there would be a misfired round in the breech, so I wound the lock back and forward again. This would put a new round in the breech and the misfired one into the ejector tube.

In action, one then carried on firing and the misfired round was pushed out by the empty cylinders. There was a very slight risk of it falling on its head and exploding, but, in action, the risk was not taken as it was in trial firing. It had to be pushed forward with a brass-tipped cane into awaiting hands. When the shell plopped into my hands I could see an indentation on its base, proving it to have been struck. I held it up to the bridge to signify misfired charge and threw it overboard. We then tested the gun a second time, satisfactorily.

The operation had taken no more than three minutes but, in that time, I had had to work with bare hands in icy, lashing spray, and my hands were blue with cold. We then got permission from the bridge to fall out and when I came aft I continued down to the funnel, unseen by the bridge, to get the circulation back in my hands. Just as I arrived there, the Gunner's Mate came out of the gunnery transmitting station onto the flag deck above me and asked me why I was not at my station. I explained what had happened and, while he sympathised, he ordered me back onto the fo'c'sle. The need to maintain discipline had crushed any sentiment he might have had, but at least he was not devoid of sympathy. I returned to the fo'c'sle still with numbed hands, but heard nothing further of the incident.

In all but very rough seas, however, the gun was manned. We had to grin and bear the head wind and spray for up to eighteen hours. In the coldest weather we would watch the fo'c'sle start icing up, each successive shower of spray freezing on top of the preceding one, until the ship was like a birthday cake and the wire guard-rails became three-inch diameter ice tubes. The upper deck of the fo'c'sle was soon a solid sheet of thick ice and the capstan a solid ice block. Only our constant movement, such as jumping on the spot, prevented the same thing happening to us; even then our outer oilskins became stiff with an icy film and the wool of our balaclavas became sea-spangled.

On the coldest night of the winter (excepting an area of deck around the base of the funnel), the whole of the ship was iced-up to the extent that, to anyone seeing it from a distance, it would appear as a ghost ship from some mediaeval Norse legend. As we turned into the Harwich estuary the forward 4 inch gun's crew began to break the ice from the capstan with the capstan bars. No one had ordered them to do it; firstly it exercised frozen bodies and, secondly, an ice-free capstan meant there would be no delay in securing to the buoy when we reached harbour. We were somewhat perplexed, therefore, when John Barnes poked his head over the top of the bridge and shouted to them to desist. Later, the bridge signalman reported that the Captain had turned to the Officer of the Watch and said, 'I want the rest of the flotilla to see what conditions we've had.

During this period of extreme cold the pom-poms froze up. They were water-cooled, with glycerine added as an anti-freeze, but this did not prevent their freezing-up in arctic conditions and that is what we were experiencing. The answer was to fit the barrels with electrically heated jackets and this was done. Then, unless we kept our eyes on them, they tended to overheat, boil the water and blow out the overflow plugs. The drill was to switch them on for ten minutes every half hour. Undoubtedly our worst experience of the North Sea was one autumn night in 1942, while acting as close escort to a north-bound convoy. The wind had sprung up in mid-afternoon and by the small hours the storm was at full fury.

> 'And now the storm blast came, and he
> Was tyrannous and strong:
> He struck with his o'ertaking wings,
> And chased us south along.'

It was, in all respects, as Coleridge describes in 'The Rhyme of the Ancient Mariner' except that he was chasing us north and he had us well and truly in his grip.

At convoy speed we were very vulnerable. The wind was blasting and howling like a banshee – so strong that voices were plucked from lips and dissipated on the night air. Conversation was impossible; communication necessitated putting one's mouth close to an ear and bellowing. The merchant ships with deeper draughts, broader beams and bigger rudders were able to battle it out far better than we could, and we were in considerable difficulty.

Our problem was that we were being driven before a tremendous following sea, which repeatedly crashed onto the quarter deck, driving it under water and causing the bows to rear up. Owing to our slow speed, our rudder was virtually useless and we began to corkscrew. We were then in grave danger of presenting our beam to the sea, broaching-to and foundering. There was only one course open to us – to turn head-on into the gale and increase speed in order to have an effective rudder. This, of course, meant leaving the convoy, but there was no alternative if we were to survive. The convoy would, in any case, manage without us: no E-boat could survive in seas like that. John Barnes accordingly sent the following signal,

> From: *Hambledon*
> To: Flag Officer in Charge, Harwich.
> 'Am unable to steer at convoy speed. Request permission to return independently.'

There was no delay in the answer. Back came the signal, 'Request granted.' We turned into the teeth of the gale, increased speed, and for the remainder of the night rode it out.

> 'The ship drove fast, loud roared the blast,
> And southward aye we fled.'

It was the North Sea at its worst. The wind seemed to be coming from all directions at hurricane force, swirling, screeching and howling, and the ship was alternately dipping and tossing her bows like a demented rocking horse. The wind tore through the rigging and set it squealing like a diabolical, stringed instrument playing off-key, the note rising and falling as the gusts rose and fell. It was so eerie, frightening and awe-inspiring at the same time. One felt puny, powerless and insignificant in the face of it. All night long it blew; at dawn it had begun to slacken, but even when we entered Harwich harbour we left a force eight gale behind us. I always had great faith in British shipbuilders that our ships would weather anything the elements threw at them. But stout ships are of no avail unless they are well handled and I had equal faith in my three Commanding Officers. Both Russia and America lost destroyers in the last war due to storm damage in heavy seas. I knew of no British destroyer suffering a similar fate.

The rough weather, at least, kept the E-boats in their home ports. Apart from the hazardous trip across and back, the accurate launching of torpedoes is near impossible in rough seas. Neither did they come under a full moon, when it was possible to see the horizon. Under those conditions any vessel is thrown-up in full relief, so the E-boats stayed at home. On these occasions we went into defence stations and it was akin to being given a holiday. The watch below, however, did not sling hammocks. We slept fully clothed on the lockers and the deck, ready to rush to action stations at the clamouring of the alarm bell.

It would be on a night in January 1942. We had come in from sea during the forenoon and shore leave had been given to one watch from 1300 to 2100 hrs. Pipe-down came at 2200 hrs and all except watchkeepers had turned in. At 2300 hrs we were awakened by the bo'sun's pipe; 'Both watches of the hands fall in; away sea boat's crew; special sea dutymen to your stations.'

So, we were going back to sea! There was much groaning as men, who had been in deep sleep, tumbled reluctantly out of their hammocks and began dressing. It was a very rare occurrence to be sent to sea after the harbour boom defence had been closed for the night, so we knew there must be some kind of emergency.

The Officers had male and female guests in the wardroom when the signal came to proceed to sea and the motorboat's crew was called away to get the visitors ashore. While it was away, the ship was unbridled from the buoy and held by a slip rope, and when the boat returned, it was hoisted inboard. Then the slip rope was pulled through the buoy ring and we were under way, heading down river to the harbour entrance. The boom defence vessel had received a signal to open and, as we neared it, a small searchlight was switched on to light us through.

Ships leaving harbour always went through the boom very sedately; but this night we shot through it like a cork from a bottle. John Barnes then ordered emergency full-speed, and I never knew *Hambledon* to pick up her skirts as she did on that occasion. The engine-room artificers later told us that, with a strong following sea, we were peaking at 31½ knots (35½ mph) and there was evidence of the fact next day when we found all the paint on the funnel was blistered. We had been piped to action stations immediately on leaving harbour and a message came from the bridge that E-boats were attacking a convoy north of Harwich, and the close escort destroyers had asked for reinforcements, On the forward pom-pom we could tell by the headwind we were making that the ship was steaming flat out and were thankful the sea was reasonably calm.

The convoy was a southbound one and we were going north to meet it. Eventually the first ship in the convoy was spotted by the bridge lookouts. We steamed past it to seaward and continued north still at full speed, passing ship after ship on our port side. There was no sign of any action – no star shells, no tracer. At the tail end of the convoy, the Captain decided to turn south. He would wish to remain to seaward from where a second attack was most likely to come, and the order was given for a turn to port. As the ship answered the helm, we were still at full speed and she heeled over to starboard at an alarming angle, our guardrails almost horizontal and the sea lapping over the iron deck.

Then begins the turn with the ship's head sweeping round, and the heeling continuing until we have completed the half-circle and the wheel is put amidships. When we were well into the turn, there was a merchantman some distance from us on our port side, and I felt it to be rather too close for comfort. John Barnes must have satisfied himself that he had sufficient room, but distances in the dark can be misleading and the merchantman began to loom ominously close, until I felt sure we were on a collision course. I told the other two pom-pom crew members to sit flat down on the deck so that we would not be knocked off our feet when the collision came.

The ship had now reached a point of no return; a slackening of speed would have increased the turning arc to the point of a definite collision. The Captain had no alternative but to complete what he had set out to do. I have already mentioned how well the Hunts responded to the helm and it was probably our saving grace. She did come round and we did complete the half circle with literally nothing to spare; in fact we needed about two feet more room than we had. Our starboard side brushed the Merchantman's port side amidships and we bounced off her.

The brunt of the impact was taken by our motor boat hanging in its davits, which acted as a fender and saved any metal-to-metal contact. Just as the two ships came together, the Skipper of the Merchantman (who had doubtless been watching the incident with bated breath) came out onto the port wing of his bridge a dozen feet from where we were sitting on the fo'c'sle and bellowed an angry oath at us as we ploughed on past him, still at full speed.

Eventually, speed was reduced to that of the convoy and the night passed uneventfully. The incident was much debated on the seamen's mess decks on our return, and it was assumed that having been ordered to sea in the middle of a wardroom party, the Captain may possibly have had one gin too many. Whether that was so or not, John Barnes' impeccable ship handling, particularly the timing of his turn, was not up to his usual high standard that night. The motor boat was a complete write-off so much so that it could not be launched and we had to go alongside for it to be lifted off by crane. There was no immediate replacement and we had to make do with a whaler for three weeks. When the replacement did arrive it was a far better boat than its predecessor, in fact the most resplendent motor boat in the flotilla.

Harwich mine sweepers were kept busy sweeping the estuary and the sea lanes on their section of the east coast. The minesweeping trawlers always tied up two and three abreast alongside Parkestone Quay, leaving the buoys for destroyer use. They left at dawn to sweep the estuary and its approaches in case mines had been laid by aircraft or E-boats during the night. The Admiralty had requisitioned whole fishing fleets at the commencement of the war – including their crews – who were almost literally in mufti one week and uniform the next. The Skippers and first mates were commissioned in the Royal Naval Reserve and wore the interlaced gold braid rings on their uniform jacket sleeves. Their accents ranged from Grimsby to Lowestoft and from Cornish to Scottish. These men did a mammoth, unenviable job throughout the war all over the world. Some trawlers were fitted with Asdics and played the role of U-boat hunters. Forty years after the war I went into the Fisherman's Chapel in Grimsby Methodist Central Hall and was deeply moved by the many memorial plaques lining the walls, bearing the names of Grimsby fishermen who had lost their lives serving in trawlers.

It was only to be expected that odd mines were missed, despite all their efforts, and, within an eight-hour period in April 1942, two of our four Hunts were mined. Ironically it was 20 April – Hitler's birthday. The mines were, in all probability, laid by enemy aircraft in the estuary the previous night and had not been swept. *Quorn* detonated one going out on patrol in the morning, and *Cotswold* another, returning in the late afternoon. Fortunately, neither ship was badly damaged – *Cotswold* came off worst, but it meant that we lost them both for several weeks and we were already minus *Worcester*, which meant extra work for the remaining six ships of the flotilla. It was after this incident that an order was made that all ships entering or leaving harbour were to clear lower decks and batten down hatches. All men not on watch had, therefore, to vacate their mess decks, which was a nuisance, but a wise precaution.

Ships in the flotilla went out in pairs to do practice AA shoots and, in daylight and not under attack, many eyes were on the drogue, ready to criticise indifferent shooting. Occasionally the whole flotilla went out doing evolutions; practising towing another ship and being towed; rigging collision mats and lowering sea boats and so forth. Some evolutions were timed and there was keen competition to see who hoisted the first pennant, signifying evolution completed. On the rare occasions ours wasn't hoisted first, John Barnes was most displeased.

Best of all were the flotilla manoeuvres, when the only people involved on deck were the signalmen, who were kept on their toes sending messages by Aldis lamp and bending-on and hoisting bunting, There was nothing more pleasing to my impoverished eye than to see a flotilla of destroyers manoeuvring at full speed, changing from line ahead to line abreast, or into echelon formation, each cleaving the water with billowing bow waves. All helms were put over at the drop of a pennant and ships changed course as though linked together. Nicholas Monsarrat, in *The Cruel Sea*, describes two newly-built destroyers joining a convoy at full speed, 'signalling in three directions at once and refusing to stay still in any one position for more than five minutes.' It was a typical destroyer scene, as was the snort of envy it evoked from a corvette signalman, 'Proper show-offs! All very well for them to dash about like a couple of brand-new tarts – they haven't had the last week along o' this lot.'

In their way, some flotillas were as skilled at manoeuvre as the RAF Red Arrows. My admiration for our Merchant Seamen was unbounded. Royal Navy sailors were, after all, in the business of making war at sea, and had weapons and equipment with which to protect themselves – to say nothing of speed. Most of our merchantmen carried light AA guns, but war-making was not their primary business, and they had the least glamorous task. They had no uniform, for instance, other than a small enamel lapel badge and must have felt neglected and crestfallen in pubs in Liverpool, Southampton, on the Tyne or on the Clyde, surrounded by uniformed servicemen, after sweating it out for three weeks in the Atlantic.

In addition to the lack of glamour, many of them had to endure terrible conditions at sea in unseaworthy ships with appalling living accommodation. Between the wars, the country hardly knew they existed, even though Rudyard Kipling had warned his countryman in his poem, Big Steamers that, 'If anyone hinders our coming – you'll starve.'

Yet little thought was given to the pay and conditions of Britain's merchant seamen between the wars, and even throughout the war there were cruel anomalies. Merchant seamen, for instance, signed on for every voyage. Their contracts came into operation when their ships sailed and terminated when they returned. But, if a ship went down through enemy action, the contract ended there and then. Thus, if men were cast adrift in the Atlantic, they got no pay and, indeed, no further money was forthcoming until they signed on again. Despite all this, merchant navy men signed on again and again all through the war. Many tramp steamers were still coal-fired and the stokers had to feed the furnaces in raging storms in a U-boat-infested Atlantic. I used to watch the tankers in convoy – always recognisable by their bridge and funnel right aft – and marvel that men could sweat it out day after day in a ship full of oil fuel or – worse – high-octane spirit. The same went for the crews of ammunition ships. It cannot have been beyond their ken to have gone ashore and taken up essential war work in factories; but, of course, they were sailors, and sailors went to sea.

When it was all over, then came the plethora of books on the war at sea – the Atlantic, Mediterranean and Russian convoys. And, with few exceptions, the glamour went to the warships, with the merchant ships mentioned in passing, or quoted as statistics. One can get bogged down with statistics (e.g. in 1942 we lost 16 million tons of shipping) and lose sight of the loss of human life involved in it. The battle of the Atlantic did not only involve U-boats against men-o'-war and aircraft. It also involved merchant seamen and, without their fortitude, the war would have been lost and nothing the three fighting services could have done could have altered that.

We joined the convoy on a sunny day in July 1942 early in the morning, and by mid-day the sun was out in full strength and the sea so flat calm we could have been on a peacetime cruise. I had the afternoon watch and, looking back on it, it was probably the most pleasant summer day I spent in the North Sea. But, of course, it was wartime. At 1500 hrs, there was an ominous underwater crump and we knew someone had struck a mine. Seconds later, the screws thrashed and we increased from 7 knots to full speed. We overhauled ship after ship – then we came upon her settling by the stern. In a very short time after our arrival her bows went high in the air and, with a loud hissing of steam as the water found its way down the funnel, she was gone. The name I read on her side as she vanished was SS *Dynamo*. She was travelling north in ballast and, shortly after she disappeared, empty wooden beer barrels began plopping to the surface – dozens of them.

In amongst them were the survivors. One good thing to be said for coal-burning Tramps is that survivors do not have to swim through oil fuel. There was coal dust on the surface, but no oil fuel to clog mouth and nostrils and to rob men of their sight. The ship moved in closer and men began to swim towards it. As they drew near, the scramble nets were unfurled and fell down the ship's side and, eventually, the stronger swimmers reached us and scrambled up the net. Others following, exhausted through their exertions, were helped on board. There had not been time to lower boats, but coming towards us was a wooden raft, about four feet square. A merchant seaman sat on either side, each paddling it along, his feet in the water; and standing upright between them was the Skipper. This man epitomised the average lion-hearted merchant seaman.

He was short in stature, slightly rotund and with white hair. He could not have been a day under seventy. He was wearing black trousers and waistcoat, and a blue, smock, artisan's jacket. In appearance, he could have been any young man's grandfather. At about twenty yards from the ship he took his steel pocket watch from his waistcoat pocket, looked at it and replaced it with seemingly as little concern as though standing on a raft in the Serpentine. When the raft bumped the ship's side he was helped up the net onto the deck. He was wet, but not dripping; the hot sun had dried his hair and face, and as he ducked through the guardrails I heard him say, 'That's the fourth one I've lost.'

It goes without saying that that Tramp Skipper would go back to sea; indeed, he would probably be back again a week after getting ashore. That was the spirit which won for us the Battle of the Atlantic.

Two of the survivors died on board. It was not uncommon for survivors to appear fit and uninjured – even to need no help up the ship's side – then to die later from shock or internal injury. The bodies were stitched up into canvas shrouds and weighted with 4 inch shells. Then, after appropriate prayers, read by the Captain from the prayer book, the bodies slid from under the Union flag and were committed to the deep from the quarterdeck. This description is typical of several instances of the burials we carried out at sea of our own and of enemy seamen.

I witnessed the loss of many merchant ships, flying the flags of all our allies, whose names I never knew or have forgotten. Only the name of SS *Dynamo* remains in my memory. Naval losses were always promulgated in the media – sometimes long after the event: 'The Board of Admiralty regrets to announce the loss of HMS…' whether it be a battleship or a humble corvette. No such promulgation was made regarding lost merchant ships, probably because it was not considered prudent to let the enemy or the British public know just how grave were our losses at the height of the battle of the Atlantic. The only time merchant ships made the headlines was when they made a spectacular return to harbour against all odds, after being bombed or torpedoed. Consequently I always saw our merchant seamen as unsung heroes and admired them immensely.

Chapter 10

Salmon and Gluckstein

On 12 February 1942, the *Scharnhorst* and *Gneisenau* made their dash through the English Channel from Brest. They were accompanied by the heavy cruiser *Prinz Eugen*, screened by destroyers, E-boats and torpedo boats, and they had an air umbrella of 250 aircraft, some of which were to be detached to carry out diversionary bombing attacks.

These two ships were battlecruisers and some thought had gone into their design, in that they could outpace our heavier-gunned capital ships and outgun our cruisers able to match them in speed. However, they had had little success in their role as commerce raiders, and in every instance, where our heavier-gunned units appeared on the scene, the two enemy ships withdrew, making use of their superior speed. The only way they could be brought to action and destroyed was for the Navy to have on hand the correct mix of ships. This, ideally, was cruisers to shadow and harass until heavier units could be called up with their screening destroyers – as indeed happened with *Bismarck*. So while any success they had was limited, they did constitute a menace, and heavy units of the fleet had always to be kept in readiness to be deployed against them.

Because they always acted in concert, they were sometimes referred to disparagingly by British sailors as Salmon and Gluckstein but no-one ever took them for granted, or had any illusions of the terrible damage they could inflict on warships, or the havoc they could wreak on merchant shipping. They drew blood quickly in November 1939, when they found and sank the armed merchant cruiser *Rawalpindi* in the Atlantic. When *Rawalpindi* had been sunk, the cruiser Newcastle appeared and she would have been easy meat to the two battlecruisers. However, assuming she was the forerunner of heavier reinforcements, they beat a hasty retreat.

They were sent to Narvik as decoys to draw off British units from the German landings. Here, the battlecruiser *Renown* found and engaged them and salvoes were exchanged. Both *Renown* and *Gneisenau* suffered damage in the action that followed, but when *Renown*'s attending destroyers formed up to make their torpedo attack, the two German ships cleared off into the murk at high speed. The enemy destroyers left behind then came in for a severe mauling from British destroyers in the first Battle of Narvik, and from the battleship *Warspite* in the second battle. Ten German destroyers were sunk at Narvik after being left to their fate by the two battlecruisers. German naval strategy decreed that action was not to be sought with equal or superior British naval forces.

Later, the two ships were sent to harry the withdrawal of British troops from Norway but never arrived there. The German Admiral detached the cruiser *Hipper* to Norway and, himself, went commerce-raiding in the Atlantic with the two battlecruisers. Eventually they came upon the aircraft carrier *Glorious*, escorted by the destroyers *Ardent* and *Acaster*. The two battlecruisers opened fire on *Glorious* and she took a shell from *Scharnhorst* in her hangar early in the action, which prevented her flying-off her torpedo-carrying Swordfish aircraft.

With no heavy guns to defend herself she was soon ablaze and sinking. In the meantime the two destroyers were steaming full speed at the enemy in their torpedo attack. *Ardent* did not make it; she was sunk, with one survivor. *Acaster*, however, managed to launch her torpedoes, one of which struck *Scharnhorst*, before she too was destroyed, again with one survivor. Both destroyers had thrown themselves at the battlecruisers with almost careless abandon, been badly mauled in the process and lost a combined complement of some 300 men. *Ardent* and *Acaster* exemplified destroyer tenacity at its very best.

During a two-month foray in the Atlantic in February and March 1941, the two ships sank twenty-one merchant ships. Throughout this period they had kept well clear of engagement with any British warships, clearing off at high speed when any appeared on the horizon. At the end of the two months, the two ships made for Brest, and it was to be virtually the end of their useful lives as commerce raiders. They reached Brest on 22 March 1941, and were not to emerge into open seas again until 11 February 1942.

While in Brest they were under constant RAF attack. *Gneisenau* was bombed and torpedoed, and it was decided to move *Scharnhorst* to a safer haven while *Gneisenau* was undergoing repairs. The harbour chosen for *Scharnhorst* was La Pallice, but it proved no safer than Brest. She was located by the RAF and bombed twenty-four hours after her arrival. Consequently she was taken back to Brest and both ships were now out of action. *Prinz Eugen* had also sought refuge in Brest after the *Bismarck* action and she too was disabled by RAF bombing. While the repair of all three ships was taking place, a plan was devised for them to make a dash through the Channel back to Germany, eventually to join the battleship *Tirpitz*, which was lying in Trondheim. With these four ships on the loose, no Atlantic or Russian convoy would be safe. It was known in the German Navy as the 'Z Plan', and *Bismarck* was to have played a part in it.

At the end of January 1942, all three ships were ready to put to sea, and the commanding Admiral planned to break out of Brest under cover of darkness. This would mean passing through the Channel in daylight, but he considered the long voyage in the dark before reaching the Channel was worth the risk. Admiral Raeder, C. in C. of the German Navy, was opposed to the idea, but Hitler overrode him. His reasoning was that the British would be taken by surprise and he considered them to be not good at making lightning decisions!

The British were indeed taken by surprise but it was due to ill-luck on a massive scale rather than bad planning. Lightning decisions were also taken, but with the paucity of equipment at our disposal, this availed little or nothing. It was debated at the time that, if it was expected that the ships would leave Brest sooner or later, why were not heavy naval units moved south from Scapa Flow to be deployed against them when they did so? The answer was, of course, that if the RAF could play havoc with enemy ships in Brest, obviously the Germans, with their preponderance in air strength, could certainly do likewise to any of our capital ships held in readiness on the south coast. The feasibility of a Channel dash in daylight had also been noted, but it was not thought likely. Nevertheless, dispositions by both the Navy and RAF had been made with the resources available, which, throughout 1941, were little enough.

What followed after the three ships left Brest was a situation compounded of a series of unfortunate mishaps, inadequate resources, and some muddle due to surprise. A submarine patrol had been instigated off Brest and, at one time, no less than seven were deployed. At the time of the breakout, *Sealion* was on station, but she was caught on the surface, recharging her batteries, and depth-charged by a patrolling enemy aircraft. *Sealion* crash-dived and drew further out to sea and, while submerged, the three ships passed through her patrol area and escaped detection. This was the first stroke of bad luck; the ships had left Brest at 2345 hrs on 11 February, and no-one in Britain was aware they were at sea.

Coastal Command had been flying repeated sorties over Brest. Three aircraft were allocated to the approaches every night, one relieving another, and, on the night of the break-out, the patrolling aircraft's radar set had malfunctioned and the pilot had returned to base. In the interval between his departure and his relief's arrival, the German ships slipped through the gap. Towards dawn on 12 February, yet another patrolling aircraft might well have spotted them. Unfortunately, he was recalled to base an hour early because of the mist which was threatening to envelop his base. The enemy ships had now been at sea, undetected, for eleven hours.

The first intimation came from a coastal radar station, which picked up echoes from surface craft off Cap Gris Nez at 1015 hrs on 12 February. Two Spitfires were sent to investigate and, at last, Britain woke up to the fact that an enemy fleet was on its doorstep. It was now too late to synchronise the available forces, and these had to be thrown in piecemeal. Our heavy units were deployed in Scapa Flow and Iceland against a break-out by *Tirpitz* from Norway, but the enemy fleet was now sweeping through the Straits of Dover almost unopposed. Five MTBs were despatched from Dover, but they never came near to attacking the enemy capital ships. They had no fighter cover, and the screen thrown around the three heavy units was too formidable. They were set upon and mauled by E-boats, and their mission was a total failure.

Another piece of ill-fortune was that a squadron of RAF torpedo carrying Beauforts had been ordered south to East Anglia from Scotland in anticipation of a break-out, but bad weather had kept them grounded. The only other torpedo-carrying aircraft available was a squadron of Fleet Air Arm Swordfish based at Manston, and these flew off to attack – an attack which would prove to be ineffective. The RAF Spitfire escorting the navy torpedo bombers soon found itself hard-pressed in its own defence from enemy fighters, and, when the Swordfish levelled off to attack, the German sailors stared at them in disbelief. These small canvas-and-wire aircraft were all that could be mustered, and they were described as seeming to be hanging in the air rather than flying, such was their slow flying speed. They flew into a murderous barrage of AA fire, and every single one was shot down. None of their torpedoes found a target. The German Admiral's praise was unstinting: 'The pilots of these ancient aircraft have shown a bravery which surpasses any action by either side this day.' Another German Officer described the attack as, '…so devoted and incredible, one was privileged to witness it.' The enemy fleet was now safely through the Straits of Dover, and the German sailors could not believe the opposition had been so puny. In fact, many would convince themselves the real opposition must be still to come!

We had returned to Harwich from patrol on the forenoon of 11 Febrauary to find two destroyers from the Sheerness flotilla alongside Parkestone Quay. One was *Campbell*, the 21st flotilla Leader, the other *Vivacious*. We assumed the Captain of the 21st was paying a courtesy visit to our Captain, but there was more to it than that. The two Captains had come together to carry out exercises at sea against a break-out which (unknown to them) had already occurred! So their exercise would eventually become the real thing! When we came on deck on the forenoon of 12 February, the two afore-mentioned destroyers had gone, together with *Mackay*, *Whitshed* and *Worcester* of our own flotilla.

All ammunition had a safety dateline, after which it was likely to be increasingly unstable. Some of ours had exceeded its dateline and the seamen had come on deck to find the full ammunition lighter on the starboard side and an empty lighter on the port. The emptying and refilling of the magazines usually constituted a day's work, but on this occasion it was completed in half the time. By the end of the forenoon all the old ammunition had been de-shipped, and the new had begun to come inboard when we fell out for dinner. We resumed at 1315 hrs and at about 1400 hrs all hands were piped to muster amidships. The First Lieutenant then informed us of the break-out and we learned that Salmon and Gluckstein, together with *Prinz Eugen* were already through the Straits and off North Foreland. He added that the five V and W Class destroyers Were on their way to intercept, and all the Hunts were ordered to follow and give them AA cover.

We were at instant notice for steam and, in no time at all, had slipped from the buoy and were going through the boom defence to rendezvous with five other Hunts. When we left harbour, the majority of the new ammunition was stacked on the upper deck, and there was a mad scurry by every available hand to get it into the magazines. An order came from the gunnery director for the 4 inch guns to be loaded with semi-armour piercing shells and for replenishments to be to hand. The main armament was usually loaded with anti-aircraft shells so, obviously, contact with enemy destroyers was thought to be likely.

When all the ammunition was safely off the upper deck, I took up my action station on the forward gun. All six Hunts were steaming eastwards in line ahead at full speed, and I was thankful for a reasonable sea. I was well aware that no matter how rough it blew, there would be no coming aft on this trip. Another thing I was aware of was that we would be negotiating our own mine barrier, and I just hoped that the navigating Officer on the leading Hunt had got his facts and figures right! Eventually, night came as we ploughed on in the gloom, keeping perfect line-ahead formation. I remember thinking the first lines of Drake's Drum by Henry Newbolt:

> 'Drake is in his hammock
> An' a thousand miles away'.

But who was drumming whom up the Channel this night? Finally total darkness came and only the ship immediately ahead of us was visible without binoculars. The six Hunts were *Hambledon*, *Eglinton*, *Quorn* and *Cotswold* of our own flotilla, and two others from the Sheerness flotilla.

Exactly when the dawn of realisation came that their intended exercise had evolved into the real thing I cannot say, but, when it did, the V and W destroyers struck out eastwards at full speed. Old as they were, the two Leaders were capable of 36 knots and the other three 34 knots. When they sighted the enemy fleet at 1547 hrs it was some fourteen miles off the Dutch coast, and our own destroyers were now operating in unfamiliar mine-infested waters. When the sighting took place at a distance of approximately four miles, the V and Ws were immediately attacked by enemy fighter-bombers and all the German ships opened fire. In face of this inferno, they had as close as three miles in order to get into torpedo-launching range, and the amazing thing is that only one ship suffered extensive damage. The Germans must have been jittery; their gunnery was not up to its usual high standard on this occasion.

With all guns firing, four of the five turned to launch their torpedoes at a range of 3,300 yards. *Worcester* held on course for a further 300 yards which, at a speed of 34 knots, is quickly covered, but which, in the event, amounted to a further agonising sixteen seconds. It is possible she had already been hit during her run-in, but now she took an extra battering from *Gneisenau*. One shell shot away half her bridge and two more exploded in two of her three boiler rooms. Her torpedoes launched, she swung around to withdraw, only to present herself broadside-on to *Prinz Eugen* who slammed four more shells into her. Her torpedoes seemed to be running true and the attackers claimed to have heard two underwater explosions, but the fact is, no torpedoes struck home.

All five destroyers were now racing back, four of them largely unscathed. One wonders why the enemy destroyers and E-boats did not harry them or, indeed, pursue and attempt to destroy them. The whole German fleet, sweeping along at 30 knots, held formation, the smaller units protecting the larger, and the former showed no inclination to chase and kill. So the five destroyers came through the melee but the greatest miracle was *Worcester*. All her main armament was knocked out and only a single barrelled pom-pom remained firing. The Captain of *Gneisenau* certainly gave her no chance whatsoever of survival. He wrote in his report, 'I watched our heavy guns score direct hits on the English destroyer and she heeled so far over that she nearly capsized. I ordered our guns to cease firing, there seemed no point in wasting shells on a ship already sinking. No ship of that size could be hit so heavily and survive.'

The Hunts were now in the middle of the North Sea, hoping to rendezvous with the returning V and Ws. It was never expected that they would come to grips with the main body of the enemy fleet; they were sent out far too late for that. We did, however, expect E-boat and destroyer harassment of our surviving destroyers, but it was something that did not happen. *Hambledon* was detached from the other five Hunts, with orders to find *Worcester* and to take her in tow. It was perhaps assumed that she could no longer make steam. Despite a fog which came down in the small hours of 13 February, we did find her, and a message was flashed to her asking if she required assistance. She was making steam on her remaining boiler and travelling at about 8 knots. She replied courteously, 'Thank you. I've made it so far and hope to manage the rest.'

We circled her all night in case E-boats found her and, when dawn came, marvelled that a ship so badly damaged was not only seaworthy, but was actually still able to steam. Of her company of 130, 100 had been killed or wounded. Looking at her on that morning we knew by the state of her how much carnage there must have been, and that made us very sad, but we were immensely proud of her as a sister ship of our flotilla. *Worcester* earned for herself a place in naval annals, not only for the tenacity of her attack, but also for her doggedness; for her refusal to give up the ghost, as the Germans were convinced she assuredly must. It took Chatham dockyard many months to repair her damage, but she eventually emerged again to play a part as escort to several Russian convoys.

Before the V and Ws attacked, the RAF Beauforts managed to get airborne from Scotland. They landed in Norfolk for refuelling and flew off to the attack. On their way in, one pilot spotted *Campbell* and *Vivacious* picking up survivors from *Worcester* after an order, 'prepare to abandon ship' had been mistakenly interpreted as the order to abandon. A torpedo was launched at them which caused *Campbell* to go astern in order to avoid it. Due to his bad ship-recognition, one pilot had added insult to injury. The Beaufort attack was also a failure. No torpedo found its mark.

What our attacking destroyers did not know was that *Scharnhorst* had struck a mine at 1431 hrs, shortly before they arrived on the scene, and the damage she sustained was sufficiently extensive for the German Admiral Ciliax to transfer to a destroyer. At 1955 hrs that evening, *Gneisenau* also touched off a mine and, less than two hours later, *Scharnhorst* struck yet another. It was ironical that all our attacks had proved fruitless; the only consolation for our efforts was that the mines in question were, in all probability, RAF laid.

The German Navy achieved little from their Channel dash. In fact, it was the beginning of the end of their Z Plan. *Gneisenau* never put to sea again. She limped up the Kiel Canal for repairs, and two weeks later the RAF found her. She was bombed and set ablaze, and in June 1942 she was paid-off and her guns dismantled. Hitler by this time had become disappointed in his big ships. He ordered them all to be paid off and dismantled, complaining that their crews lacked the fighting spirit, the British traditions and long naval history. Admiral Raeder resigned on the issue and his successor, Doenitz, pleaded one further chance to unite *Scharnhorst* with *Tirpitz* and harass the Russian convoys to which Hitler grudgingly agreed.

Scharnhorst was eventually sacrificed at Doenitz' attempt to redeem the big ships' fall from grace in Hitler's eyes. All previous caution was discarded when she was sent to attack a Russian convoy when it was appreciated that it was likely to be well protected. The mix of British warships escorting this convoy was based on likely attack by an enemy capital ship, and *Scharnhorst* fell into the trap. She came under the guns of battleship *Duke of York* with her cruisers and the escorting fleet destroyers. This time destroyer torpedoes did find their mark and *Scharnhorst* was slowed and battered by *Duke of York*'s 14 inch salvoes. She was sunk on Boxing Day, 1943.

Of Germany's battleships, only *Tirpitz* now remained, Although she never fired a shot in anger, while ever she lay in the Norwegian fjords she posed a threat, and our capital ships had always to be held in readiness against her breaking out. The mere fact that she was thought to have done so caused the scattering of convoy PQ17, with tragic losses of ships to aircraft and U-boats. For her part, she was given no peace. She was disabled by midget submarines and by Fleet Air Arm aircraft. Finally, she was bombed and sunk by RAF Lancasters in 1944. Ludovic Kennedy described her as, 'an invalid in life and a cripple in death.' It was an apt description.

Chapter 11

Life Onboard

In June 1942, a second AA2 gunnery rating joined us, who took over captaincy of the forward pom-pom. This enabled me to return as gun layer of the quadruple pom-pom in the more sheltered position aft. But nothing is perfect. Here, on our elevated platform, we were subjected to sulphurous fumes from the funnel. Some days were worse than others. At convoy speed with a cross wind, the fumes were carried away from us, but when we were patrolling and steaming at a reasonable speed, we got the lot. The sulphur lodged in the back of the throat and made the eyes sting, and there were also smuts which covered our clothing. Sometimes when we had been laying smoke to cover shipping, we came off watch looking like chimney sweeps.

By the Spring of 1942, after a gruelling winter in the bows, I began to suffer from carbuncles. I suppose I was still not yet fully out of puberty, but the travail I had undergone from November to March had not helped, and I had become thoroughly run-down. All ships' doctors in the Navy are termed Surgeons, a term inherited from the sawbones of the old sailing ship era. Not all of them were actually surgeons; some were physicians, others called-up GPs, but *Hambledon* did have a doctor trained in surgery, who was very keen to practise his art. One of the wags warned that anyone reporting to the sick bay must be prepared to face the scalpel, even if they only required cough medicine! For this reason, when a boil appeared on my right wrist, I decided on a self-cure. When it was ripe, I turned in one night after applying a bread poultice. The next morning I took a clean linen handkerchief and nipped out the core. It was a painful experience – but at least I had evaded the scalpel ! The removed core left a hole large enough to take a small pea, and needed bandaging. Accordingly, I attended sick parade. When I proffered my wrist, the surgeon was somewhat taken aback with what I took to be intrigue at my surgical skill.

'How did you get the core out?' he asked.

'I put a bread poultice on it and nipped it out with a clean handkerchief, Sir.' I said proudly.

At this he almost hopped with anger, saying, 'You fool! Don't come here with your old wives' remedies unless you want to lose your hand.' He ordered his Assistant to bandage the wrist and to include a splint. I was then given light duties in harbour until the splint and bandages were removed.

A week later, a carbuncle appeared on my right buttock and, when I reported again, the surgeon told me to report back the next day. Obviously it was not yet ripe enough for his ministrations! The following day he selected a scalpel, probe and tweezers and dropped them into a bubbling, stainless steel steriliser. I swear there was a look of rapture on his face as he pulled on his rubber gloves.

He had placed a wooden dining chair in the middle of the deck and demonstrated how I was to stand behind it, bent over, with the top of the chair back in my midriff, while gripping the seat. He then squirted something excruciatingly cold all over my buttock, which, as a local anaesthetic was only partially successful, in that I did not feel the incision he made with the scalpel, but I certainly felt him digging out the core. When I straightened up in pain, lifting the chair from the deck, he said testily, 'I'm not hurting you. Put the chair down and don't act like a baby!'

Two weeks later another appeared, followed by another, then a third, each one bigger than its predecessor, and all on the right buttock. Each time, over the chair back I went, and suffered agonies rather than be scoffed at. For several weeks I was only able to sit on the left side of my posterior, but was not excused any duties, and kept all my watches at sea. Eventually, another carbuncle manifested itself which dwarfed all the previous ones, whereupon the surgeon decided to operate with a full anaesthetic. This required the presence of a second sawbones, so a signal was sent to another destroyer in the flotilla, whose surgeon duly arrived onboard.

I had been instructed to bath, put on clean underwear, and report at 1500 hrs, which I did. I was then ordered to lie face down on the couch, after which I was given a shot of pentothal in my arm and told to count up to twenty. When I reached twenty, all my deference and inhibitions had vanished and I said cheekily, 'There's your twenty and it's twenty not out.'

A voice said, 'Try twenty more.' At ten I zoomed off into oblivion. I regained consciousness lying on my side, with my right buttock bandaged and strapped with sticking plaster.

'Are you all right?'

'I think so, Sir.'

'Good. Lie there for a while. You can leave when you feel like it, but make sure you're good and steady on your feet. OK?'

With that, they both departed having had, I suppose, the time of their lives. I lay there thinking what an improvement it had been compared with the chair back, when the sliding door slid open and Able Seaman Davies poked his head in and said, 'Are you going ashore at 1600 hrs?'

'Does it look like it? Come off it man. I've just been operated on.'

Without batting an eyelid he said, 'Will you sub for me then?'

I grudgingly agreed, whereupon he said, 'Thanks, mate. You're a toff!' and the door closed. He had made no enquiries about my condition and proffered no condolences. I had the feeling he might well have made the same request had I had a limb amputated! Two weeks later, two carbuncles appeared together and this time the surgeon decided (belatedly, I thought) that I needed rest and hospitalisation. He arranged for me to be admitted into the hospital in *Ganges*.

It was a hot June day when I left the ship with my kitbag and hammock and landed at Shatley pier. I felt so weak and ill that I could not manage to carry kitbag and hammock together and had to make two trips from pier to hospital. After admission I was given a hot bath and put to bed close to the bay window of the ward, from where I could see the harbour. It was late afternoon and the sky had become ominously dark. Suddenly, through the window I saw *Hambledon* making the turn to starboard which would take her through the boom and out to sea. At that moment there was a brilliant flash of lightning, followed seconds later by an almighty crash of thunder as the heavens opened, releasing a heavy deluge of rain. A sailor in the bed opposite, seeing my interest in what was happening on the river, said, 'That your ship just going out, Lofty?' 'Too right,' I said, and may God protect her and all who sail in her.'

I lay back contentedly and pulled the crisp linen sheet up under my chin. The following day I was seen by a hospital surgeon who examined me and ordered a daily treatment of Litz baths and staph vaccine injections, together with regular hot fomentations – a more up-to-date version of the old wives' remedy! The treatment and rest worked like magic. The two carbuncles eventually came to a head and burst, and there were to be no more. The physician's art had proved far more successful than the surgeon's, whose ministrations might have continued interminably for all the good they were doing.

On the seventh day I was discharged and took my kit back to Shatley pier to catch the boat which ran between Harwich and Parkestone Quay via Shatley. When it arrived, there were several sailors and two Wren passengers onboard and, after I boarded, we set off up-river for Parkestone Quay. As we arrived, I saw *Hambledon* coming down-river to go to sea. She had been out, come back, and was now off again. 'Good, I thought.' Kit into Badger (the shore establishment on Parkestone Quay) and two days' leave for yours truly, with perhaps a third if I'm watch ashore when she returns. My reverie was broken by the Petty Officer Cox'n of the boat saying, 'Where are you for then, mate?'

With more than a hint of glee I replied, 'I was for *Hambledon*, but I'm too late – she's on her way to sea,' pointing in her direction. Then to my chagrin he said, 'You're not if I can help it,' and he gave two blasts on his whistle to the engineman. As the boat began to move I said pleadingly, 'Play the game. I've just been discharged from Shatley hospital.'

He muttered something above the engine noise about my being fit or I wouldn't have been discharged, and the boat ploughed on. As we neared the ship he began to turn until eventually he was running on a parallel course. He closed the gap and throttled back until the boat was running at the ship's speed about a foot from her port side midships. Piqued as I was, I had to admire his boat-handling. He shouted, 'Get your kit aboard and get ready to jump.'

I hurled my kitbag and hammock onboard and they landed at the feet of the Sub-Lieutenant who, with a bemused look on his face, had appeared amidships to investigate what all the commotion was about. I then stood on the gunwale of the boat, took a leap upwards, grabbed a guardrail and pulled myself onboard. I saluted the Sub-Lieutenant who said, 'You managed that very nicely. Better report to the Captain.' I climbed the three ladders to the bridge, to be confronted by John Barnes, telescope under his arm, hands in duffel coat pockets, looking at me with his pale blue eyes under the cap peak with its exaggerated curve and, grinning broadly.

Giving him a smart salute, I said, 'Able Seaman Saxton reporting back onboard for duty, Sir.' He returned the salute and, still grinning, said, 'You mistimed this one, didn't you, Saxton?' to which I replied, 'I didn't, Sir. The Cox'n of the boat did.' He asked, 'Are you quite fit?' 'Considering I've missed my recuperation, yes, Sir.' He was still grinning when I saluted him and left the bridge, so I had got away with the sauce. At the foot of the bridge ladder I met the Sub-Lieutenant who said, 'You can't get your gear below, we've battened down, but get it off the upper deck into the after screen.' An off-watch stoker, turfed out of his mess deck, appeared, grabbed my kitbag, and said, 'Good to see you back, mate.'

With my kit off the upper deck, I climbed the ladder up to the pom-pom deck and as soon as my head appeared there was raucous, sarcastic cheering.

'You idiot, why didn't you give it another five minutes?'

'Can't bear to be parted from us, can he?'

'Trouble with him, he thinks we can't manage without him. He's even come on watch in his number-one suit; best dressed sea-going sailor in the flotilla.' Of course, it was all good-natured ribbing. Eventually it petered out and changed to, 'You fit again, mate?', 'Glad to see you back,' and so on.

I stayed on to test the gun, then, when the hatches were opened up, went below to change into sea rig. I had enjoyed seeing her going to sea in a thunderstorm; but, somehow, I felt that for me to be ashore and fit, and the ship at sea, would hardly have been cricket. The Navy in wartime was a far different proposition from the Navy in peacetime, as can be imagined – especially on the east coast. We had, of course, ratings with us who had served in the peacetime Navy in the Home Fleet and overseas, and their accounts of life in the peace time Navy made us green with envy. Little sea time, plenty of shore leave and, when at sea, always at cruising stations, with two-thirds of your time off watch. Naturally that did not mean time off. The ship's routine of cleaning had to be carried out even at sea but it was a far cry from all-night action stations and defence stations during daylight. In harbour, all hands were piped at 0615 hrs to lash up and stow. At 0630 hrs came the pipe, 'Hands to breakfast and clean.'

After breakfast, the mess had to be scrubbed out, including tables and lockers. There was no cooked breakfast on a small ship. If you were hungry there was bread and jam, but most were content with a cup of tea and a cigarette. Both watches of the hands were then piped to fall in and were put to work. Some had regular jobs which they did unsupervised; others were paintwork cleaners and deck swabbers, supervised by Leading Seamen.

Occasionally there would be 'paint ship' when all hands were pressed into service with stages rigged around the ship's side, the mast and the funnel. We had a ten-minute' stand easy at 1000 hrs.

'Up spirits' was piped at 1100 hrs. Rum is no longer a feature of the Navy. It was so weighted with tradition that there must have been much heart-searching by the Admiralty before the decision was made to withdraw it, but I imagine the Navy is better off without it. Throughout my first ten months in the Navy, when I was under-age, I was not eligible for grog. During that time I resolved I would never draw my rum ration because of the trouble it caused. It was a liberal tot and a double amount of water was added to it. This left a man with three parts of a tumbler full of grog – a potent mixture. It led to arguments and squabbling – even fighting by the firebrands – and it certainly turned me from wishing to be part of it.

Temperance ratings were given three old pence a day in lieu of rum, but I certainly did not decline it in order to get that. The rum was kept securely locked in a compartment below the stokers' mess deck. It came aboard in either one-gallon stone jars or five-gallon wooden casks. There was no ventilation in the cramped compartment and the fumes the rum gave off when being drawn were potent enough to cause giddiness. The casks were lowered by ammunition whip from the fo'c'sle through the forward seamen's mess deck down to the stokers' mess deck below it. There was one occasion when one of the casks slipped out of the bale-sling just as its weight had been taken by the whip, whereupon it went hurtling down through two decks. The unfortunate seaman who was waiting to receive it heard the ominous cry, 'Under below!' and turned to run.

He was a fraction too late and the hoop of the cask struck him at the top of the right buttock. Two stokers escorted him to the sick bay, bleeding profusely, where his wound required twenty-two stitches. When the cask hit the deck, one of the staves split and its contents began gurgling out over the deck which (fortunately for the stokers) had just had its morning scrub. There was a brief second of intrigued fascination from the onlookers then, acting as one man, they ran to their respective lockers for any clean linen they could lay their hands on.

When the cask had been deemed to have gurgled long enough, it was rolled with the damaged stave uppermost and the mopping up operation began. Clean handkerchiefs, towels and vests were brought into play and the prized liquid was squeezed into a large mess kettle. Time was of the essence before the Officer of the Day put in an appearance to make his decision about the disposal of the damaged cask. When he did so there was, of course, no sign of the mess kettle, and he must have been impressed at the speed with which the spilled ullage had been mopped up. For weeks after the event, the stokers' mess deck exuded the heady aroma of a rum store in the victualling depot!

The tobacco allowance was, perhaps, too liberal and there were surprisingly few non-smokers. There was not the taboo against smoking that there is today, and the liberal allowance possibly induced men to smoke who otherwise might not have done, or at least, made it possible for smokers to smoke more. Every man was allocated 1lb weight of either cigarette or pipe tobacco a month, for a shilling. In addition, packets of duty-free cigarettes could be purchased from the NAAFl canteen for six old pence for twenty. Ashore, during the war the price of the same packet, non-duty-free, rose to twenty-eight old pence. I have often wondered how many sailors developed drink problems through their daily rum ration; and how many smoking-related health problems due to plentiful and cheap tobacco.

The two main meals were dinner at noon and supper at 1830 hrs. Tea was, like breakfast, merely a snack which kept us going to the next main meal. We ate well and did not suffer the stringent rationing experienced by civilians. Meat was plentiful, although I have my suspicions that in the Mediterranean, the 'lamb' we were eating was goat and the 'beef' horse! In general the ship's company was an excellent crowd and I enjoyed my life onboard. Sailors share a common danger – the elements – and in wartime an obvious other danger was added to that. Well might the naval prayer carry the plea, 'Preserve us, we pray Thee, from the dangers of the sea and the violence of the enemy.'

Any trouble-makers were drafted. When men are living cheek by jowl, nothing is mare calculated to wreck their contentment than the odd misfit who would make trouble in any company or situation, So the persistent drunkards, the pugilists and the malcontents were discreetly drafted. There were the usual crop of comedians and these were the leaven in the bread. No-one was addressed by his Christian name. Those who did not acquire a nickname were addressed by their surnames. There were the obvious Chalky Whites, Taffy Williamses and Johnnie Walkers, and others took the name of the job they did. A stoker was always Stokes, a cook, Chef, a wireless-telegraphist, Sparks. Nicknames arose naturally. One rating had served on the ex-Yankee and had found an anorak with the name 'Crawley' emblazoned on the back of it. His name was Claire but he was always referred to as Crawley.

Another rating was always begging old trousers and jumpers to wrap around his 4 inch pull-through. He was quickly dubbed Serge. Paddys and Jocks also abounded, but if a man did not acquire a nickname, his surname was automatically used.

The best comedian was Gordon Chipeau (Chips) from Dover, of French extraction. Apart from being an excellent mimic, he never seemed to have to think for the witty back-answer. We had recognition signals for aircraft and minor war vessels operating at night. These signals were changed at midnight and a message along the following lines would be passed from the bridge to all guns:

> 'Aircraft recognition: white over red;
> Minor war vessels: red over green.'

Chipeau was in the opposite watch to me and I met him one night at the top of the mess deck ladder, coming off watch, and asked him what the recognition signals were. Quick as a flash he replied, 'Aircraft: old gold over heliotrope; minor war vessels: blush pink over magenta.'

The CPO Cox'n on a destroyer is the regulating NCO responsible for discipline. Ours had a very gruff voice which Chipeau could imitate. He would say in the Cox'n's voice, 'It isn't the rum that makes my voice gruff, it's the water they add to it.'

The only form of gambling permitted was tombola, officially run by the Canteen Committee. But that did not prevent Jack from gambling. A blanket would be spread on the table to deaden the sound of chinking coins and pontoon or brag would be played. One night the pontoon school was well under way when the Cox'n's voice shouted down the hatch, 'I can hear the jingle!' and there was a mad scurry to hide the cards and get rid of the money. Then two legs appeared descending the ladder, but the body attached was Chipeau's! The card school groaned in exasperation, jeered and pelted him with locker cushions.

Eric Gee (the Horse) was the noisy type. He would stamp around in his heavy leather sea boots and, if there were anything to fall over, he would find it. The ladder into the mess deck stood at an angle of 75° from the horizontal and Gee would descend it without using the treads. He would grip the tubular handrails and slide down backwards, landing with a thump, to everyone's annoyance – especially Hedley Woodruff. Hedley was a qualified Chartered Accountant from Sheffield, who was eventually commissioned. He was normally well-spoken but, when annoyed, would vent his anger in broad Yorkshire. Gee once referred to him as 'Headstrong Dandruff' and, with unconcealed disdain, Hedley came back, 'Tha looks like a horse, tha cavorts around like a horse and, furthermore, tha's got the brains of a bloody horse!' Gee, to his credit, laughed louder than anyone, although Woodruff had certainly not meant his invective to be amusing.

Arthur Charles Edward Brown from Watford was dubbed 'Ace' for obvious reasons. He was trainer to my gunlayer of the quadruple pom-pom, and we forged quite a skilled partnership, each knowing instinctively the other's mind and intended moves. That apart, we were also good friends in the mess. Brown used to claim he had worn a sailor's uniform longer than anyone on the mess deck. When challenged to prove it, he would recount having been sent to the boys' training ship *Arethusa* as a child and, from there, sent as a boy entrant into the Navy.

The *Arethusa* came under the Shaftesbury Homes which took in orphans, but Brown was not an orphan; he had no father, and his mother could not afford to raise him, so Brown had been put into a sailor suit at a very young age. This early experience had not soured him, but it had certainly instilled in him the conviction that the decisions of those in authority over him were not always for his good. He had served in the cruiser *Dido* and the destroyer *Eskimo*. Consequently, he was an experienced seaman, even though only twenty-two years of age. While in *Dido* he had turned his back and walked away from an officer who was verbally abusing him. He was charged with silent contempt and served ninety days in Barlinnie prison.

Such was naval discipline at that time, and it did nothing to endear Brown to his superiors. Yet he was not a malcontent; rather the end product of a child who had drawn a poor hand. He would tell of how he once came home on leave after a two-year spell of absence abroad, to find his mother rolling out pastry with a cigarette in her mouth. She looked up from her task and said, 'Brought any fags?' The story was not related with any bitterness. That is how life had dealt with him and he meant it to be good for a laugh.

Tubby Bishop came from the Midlands and had a pronounced Birmingham accent. He was as round as a barrel, with a jolly, carefree disposition. Occasionally, for reasons known only to himself, he would get very drunk, but even then he caused no trouble. One of the trouble-makers was Ginger, a Tynesider. Ginger was short and wiry; he had a temper and would resort to fisticuffs with little or no provocation. There was an occasion when liberty men had been piped to fall in, and Ginger could not find his cap. Time was running out and he grabbed the first cap to hand which happened to be Tubby's. Tubby remonstrated that he intended going ashore himself later and needed the cap, whereupon Ginger attacked him, blacking his eye. Tubby did not go ashore and there was much sympathy for him and much disdain for his attacker.

Six months later we were guard destroyer standing by for emergency and no leave was given. Consequently every man was aboard and the mess deck was crowded. Suddenly two pairs of boxing gloves were thrown down the hatch, landing with a thud at the foot of the ladder. Tubby waddled over to them, picked them up and going to Ginger said, 'Fancy a couple of rounds?'

Ginger couldn't believe what he was hearing, and everyone almost gasped – it was like the mouse challenging the cat. No-one who witnessed it is likely to forget what followed, As the gloves were being laced up there was a deadly quiet and not a little apprehension on Tubby's behalf. When they came out sparring, Tubby changed from being a small hippopotamus into a ballet dancer. He waltzed around Ginger and gave him the hiding of his life. Try as he would, Ginger did not manage to lay a glove on his opponent, took a severe mauling and eventually cried off.

Tubby requested his gloves to be unlaced and (after congratulating Ginger on a good fight) returned to resume the letter he had been writing. It was obvious that Tubby had acquired pugilistic skills but, owing to his love of food, had run to seed. Nevertheless the skills were still there and he had used them to pay off a score of six months' standing. He never referred to the incident again and, shortly after the incident, Ginger was drafted from the ship.

The mess loudspeaker served several purposes. It could be hooked up to the radio or the gramophone and could be used by the Captain to broadcast messages. Mostly it was a radio speaker, but, occasionally, someone would play records. We had a selection of records bought from canteen funds but they were mostly swing or jazz in which I had little interest. The American jazz aristocracy reigned supreme in Earl Hines, Count Basey, and Duke Ellington. I enjoyed classical music, but I was very much in the minority and was irritated beyond words when someone switched off, say, a broadcast promenade concert, as not being worth listening to. Occasionally, I stood guard aver the loudspeaker and insisted on fair play. Eventually, I found a way around the problem.

A radar rating joined the ship – a Londoner called Hooper. Shortly after he arrived onboard he established himself as the ship's gramophone librarian. This meant that he was permitted to buy records from canteen funds. Naturally, he had to pander to popular taste, but he did manage to come back with the odd classical record and I discovered him to be a classical fanatic. He had a large collection at home and returned from each leave with half a dozen or so. When he learned of my interest, he devised a way for us to listen to records together privately, without fear of interruption or objection.

The record player was housed in a tiny compartment adjacent to the wireless-telegraphy room. The compartment housed other wireless telegraphy equipment and there was then only sufficient space left for two standing or crouching bodies. This did not deter us; we would repair there after supper, unplug the gramophone to the mess deck speakers and plug in the radio. We then had the gramophone to ourselves, playing through the one speaker in the compartment. By dint of his own record collection, and attending every concert he could in London, Hooper's knowledge was prodigious and, from him, my own knowledge increased by leaps and bounds.

Sometimes we broke all regulations by continuing our recitals long after 'pipe down.' He knew his composers, and before playing, say, a symphony, he would give me a run-down of the passages and the highlights to listen for. He also knew his conductors (his favourite being Toscanini) and he would play the same work under two different batons, first explaining how each would interpret it differently. I have fond memories of him drumming his fingers to the beat, visibly stiffening in expectation of a rousing crescendo, anticipating in mime the cymbal clashes and drum rolls. He would lean back with his head on the bulkhead, his eyes closed, floating in rapture at some enchanting slow movement. They were the old 78 rpm wax records and there were times when, as one side terminated and cut off, he would turn it over at lightning speed so that the spell that had been cast should not be broken. At the end of the last record he had drifted into a reverie and needed several seconds before he could rouse himself.

Hooper was a classical-music fanatic. He played no instrument but his knowledge was formidable, and most of the knowledge I acquired came from him. He revelled in having a pupil of kindred spirit; it seemed to enhance his own enjoyment, and he would seek me out on every possible occasion to join him in the compartment. His records were sacred objects and he handled them with a care amounting to veneration, holding them with the tips of his fingers pressed to the rims. They were wiped with a special cloth before being played and again before being returned to their sleeves.

Life onboard was never dull. There were times during the winter when I would let a shipmate take my shore leave and stay onboard to write letters, listen to records, or just enjoy the company, rather than go groping in the blackout and sitting in pubs. I am told that hammocks are no longer used in today's Navy, and that every sailor now has his own bunk, I also read recently that efforts have been made to make mess decks more attractive and comfortable, some, I gather, even running to simulated wooden wall-panelling,

Our mess deck was no more than a large steel box with portholes, the lower half of it being below the water line. There was nothing domestic about it and by no stretch of the imagination could it be seen as comfortable and attractive. There was no comfortable seating, no armchairs or chairs of any description, no carpets, no decor. The only thing approaching the domestic were the bare wooden tables and the lockers which doubled as seats. For the rest it was the lower deck of a man-o'-war, given over as living space, and such was evident by the electric cables and piping that ran through it, by the 4 inch gun support which swallowed up precious space and the ammunition chutes under which one had to duck.

Nevertheless, it was more home to us than our actual homes. The latter were only accessible to us for about three weeks every year; for the rest, the mess deck was home in most other respects and I have fond memories of it and the comradeship I enjoyed in it. There was a particular sadness in watching a ship go down, a sight I witnessed many times. The emotions roused through loss of life were but there were other emotions of a different order. When the sea claimed a ship, it was also claiming sailors' homes. All their intimate and precious possessions went with it, and they had to begin again with only the dripping garments they were rescued in. A bachelor sailor with no other home ashore (and there were many of them in the merchant service) lost everything he possessed, every bit as much as bombed-out families did. There is, however, an aspect about ships that a landsman might find difficult to comprehend. To a sailor, a ship has a life of a kind that no house has. Be it a spick and span warship or humble tramp, its throbbing, pulsating, living ambiance gets under his skin and becomes a part of him. As sailors watch the sea claim a ship, the feeling is akin to that in a funeral parlour. And the sailor whose ship it is, mourns its loss as no householder would mourn a lost house. In addition to losing his possessions, part of himself has gone down with his ship.

Chapter 12

Accolades and Bottles

In the summer of 1942, the First Lieutenant, Eric Pilditch, left the ship, and Nicholas Fitzherbert was promoted to Lieutenant and took his place. Nicholas was reputed to come from a titled family and his name seems to bear that out. The term, 'an Officer and a Gentleman' is sometimes a misnomer because not every officer was a gentleman and, incidentally, there were some gentlemen on the lower deck. However, Nicholas Fitzherbert was the epitome of an officer and a gentleman and he was slim and dark with the good looks of a film star.

Then, later that same autumn, John Barnes also left. He was piped over the side and, as he drew away in the motorboat, we lined the guard rails and gave him three rousing cheers. He was reputed to have said that *Hambledon* was not his first destroyer and that he might command a bigger one, but he would never command a better, which was a tribute to the ship's company rather than the ship. He did command a bigger one. He was promoted to Commander and given one of the Navy's best destroyers – *Ashanti* – a Tribal class in which he escorted many Russian convoys. I suppose we were fortunate in having him for eighteen months. He was certainly a first-rate destroyer Captain.

There is no such thing in the Navy as a retiring Commanding Officer remaining on board to show his successor the ropes. A ship cannot have two Captains on board at one and the same time. Our interregnum lasted less than an hour before the new one was piped on board and, shortly after his arrival, all hands were piped to muster on the fo'c'sle. Immediately we had assembled, the new Captain appeared, and we were called to attention by the First Lieutenant who saluted, and reported, 'Ship's Company present, Sir', and was ordered, 'Stand them at ease, Number One!' Lieutenant Commander Gordon MacKendrick, RN, then mounted the capstan, took off his cap, thrust it under his left arm and said, 'I've cleared the lower deck to let you see what you've got this time.'

He was as tall as John Barnes was short, with light brown hair and a weather-beaten face. It is difficult to place a man's age at this distance in time, because a twenty-year-old tends to view a man of forty as well advanced into middle age, but I imagine him to have been about thirty-eight. The gist of his speech was that although *Hambledon* was his first command, he had had extensive destroyer experience with the hierarchy.

He was referring to the fact that he had been First Lieutenant in a flotilla leader and, in fact, we knew he had come from the leader of the 21st Flotilla. It is not given to the lower-deck sailor to know the twists and turns of a Commanding Officer's career. All we had to do was to wait and see what sort of captain Gordon MacKendrick would make. If his speech was anything to go by, he was a firebrand who wanted to be where the action was, and this turned out to be true. He also said *Hambledon* had a good sea reputation but that our punishment returns were the highest in the flotilla and something had to be done about that. He warned us that all future leave-breaking would be dealt with severely.

Gordon MacKendrick turned out to be a good Captain. He was not the ship-handler John Barnes was, and no-one expected he would be. The first time he took the ship alongside Immingham pier, the engine room personnel reported him as requiring three times the number of screw movements that John Barnes had needed. But we seamen hardly needed to be told that, because we were handling the berthing wires and could see every move made. Nevertheless, he improved, took us into plenty of action and always brought us out intact. He was extremely conscientious and spent untold hours on the bridge. He did not suffer fools gladly and could be crotchety when things went wrong because of someone's foolishness. He was reputed to have survived a brain tumour and, whether this was true or not, the fact is that his hair did not grow in the nape of his neck, and there was evidence of his having undergone surgery there.

His reference to high punishment returns resulted from a minor mutiny having taken place when the aftermess deck refused to obey the pipe to fall in after dinner one day in the summer of 1942. We had been in the habit, after two nights at sea, of being given a 'make and mend' (the afternoon off) on returning to harbour, and when the privilege was withdrawn, the aftermess deck personnel objected. The result was that there were about forty cases registered on the punishment returns as, 'Did not immediately obey an order, namely, Hands fall in at 1315 hrs.'

There is no doubt that the personality of a ship's Commanding Officer is reflected in the ship's company. At all times he wields tremendous power – especially at sea – and his every mood permeates the ship. Both Officers and ratings pick up the nuances of his temperament and this can lead to amusement or irritation, according to prevailing circumstances. Gordon MacKendrick quickly became known for his crotchetiness and this resulted in many amusing stories circulating the mess deck. The Asdic set was housed in a small cabin tucked into a corner of the bridge. From here the operator was able to communicate his under-water tracking to the Captain directly, without recourse to communication equipment, but since the Asdic were seldom used on the east coast, the cabin was often unoccupied.

It was just large enough to take the seated operator and Gordon would occasionally take refuge in it during the long night watches, resting his legs and sheltering from the wind, when many other captains would repair to their cabins. Gordon was sitting in the cabin one night, with his knees protruding, and resting on one knee was his hand holding his fleece-lined mittens. A bridge look-out, coming on watch, saw the mittens, and, thinking was the Asdic operator, grabbed them saying, 'You don't need those in there – I'll borrow them.' Gordon did not let go and a short tug-o-war-developed. Suddenly Gordon bellowed, 'Who is that man?' The look-out, realising his awful error, sped away in the dark to his position in the corner of the bridge. Gordon pursued him and sniffed him out.

'What the hell do you think you're doing? Have you come on watch to play holding-handies?'

The luckless rating spluttered, 'I'm sorry, Sir. I thought you were the Asdic operator.'

Gordon knew full well how the mistake had occurred, but that did not mitigate his wrath, and he went back into the cabin, fuming and muttering. The term 'holding-handies' was repeated with mirth over and again in the mess deck.

Captain of the Flotilla Leader reserved the right to go to sea whenever he chose and, compared with her sisters, HMS *MacKay* put in little sea time. After languishing in harbour for what seemed ages, one of our comedians ventured that she would never go to sea again because she was aground on the empty bottles and tin cans she had thrown overboard! Destroyer sailors were always keen to see other ships do their share of sea time. During the war, Captains went to sea with sealed orders, to be broken open when clear of the harbour. Thus, Jack never knew his movements until the last minute, and this led to wild speculations and rumours (known as 'buzzes') spreading throughout the ship. There were buzz merchants who claimed to know all that was to happen, and occasionally they got it right. Mostly they were hopelessly wrong, and had to suffer ridicule, but this never seemed to deter them. Leading Seaman Tubby Dutton was a buzz-merchant and, one night in the mess he said, 'I've heard a buzz we're going out tomorrow on a northbound with *MacKay*.' Somebody else said, 'Us maybe, but not *MacKay*.'

But this time Tubby's clairvoyance was accurate; as we made preparations to slip from the buoy, we could see *MacKay*'s fo'c'sle party doing likewise. The senior ship always leads in or out of harbour, and *MacKay* preceded us down river and through the boom. Just north of the estuary, landward from us on the port side, was the wreck of a merchantman. This ship had probably been bombed or mined in 1940 and her Captain had probably been aiming to beach her, because she was well off the swept channel. If that were so, he had not quite achieved his aim, because she lay on the bottom with only her steel foremast visible. *MacKay* opened fire as she drew abreast of it and, as we watched the fall of shot, we considered it to be indifferent shooting. Then, as we in turn drew abreast, the communication number transmitted the order from the bridge, 'For exercise – red 90 – U-boat periscope – open fire!'

We had fired at it before, but it had never been designated a U-boat periscope. Gordon was indulging his fancy somewhat! As Brown spun his handwheels and began to train the mounting to port, a second message came through from the bridge, 'Show *MacKay* some good shooting!' and just for devilment I shouted to Brown, 'OK Brownie. Chink of daylight down the trailing edge and we'll hit it this time.' Brown replied, 'My oath we will.' whose interpretation in naval terms is ironic.

What Brown meant was 'you'll be lucky', because both of us knew that the odds against our scoring a direct hit were high. Gordon was asking for accurate ranging and grouping but even he was not prepared for what followed. Brown gave me the chink of daylight to allow for the ship's speed and I positioned both our horizontal cross wires as far up the mast (which presented as no more than a knitting needle) as I deemed necessary for range and curvature of trajectory. I then called, 'Layer target!' and Brown immediately pressed the trigger. The smaller, nimbler forward pom-pom was already blazing away and placing some well-aimed shots, as was the port Oerlikon, when we too opened fire. Our gun barked six times discharging a stream of tracer shells, then, as we paused between salvoes to adjust our aim, the impossible happened. There were two orange-coloured flashes as two shells struck the mast, while the remainder of our salvo burst in black puffs around its watery base.

There was a chorus of cheering from the off-watch stokers lining the guard rails, and they all turned as one man to look up at the gun platform with their thumbs in the air. We were about to fire a further salvo when the 'cease-fire' gong sounded and the communication number shouted, 'Cease firing, train fore and aft, gun layer report to the bridge!'

When I reached the bridge, Gordon was sitting in his high chair, wearing a sheepskin coat, which came down well below his knees. He sprang out of the chair to return my salute and, trying hard not to be too effusive said, 'Excellent shooting. Leaves nothing to be desired. Keep up that standard and we'll win the war. Send the gun trainer up here!' When I got back, I sent Brown off to receive his pat on the back and, two minutes after his return came another message, Gun Layer report to the First Lieutenant's cabin!'

Once again, I left the gun platform and made my way to the First Lieutenant's cabin in the bridge superstructure. Nicholas Fitzherbert had been on the bridge when I had reported and, after Brown left, must have decided to take Gordon's congratulations a stage further. I knocked on the cabin door and he shouted to me to enter. He was standing alongside his bunk and said with a smile, 'I'm pleased you put on a good show for *MacKay*'s benefit – here's your prize for good shooting.'

And drawing his hand from behind his back he held out a packet of twenty Craven-A cigarettes. I had made my way to the cabin expecting a repeat performance of Gordon's verbal congratulations, so was quite taken aback. Nicholas' psychology was admirable. He had decided that our performance warranted something more tangible. The 'prizes' were worth six pence in the NAAFI canteen, but the thought behind them, and Nicholas' demeanour set them beyond price. In fact, I never smoked mine. I kept the packet in my locker as though it was a medal, until the

Two Hunt Class destroyers at anchor.

Portrait of Fred Saxton taken in Redcar in 1942.

This picture postcard purports to be of H.M.S. *Hambledon* - but it is not! It is in fact H.M.S. *Tynedale*, another Hunt Class destroyer (L 96). H.M.S *Hambledon* was her sister ship (L 37.) *Tynedale* was sunk by a U-Boat torpedo in the Mediterranean in 1943. It may be that the photograph was taken *from* the *Hambledon*.

Standing beside a four-barrelled pom-pom. Made by Vickers they were primarily anti-aircraft weapons, and technically were automatic cannon firing explosive rounds. They came in four or eight barrel models, the eight barrel models being referred to as "Chicago Pianos". They had a range of 1000yards and a rate of fire of 120 rounds per minute. They could be depressed to engage surface ships and Hambledon had a single barrelled "bow chaser" for use against E-Boats.

Four barrelled pom-pom, its barrels in depressed position.

Fred and Margaret on their wedding day in February 1945. Mother was a WRNS Petty Officer.

A Hunt Class destroyer at anchor.

Artist's impression of a Hunt Class destroyer being refitted in dry-dock. The single barrel pom-pom bow chaser is evident on the prow of the ship.

Unidentified [Hunt] - class destroyer of the Royal Navy bombarding Dieppe during Operation JUBILEE.

A Hunt Class Destroyer lying at anchor.

HMS *Eridge*, a hunt class destroyer, brought back to harbour battle damaged.

HMS *Brocklesby*, in a hurry.

Sky watch, a four barrelled pom-pom.

Photograph of British Hunt class destroyer HMS *Belvoir*.

The U.S. president Harry S. Truman and foreign minister James Byrnes acknowledge honours rendered by the British Hunt-class destroyer *HMS Hambledon (L37)* which had escorted U.S. cruiser *USS Augusta (CA-31)* to the River Scheldt in the Netherlands on 15 August 1945.

tobacco went green with mildew. There were good reasons for the jubilation shown by the stokers. In their unenviable job in the bowels of the ship, it must have been some comfort to them to know that the gunnery ratings up top could hit their target. Summonses to the bridge, however, were not always so pleasant.

Gordon was always keen to keep us on our toes and, passing any wreck, he was likely to call for an exercise shoot. Woe betide us if we were caught flat-footed and were slow in opening fire. One day he hit on the idea of discharging a distress rocket from the bridge, which exploded in midair and released a flare suspended on a small parachute. Its time suspended was only about half a minute, so we had to work fast to get the gun trained onto it.

The after-galley was built under part of the pom-pom deck, and the funnel from the coal-fired range came up through the deck and stood about six feet tall in the corner. Whenever the range was lit and food being cooked, it gave off smoke, but, being aft of the gun mounting, the smoke was no problem, because the wind blew it away from us. When we were firing, however, the funnel became an obstruction, so it was hinged at the bottom and kept in place by a butterfly nut and bolt. When the alarm went, one of the ammunition numbers would run to the funnel and lower it into a horizontal position flat on the deck.

On the first occasion of a rocket being fired, we got the order, 'For exercise, enemy aircraft, red 30, open fire.' He had fired it fine on the port bow, so Brown had to do some rapid traversing. The forward pom-pom had no such problem and was banging away before we got round onto the bearing. As the mounting was revolving, an ammunition number dutifully ran to the galley funnel and lowered it, and we still had reasonable time to get in some shots. Eventually, we were on target and the firing trigger was pressed, but neither Brown nor I was prepared for what happened. As the guns fired, a cloud of soot came from the galley funnel and blinded us. It had obviously not been swept since we commissioned and there was an eighteen-months' accumulation of soot inside it, which dislodged at one go.

By the time it had settled and we were able to see again, the parachute was in the sea and we had only fired one burst. Down came the order, 'Cease firing, train fore and aft, gun layer report to the bridge!' I arrived on the bridge, covered in soot, and this must have surprised the Captain, so I was confident he would see the state I was in and accept what had happened – but I was wrong. He said angrily, 'Why did you cease firing?'

I replied, 'We we're blinded with soot from the galley funnel, Sir.' Then he said, 'So, we are attacked by enemy aircraft and you cease firing because of soot? I don't care what conditions are prevailing down there, you keep that gun firing. Do you understand that?'

'Yes, Sir.'

'Good. Then don't forget it.'

I was dismissed. The naval term for an admonishment is 'getting a bottle' so I had to return to the gun and tell them I'd been well and truly bottled. I resented the admonishment because Gordon was in error. Before the advent of close-range AA weapons, the gun layer on the larger calibre guns under local control always had the firing trigger – indeed, they still did so. Gordon, as a cadet, would undoubtedly have undergone gunnery training on the larger calibre guns, and the fact that the gun layer fired them would be firmly fixed in his mind. He had obviously forgotten that, on close-range AA mountings, the trainer was given the trigger, because it was he who (except in dive-bombing attacks) calculated aim-off. I had taken his, 'Why did you cease firing?' to be plural rather than singular, and had answered accordingly.

After that, there was no way in which I could absolve myself. Trying to correct the grammar of one's Captain by telling him that he was rebuking the wrong party as it was the gun trainer, as captain of the gun and the man with the trigger, who was responsible. Consequently, I had to accept the rebuke. There was no future in doing otherwise.

It was not only gunnery ratings who got the bottles from Gordon. Any branch falling short got them – including the Officers. The Captain was not a tyrant; irascible, perhaps but Gordon MacKendrick was keen to get at the enemy and at pains to give him no quarter. That meant that guns' crews had to keep on their toes. On patrol, the tiniest blip on the radar screen was investigated and, on several occasions, our own destroyers, which had strayed into our area of patrol, had been illuminated by our star shells, The usual procedure was to challenge a suspect and get a recognition signal from him. Gordon preferred to get a good look at them without revealing his own position.

There was one occasion when another destroyer illuminated us, and there was nothing more disconcerting than suddenly to find yourselves naked to the world, under a brilliant pool of light, and wondering whether the star shells had been fired by friend or foe.

We discovered that, even in his admonishments, Gordon could be very amusing. In the winter of 1942, we were patrolling ahead of a northbound convoy, doing a zigzag off the Lincolnshire coast. It was long after sunset and, in the blacked-out wheelhouse directly below the bridge, four ratings were on watch; the helmsman, two telegraph operators and the plot operator. The plotter (as its name implies), plotted the ship's course and recorded distances covered. It consisted of a mechanically operated pen, which drew a line on a chart spread out on the chart table. This line reproduced the geographical course of the ship in miniature and the plot was linked to, and operated by, the gyro compass.

It could be used to indicate course changes when zigzagging. The ringing of a bell indicating when the course had to be changed from zig to zag. The chart could be seen from the bridge through the 'view plot', which was a window about one foot square, set in trunking directly above the chart table. In theory, once the plot mechanism had been set up, it should continue operating until switched off. *Hambledon*'s plot, however, could be capricious and occasionally it would jump a cog and go haywire; close attention was needed. One night, close attention was the last thing the plot was getting. Andrews, the helmsman, was spinning one of his fabulous yarns and had the undivided attention of his three shipmates, during which time the plot chose to jump a cog. Suddenly, the Captain's voice bellowing down the voice-pipe put an abrupt end to Andrews' peroration.

'How many of you are on watch down there?'

'Four, Sir,' replied Andrews jauntily, pleased that no-one had slipped away and he was able to tell the truth!

'Have any of you four ratings ever heard of Euclid?' asked the Captain with rising anger. No-one had heard of Euclid. 'Are you all wearing caps?'

Andrews, mystified as to what Gordon was leading up to, replied, 'Yes Sir.'

'Then,' bellowed the Captain, 'I suggest you show some respect and remove them at once, because according to that damn plot we're steaming straight up the nave of Lincoln Cathedral!'

When the plot was set up correctly, Gordon, now satisfied, was heard to say, 'It really is enough to give anyone a bloody sick headache.'

In November 1942, I went on a boiler-cleaning leave and, on the day I was due to return, my five-year-old nephew was diagnosed as having contracted scarlet fever, Since I had been in contact with him, the GP refused to let me return until I had received instructions to do so. Not without some glee, I wired the following message to the ship:

'Commanding Officer, HMS *Hambledon*, c/o GPO London.
In contact scarlet fever. Doctor advises remain and await your instructions,'

The telegram arrived next day, 'RETURN FORTHWITH.'

I returned armed with my Doctor's note and was examined immediately by the surgeon, who ordered me to report back to him if I ran a temperature or if any rashes appeared. Had I contracted the disease, the ship would have been put in quarantine, which meant that, while she could still operate, no shore leave would be permitted. Consequently, throughout the following week, I was under close scrutiny from my shipmates and I feel that I would have been very unpopular had I succumbed. Gordon had warned that all future leave-breaking would be severely dealt with and he was as good as his word. Missing the liberty boat *Brightlingsea* at Harwich pier entailed catching a local train to Parkestone Quay and getting onboard an hour late. Such an infraction with John Barnes warranted two weeks' stoppage of leave. Gordon doubled the punishment to one month. Stoppage of leave included shore leave and long leave. Consequently, if boiler cleaning leave took place during the month's stoppage, it was forfeited.

Occasionally during the summer months, the watch ashore was granted afternoon leave from 1300 hrs to 1700 hrs. It was a sunny April afternoon and I had gone ashore to enjoy a country walk with my Wren girlfriend. Neither of us had wrist watches (they were hard come by during the war) and we had taken our time from Dovercourt station clock, giving us, as we thought, reasonable time to get to Harwich pier. Whether the station clock was slow, or the Cox'n's watch was fast we never discovered, but when we reached Harwich pier, *Brightlingsea* had just departed and I arrived onboard an hour late. Losing a month's shore leave was going to be bad enough but, worse, a refit with long leave was in the offing and I was likely to lose that too.

When I arrived on board, the Officer of the day placed me in the First Lieutenant's report. Two days later, I appeared before Nicholas and he automatically referred me to the Captain. There, until Captain's Defaulters, the matter rested. No-one gave a fig for my chances when I confronted Gordon.

The *Brightlingsea*'s PO Cox'n lived ashore and had a nodding acquaintance with my girlfriend. On meeting him in the street a couple of days later, she accosted him and accused him of leaving Harwich pier early. She insisted that Dovercourt station clock was reliable and his watch must have been fast. She agreed that the margin was two or three minutes, but that vital period would cost her boyfriend a month's leave. To his credit he was sympathetic with her obvious upset, came onboard the following day and accepted liability for leaving the pier slightly early. The first I knew of the matter was when Nicholas Fitzherbert sent for me and informed me he had struck my name from his Defaulters' list. He tried hard to hide his pleasure at being able to do so by giving me a slight wigging for cutting my return to the pier too fine. Gordon, of course, never got to hear of the incident and, two weeks later we went in for refitting! A stoker who was also in the Captain's report for leave-breaking observed ruefully, 'I suppose I shall get clobbered with a month's stoppage. Unlike Lofty Saxton, I don't have a good-looking Wren to plead my cause.'

The destroyers' liberty boat *Brightlingsea* is still in service at Harwich, taking holiday-makers on trips around the harbour. Although sixty-four years old, she shows no sign of age, indeed, after being demobbed, she shed her drab brown livery and is now attractively painted in blue and white. I took a trip on her across to Felixstowe very recently to see what is now reputedly the fourth busiest container port in the country. Felixstowe shoreline bordering the Orwell side of the estuary was open beach and scrubland up to twenty years ago. It is now fronted with jetties and overhead travelling cranes. Harwich has altered little, except that its harbour front has been made more attractive and it looks more prosperous than it did during the war. The environs of Parkestone Quay, that is, its approaches and buildings, have been considerably enlarged and extended to cater for the vast increase of continental traffic and passengers using the North Sea ferry services.

Chapter 13

Invasion of Sicily

By May 1943, I had been at sea two years and could be considered a competent seaman and gunnery rating. Sinkings on the east coast had fallen steadily since May 1941 as the country gathered strength on the sea and in the air. The Nore Command had now at its disposal more escorts including destroyers – and although there was never enough and to spare, convoys were better protected than they had been in the first two years of the war. That we were gaining strength in the air was obvious. Whereas in earlier times we were only allocated the odd Spitfire or Hurricane occasionally circling some part of a convoy at dusk, we were now assured of them. They came, if not in strength, at least regularly and sometimes even in daylight, from airfields in East Anglia, to stay until their diminishing fuel supply made their return imperative. Some pilots would swoop down and fly past us singly or in pairs, at sea level, waggling their wings audaciously before reaching again for the sky. All this had its effect on enemy aircraft and E-boat activity until, by May 1943, both ventured across the narrows at their peril.

I was past suitability for promotion in both seamanship and gunnery for several reasons. Firstly, I had no hankering for the responsibility of a Leading Seaman. Secondly, promotion in gunnery meant going back to gunnery school, and I had no wish to leave the ship and run the risk of not getting another destroyer. I had also done my share of deck swabbing and paintwork washing and had achieved job satisfaction.

Under the Chief Bosun's Mate, I was made responsible for the ship's wire ropes and cordage. This included splicing and renewing berthing and rigging wires, and blocks and tackles. I was also a buoy-jumper. When the ship came into harbour, the whaler was slipped as we closed the buoy. The two buoy-jumpers then leaped from the bows of the whaler to shackle on the bridle. In a choppy sea, leaping from a bouncing boat onto a bobbing buoy needed careful timing if the buoy-jumper was not to find himself in the drink. All buoy-jumpers wore cork life-jackets.

There was another reason I had no wish to leave the ship and that was an attractive Petty Officer Wren girlfriend ashore. So, it could be said that I was paying court to two females and was playing my cards judiciously to avoid being separated from either or both.

In our final year at Harwich, an electro-mechanical dome teacher was constructed on Parkestone Quay. It looked like half a large igloo made of plaster, on a wire-mesh frame. Inside it, the curving wall and roof represented the horizon and sky as seen from a ship, and onto it was projected a film of a four-engine Focke Wulf Condor attacking a convoy. It was an authentic attack filmed at sea with all the sound effects – aircraft-engine noise and the sounds of gunfire from ships in the convoy. The practice gun was a simulated one-man-operated Oerlikon and, when the trigger was pressed to open fire, the banging of a gun could be heard in the loudspeakers. The Condor appeared initially as a speck on the horizon and it had obviously attacked the ship from which the film had been shot, or one adjacent to it. In it came, looming ever larger, the engine noise increasing, while the operative positioned it in his sight, waiting to 'open fire' when it came within maximum effective range of his gun.

Aim-off was by an amber spot projected onto the 'sky', but only the instructor and the other onlookers could see it, since the operative was looking through an amber filter. The range of the aircraft was also evident from figures (in yards) also projected in amber, decreasing as the aircraft drew nearer. The operative could see nothing except the aircraft, but the instructor and other onlookers had all the evidence of good or indifferent shooting, including too early or too late opening fire. As a piece of training equipment it was first class and AA ratings were sent to it on a regular basis. While there, we also mugged-up on our aircraft recognition. Dome teachers were constructed in most naval bases and l was later to practise on one in Scapa Flow, in Alexandria and this one in the gunnery school.

Hambledon had now been in commission for two years and was overdue for refitting and modifications. Rumours were rife that, after refitting, we should be assigned to a different sphere of operation, although there was no hard and fast reason why we should be. The feeling was engendered, I suppose, because of the fact that the Allies were no longer on the defensive in the western hemisphere. A landing had been made in North Africa in November 1942 and, simultaneously, Montgomery had begun his irresistible push from Alamein. By May 1943, two allied armies were converging on the enemy and the writing was on the wall for the Axis in North Africa. The buzz-merchants were assured we would eventually be sent to the Mediterranean; especially if Gordon MacKandrick had any choice in the matter.

Our refit, when it came, took place in Sheerness dockyard. We arrived there on 8 May 1943 and the refit was to take five weeks, during which we were all given twenty-one days' leave. It was by far the longest leave I was given while in the service and, during it, my girl friend and I became engaged. When I returned, the refit was in its final stages and the ship had been camouflaged in Mediterranean colours – or so the buzz-merchants insisted. Later, when we left the dockyard, we were issued with white tropical kit. That settled the matter; we were going foreign. She was not the ship we had commissioned two years earlier. The searchlight had gone and, in its place was the latest Type 271 surface radar. It consisted of a steel cabinet which housed the operator, topped by a circular perspex lantern inside which was the revolving aerial; the whole thing like a miniature lighthouse. It registered a 'high-definition' echo which could pick up a buoy at seven miles. Anything inside that radius was clearly visible on the scan.

So we had three of the most up-to-date radar sets. 'Searcher' atop the foremast was for all-round aircraft searching. 'Hunter' in the miniature lighthouse was for hunting surface craft and 'Ranger' as an adjunct to the visual rangefinder, enabled us to find and range our guns on enemy ships at night, as our battleships had done at Matapan. The Holman projector had gone and two Lewis guns were installed in its place. The forward pom-pom was also missing and I assumed we had had to forfeit it since we were not going back to the east coast. When I got onboard, however, I found it securely lashed down amidships. It took little deduction to figure that it had been removed for a trip across the Bay of Biscay.

Changes in the ship's company of ratings, Officers and NCOs had taken place, but it had been at a gradual rate so that efficiency had not been impaired. The Officer element was becoming more RNVR but most of them had two to three years of war experience and the same applied with the lower deck. When the war began, hostilities-only ratings (HOs), with their meagre training, were looked upon with some disdain by the time-serving ratings, who saw them as having to be carried, but not anymore. HOs joining in 1939 had now had rising four years' experience, those in 1940 three years, and those in 1941, two. In addition, they had spent far more time at sea than peacetime ratings would, and were all competent seamen. A final point was that a fair proportion of them came into the service with a higher standard of intelligence than the average peacetime volunteer. They were men who would not have considered the Navy as a pre-war career, simply because they had better-paid careers in civilian life.

The day following our return, lower deck was cleared and Gordon addressed the assembled ship's company. It was rumoured that he had spent his leave on a course and his opening remarks tended to confirm it.

'You have all had more leave than is good for wartime sailors! You will also doubtless be wondering where we are going from here. Well, even I don't know that; but this I can assure you, whenever and wherever the second front starts, this ship will be at the forefront of it.'

I believe Gordon knew very well where we were going but that was more than he could divulge. He continued, 'You will have seen all the new equipment. The ship is in tip-top condition, but she is not helping the war effort in the dockyard, so let's have her cleaned up and be off back to sea where we belong.'

Gordon was right. The ship was in tip-top condition. Her engines, boilers and armament had all been overhauled and she had a fully trained ship's company. We left for Scapa Flow on 12 June 1943, but this time not for rubbing-up trials as two years ago, but as a highly efficient fighting unit. Six other Hunts left the Home Fleet at around this time, all loaned (as we were) to the Mediterranean Fleet. They were: *Mendip*, *Atherstone*, *Cleveland*, *Quantock*, *Tynedale* and *Whaddon*.

As on our previous trip to Scapa, we had no duties en route, and we arrived without incident. From now on, the punishing east-coast routine of all-night action stations was relaxed and we went into defence stations. During periods of enemy activity in the Mediterranean we should, of course, revert to all-night action stations, but it would never again become normal routine as it had been on the east coast. Our stay in Scapa was short. We arrived on the Sunday evening of 13 June and the following day all AA ratings spent the day on the AA range on the west of Orkney.

This range had been opened since we were last at Scapa and it had the usual guns and a dome teacher. The following day we spent at sea doing high – and low-angle shoots and bombardment practice. Before leaving at midnight on 16 June, we joined a new flotilla which later became part of V striking force in the assault on Sicily. It was made up of the following ten destroyers: *Blencathra, Hambledon, Mendip, Blakeney, Brecon, Woolston, Viceroy, Anthony, Arrow* and *Wallace*. The First Lieutenant of *Wallace* was the Duke of Edinburgh, then known as Prince Philip of Greece.

The flotilla went through the Pentland Firth in the dark, rounded the north of Scotland, turned through the Minch and into the Western Approaches, then on to Londonderry, where we all anchored in Loch Foyle. We arrived in the afternoon of 17 June and, after Scapa Flow, the Irish landscape looked green and lush. The south bank of Loch Foyle, being in Ulster, was, of course, blacked out that night, but we were intrigued to see lights on the north bank in Donegal.

Another new item of equipment that had been installed, and which proved to be a real boon towards good communication, was an extension speaker fitted at deck level on the pom-pom deck. Through it, we could hear all the reports made by Searcher, Hunter and Ranger to the bridge and the bridge's responses. So, we were aware of everything that was taking place and could have the guns trained round onto the bearings given by the radar sets without the bridge having to communicate them. The main armament 4 inch mountings also had their extensions, so all guns could react quickly to what was happening. We still retained lookouts in each corner of the bridge and at all guns, but Searcher and Hunter were able to pick up aircraft and surface vessels before they could be seen with the naked eye. On the radar screen, however, they are only blips, so the human eye was still needed to interpret finally what the blips were. Previously we knew nothing about reports being passed to the bridge, or orders issuing from it. Now we knew everything, as this illustrates,

'Hunter bridge.'
'Bridge Hunter.'
'Small echo, Sir, at Green 45.'
'What's the range?'
'About twelve thousand yards, Sir.'

'What's it look like?'
'It's stationary, Sir. Could be a buoy.'

We would then hear the Captain saying to the navigator,

'Is there a buoy at Green 45, pilot?'
'Bridge Hunter. There is no buoy on that bearing; keep your eye on it and report back if it moves.'
'Aye, aye, Sir.'

Or, again, from Searcher,

'Bridge Searcher. I have some aircraft at Red 60, Sir, flying from left to right, range about 25,000 yards.'

Slight pause, then,

'Disregard Searcher, they're friendly.'

We had an IFF set on board (Identification Friend or Foe) which received a signal from sets in all our aircraft identifying them as friendly. If they were not, all guns went round onto the bearing indicated ready to open fire. Hearing all this as it flowed backwards and forwards constituted a tremendous improvement in communications.

The code word for the invasion of Sicily was 'Husky', although we were not to know this until a few hours before we arrived there. The planner of the naval side of the operation was Admiral B.H. Ramsay, who had supervised the withdrawal from Dunkirk and was eventually to plan the naval operations for Normandy. The flotilla weighed anchor and proceeded to sea at 0600 hrs on 20 June.

We went east from Londonderry, then turned south into the Irish Sea and on into the Atlantic, where we rendezvoused with a large troop convoy, and took up stations around it. As the ships in the convoy were all ex-passenger liners, we were able to maintain a reasonable speed, and with the destroyers ahead and astern and on either flank carrying out Asdic sweeps and searching the air with radar for enemy aircraft, the troops must have felt reasonably relaxed. For the first two days, the Atlantic was very choppy, but we had certainly experienced worse in the North Sea and, after two days, it became apparent that the removal of the forward pom-pom had been a wise precaution but unnecessary. By noon on 22 June, the sea had moderated and the temperature become noticeably warmer. At 2000 hrs, we were on an even keel and were congratulating ourselves that we were going to get through the Bay without the usual buffeting. During the next two days we had glorious sunshine and on 25 June we changed into tropical rig. Before reaching Gibraltar we were detached from the convoy to go ahead for oil. We housed the Asdic dome, picked up speed and soon left the convoy well behind.

As we neared the Rock we saw a sight none of us had seen for almost four years. Tangier was ablaze with light on our starboard hand. It looked out of this world and we gazed fascinated at a spectacle we had almost forgotten. Gibraltar was, of course, blacked out and, apart from its towering dark shape, we saw no sign of life. We slipped into the harbour and went alongside a mole where we took on oil and provisions. It was two weeks since we had left Sheerness and we needed bread and fresh vegetables.

While we were in Gibraltar, the convoy had passed through the Straits into the Mediterranean and we left at 0430 hrs to rejoin it. By noon on the following day, we were off Algiers and were detached from the convoy to kick our heels in the bay until we finally entered Algiers harbour at 1700 hrs. As we approached Algiers, I purposely did not look ahead to see it come into view gradually. I waited until we were in the harbour entrance so that my first view of this fabulous place would be close up. I was not disappointed. Its waterfront, with the sun gleaming on its white, irregular buildings and mosque minarets, was exactly as I figured it would be,

What happened in Algiers was something that happened to us many times in the coming months. We came, we saw from the upper deck, and then we left without getting shore leave. The following day we were on our way again, with another convoy, back to Gibraltar. When we arrived off Gib on 30 June, this time it was daylight as we approached, and we all had a good look at the Rock through our binoculars. After oiling, we went alongside the aircraft carrier *Indomitable* to make use of one of her cranes to lift the forward pom-pom from amidships and place it back on its base, where two dockyard workmen bolted it down. Although aesthetically the 'biscuit' spoilt the lines of the ship, we had grown so accustomed to seeing it that the ship looked peculiar without it, and we were glad to see it back. We felt it highly unlikely that we would see E-boats in the Med, but in any case, it was a useful extra weapon and we looked upon it as the East Coast Hunt badge which we wore with pride. The following day, I was in the watch ashore and was able to enjoy looking around the Rock and, as I had not been ashore since leaving Sheerness, I was ready to stretch my legs.

After two days in Gibraltar, we joined a convoy which had come direct from the UK and proceeded eastward along the North African coast, arriving at Bone some 800 miles east of Gibraltar on 7 July. We left the convoy and went into Bone for oil during the forenoon, leaving again in the afternoon with another convoy which had formed up there. There were plenty of escorts and they took the opportunity of keeping their oil tanks replenished by darting away in their turns into the North African ports. Although we were not aware of it at the time, we were now on the final lap for Sicily, and shipping between Bone and Malta was 'thicker than pilchards at Looe'. Two days later we were off Malta and went in there for more oil, but this was merely to top-up ready for a long stay at wherever the landing was going to be. Although we did not go ashore, we were appalled at the bomb damage done to Malta. From the upper deck it looked little more than a mass of ruined buildings.

We left immediately we were topped-up and it was now 1700 hrs on 9 July. Malta is only sixty miles from Sicily and the convoy we were assigned to was timed to get there before dawn on 10 July. In order to confuse the enemy, it was routed round Cape Bon, travelling away from Sicily to make a wide sweep to the south of Malta where it split, one half of it travelling to the west of Malta, the other half to the east, as each half then turned north heading straight for Sicily. By this time it was of mammoth proportions. Some ships had come direct from the United States, some direct from the UK, while others had come from Oran, Algiers, Bone and Bizerta. Ships had also come from the eastern Mediterranean, from Port Said, Alexandria and from ports along the Tripolitanian coast. Wherever we looked, there were ships as far as the eye could see.

Eventually, the news of our destination was broken to us. By this time, the course we were on made it obvious where we were bound for. All ships received the following signal from Admiral Ramsay, 'We are on the crest of the wave, while the enemy is in the trough. We have an opportunity to hasten his downfall.'

It was an appropriate signal because it echoed what everyone was feeling. It was now dark, the sea was decidedly choppy and there was a fresh wind. We began to be apprehensive as to whether a storm was in the offing but, fortunately, by dawn on 10 July, the wind had fallen and the sea had flattened out.

The planning for the operation must have been prodigious. In that initial assault, there were 2,000 vessels, with 3,000 in the operation as a whole. They had come together seemingly so effortlessly and it had happened without a discernible hitch. Each time we had darted away for oil the convoy had, on our return, increased in size until we marveled at where all the ships were coming from. We were to see it happen again at Normandy, but by that time we had grown accustomed to seeing masses of shipping and it no longer gave us the thrill the Sicily invasion had done. We had been thrown out of France, Norway and Crete, principally because of the enemy's superiority in arms. This time it was the reverse. We had done with bitting and piecing; done with making do with inferior weapons; done with fighting an enemy with a surfeit of everything.

It was obvious to everyone who saw that Sicilian invasion armada that the tide of war – turned at Alamein – was now in full flood. It was rolling towards Sicily and no power on earth could halt it; its might would roll over anything in its path. Admiral Ramsay had hit exactly the right note. We were on our way to strike at what Churchill had termed, 'the soft underbelly of the Axis' and at last we had the right weapons.

We arrived off the beachhead at dawn on 10 July. The Americans were making their landing to the west of us between Licata and Scoglitta, and we went in with the 8th Army under Montgomery, whose objective was to land on either side of Cape Passero. We found ourselves off the beach at Pachino, which was to be the first objective of the Canadians and the Scottish 51st Highland Division. We were seeing for the first time what would later become a common sight; all manner of invasion craft were making an assault of the beach. The large, tank-landing ships were ranged along the waterline, their bow doors open, disgorging tanks, Bren-carriers, trucks and guns and Jeeps onto the beach. The troop ships anchored in the bay were embarking troops into infantry landing craft, which were to do a shuttle service all day, taking troops right up to the beach where their ramps would drop and the soldiers swam ashore. Then there were the amphibious vehicles, the DUKWs (Ducks) skimming past us to the shoreline where they disengaged their propellers, engaged their wheels and drove off inland.

An infantry landing craft passed us within a few feet, crammed with soldiers in full battle order, some shouting and giving the victory sign. A cheeky member of the after-4 inch gun shouted, 'Are you going to make it this time? We shan't have to come back and take you off shall we?' Back came the reply, 'Not this time, Jack. We're going ashore and the next stop's Rome.'

Everywhere was a hive of activity and we could detect no opposition whatsoever on the beach. This was not surprising because there were two lines of warships bombarding. Our fleet destroyers with their 4.7 inch guns were close inshore, while further to seaward and firing over the destroyers were the cruisers, each pouring salvo after salvo ahead of the advancing troops who directed the shooting by short-wave radio.

Our assignment was to give AA cover to the shipping, but there was little for us to do. We had never seen so many friendly aircraft overhead – both British and American. The fighters came in in wings, swarming around the sky as though inviting the enemy to come and mix it with them, and bomber squadrons flew over us with their fighter escort on their way to bomb inland targets.

The Italian fleet had shown little inclination to fight since Italy's entry into the war, but with their homeland invaded, everyone expected it would surely come into action now. Battleships *Warspite*, *Valiant*, *Nelson* and *Rodney* were in the vicinity, while our two latest battleships *King George V* and *Howe* were held in reserve at Algiers. As a further precaution against break-out, the aircraft carriers *Formidable* and *Indomitable* were cruising the Ionian Sea with their destroyer screens. But there was no sign of the Italian fleet. It remained securely locked up in its home ports.

There were two cruiser squadrons at Sicily, the 12th, comprising *Aurora*, *Penelope*, *Cleopatra*, *Euryalus*, *Sirius* and *Dido*, and the 15th, comprising *Newfoundland*, *Uganda*, *Orion* and *Mauritius*. Many of these ships had been torpedoed or bombed between 1939 and 1943, yet here they were, bombarding as though giving back with a vengeance the hammering they had undergone in times past. *Penelope*, for instance, had been badly crippled in a Malta convoy and had staggered into Malta for repairs. While there she had undergone repeated bombing attacks and had actually fired her 6 inch guns while in dry dock. She had so many shrapnel holes in her that she was nicknamed 'HMS *Pepperpot*' and had left Malta with dozens of wooden plugs in her holes. Yet here she was, back in action, dishing it out.

We had an HQ ship in the bay – the *Hilary*. Onboard her was Admiral Ramsay and his staff, and she was crammed with wireless equipment. It was from *Hilary* that directives were given to the warships; thus a request from the Army ashore for bombardment was sent from *Hilary* to the warships, with bearings, and off they would go to bombard. One cruiser, later in the action, slid a salvo of 6 inch shells into the mouth of a cave where a heavy gun was holding up the advance.

We spent the whole of 10 July off-shore, our guns pointing skyward, waiting for air attacks and watching the ceaseless activity of troops and material piling ashore. It was hot and sunny, with a flat calm sea and, since there was no retaliation from the enemy, we assumed that after his initial surprise, he had opted to make a stand further inland. When dinner time came, half the ship's company was piped to dinner, followed an hour later by the other half. So, for two hours, we were actually at defence stations, having our meal, and fully expecting the action stations bell to begin its nerve-jangling clamour. The first air attack of the day came at 1700 hrs and, as the black puff balls appeared in the sky to port. One gun's crew member said, 'Gerry's woken up at last!'

About twenty Junkers 88s came roaring in and proceeded to bomb the shipping, including a clearly marked hospital ship, which was well and truly straddled. The aircraft did not present a good enough target for our guns, but two were shot down and they did not seem to have scored any hits on the shipping. By this time the troopships had disembarked their passengers and were forming up to depart. The tank-landing ships, too, were hauling themselves off the beach and, as they left, full ships arrived to sustain the beachhead. At dusk, the Italian Air Force arrived at high level, but it was a faint-hearted sally. The AA barrage was too daunting for them and they quailed in the face of it, dropping their bombs indiscriminately and sheering off.

When darkness came, we withdrew to seaward to carry out an all-night, anti-submarine patrol and, as we left, we learned our troops had entered and captured the port of Syracuse. The second town to surrender in the

Sicilian campaign fell to the Royal Navy! The two Hunts, *Brissenden* and *Blankney*, had been close inshore off Pozzallo on the afternoon of 11 July, shelling enemy gun emplacements. *Brissenden* had reported to Admiral Harcourt in charge of the cruiser squadron further to seaward, that Italian soldiers on the beach were waving white flags, whereupon Admiral Harcourt ordered the *Brissenden*'s Captain to accept their surrender. This he did; consequently, the second town to surrender in the Sicilian campaign did so to a Hunt Class destroyer!

It so happened that later that afternoon, our patrolling took us into the Pozzallo area and we came within hailing distance of *Brissenden*. Both Captains began conversing with each other over their loud hailers and *Brissenden*'s Captain gave Gordon an account of the surrender. He finished by asking Gordon if he would relieve him of some of the Italian soldiers he had taken on board. Gordon declined; he had only slightly more love for Italians than for Germans. His reply to the request could be boiled down to, 'I don't want to soil my ship with them. You've got 'em; you keep 'em.' And he switched off his loud hailer and turned his ship away.

On the night of 11 July, we continued on patrol, returning to the beachhead before dawn to add our weight to any dawn attack. It materialized in the form of twelve bombers flying in close formation which again attacked and near-missed another hospital ship, damaging its upper deck. The hospital ships always anchored clear of the mass of general shipping, so it was obvious that they were being singled out as large, non-belligerent targets, quite contrary to the articles of the Geneva Convention. The few attacks on the massed ships at Sicily were seldom pressed home and it certainly gave us a misguided notion that all future landings might follow the same pattern.

When the sun was fully up, we went back again on patrol using our Asdics and making sweeps on the outer perimeter of the landings off the southeastern corners of Sicily. This was our role for the next three days – in for the dawn attack, out again on patrol. There was news of E-boat activity during the night in other sectors, but none came into our patrol area. Then on the night of 14 July, the beachhead sustained a heavy air attack, but we were sweeping to seaward and were left watching the tracer going up and hearing the muffled gunfire. We had seen little action and were getting bored, principally because we were all very tired. Action kept the adrenaline flowing, but to be at constant action stations, without the action, brought on tiredness.

When the empty ships had departed, some destroyers had gone with them, and other fresh escorts had arrived with the full ships, so it was only a matter of time before our turn came because we needed oil and stores. On the forenoon of 16 July, we were ordered to return to Malta and we arrived at noon to stay overnight. It was the first time we had seen our hammocks since we left Gibraltar on 2 July – our first full night's sleep for fifteen nights. There was no shore leave. The next day saw us escorting a full convoy back to Sicily.

After the capture of Syracuse on the eve of the first day of the landings, Augusta fell to our troops just before dawn on 13 July. It was a splendid anchorage for ships of all sizes and we put in there at 0730 hours on 18 July for oil. At noon we departed with another small convoy which was eastbound – probably to Alexandria – with another Hunt – *Blencathra*. When off Malta, the convoy continued east with other escorts and we turned south with *Blencathra* for Tripoli.

We never knew exactly how the many escorts were assigned their duties. It sometimes seemed as though there was a gigantic table chart somewhere with convoys and escorts on it, with someone pushing escorts towards convoys like a croupier and eventually clawing them back again and pushing them somewhere else. We imagined someone saying, 'This one needs a rest,' or 'This one is overdue for boiler-cleaning.' Sometimes everything seemed to articulate, but occasionally (especially when we had gone in to oil and were looking forward to a night's sleep, only to be dispatched immediately) there were howls of fury at the unfeeling planners.

We spent two nights in Tripoli and I was able to get ashore and have a look at this ex-Italian possession. I was impressed with the town, but more impressed with a contingent of Scottish soldiers who marched through the town in a pre-embarkation parade. They were preceded by pipers and were the more impressive because they were not dressed to kill. They wore Tam-o'-Shanters, khaki cotton shirts, shorts, and stockings with gaiters. Some of them had probably been in the desert for two years. Most would have started at Alamein. They were all a picture of health with an attractive golden tan to their bare arms, legs and faces, and they swung along to the tune of the pipes with a jaunty gait. Some of their comrades would have landed at Sicily and these men would shortly be going to join them. It was their jaunty, almost arrogant gait which impressed me, and I contrasted their skirling pipes with the oompah of a German military band and goose-stepping German troops. The young men I was seeing march past were a match for any troops anywhere in the world.

We left Tripoli at 0500 hrs on 21 July and proceeded with a convoy to Gibraltar where we arrived six days later. After oiling and provisioning we passed through the Straits to meet another convoy in the Atlantic. Having met it, we turned and accompanied it back through the Straits to Tunis, arriving there on 2 August. Off Tunis, we left the convoy and proceeded to Bizerta for oil. Arriving at 1600 hrs, we were under way again at 1930 hrs, this time back to Sicily.

At sea on 3 August, I was one of the Captain's 'request men'. I had requested to the Captain, through the First Lieutenant, to discontinue shaving. After saluting him, the Cox'n read out the request, 'Able Seaman Saxton, Sir, requests to discontinue shaving.' I was the first one onboard to do so and Gordon, expecting a crop of such requests, had made up his mind that only beards worthy of the name were going to be permitted. He said, 'Can you grow a beard?' I replied, 'I think so, Sir.'

I'll grant your request for two weeks, after which I'll see you again and make a final decision." The Cox'n repeated, 'Request granted for two weeks.' whereupon I saluted, about-turned and departed. Two weeks later, after close scrutiny from Gordon, my request was granted. A request to continue shaving could not then be made for at least six months.

We arrived in Syracuse on 4 August, where my watch was given three hours' shore leave, and we were able to set foot for the first time in captured enemy territory. The following day we left for Bizerta, where we oiled and proceeded to Ferryville for boiler cleaning. From leaving Scapa Flow on 16 June we had been almost continuously at sea, with only three short periods ashore in seven weeks, but operation Husky, as far as we were concerned, was now over. On 22 July the capital, Palermo, had fallen to the indomitable General Patton. On 25 July, Mussolini was deposed. Only Catania and Messina were now proving stubborn and *Warspite* was ordered to soften up Catania, which she did.

By 17 August, both armies met at Messina and Sicily fell five and a half weeks after the first troops landed. As far as the navy was concerned, Sicily had been a piece of cake. Admiral Harcourt had observed to a newspaper correspondent that what he had anticipated would be a 'battle' for Sicily reminded him more of a Thames regatta.

Before the ports were captured 160,000 allied troops, 14,000 vehicles, 1,800 guns and 600 tanks had been landed over the beaches with surprisingly few losses. The two submarines *Parthian* and *Saracen* were lost just as Sicily capitulated, but since the former was presumed lost in the Adriatic and the latter lost off Corsica, they were not strictly losses attributable to the actual assault on Sicily. Losses were confined to a few landing craft and MTBs. The two cruisers *Cleopatra* and *Newfoundland* were both torpedoed by U-boats, and the aircraft carrier *Indomitable* hit by an aircraft-borne torpedo, but all three reached Malta for repairs. We were soon to discover that the next landing was to be a far different kettle of fish.

Chapter 14

Surrender of the Italian Fleet

We had a welcome six-day respite in Ferryville while our boilers were being cleaned. There was little there to interest us, but trucks were laid on to take us up the coast road to Tunis where we were able to spend a whole day taking in the sights – including the ruins of Carthage. On our return, the truck stopped in the middle of a vineyard and we helped ourselves to bunches of black grapes, despite heated protestations from an Arab. He must have been used to this sort of thing from soldiers, but would be somewhat nonplussed as to what sailors were doing on the Tunis road!

It was in Ferryville that I held in my hand a strange medal. Rommel's push in 1942 had been so irresistible that the Axis must have been assured of his eventual conquest of Egypt. It is well known that it was Mussolini's intention to head a victory parade through Cairo, riding a white charger, and a medal had been struck in anticipation of the coming 'victory'. An enemy ammunition ship carrying a consignment of these medals had been bombed and the medals widely scattered when it blew up. A member of the ship's company came by one ashore and brought it back to the ship. On one side it carried the heads of the two dictators and, on the other, a German and an Italian soldier were jointly stabbing and wringing the neck of a Nile crocodile. It was a classic example of 'the best laid schemes.'

On leaving Ferryville to return to Bizerta we struck an underwater obstruction and damaged our screws. We now needed dry docking, but since we could still steam there was no urgency. Our speed was cut by 8 knots and any attempt to steam faster than 22 knots set up an unacceptable vibration The speed we had was adequate for a sloop or a corvette, but it was not destroyer speed and we felt restricted without the extra 8 knots.

Unless the ships in a convoy were troopers or tankers, we seldom knew what cargoes they were carrying. Ammunition ships left us in no doubt – they flew red flags. We knew whether ships were full or empty according to whether they rode high or low, but generally we were in ignorance of their cargoes. I mention this in view of the following incident.

On 16 August we left with a convoy bound for Bone, 175 miles to west of Bizerta. We joined the convoy at 2000 hrs, and it was to travel through the night at 11 knots to reach Bone by noon the next day. At around 0400 hrs the following morning, the convoy was attacked by Italian bombers. Tracer shells were going up ahead of us and we could hear the sound of aircraft engines. The forward pom-pom and twin 4 inch main guns opened fire on a target dead ahead which was obscured by the bridge superstructure.

Suddenly we saw torpedo tracks. One was twenty yards from the ship; the other ran within a few feet of the starboard side, leaving a phosphorescent glow in the wake of its propeller. Seconds later there was an explosion astern of us. As dawn broke we left our position and came up close to a torpedoed liberty ship which was listing slightly. She hove-to and we went alongside and made fast. She had been hit by one of the torpedoes, tragically, in one of her holds, which was crammed with Italian prisoners of war, captured in Sicily. One of our seamen who had gone on board to take our berthing wires, looked down a hatch into the hold and wished afterwards that he hadn't. He described it as a charnel house. We took on board the survivors and most of them were in poor straits. Some, in their panic, had jumped overboard, then got back on board, covered in oil fuel which was making them retch. Others were obviously suffering from internal injuries.

We left the convoy and made for Bone at full speed, sending a signal ahead of our estimated time of arrival and of the passengers we had onboard. During the passage, our own Surgeon and sick-berth attendant were attending to the most serious cases and, when we arrived, three Officers came aboard. Eventually all the casualties were attended to and taken ashore, some into ambulances drawn up on the jetty. It was one of the cruel anomalies of war that all this maiming and loss of life had been brought about by a torpedo launched by an Italian airman who would little realise that he had killed and wounded his own countrymen.

We left Bone at 1300 hrs to drop anchor eventually off Djidjelli, where we stayed the night awaiting two large troopships which were taking on troops in the harbour. Both ships left at 0600 hrs, crammed with soldiers, and one of them was named *Ulster Monarch*. It was a precious small convoy and, at that period of the war, it should have been allocated more than one escort. By midnight we were off Cape Bon under a magnificent full moon. Conditions were ideal for us to be spotted from the air and, sure enough, enemy aircraft found us. Cape Bon had always been a trouble spot, due to enemy airfields on Sicily and Sardinia and, although Sicily was no longer a threat, Sardinia was still in enemy hands. Bright moonlight is ideal for aircraft looking for ships at night, because they appear as black silhouettes on a silver sea. What we needed, and what we sorely missed, was our chummy ship, the Hunt destroyer *Blencathra*, which had done several trips with us. Had she been in position on the other side of the troopers, the aircraft might have been deterred from attacking twice.

We beat off the first attack, but they flew round and came in a second time, flying through our barrage. *Ulster Monarch* was near-missed by three bombs, then hit by a fourth – a delayed-action one – on the stern. It hit her gun shield, was deflected onto a bollard, then pierced the upper deck and exploded in the deck below, setting fire to some drums of petrol. Then ready-use ammunition began to explode and there was danger that a nearby magazine would go up. However, inside half an hour the fire party had the fire under control and the ship reached Tripoli safely on 19 August. One destroyer for two large troopships crammed with soldiers was taking a risk – a risk that was not repeated.

Four days later, another troopship, *Letitia*, sailed from Tripoli for Algiers. She was half loaded and was to put into DjidjellI en route to pick up more troops. This ship was given three Hunts as escort – *Hambledon*, *Blencathra* and *Blankney* and we were again attacked in bright moonlight off Cape Bon. The moon came up at 0130 hrs and from then until dawn we were persistently attacked. This time, however, the barrage from the three Hunts was such that the enemy pilots were either so shaken up in their attack as to miss their targets or were driven off altogether. There were no hits on trooper or escorts and *Letitia* arrived in Djidjelli safely next morning to pick up her extra complement. We then saw her through to Algiers, arriving there at 0630 hrs next day.

Throughout the trip, with *Blankney* ahead of *Letitia*, *Hambledon* and *Blencathra* on either side of her, the attackers were facing a combined barrage of seven twin 4 inch guns, four quadruple and two single pom-poms, seven Oerlikons and at least twelve Lewis guns. *Letitia* was also armed with AA weapons so, by any reckoning, the attackers were meeting a formidable barrage. The Hunts were well equipped to cope with air attack of this nature and, had the same three ships been guarding *Ulster Monarch* four nights previously, the chances of her being hit would have been much less.

On arrival in Algiers at 0630 hrs on 26 August, we oiled and anchored in the outer harbour. A boat was sent away for provisions but there was to be no shore leave. At 2000 hrs we were ordered out to patrol the harbour entrance and the reason why was plain to see. Two of our latest battleships – *King George V* and *Howe* were moored inside. At 0400 hrs the following morning, Algiers was attacked from the air and I never saw a city throughout the war which seemed so strongly defended. I question whether even Gibraltar could have equalled the Algiers barrage. There were dozens of searchlight beams probing the sky and, once caught in them, the attacking aircraft were doomed. Not only was the port area bristling with AA guns, the two battleships added their weight to a tremendous barrage. Aircraft trapped in the searchlight beams twisted and dived to no avail. Some blew up, some came spiralling down. We could see and hear the battleships' eight-barrelled 'Chicago Piano' pom-poms and our own guns added weight to the barrage. We made smoke to cover shipping in the harbour.

At 1230 hrs the following day, the two battleships emerged with their destroyer escorts which we were ordered to reinforce. Taking up station with the other destroyers, all the escorts began Asdic sweeping and, during the night, the two battleships carried out a practice night shoot. At 0600 hrs the following morning, our two consorts made back to Algiers and we were released from our duties at 0700 hrs to join a convoy. As we sped away, one of the pom-pom crew echoed all our sentiments, 'Who the hell wants to be escorting battlewagons in the middle of a war?'

On 30 August, after escorting a convoy from Philippeville to Oran, we received a signal to proceed independently to Algiers. When receiving such an order there was always speculation as to what lay in store at the end of this journey. Some secret mission? A convoy already forming up? VIPs taking passage? It wasn't any of these things; it was much more pleasant than anything we imagined. Our name had come to the top of the dockyard repair list and we were going into dry dock for new screws. Since the rifling of our 4 inch guns was badly worn, we also needed new barrels, so we went first alongside the gun wharf for armament overhaul. That having been done, we went into dry dock.

During two days in dry dock, the French dockyard workmen toiled round the clock twice to get the job done. During the hours of darkness, arc lights were rigged and one shift followed another. We were very impressed with the efforts that were made to get the work completed and one of the wags said, 'I don't think the Frogs like us very much. They can't get us back to sea sharp enough.'

Both screws were found to be damaged, the port one quite badly, the starboard one less so. When two new ones had been fitted, the dock was flooded and, with the Base Engineer on board, we went outside the harbour for trials. These proved far from satisfactory; there was still vibration at speed, so back we went into dry dock. Since only the screws were damaged and not the shafts, it is possible that the screws we were given were not Hunt class destroyer screws. Back in dry dock a decision was made to refit the slightly damaged starboard screw, after which, out we went again for further trials. This time the vibration had gone and the Base Engineer was satisfied. His opinion was that we would be a couple of knots short of design speed, but would have to settle for that until our name came up again for dry docking. When we eventually got back to sea our speed was little impaired.

The pom-pom barrels had been renewed in Sheerness, so every gun barrel on the ship had now been changed and they were soon to be put to good use. We were in Algiers dockyard nine days, during which time each watch managed three days' shore leave. We also hoped to get mail from home, but did not and we assumed it was chasing us around the Med. While in Algiers, news came through of the Italian surrender and there was much jubilation. Our joy exceeded that of the later German surrender amongst naval personnel, because the Mediterranean fleet had been hard-pressed since Italy entered the war in 1940, and had suffered terrible casualties. Another reason was that it came so suddenly and so quickly after Sicily, whereas the German surrender – although inevitable after Normandy – took a year to come and, during that time, the U-boats had been withdrawn and all Germany's big ships sunk.

Although we were not to know it at the time, our striking of the underwater obstruction was a fortuity which had a far-reaching sequel.

While we were still in dry dock, the invasion fleet was on its way to Salerno. In fact, Salerno's D-day was 9 September, the day we left Algiers and, but for the repairs, we would undoubtedly have been part of it. Secondly, our being at the right place at the right time resulted in *Hambledon*'s name appearing in all the news media – newspapers, newsreels, magazines and radio – and it ensured her a place in naval history.

We left Algiers at 1400 hrs on 9 September and proceeded to Bizerta independently. On arrival in the small hours of 10 September, we anchored outside the harbour till dawn, then went in to oil. While we were oiling, the whaler went inshore and returned with several sacks of mail – the first we'd had since leaving England. During the forenoon, while cleaning ship, we were informed that we would be piped to early dinner because the Commander in Chief was coming aboard at 1300 hrs. For what reason was not divulged, but it was not often that an Admiral of the Fleet chose to board a destroyer and we were all agog.

What follows is conjecture, but it is probably near the mark. The invasion fleet had sailed for Salerno twenty-four hours previously and there was not a single man-o'-war in Bizerta when we arrived there. All other destroyers would be either escorting the invasion fleet or convoying and patrolling in other areas. The only unit not assigned to a specific duty was *Hambledon* who, her repairs completed, was due to leave Algiers. The Admiral would, of course, be informed of this and it is possible that *Hambledon* was summoned to Bizerta on his instructions for a specific purpose. I could imagine him enquiring of his staff if there were a non-assigned destroyer in the vicinity and being informed that *Hambledon* was due to leave Algiers, whereupon she would be ordered to proceed to Bizerta.

At 1300 hrs, the Admiral's barge swept alongside and the Admiral, dressed in white from head to foot, was piped aboard followed by his aides. Immediately the Union flag was hoisted to the top of the foremast – a privilege only vouchsafed to Admirals of the Fleet. We then slipped from the buoy and went alongside the jetty, whereupon speculation rose even higher. Hardly had we made fast and the gangway run out when, amid a swirl of dust, a retinue of cars screeched to a halt alongside – the leading one flying a small Stars and Stripes flag. An American army officer leapt from the passenger seat of the leading car, opened the rear door and out stepped General Eisenhower!

He was dressed in a light khaki drill uniform (trousers and shirt) with a Glengarry-type cap, and had a small leather baton under his left arm. He came over the prow, grinning broadly, followed by his aides and several newsmen. There was no ceremony: everything happened surprisingly quickly. I had been assigned with others to running out the gangway and we had barely got it into place when the cars arrived. I stood to attention as he passed within a yard of me, Little did I realise that this man would eventually become President of the United States. Admiral Cunningham was on the bridge awaiting his visitor and the General was conducted there by *Hambledon*'s Officer of the Day. One of the newsmen later reported that when he reached the foot of the bridge ladder in Eisenhower's wake, a rating had said to him, 'There's tons of gold braid up there'.

There was no further delay. The gangway was run back inboard, the berthing wires cast off and we were under way, the Union flag streaming from the highest point of the foremast and the white ensign fluttering from the stern. At this point we were told what our mission was – to accept the formal surrender of the Italian fleet – and I was able to witness all that followed from an elevated position on the pom-pom deck.

When Italy secretly negotiated terms of surrender with the Allies, one of the stipulations made to the Italians was that their fleet should not be allowed to fall into German hands. A plan was made to get it into North African ports without arousing German suspicion. It was to leave Spezia and Taranto immediately on the announcement of surrender and move south to North Africa. We were on our way to meet the Spezia fleet and, in addition to it, two battleships, two cruisers and a flotilla of destroyers had already left Taranto. These ships arrived in Malta before the Spezia fleet.

The ships from Spezia sailed in the late afternoon of 8 September and, during the night, they were joined by cruisers and destroyers from Genoa. On the morning of 9 September, this combined fleet was seen by our air reconnaissance steaming down the west coast of Corsica. Although they had managed to slip away without German interference, when their late allies realised the birds had flown, they attacked them from the air using their newly-introduced radio-controlled glider bomb, sinking the battleship *Roma* and damaging another. The Italian Admiral Romeo Oliva transferred his flag from the damaged battleship to the cruiser *Eugenio di Savoia* which then took up a position in the van of the fleet. Two naval officers from Admiral Cunningham's staff put out in a small boat from Bone as the fleet steamed eastward towards Malta and boarded the cruiser flagship. Their orders were to ensure the ships reached Malta by ironing out any navigational problems.

Our two battleships *Warspite* and *Valiant* were at sea supporting the Salerno landing and, before their departure, the commanding Admiral (Admiral Bissett, flying his flag in *Warspite*) had been given sealed orders which were not to be broken open until the Italian surrender. These orders, which were broken open on 8 September, informed Captain Packer, Commanding Officer of the *Warspite*, to proceed to the North African coast off Bizerta, together with Valiant, there to rendezvous with the eastward-steaming Italian fleet. The two British battleships with their destroyer escort met the Italian fleet at 0600 hrs the morning of 10 September, and a signal was sent from Admiral Bissett to the Italians to form into column. When this had been done, *Warspite* and *Valiant* took up station ahead of a triple column of two Italian battleships and five cruisers flanked by their destroyers. Outflanking the latter were the British destroyers.

After an hour's steaming time from Bizerta, *Hambledon* sighted the fleet in perfect formation, led by the unmistakable *Warspite* with her solid fort-like bridge superstructure. As we drew nearer, *Warspite*'s Aldis lamp began to flash in answer to signals sent by Admiral Cunningham from *Hambledon*'s compass platform atop the open bridge. As the distance closed, we could see that all the Italian ships were flying black pennants at their mastheads, signifying their agreement to surrender as instructed. Admiral Cunningham's feelings during his time on *Hambledon*'s bridge are recorded in his memoirs. He had commanded the Mediterranean fleet throughout the war. Fleet Air Arm planes had attacked and crippled two battleships and a cruiser lying in Taranto in 1940. He led the night action off Matapan in *Warspite* with *Valiant* in attendance in 1941. He had suffered the agony of losing an inordinate number of his ships, due to insufficient air cover, keeping the desert army supplied, evacuating our forces from Crete and fighting the convoys through to Malta. Many times, he had trailed his coat around the Mediterranean, hoping to bring the reluctant Italians to battle, to no avail. Now, here was a major part of their fleet, spread out before him in surrender. He writes:

'To me it was a most moving and thrilling sight. To see my wildest hopes of years back brought to fruition, and my former flagship *Warspite*, which had struck the first blow against the Italians three years before, leading her erstwhile opponents into captivity, filled me with emotion and lives with me still.'

He had instructed *Hambledon*'s Yeoman of Signals to send the following signal to *Warspite*, 'From C. in C. : Congratulations on your proud and rightful place at the head of the line.'

Hambledon was now drawing abreast of *Warspite* on an opposite course and she was to enjoy the full benefit of naval ceremonial as each British ship paid her respects to the C. in C. As we finally passed *Warspite*, her marine buglers saluted us with a short fanfare, *Hambledon* acknowledging the salute by bos'un pipes, to be followed once more by Warspite's buglers. The junior ship always gives the salute first, is answered by the senior ship, then the salute is closed by the junior. On we swept to receive the same courtesy from *Valiant* by bugle, followed later by the double-trilling from the British destroyers as we drew abreast of each.

Every sailor on the British ships would know the C. in C. was onboard by the Union flag flying at our masthead. They would not know Eisenhower was with him until they heard it on the BBC news later, but every sailor on *Hambledon*'s upper deck that day was in no doubt that he was witnessing history being made. We had come from the east coast on loan to the Mediterranean fleet and scooped the pool. Every man-jack from the Captain downwards was bursting with pride. Gordon had said, 'I can assure you that when the second front starts, *Hambledon* will be at the forefront of it.' but even he had not expected an honour like this.

Eventually we reached the rear of the five-mile-long column, and the helm went over for us to turn about and steam down the opposite flank, thus completing the encirclement. There were seamen lookouts in each corner of *Hambledon*'s bridge who heard the various conversations and remarks, and who reported what was said. One newsman had asked the Admiral where the other ships were. He had informed them about the Taranto fleet already on its way to Malta, and other ships reported being at Bone, Malta and other North African ports. He said that submarines were also popping up all over the place.

General Eisenhower was as exuberant as a schoolboy on a school outing. At one point he was sitting on top of the Asdic cabin, swinging his legs and, as we turned to reverse course, and seeing all the columns in perfect alignment from astern, he said 'What a sight! Just the way you see them in reviews in the movies.' He had accepted the Admiral's invitation at relatively short notice and was enjoying every minute of it. Another reporter asked if there were any British personnel aboard the Italian ships.

Admiral Cunningham replied, 'There are two aboard the Italian flagship, just to make sure they don't take the wrong turn.' at which Eisenhower, with his usual broad grin, nodded towards *Warspite* and *Valiant* and said, 'I'm sure nothing would please those boys more than to have them make a try at it.' The reporters asked the Admiral for a statement on the surrender. He thought for a moment then said, 'You may send this, but it must not appear until 9 o'clock tomorrow, "The Italian battlefleet is now anchored under the guns of Malta".

It was an abridged version of a signal he was later to send to the Admiralty, which was more Nelsonian in its tone, 'Be pleased to inform Their Lordships that the Italian Battlefleet now lies at anchor under the guns of the fortress of Malta.'

In putting an embargo on his abridged message, he was making sure that the Admiralty had the news before it appeared in the press. Next morning the Spezia fleet reached Malta to join the Taranto fleet which had arrived in the small hours, commanded by Admiral Da Zara, the senior Admiral, who eventually went ashore for a conference with Admiral Cunningham. Admiralty House overlooked the docks and could be reached by several flights of steps. Admiral Da Zara was not taken that way.

He was taken by car a longer, more circuitous route so that he could see the appalling damage his countrymen and the Germans had inflicted in their attempts to subdue the island. Now Malta had the Italian Navy under its guns and the islanders were jubilant. Admiral Cunningham could have ordered the Italian fleet to make for any harbour he chose on the North African coast. It could have gone to Algiers, to Bizerta, to Tunis, to Tripoli – to Alexandria, even. There seems little doubt that he chose Malta for two reasons. Firstly, because it was no less than the Maltese deserved for what they had suffered in defence of their island. Secondly, to bring it home to the Italians that their three-year effort to conquer the island had failed and, in anchoring their ships under Malta's guns, he was making manifestly clear their failure to the whole world.

We, of course, did not go to Malta. We returned to Bizerta to disembark our distinguished passengers at around 1630 hrs. We had had our short period of glory and, still heady with it, we went back to the business of the war at sea. Six weeks after the event we received the following signal,

> 'From: C. in C., Nore Command
> To: *Hambledon*.
> I was delighted and proud to read in the papers of the prominent part played by a unit of the Nore Command in the formal surrender of the Italian fleet.'

Our families had also seen it in the papers, heard it on the wireless and seen it in the newsreels.

Chapter 15

SALERNO: A Near Disaster

The code word for the Salerno landings was 'Avalanche' but, initially, such avalanche as there was came from the Germans and fell upon landing parties. The C. in C. of the operation, the US General Mark Clark, described it in his memoirs as a near disaster. The invasion armada was on its way when the Italian surrender was announced on 8 September but if the troops involved imagined this would make for an easier landing, they were under a grave misapprehension. The Germans had pulled out all Italian troops in the area and replaced them with a Panzer division. Right from the start, operation Avalanche was in serious trouble. Two landings were made, the British one, three miles south-east of Salerno, designated 'Avalanche North', while the American sector fifteen miles further south was named 'Avalanche South'. The final objective was the capture of Naples; the immediate objective a bridgehead forty miles deep, including neighbouring airfields.

The first wave, which went in in the early hours of 9 September, met considerable opposition, despite which, by nightfall, the beachheads were reasonably secure. Then the enemy counter-attacked on 11 and 12 September to drive a wedge between the two landings and a precarious situation developed. By 13 September there had been no penetration deeper than six miles. Both British and American contingents were pinned down on their respective beaches, each subjected to enemy artillery fire from the hills, and a two-mile salient was driven between the two landings. This was the situation prevailing when we arrived at Avalanche South – the American sector – at 1600 hrs on 12 September.

Before leaving Bizerta the previous day, we had taken onboard much smoke making equipment in the farm of canisters and smoke pots, which would be used to cover shipping at the beachhead. On arrival, we went alongside the HQ Ship *Ursula* to tranship it, after which we visited an oil tanker anchored in the bay to top-up our tanks. It was a relief to slip from the tanker. Apart from her being a vulnerable target, while alongside her our arc of fire was considerably restricted. Eventually, with a full replenishment of oil, we cast-off and began patrolling the bay, weaving in and around the anchored ships.

The amount of shipping in the bay was not, of course, as dense as it had been at Sicily. The invasion of Italy had been made across the Straits of Messina and Salerno was seen as a landing in force, to get behind the enemy who was confronting the 8th Army under Montgomery. Progress up the leg of Italy was proving painfully slow and it was hoped to relieve the pressure on Montgomery by getting behind the enemy forces holding up his advance. However, the bay was crowded with shipping, with invasion craft coming and going, ferrying men and material onto the beach.

There was the hospital ship *Leinster* lying in the entrance to the bay, which would eventually embark many wounded. All hospital ships were painted white overall, emblazoned with red crosses and fully illuminated at night, despite which the enemy aircraft had bombed and sunk the hospital ship *Newfoundland* the day before our arrival in the Gulf. Days after the event we were seeing wreckage from her in the form of floats and boxes, many with the Red Cross insignia on them. It had happened at Sicily: it happened more devastatingly at Salerno. From our arrival till dark, we were constantly under air attack from fighter bombers, which came in over the hills, swooped dawn, selected their targets and hurtled across the bay, dropping their single bombs. They would then fly out to sea, make a wide detour to evade the AA fire, return to the airfields, load up and return.

The problem with Salerno was that it was at maximum range for fighter cover. Sicily was only sixty miles from Malta, so our fighters were buzzing around all day, whereas Salerno was outside the range of most allied fighters from Sicilian airfields. Only the more modern American ones could be used and even they had only a bare twenty minutes of airtime on arrival in the battle area. We had twin-boomed, American P38 Lightnings over us, but they did not always co-ordinate their arrival and departure, and often we looked in vain for them. At other times they would circle the bay, then fly off to the British landing grounds. It sometimes seemed as though the Germans were waiting for them to go because as the Lightnings departed, in came the Focke Wulf 190s.

The following day the attacks increased. During lulls, we always gathered up the empty cartridge cylinders to get them from under our feet and after the dawn attack we had fired 750 rounds. In mid-forenoon, an American P-39 Airacobra fighter flew in from seaward and was shot down by gunners on the American merchant ships. It was obvious by its leisurely speed that it was not hostile but, presumably because it was not twin-boomed, one ship assumed it was enemy and opened fire. Others joined in and he was caught in a crossfire and plunged into the sea. There was scarcely a splash and no sign of wreckage or pilot. It was as though the waters had opened and swallowed up man and plane.

There was no let-up on the third day. The attacks were all coming from the sun, and it was hot and blinding. I remembered the words of the Gunner's Mate in Chatham Gunnery School: 'They'll came at you out of the sun, lads, and you won't see them.'

Many times we carried out his advice, pointed our gun into the sun and opened fire – and one occasion to have the gratification of seeing an aircraft spiral down out of it. No twin-engine bombers came in daylight – they would not have survived the barrage. What we got were fighter-bombers which hurtled across the bay so fast that only the single-manned Oerlikon cannon and Lewis machine-guns were nimble enough to deal with them. The quadruple pom-pom was only effective if our barrels were already pointing in the direction of attack. Other than that, we had a few brief seconds as they sped away.

Sometimes they came in in threes, flying in line ahead and dropping their bombs one after the other an a target chosen by the leader. When we were singled out for this treatment, I did not see them come in. Brown and I were firing at an entirely different target and these three came in behind our backs. The leader's bomb fell short, the second close to the ship's side, the third just over. They had straddled us and the second bomb exploded on impact with the water and showered the ship with shrapnel. Two ratings were wounded, one on the forward, the other on the after 4 inch guns, both lacerations to their backs. In the next attack a merchantman was hit and subsequently abandoned. This went on all day and we ate our food at the gun. Fortunately, we had a quiet night and were able to snatch some sleep, but still on the gun deck.

On 15 September (the fourth day) twin-engine bombers flew over us, but at such a height as to be out of range. However, when they dropped their bombs (they certainly were not aimed from that height) they scored a lucky hit on a tank-landing craft. It was making a trip into the beach full of jerricans of petrol which began to burn; the crew quickly abandoned it. So there it was, still afloat, burning fiercely as the jerricans exploded in the scorching heat. Apart from making an excellent beacon, it had become a danger to shipping and we received a signal from the HQ ship to sink it. We stood off, and riddled the waterline with shells until it sank lower and lower in the water.

Then, to our amazement, it rolled over and remained floating with its flat bottom up – and there it stubbornly remained. Gordon was not amused – he decided to put a depth charge under it. We went astern to work up some speed, then went ahead and lobbed a depth charge close to it, set at the shallowest depth setting. When it exploded, the craft was lifted clean out of the water – we could see daylight under it. It dropped back with a mighty splash and disappeared momentarily, only to reappear. Twice more it received the same treatment and twice more it refused to go down. Gordon must have realised a lot of telescopes and binoculars were bound to be watching, so he decided to ram! Once again we went astern, stopped, then went ahead, picking up speed. About fifty yards distance from it, just as the situation was getting very interesting, it decided to give up the ghost and disappeared. When we ran over where it had been it was below our keel.

The late Peter Bull, the actor, was the Commanding Officer of one of these landing craft and he watched with some amusement our efforts to sink her. In his memoirs, *To Sea in a Sieve*, he writes,

> 'I steered my way in trepidation, passing a burning LCT (Landing Craft Tank) from which the crew had been rescued. It cheered me enormously to note that a destroyer was finding it impossible to sink her at close range. Time after time a direct hit was scored and the craft just sank a little lower in the water.'

Obviously, Peter Bull had left the scene before we started depth charging. Later in the action we went alongside him, and our WT ratings repaired his defunct radio. The Officer complement was invited onboard for sherry and left with bread and other victuals. Peter Bull writes,

'She was a delightful ship, who reminded me of the *Hesperus*.'

The whole area of the beachhead was now under constant attack from Panzers and heavy artillery, and it was touch and go as to whether a withdrawal might have to be made. There were calls from the army for naval gunfire to break up the enemy tank and artillery concentrations, so some cruisers and destroyers lined up off-shore and began bombarding. We were never called on to bombard; our high-angle guns were considered more useful as anti-aircraft weapons.

During the early afternoon, the large bulks of two battleships were seen and, eventually *Warspite* and *Valiant* steamed slowly into the bay. They stopped about 2,000 yards from the beach. There was some delay while spotting Officers were sent ashore, then the two ships began to slew broadside onto the beach on their screws, and to swing round their combined sixteen 15 inch guns. It all seemed to be happening so casually, like a film in slow motion. Suddenly there was an earth-shattering roar from *Warspite*, followed by another one from *Valiant*. A sheet of orange flame shot from each ship, followed by billows of brown cordite smoke. The surrounding hills threw back the roar of the broadsides in booming echoes. As broadside followed broadside, the bay became enveloped in infernal noise; crash – boom, crash – boom, crash – boom ... Nemesis had fallen on the enemy and someone ashore must have been getting a terrible headache! It was so awe-inspiring our eyes were drawn to it, until the older and wiser Leading Seaman Captain of the Gun said, 'Never mind them. Keep your eyes on the hills. Gerry's not going to put up with that for long.' How right he turned out to be!

In the late afternoon, the two battleships withdrew with their destroyers, not wishing, I suppose, to be in the bay at dusk. The next day (16 September) they came back and again, took up bombarding positions. After the third salvo, there were aircraft overhead – twin-engine bombers – but they were no bigger than flies, out of range. We waited for them to dive down but they didn't. Suddenly I saw what appeared to be a fighter aircraft, with its wings shot off, coming down in flames. Down it came at a terrific speed above *Warspite* and, when it crashed onto her, I was still convinced it was a shot-down fighter. Only later did we discover it was the latest German secret weapon – the radio-controlled glider bomb. Later, too, we discovered this was the type of bomb which had sunk the Italian battleship. The two battleships then withdrew and, when they were well out to sea, we could hear *Warspite's* pom-pom ammunition exploding like a gigantic jumping cracker. She had been hit amidships and the bomb had penetrated a boiler room and blown a hole below the water line. She was taken in tow by one of her destroyers until two tugs reached her and took over. She was towed to Malta, patched up, then made her way to Gibraltar for final repairs. When she had gone, fighter-bomber attacks resumed and we were kept busy fighting them off.

On the following day, the crisis ashore was over. Montgomery's 8th Army linked up with the American 5th Army and the Germans withdrew. It had been a close run thing. Before the naval bombardment, the German counter-attack had penetrated within three miles of the beach. Monty was convinced his push had caused the withdrawal and stated so in his memoirs. But General Alexander did not agree. His opinion was, '… the battle was won before the 8th Army arrived, mainly as a result of heavy naval gunfire brought up in support of the counter attack, the air support and the sterling quality of the troops.'

The American Admiral Hewitt discounted any other arm than the Navy: 'The margin of success in the Salerno landing was carried by the naval gun.' The Germans agreed with him, and Naples fell on 2 October.

The Germans wreaked considerable havoc with their new glider bomb. Two days after sinking the Italian battleship, they hit the US cruiser *Savannah* and so badly damaged her that she had to withdraw. Then the British cruiser *Uganda* was hit and the bomb penetrated all her decks and blew a hole through her bottom, fortunately without sinking her. Following their hit on *Warspite*, they came back and near-missed the US cruiser *Philadelphia* slightly damaging her.

We had now been in the bay six days at action stations, keeping endless watch skyward into a blinding sun, and were feeling very weary. Most of the American warships were making smoke, but its value was dubious. It dissipated too soon to cover the shipping and tended to restrict our sight of attacking aircraft. We were still only getting sleep where we could around the gun at night. Then, to add insult to injury, the heavy bombers did arrive – but in the dark. They came at 0200 hrs on 18 September in low cloud and flew over us to drop their bombs inland. So, because of cloud, the slow-moving targets we yearned for were denied us.

At daybreak we had the usual dawn fighter-bomber attack. Then we went to an American tanker for oil. Much to our surprise, the tanker Captain refused us because we were British! Consequently, we took ourselves off to the British landing and arrived just in time to participate in their first air attack. We refuelled alongside a British tanker and returned to the American sector at noon. On 19 September, I spent my twenty-second birthday at Salerno, wondering if I had any more birthdays coming to me. Possibly my best birthday present was that the attacks were now easing off, which was a good thing because our magazines were getting very low.

Apart from his ablutions, the Captain had never left the bridge. His meals were taken up to him and at night he threw himself under the gunnery director at the rear of the bridge, wrapped himself in his voluminous sheepskin coat and endeavoured to snatch some sleep. On the sixth night the signalman went to him and said, 'Captain, Sir, from the American cruiser – she requests we make smoke.' Gordon poked his head from under the sheepskin and said irritably, 'Tell them to go to hell.' then turned over and went back to sleep. We had to admire him. His rages were magnificent and he seemed indefatigable, but he did not relish being under American command.

On 21 September, U-boat activity in the gulf saw us outside the bay, Asdic sweeping. A US merchantman had been torpedoed and was on fire. The crew abandoned it. A British tug came out, went alongside it and fought the fire with hoses, but it was too far advanced and eventually it was lost. This patrolling was to continue up to 2 October, by which time we had been at sea (mostly at action stations) since 11 September. There were few problems getting oil, but our fresh water had run out and we were having to make fresh water from sea water. Consequently, it was rationed. The pumps were turned on one hour in the forenoon and one hour in the afternoon, bathing was forbidden and no clothes could be washed. Eventually our potatoes, frozen meat and bread ran out and we were left with corned beef, biscuits and lentils.

The Captain's steward went up on the bridge one day and said, 'Your dinner, Sir.' He handed over a plate on which were two slices of corned beef, a dollop of peas pudding and two dry biscuits riddled with weevils. Gordon made absolutely no comment. He simply took the plate, tendered his thanks and began to eat it.

When the allied troops entered Naples on 2 October, they discovered that the retreating Germans had contaminated the water supply before pulling out. Typhus had broken out. They also left a time bomb under the main post office which blew up, killing and maiming dozens of civilians. All water in Naples was suspect and it was this that got us away from Salerno after a stay there of three weeks. The military authorities in Naples acted quickly to stem the typhus outbreak. A decision was made to send a water tanker to Palermo in Sicily to get fresh water for the Neapolitans, and we were ordered to escort it. It came as a welcome break after twenty days of continuous strain and we were not sorry to get to sea. We left at 1100 hrs on 2 October, rendezvoused with the tanker off the Gulf of Salerno and proceeded south for Palermo – a distance of about 220 miles. The tanker was making 10 knots and the further south we went, the more relaxed we became. We were doing an Asdic sweep; U-boats were known to be operating in the area and the safe return of this tanker as soon as possible was vital to the health and well-being of the Neapolitans.

Night descended without incident. Then, just before midnight there was a hissing from our loudspeaker extension as a microphone was switched on.

'Hunter, Bridge.'
'Bridge, Hunter. Several small echoes, Sir, at extreme range on green 30.'
'Report back if they get closer, Hunter.'
'Aye-aye, Sir'.

Fifteen minutes later, another hissing.

'Hunter, Bridge.'
'Bridge, Hunter.'
'Same bearing, Sir, much closer, clear echoes, about six small vessels.'
'Very good'.

Surely these couldn't be E-boats. Their nearest base was Leghorn, 200 miles north of Naples. If they were E-boats, they must be at their extreme range of operation. As we deliberated we heard the 4 inch gun communication number below us shout, 'Stand by star shell!'

Gordon was going to have a look at what was out there. I heard both breeches being opened to remove the loaded AA shells followed by the clop, clop, as the breeches closed when the star shells were loaded. Then came the cry, 'Star shell spread – Commence! Commence! Commence!'

The report from the gun when star shells were fired was much kinder on the ears than the AA shells as they had a reduced propellant charge. Immediately after the report, there was the bell-like sound of the brass cylinders hitting the deck as they were automatically ejected as the guns recoiled. We waited for the first two stars hells to burst and when they did – there they were – a gaggle of E-boats lying in wait for the tanker. These E-boats could not have fallen foul of a more deadly adversary.

Of all the destroyers operating in the Mediterranean at that time, they now had to contend with one that had had two years of hard experience on the east coast and was fitted with a bow chaser gun. Although we had not encountered E-boats for five months, everything clicked into place as though we had left only yesterday. The after twin-4 inch guns barked twice more, then the helm went over and we were charging in, bows-on, at increasing speed. The forward pom-pom opened fire and as I listened to the bangs, I envied the crew. It was a warm night with a flat calm sea, no biting cold, no freezing spray whip-lashing their faces. Having got in an initial burst of fire on the after pom-pom, we lost the target as the ship turned bows-on. The bridge superstructure then masked our view of what was going on ahead and it seemed an eternity before our chance came a second time. The Leading Seaman echoed what we were all thinking when he said, 'Come on, Skips. Turn her and let somebody else have a bang.'

It was almost as though Gordon heard him because, as he finished speaking, the helm went over and we began to slew broadside on. As the scene presented itself once again, the after twin-4 inch began putting up more star shells and the after pom-pom and starboard Oerlikon opened up. The E-boats were scattering in all directions. It was as though we had raised a covey of partridges and there were several flashes as our shells struck home. They would know the bearing we were on as our tracer bore in upon them, but they showed no inclination to come and attack us across the deadly pool of light. Instead, they fragmented and veered off in all directions at full speed, seeking the blessed relief of darkness in which to lick their wounds. Eventually the last flare went out and it was dark again, as though a light had been switched off.

'Bridge, Hunter. Where are they now?'
'They've scattered, Sir. I've got them all over the scan, but the range is opening.'
'Let me know if they form up to come back!'
'Aye-aye, Sir.'

They did not come back. They were routed and out-fought and I have often wondered what the crew of the water tanker thought about it all. The ship had ploughed on as though nothing was happening, but they must have had a grandstand view.

We arrived in Palermo at 0700 hrs the next morning. All of us were dog tired after three weeks of tension, but we had to spur on our bodies more yet. Our magazines were now almost empty, so we had to ammunition ship. We oiled first, then took on fresh water and provisions, then the ammunition and by that time we were virtually on our knees, and the day was over. Hammocks were slung and we turned in to get a full night's uninterrupted sleep – the first for twenty-two days. We stayed in Palermo one further day and I was able to get ashore. I do not recall anything about Palermo, only my diary tells me I went ashore there. What I remember most is the baths we were now able to have after our water-tanks were replenished. There was only one bath in the ship and that was in the Officers' quarters. The after-seamen's bathroom was about nine feet square. It had a shower which never worked, and six wash bowls, so all our baths were standing ones. Nevertheless, it was good to be able to get rid of our sweaty underclothes and have a good sluice down.

After the hard tack we had been living on, we also looked forward to some better food. Our cooks had had a go at baking bread, but they were obviously not experts at it and it had not been baked through; the centres of the loaves were doughy. Perhaps their small coal-fired ovens were not adequate for the task. Apart from fresh provisions, we had a sample of what the Americans were having. A number of large cardboard boxes were delivered to the ship, and each one contained one day's food ration for one man. There was a menu card, setting the fare for breakfast, dinner and supper. Some of the food was canned, but can opener and can-key were provided and there was also a fruit bar and hard candy bar (toffee). After our hard tack this was luxury indeed.

I discovered during our time in the Med that if the Englishman had the choice between being deprived of either bread or potatoes, he would choose to go without bread. There were periods when we ran out of both. In place of bread we had hard biscuits and in place of potatoes – yams; but we never saw the latter as a substitute potato since they were more like parsnips. Keeping RN ships, other than those in the Home Fleet, supplied with potatoes, often proved a problem during the war, and one must experience life without them to know how large they loom in the English diet. A breakfast of biscuits and marmalade instead of toast is all right, but dinner without potatoes is not. Without potatoes, we left the dinner table feeling deprived and morale suffered. This may sound strange but only to those who have never been potato-less for several weeks.

When we were a few miles from Palermo on our way in, our Asdic set malfunctioned and we had hopes that another destroyer would escort the tanker back and we would be given some extra time in harbour. It was not to be. To call in another destroyer would have delayed the tanker, but there was an Asdic trawler in Palermo and, when we left at 1600 hrs on 5 October, she came with us. She was the 'ears'; we were the 'eyes'. She could have coped with U-boats, but E-boats would have overwhelmed her. So, the three of us left Palermo and we arrived in the bay of Naples the next day after a quiet, uneventful trip.

Although Naples was now in Allied hands, the harbour was not yet cleared of obstruction and material was still going ashore at the two beachheads. We embarked Army Staff Officers from Naples the next day, and took them to the British beach, along with several bags of mail for the cruiser *Delhi*, after which we were permitted to return to Naples for the night and more rest. There was an air raid at 2100 hrs, but thereafter we had a peaceful night at anchor in the bay. The following day we were given an assignment which we thought was fraught with danger. We were to escort six fleet minesweepers who were to sweep from north of Naples up to the mouth of the river Volturno and, since the Allies occupied the south bank of the river and the Germans the north, the sweeping had to be done in darkness.

Fleet sweepers (as against minesweeping trawlers) are Admiralty commissioned, purpose-made vessels with naval crews. In other words, they are not ex-fishermen. We left Naples at 1800 hrs, escorting the six fleet sweepers, who began their sweeping in daylight immediately we turned north from Naples. The Volturno is about sixty miles north of Naples and we were timed to arrive in the vicinity well after dark. One sweeper on its own is quite capable of sweeping in the dark, and many did, but six was going to be quite something and we wondered how they were going to accomplish it.

Darkness came without incident, and gradually we drew nearer to the river mouth. All the sweepers had the tiniest of red lights at their sweep ends and it was on these that they kept station. We were now so close inshore in the river mouth that we could clearly make out the darkened houses on the enemy occupied bank. We fully expected to be illuminated and fired on at any second and were keyed up for it. Much to our relief it did not happen. We had sneaked into the enemy's backyard and come away unmolested. Eventually the sweep was completed, the fleet sweepers hauled in their gear and we high-tailed it back to Naples, arriving there in the small hours.

On 11 October, we escorted an oil tanker to Bizerta, saw it safely in the following day and left, after oiling, for boiler cleaning at Algiers. We were given a berth on arrival alongside the French destroyer *Le Fortune* who was alongside the jetty undergoing repairs. It was 13 October, the day Italy declared war on Germany. When the news was announced, it was greeted with much amusement. Gordon Chipeau pranced along the upper deck, doing a hilarious take-off of the Italian-American film actor Henry Armetta, including his crab-like walk.

We knew that when we were ready for sea again, Naples harbour would probably be cleared for shipping and the two beachheads dispensed with. Consequently Salerno, as far as we were concerned, was a thing of the past. It had been an unforgettable experience which, at one period, was very much in the balance. But we had come through it and were now looking forward to shore leave in Algiers.

Chapter 16

A Lull Between Landings

Much to my disappointment, I only managed to get ashore once in Algiers during our eight-day period in dock. We arrived at 1030 hrs on 13 October and I had shore leave from 1600 to 2200 hrs. I arrived back twenty minutes early and, having to cross the French destroyer, decided to have a look around her. I went into the fo'c'sle flat and immediately got the smell peculiar to French ships – a mixture of Gauloises and the sweet odour of garlic. There were three card playing matelots in the galley who looked up in surprise as I entered. I tendered a greeting in English, they replied in French. One of them threw his thumb over his shoulder towards *Hambledon* lying alongside behind him and I nodded. There then followed an attempt at entente cordiale which was severely restricted by language problems. There was a matelot's cap lying on the table and I picked it up, removed my own cap, and replaced it with the French one. The three Frenchmen slapped their thighs and guffawed. The cap with its red pom-pom looked so incongruous against the rest of the Englishman's uniform and it was like balm to a shock I had undergone that afternoon.

I had been standing on the jetty in overalls and minus cap, when a French dockyard workman approached me and tried to converse . When I said the one word, 'English', he realised his mistake, apologised and went on his way, leaving me somewhat shattered. My pride in my English ancestry had always been strong and the war years had tended to intensify it. I considered it a God-given concession, rather than an accident of birth, and never for a moment thought of myself as looking any other than unmistakeably English. To have been mistaken for a Frenchman came as a shock and a blow to my pride. The rankling I felt at the mistaken identity had still not receded and it was probably this fact that prompted me to don the French cap. The reaction to my doing so was all I needed to restore my youthful pride. The gales of laughter beyond doubt that, to them, I was, after all, no Frenchman.

The First Lieutenant had decided to make use of our time in dock to paint ship. Consequently, next morning every available man onboard found himself with a paint brush in his hand. The paint on the funnel was looking decidedly shabby so that had to be chipped off to bare metal and I found myself sitting on a stage at the top of the funnel with a chipping hammer. A seaman is advised to rig his own stage, then, if it collapses, he has no-one but himself to blame. I did not rig mine; it had been rigged before I came on deck by a zealous Leading Seaman and I assumed he knew what he was about. I had been chipping for about half an hour when, without warning, the plank I was sitting on turned on its side and down I plunged. I fell from a height of about eighteen feet and landed on my feet on the iron deck. Behind me was a salt-water hydrant and as my knees bent with the shock of landing, I hit the wheel of the valve with my coccyx, felt an excruciating shock of pain up my spine and passed out. Someone ran to the wardroom to get the Surgeon and when he heard what had happened he said, 'Oh, my God !' thinking I had landed on my head. When I came round he was saying, 'Carry him into the sick bay.'

I was carried in and placed on the sofa, my boots and socks removed and my feet given a thorough examination – much wiggling of toes and so on. Eventually the Surgeon seemed convinced I had not broken any bones but he decided to send me ashore to the military hospital in Algiers for X-rays. Promptly at 0900 hrs next morning a taxi arrived on the jetty and, supported by two messmates, I boarded it and was driven away.

The X-rays showed no broken bones, but two badly sprained arches. When I emerged from the X-ray department there was no sign of my taxi and I was advised by the Royal Army Medical Corps Sergeant to get the guardroom to rustle up some transport for me. I was left to walk a good quarter of a mile to the hospital gate house. I did it, walking on my heels, in excruciating pain the whole way. I was excused all duties and did no more chipping or painting, but bang went any more shore leave. So all I got from our eight days in Algiers was the first day's six hours ashore.

On 22 October our boiler-clean was finished and we left Algiers harbour at 0800 hrs and joined the Hunt class destroyer *Bedale* which had been renamed *Slazak* and was Polish-manned. The seamen, as usual, were fallen in for leaving harbour on fo'c'sle and quarterdeck and as we drew away from *Le Fortune* one of the lads said, 'When's the Froggie going to sea then?' Another answered, 'Don't worry, mate. She'll be here when we get back.'

Painted on the harbour wall in black letters three feet high was the French equivalent of 'Victory is our only aim.' The British Navy had sunk and crippled the French Western Mediterranean Fleet at Oran in 1940. It was done reluctantly after much parleying with the French Admiral who steadfastly refused to concede to several alternative demands made on him. Admiral Cunningham (then C. in C. Eastern Mediterranean) had had better success with the French Admiral in Alexandria when, again after much parleying, he agreed to de-oil and demilitarise his fleet. And there the Eastern Mediterranean French Fleet lay immobile, taking no part in the war until May 1943, when Admiral Godroy at last agreed to operate on the side of the Allies. The fact is, however, that in all our time in the Mediterranean – almost a year – we never saw a French man-o'-war at sea. Hence the sardonic rejoinder – 'Don't worry mate. She'll be here when we get back.'

My feet were by no means healed and I could do no more than hobble around. This absolved me from work duty while in Algiers, but it did not absolve me from keeping watch at sea. I could manage to scale the mess deck ladder because it had 4 inch-wide treads. The problem was the vertical ladder up to the pom-pom deck which had ½" diameter steel rungs which would have played havoc with my sprained arches. Each time I went on watch throughout my incapacity, I had to be lifted from the upper deck. Two ratings grabbed my legs to lift and raise me, while the burly Leading Seaman reached down and grabbed the scruff of my goon skin. The opposite applied when I came off watch and had to be lowered down to the upper deck.

We carried out an anti-U-boat patrol with *Slazak* for one day and one night, then returned to Algiers and tied up alongside with her. During the day, three Italian destroyers came in and tied up astern of us. These three were the only Italian ships we saw after the surrender. French and Italian warships may have operated in the Med during our time there, but we certainly never encountered any ships from either navy, other than in harbour. While in Algiers, our mail caught up with us and I received all my birthday cards six weeks after the event! The following day we went alongside the sloop *Pelican* and took from her some gold bullion. It was in wooden boxes about 10 inches square by 3 inches deep and, while it was being trans-shipped, nets were draped between the two ships in case any boxes were dropped.

Gordon was standing on the upper deck, watching the gold come aboard, when the ship's half-grown ginger tomcat, trotting along on the outside of the guardrails, chose to fall overboard between the two ships. Immediately Gordon ordered the trans-shipment to stop until the cat was rescued. It was surprising what effect this small incident had on the ship's company. Beneath his blood and thunder and tetchiness, Gordon was seen to have a tender heart after all!

The cruiser *Edinburgh* had been carrying gold from Russia when she was sunk in Arctic waters in May 1942 – gold that has recently been retrieved. Fortunately, our consignment reached its destination safely. It was destined for the Bank of Egypt and was reputed to be valued at over a million pounds. It was put under lock and key in the after magazine, under the seamen's mess deck. The buzz-merchants were then assured we were going to Egypt and, once again, they got it right!

We left Algiers at 1100 hrs to catch a convoy which had sailed at 0400 hrs that morning and, when clear of the harbour, we worked up to a brisk speed. In five hours, the convoy was sighted, and it consisted of seven large troopships with five destroyers, including *Slazak*. This convoying of troopships was a regular feature, with fresh troops going to Italy to reinforce the invasion, battle-weary troops coming from Italy to North Africa for rest, and troops being sent through the Med to war zones further east. The following year troops were also withdrawn from Italy to take part in the invasion of France. Consequently, there was a constant movement of troopers, all of which needed escorts. That night and the day following were uneventful, except that we sank a floating mine with rifle fire. Another Hunt in the convoy was *Atherstone*. We had not seen her from leaving Scapa Flow until she turned up at Salerno. It was the day *Warspite* was bombed and, just as *Atherstone* came into the bay, there was an air attack. She came in at a brisk speed, turned broadside on to the beach and, as she heeled over, fired a salvo from her twin 4 inch guns. I remember thinking that she was late on the scene but had lost no time getting into the action on arrival. While sinking the mine we were delayed and *Atherstone* (who had slipped into Malta for oil) caught up with us and signalled, 'I took aboard your mail while in Malta. Come and get it!'

So obviously there had been one batch of our mail in Algiers and another in Malta. We went alongside her, dropped down to her speed and a light line was shot across to her with the Accosting Gun. A stouter line was then bent on, hauled in by *Atherstone* who tied onto it our sack of mail. We then hauled in the line, thanked *Atherstone* profusely and the two ships separated and drew away to take up their respective stations back in the convoy.

The following day we left the convoy to top up our tanks in Tobruk harbour, and we took our oil from a semi-submerged tanker, which had been bombed and was lying on the bottom. Some of her compartments were obviously still water-tight and she was being replenished from other tankers and constituted a static oil-fuel tank.

We rejoined the convoy, and two days later arrived off Port Said, where we cruised around, waiting for the convoy to disperse, then went in and unloaded our cargo of gold bullion. After two days in Port Said, we left with *Slazak* and a convoy of merchant ships bound far Malta. The ships were probably UK – bound because other escorts relieved us at Malta and we went in to oil at Valletta. We tied up between two buoys in Sliema Creek – the destroyers' anchorage.

The Maltese had a very happy relationship with the Navy, which was to continue up to Malta gaining independence in 1964. RN ships had found Malta to be a useful haven long before it became a British possession in 1814. The island's economy was almost entirely dependent on the fleet, through the trade it engendered and through its dockyard.

The Maltese looked upon ships of the fleet as fair game for selling their merchandise and plying their trades. They would hire a dghaisa (a boat like a gondola, but not as resplendent) and come aboard to flog their wares. Tailors came to measure up and take orders for uniforms, and barbers would come and have a hair-cutting session. The story was that peace-time sailors ordered uniforms just before their ship was due to sail home for paying-off, when 'one turn of the screws homeward and all debts are paid.' I heard the story many times of the sailor who had a uniform made and decamped without paying. Five years later he found himself once more in the Med and anchored in Malta, where a tailor came on board for orders. Suddenly the cheating sailor was accosted by the tailor, who reminded him of his debt. The sailor denied he had ever been to Malta, but the tailor insisted.

'I remember you, *Rodney* 1932. You owe me £3.'

'It was my twin brother. He was in *Rodney*.'

'Then you pay your brother's debt. Give me £3.' After many denials and much haggling the tailor got his money.

We had shore leave in Malta and it was obvious as soon as we stepped ashore how much the Maltese had suffered from air attacks. There were still piles of rubble in every street, and those buildings that had not been flattened were cracked and pock-marked with bomb damage. Valiant attempts had been made to clear up and get the island back into shape and the famous Gut, with its many eating-houses, was back in business, although on a much-reduced scale. Food was still scarce for the Maltese and, occasionally, men would come aboard with their children, looking for food. They brought with them an empty 7lb jam tin with a wire handle, and would take leftovers from dinner. These were not beggars. They were clean and well-dressed and their golden-skinned children were a delight. But it proved to us that what food there was in Malta must have still been stringently rationed.

There followed a month of convoying, firstly from Malta to Augusta, where we arrived on 7 November, to find all RN ships in the harbour flying the Russian flag. It was the twenty-sixth anniversary of the Revolution. All the Sicilian harbours were now being put to good use and from Augusta we called in Messina, then Catania, in our journeyings. We also went back to Egypt and spent five days in Alexandria, where I went onboard the destroyer depot ship *Woolwich* for dental treatment. That five days was the longest spell we enjoyed in harbour while not undergoing repairs, and even our repair jobs only averaged six days. In a book about their ship, written by several members of the ship's company of the cruiser *Aurora*, one can read this: '*Penelope* and ourselves kicked our heels in Bone for some weeks and organised a regatta …'

How long, one wonders, was 'some weeks' – three, four, five even? Few destroyers during the war enjoyed that kind of lotus-eating luxury. Even when there was a welcome respite from sea-time, the powers-that-be never let us rusticate. In those five days, we painted the ship from stem to stern, carried out high- and low-angle shoots, an exercise night encounter, an

Asdic exercise and the AA ratings had more practice in the dome teacher. We were still going out of the harbour, even if only for exercises; but it did mean we got shore leave in Alexandria, which I considered the best run ashore in the Med – particularly the Fleet Club.

The attraction of the Fleet Club for sailors was the beer as much as the food. British sailors were little interested in the wine that was to be had in the French North African ports or in Sicily and Italy. They would drink it, but only because there was nothing else. I still have a small blue card with 'Fleet Canteen, Naples. One beer ration.' printed on it. In Alexandria there was no such rationing and, on one visit to the Fleet Club, we had a fabulous waiter-served meal, followed by unrationed bottled beer, and listened to a show given by Geraldo and his Dance Orchestra, with his attractive female vocalist, Dorothy Carless. The meal and entertainment were al fresco, and there were coloured lights in the trees. Sitting there under a fabulous starlit sky, on a balmy Mediterranean evening, the war seemed a thousand miles away.

We left Alexandria for Port Said on 2 December to rendezvous with six troopships bound for Taranto. The trip would take five days and this precious convoy was allocated six destroyers. There was a Greek-manned Hunt and three other Hunts: *Hambledon*, *Catterick* and *Blencathra*, together with *Inglefield* and *Fury*. We spent one night in Taranto while the six troopers disembarked their passengers and embarked others. The following day saw the six ships under way again, bound for Gibraltar and possibly the UK. Only *Hambledon* of the original six destroyers left with them – we were to boiler clean in Gib. The escort had now increased to seven destroyers: the Hunts *Hambledon*, *Calpe*, *Holcombe* and *Tynedale*, and three American destroyers *Niblack*, *Benson* and *Wainwright*. Throughout the five-day trip the weather was depressing – low-cast with drizzling rain.

We took up station astern of the convoy Asdic sweeping and, as tail-end Charlie, were very much isolated from what was going on ahead. Two days later we were off Pantellaria where the Asdic operator reported a clear ping (sonic return), and we began depth-charging. After dropping two patterns, Gordon called off the attack, presuming we were pinging a wreck. We were in an area which was a known graveyard of shipping and he was probably right in his assumption. In any case, the convoy had passed through the area without incident and its rear was now well ahead, so we sped after it and, once more, took up station.

On the forenoon of the following day (12 December) we were off Bougie and were disconcerted to receive a signal telling us that *Tynedale* had been torpedoed and sunk. There was much speculation as to how a U-boat could have got at the screening escorts without being detected. However, having now blown his cover, we imagined the remainder would summarily deal with him, and we were in little doubt the score would eventually be one all. Imagine our bewilderment and anguish, then, when during the afternoon a further signal informed us that *Holcombe* had also been torpedoed and sunk. We had lost two Hunts out of four and, apart from knowing that, we were at a total loss as to what was happening ahead. Naturally we were all eager to get into the fray, and Gordon must have been frustrated beyond endurance at our enforced inactivity. Whoever the senior escort was (it could even have been one of the Americans) must have decided that *Hambledon* should stay put, rather than the rear of the convoy be unguarded. And there we remained, straining at the leash.

The night passed uneventfully, and we had begun to think that the U-boat had got away with it, when a further signal informed us that *Calpe* had detected it, forced it to the surface and sunk it. The two-for-one score, however, rankled with us. It was, I suppose, a blow to our pride, which was added to the anguish we were feeling at the loss of the two Hunts. Only later did we discover why the U-boat had been so successful. She was U593 and had been armed with acoustic torpedoes which, attracted by the vibration of a ship's screws, need not even be on target when released. The U-boat Captain was picked up by *Calpe* and he was reputed to have told *Calpe's* Captain that, had he not made his run in to attack at the precise moment he did, his bag would have been three!

So, this was yet another German secret weapon, and it is fortunate that its advent was so late in the war at sea. By this time, the Navy had complete ascendency in the Atlantic and U-boat losses had mounted to a point where the packs were later withdrawn. They rallied with the fitting of the Snorkel tube but by then it was too late for the tide to be turned. What the acoustic torpedo could have achieved, had it been introduced in sufficient numbers earlier, leaves little to the imagination. An answer to it was found, and it was called 'Foxer.' It entailed towing noise-making paravanes astern of the ship, which gave off more vibration than the screws, thus 'foxing' the lethal torpedo.

In 1971, I read an article in *The Guardian* to the effect that the Royal Navy was seeking to buy acoustic torpedoes from the Aerojet Corporation in Sacramento, California. It was a long way and a long time after our experience off Bougie in December 1943. This does not mean that the Navy did not have an equivalent. A German acoustic torpedo was captured intact in 1944, but the Navy's equivalent was guided by wire-borne signals, and these were introduced after the cessation of hostilities.

It is an indication of the sea time we were doing that, when the convoy reached Gibraltar, we went in for yet another boiler clean. Here we found *Warspite* in dry dock, undergoing final repairs to her bomb damage. Another ship which had gone to Gibraltar for repairs was the torpedoed Liberty ship from which we had taken off the Italian prisoners. However, on her arrival, the carnage in the hold was so gruesome that it had been filled with quick lime and left, until the quick lime had done its work and the ship was in a better condition for men to begin repairs on it.

We were tied up alongside the jetty throughout our boiler clean and I was below on one of the days, washing up our after-dinner crockery. Suddenly a voice shouted down the hatch, '*Nelson's* on her way out.' I went on deck to have a look at her (even when a ship has a masculine name, she is still referred to in the feminine gender), *Rodney* and *Nelson* were unlike any other battleship in the fleet, indeed, in the world. They were referred to as 'the boots' because that is what they resembled – floating boots. They were just short of 34,000 tons' displacement and, but for the limitations imposed by the Washington Naval Treaty, would have been nearer 50,000 tons. Design alterations left them with a long fo'c'sle and the mere stub of a quarterdeck.

The 'boots' were reputed to be bitches to handle. Minus a long quarterdeck to keep them stable, they were inclined to yaw alarmingly in a beam sea, and their quarterdecks were often water-logged. They carried the largest gun in the navy – nine 16 inch in three triple turrets, all of which were mounted on their interminable fo'c'sles. *Nelson's* sister ship *Rodney* had fired repeated salvoes of her 16 inch into *Bismarck*. Despite her clumsy appearance, there was something awe-inspiring about *Nelson* as she slid past. With her three triple turrets ranged along her fo'c'sle she was the epitome of the floating gun platform.

Then a curious thing happened. Some minutes after she had passed us and had begun to recede, the wash she had made set the ship dancing. A slight movement up and down gradually increased until we were dancing a fandango and our berthing wires began to snap like pieces of string. Everyone in the vicinity ran for cover as the wires pinged and snaked lethally in all directions. The seamen then had to jump to it and get temporary wires in place before the ship (without steam) drifted away from the jetty. *Nelson* caused us a lot of work splicing eyes in new wires. One seaman remarked ruefully, 'We put in more sea time in a month than she puts in in a year, and just because she's going to sea and we are not, she breaks all our bloody wires. Isn't it the truth?'

When we left Gibraltar on 21 December, we were escort to a large convoy which increased in size as we proceeded along the North African coast until it totalled some 186 ships. We patrolled ten miles ahead of it Asdic sweeping, then on 24 December we were relieved and put into Bone. Here we discovered smallpox was rampant ashore and every member of the ship's company was vaccinated before shore leave was given. I spent Christmas in an Army camp, after being invited there by a soldier I met in Bone. There was little by way of entertainment in a bare army hut, but the soldiers were at pains to be sociable and plied me with bottled beer, while we sang carols to try and usher in the Christmas spirit.

The only food to be had were small new potatoes which were simmering in a large cooking pot on the coal-fired stove. Christmas dinner on board next day was enjoyed by all and the mess was decorated with bunting. Before dinner, a Naval Chaplain came aboard and we held a Christmas service on the aftermess deck. It was only the second time we had been so graced since we commissioned. Our festivities, however, tended to be spoilt because we knew they were going to be short-lived. A signal had arrived from the Naval Officer in Charge, Bone, during the forenoon: 'You will be able to have your Christmas dinner in harbour, but I fear your Christmas cake will have to be consumed at sea.' By 1400 hrs we were leaving the harbour and, apart from a small Christmas tree at the masthead to remind us it was Christmas day, our festivities were over. The same thing had happened on Christmas Day 1941 and 1942.

On 28 December, while at anchor in the outer harbour at Algiers, Gordon MacKendrick relinquished command. I suppose the ship's company must have manned the side and cheered him on his way, but I do not recall the incident and, as it is something I would not have forgotten, I must have been on a working-party ashore. Our new CO came aboard shortly after Gordon had departed and since I do not recall any speech from him, this seems to confirm my not being onboard at the time. His name was Lieutenant L.G. Toone, RN. He was younger than the two previous COs and, although supremely efficient, there was nothing crotchety about him. He was polite and affable, with a well-developed sense of humour.

However, we felt we had come down in the world. After two Lieutenant Commanders, we now had a young Lieutenant. A Lieutenant as CO of a destroyer would have been totally out of the question in peace time and this is indicative of the number of escort vessels that had emerged since 1939, both from our own shipyards and from America under lease-lend. Not only Lieutenants RN were getting commands but more than that, RN Volunteer Reserve Lieutenants were to be seen commanding mine layers, motor torpedo boats, corvettes and sloops. I came across more than one RNVR Lieutenant Commander in command of a destroyer.

Chapter 17

ANZIO: A Stranded Whale

We were hard-worked convoying through the month of January 1944 – mostly troopers, ferrying troops between the North African ports and Naples, and vice versa. Normally the trip between Naples and Algiers as escort took two days, but there was one occasion when we did the reverse trip with *Blencathra* independently and, at 22 knots economical cruising speed, we completed the trip in twenty-four hours. It was tiring work and mostly uneventful. During the whole of the month, shore leave was given only twice – on New Year's Day in Taranto and for a few hours in the dockyard canteen in Algiers.

In February we fared a little better. We put into the Isle of Capri on 7 February and I was in the watch ashore. Four of us went ashore together and when we were on our way back to the ship, we met three other members of the ship's company, who told us that one of our boys had been beaten-up by some American soldiers. We arrived at the ship at 2200 hrs to find Nicholas Fitzherbert standing at the head of the gangway. He said, 'You obviously haven't heard. I've extended leave by one hour. Be back on time at 2300 hrs.' He said nothing more, simply turned on his heel and went back onboard. We took the hint and all of us went back up to the Capri mainland. Anglo-American relations were not improved that night!

Also in February, we managed leave in Naples for the first time since its capture. In my view, the beauty of the bay of Naples far surpasses anything ashore. In fact, I was somewhat disappointed with Napoli and took myself off to see the sights of Pompeii. The harbour was now busy with shipping. Since the Italians had achieved much success with their underwater chariots and midget submarines it was thought the Germans might have inherited them, so we took our turn patrolling the entrance to the harbour, dropping anti-personnel charges throughout the night.

On 22 January, we heard that Allied troops had landed at Anzio and wondered what part, if any, we were going to play in it. That some of the troopships we had been escorting would eventually end up there was obvious. Anzio turned out to be a miniature Dardanelles; the troops got ashore without opposition and Rome was only thirty-seven miles to the north. It was there for the taking, but the American General commanding the operation dug in on the beachhead and consolidated his position, instead of striking out. It was only a matter of time before the Germans counter-attacked and, as at Salerno, when they did so the situation became very precarious indeed. Winston Churchill, always the one to come up with the apt metaphor said, 'I had hoped that we were hurling a wild cat on the shore, but all we had got was a stranded whale.'

Unlike Salerno, Anzio did nothing to relieve pressure on the allied armies in the south for several months. But Salerno had to be maintained and fed and it led to *Hambledon* undergoing one of the most wearying tasks of her sea war. On 18 February, after a night dropping anti-personnel charges outside Naples, we were informed that the cruiser *Penelope* had been torpedoed and sunk by a U-boat off Anzio. At 0900 hrs we left Naples and raced north at full speed to look for survivors. It seemed incredible that *Penelope's* luck had run out. She was renowned throughout the Navy as 'HMS *Pepper Pot*' and had come through countless direct hits and near-misses.

Her latest had been bomb damage in the Dodecanese not many weeks before, from where, once again, she had been nursed back into Malta, patched up, and had come out fighting once more. She had seemed quite indestructible, but here we were rushing to try to find survivors from a *Penelope* who no longer existed. We found wreckage and oil – but no survivors. The board of enquiry assumed there was no destroyer escort available, but *Hambledon* was, in fact, off Naples when *Penelope* left the harbour.

For the next six weeks we patrolled with other destroyers off Anzio. We were strung out in sectors, Asdic sweeping to keep the sea lanes clear of U-boats so that the beachhead could be maintained. News bulletins told us there was no movement from Anzio, so it was galling to be doing a boring task in atrocious weather, which amounted to feeding 'a stranded whale'. Destroyers were on anti-submarine patrol from Naples northward and there were seven off the Anzio beachhead. There were no problems about oiling; ships left in their turn for Naples, oiled, and went straight back on patrol.

As all holiday-makers will know, the Med has a delightful climate in the summer, with flat calm seas for weeks on end. In winter it is a different matter and, off Anzio, we were to experience the equinoctial gales. The weather does not have the bone-chilling bite of western climes but, nevertheless, cold it is. Neither do the Med breakers rise to the height of the Atlantic ones, but a gale is a gale in any sea, and we endured gale conditions off Anzio.

Most of the enemy air activity was off the beachhead, but that did not leave us wholly unmolested and one of our number, the destroyer *Inglefield*, was sunk by glider-bomb on 25 February. *Inglefield* had operated on convoy work with us on several occasions and when we tied up alongside her one day in Naples, I discovered an ex-schoolmate onboard her, who was lost when she went down. The threat of air attack meant that the guns' crews had to be at action stations during daylight hours but, thankfully, we were able to go into defence stations after nightfall, otherwise, we could not have sustained the six-week patrol. Other Hunts operating with us were *Lamerton, Wheatland, Cleveland, Blencathra, Brecon*, the Polish-manned *Slazak*, and the fleet destroyer *Laforey*.

At dusk one evening we sighted an inflatable raft from a crashed American bomber. On coming alongside it, we found two American airmen, one alive but wounded, another who appeared to be barely alive. The wounded man was put to bed in the sick bay and was in no danger. The second man was still warm when we got him inboard, although he had no pulse. The Surgeon had him tied to a stretcher, which was then strung up at its point of balance in the after superstructure. For an hour we rocked the stretcher up and down like a see-saw, in an effort to get his heart beating, with the Surgeon attending the wounded man and returning intermittently to give an injection to the other. The Surgeon must have had some hope of his recovery because there was no sign of any injury.

It was not to be. Despite all our efforts he died, presumably of shock and exposure. Since he was American we could not bury him at sea. His body was taken back to Naples and handed over to the US military. In 2 Kings, Chapter 4, verse 34, the prophet Elisha seems to be practising mouth-to-mouth resuscitation. Did the Ancients know more than we knew in 1944? This form of artificial respiration did not come into use until sometime after the war and our rocking of the young American airman, sadly, proved of no avail. I think it highly likely that mouth-to-mouth resuscitation might have saved him.

Day followed weary day off Anzio and I look back on it as the most soul-destroying period of my time at sea. It was not particularly the weather because, bad as it was, we had known far worse. The problem was psychological. We had lost a cruiser to a U-boat and a destroyer to bombing, but we did not seem to be achieving anything. That the beachhead needed protecting and sustaining was obvious, but that it was playing no part in furthering the war effort was also obvious, and our morale suffered.

On 6 March we got a welcome break. Our Asdics were playing up again and we went into dry dock in Naples so that the dome could be examined. It gave us two days' respite, and on my run ashore I went to the San Carlo Opera House, to enjoy the two short operas *Cavalleria Rusticana* and *Pagliacci*. There were few lower-deck sailors in the audience and the incongruity of where I had been two days previously, and where I was now, was quite stark. I returned six weeks later, this time to enjoy a performance of *Carmen*.

When we left the dry dock, we were assigned to a convoy of tank-landing ships (LSTs) bound for Anzio. We left Naples at 1730 hrs and arrived off the beachhead in the small hours. The LSTs went straight in, opened their bow doors, dropped their ramps and began disgorging their cargo of jeeps, tanks and guns. We steamed around slowly and made smoke to cover the shipping, but there was no air attack. The difference between Anzio and Salerno was that there were Allied airfields close to Anzio, whereas such had not been the case at Salerno. By nightfall the LSTs, now empty, hauled themselves off the beach and formed up for return to Naples. Other duties were then to take us away from the area, and we did not return to Anzio again before the break-out which eventually did come.

By mid-March, it became obvious that the Allies had won almost complete ascendancy in the Mediterranean. There was still U-boat and some E-boat activity, but the large surface ships had gone with the surrender of the Italian Fleet. Except in the Naples area of Italy, enemy air activity was now practically nil on the North African coast. The airfields on Sicily, Sardinia and Pantellaria were all now in Allied hands and south of Naples we went into a three watch routine. This meant we could use our hammocks at sea, something not before known, and every third night we could have a full night's sleep below decks. This was luxury indeed and, further, the short Mediterranean winter had run its course. We were enjoying some sunshine again. The emphasis was now on the Asdic, with the guns getting a welcome respite. The biggest danger was more under the sea than over it.

With Anzio behind us, we went back to convoying troopers again, chiefly between Augusta and Naples. On 18 March we anchored off Capri overnight and, while there, Mount Vesuvius began erupting. We left the following day to carry out a patrol with *Blencathra* north of Naples and, on our return, came upon a semi-submerged tank-landing craft. Both ships had a fine old time sinking it. It was the first bit of anything like action we had had for several weeks, and we both made depth-charge runs at it and riddled it with shells until it sank.

On our return to Naples on 20 March, the Vesuvius eruption was in full spate, with flames leaping from the crater and streams of molten lava running down the volcano's slopes. Reports were that Vesuvius was angrier than it had been for seventy years, and the situation had become so crucial that a small town and some villages on the slopes had been evacuated. The fireworks continued for five days and, when they subsided, clouds of lava dust were emitted from the crater. They ascended into the sky then disintegrated and fell as a fine red-grey ash like fine sand. This ash rain began in the afternoon and, when we came on deck at 0630 hrs the following morning, it had covered the upper deck and all the superstructure to an inch in depth. Fortunately, we were lying at Capri and the wind was blowing away from us. Even so, every square inch of the upper deck, the bridge, guns, lockers, capstan and so forth had to be hosed down and cleaned, which was not as easy as it sounds. With the addition of water, the ash became a pumice sludge, which was difficult to remove.

After Sicily, when V striking force broke up, we had been itinerant free agents under the Flag Officer, Western Italy. Mostly, we operated as a twin with *Blencathra* until after Salerno in November, when she went to operate in what became a graveyard of British destroyers – the Dodecanese islands. However, *Blencathra* survived the Dodecanese and we came back together again. We often tied up together, and Officers and men of both ships intermingled. She was junior ship, so we always preceded her out of harbour, but on one occasion leaving Ferryville she was on the outside of us, so had to leave first. As she preceded us down the small gulf to Bizerta she was playing the 'Post Horn Gallop' from her gramophone, through her upper-deck extension speakers, and we thought how apt a signature tune it was for a Hunt class destroyer. At around this time, five Hunts were formed into a small flotilla, known as the 58th Division and placed under the C. in C. Levant. The ships, in order of seniority were: *Blankney* (Leader), *Hambledon* (Half leader), *Mendip, Brecon* and *Blencathra*. That our Lieutenant Captain was second in seniority proves the young age of destroyer commanders at that stage of the war.

It was during the Anzio period that the First Lieutenant, Nicholas Fitzherbert, and the Surgeon left the ship. We had come in from patrol for oil and provisions when, without any preliminary warning, their kit appeared on the upper deck and they had departed in the motorboat. Both were popular with the ship's company and we were sorry to see them go. Eighteen months later I heard that Nicholas had lost his life in an air crash. The news came to me by word of mouth and, if true, the Navy lost a potential Admiral. His replacement was a Lieutenant RNVR as were most of our Officers by this time. Shortly after he arrived, I spent some time with him, making an inventory of our stock of hemp and wire ropes in the tiller flat. He was interested enough to ask questions about my life pre-war and my career to date in the service. One thing that intrigued him was his discovery that I had a very retentive memory; and he would fire destroyer pennant letters and numerals at me to see how many names I could come up with. My memory today is such that I do not even recall his name!

He was, of course, a civilian in uniform. No RN Officer of that period would have been as approachable as he was. He relinquished no authority in the process of presenting as a warm human being. With pre-war Dartmouth-trained Officers, the class demarcation line between themselves and the lower deck was clearly and rigidly drawn, and this fact did not engender easy relationships. John Barnes and Gordon MacKendrick were classic examples – of how difficult it was for a pre-war RN Officer to acquire the common touch. Nicholas Fitzherbert acquired it, possibly without realising he had done so but others of higher rank might have seen it as erosive of authority.

A clear example of class demarcation was an order which was made to Liberty men every time we had shore leave at Harwich. After they had fallen in and been inspected, the leave expiry time was given, together with a warning of the maximum number of duty-free cigarettes or tobacco we were permitted to take ashore. The final injunction was as follows: 'The saloon bar of the Alexandra Hotel, Dovercourt, is out of bounds to naval ratings.' This rankled to such an extent that all ratings – including NCOs – boycotted the entire hotel. Thus, what the owners gained in Officer-patronage of the saloon bar, they more than lost through the other ranks' boycott of the place because of what they could only see as a snobbishness.

I have the feeling that what I have described no longer appertains in the post-war Navy. After I was demobilised I went into the Royal Fleet Reserve and, seven years after the end of the war, I was called up for two weeks' training. During that time, I was agreeably surprised to find a different atmosphere from the one I had experienced, in that relationships were much more relaxed. The discipline and the efficiency were still there, but there seemed to be a comradeship between Officer and rating almost unknown to me during the war. Perhaps the sharing of wartime hardship and danger had brought about change, a change which resulted in a bond being struck that eventually came to fruition. Perhaps, again, the greater egalitarianism resulting from the first post-war Socialist Government – which servicemen in their hundreds of thousands voted for – had something to do with it. Whatever it was, the difference was very noticeable, and since that time the Navy has become inundated with ex-grammar school graduates. Consequently, I imagine the demarcation line will now be somewhat blurred, if not erased altogether.

On 24 March we left Naples with *Blencathra* as escort to a convoy of six tank-landing ships to Ajaccio, the capital of Corsica. We steamed to the east of Sardinia to pass through the Straits of Bonifacio and arrived at Ajaccio on the west coast of Corsica at 2000 hrs on a beautiful and tranquil Saturday evening. Spring was now well-advanced, and the greenery and hills surrounding the harbour were breath-taking in their beauty. The following morning a church service was held on the aftermess deck and in the afternoon I went ashore in Napoleon's birthplace.

We were never permitted to remain in idleness anywhere very long and next day saw us on our way back to Naples with the same six ships now empty. At the time we wandered why war material was being unloaded in Corsica, because we were to return there with more LSTs. When Southern France was invaded after Normandy, the reason became plain.

We arrived back in Naples at 1900 hrs on 28 March and the following day were allowed to lie idly at anchor with *Blencathra* all day in the bay. The day fallowing, however, the call to action sounded in our ears and we were, as usual, at immediate notice for steam when the call came.

Chapter 18

An Eye for a Tooth

We were not aware at first that it was a call to action as such. We had had many so-called emergency dispatches, with nothing at the end of them, such as our midnight dash from Harwich, which had proved fruitless. However, at 1000 hrs on 29 March we were ordered to proceed with *Blencathra* to a position north-east of Palermo to assist in what we thought might evolve into an anti-U-boat sweep. Perhaps an aircraft had seen a surfaced U-boat well ahead of a convoy, and the powers-that-be had decided to reinforce the escort. All this we pondered, until news came from the bridge that a U-boat had definitely been run to earth and that we were to reinforce the attacking destroyers.

The position we had been given would take us in the vicinity of the small island of Filicudi in the Lipari group, about 135 miles south of Naples. Both ships quickly worked up to a speed of twenty-five knots and, when dinner time came, each watch was able to partake of it in plenty of time before we reached our destination. I had the afternoon watch and, until the other destroyers came into view at 1530 hrs, we were at defence stations. When we arrived on the scene, three destroyers were already there and all were flying their 'Submarine in Contact' flags. They were *Laforey* and *Tumult* – two fleet destroyers – and the Hunt *Wilton*. *Laforey* was one of the Lightning class, the Navy's fastest, most heavily armed destroyers. In the First War she would have been classed as a light cruiser. She had sped to the scene from Naples to join the other two, then called for extra reinforcements in the shape of *Hambledon* and *Blencathra*, so the 'finder' would have been *Tumult* or *Wilton*.

Laforey was commanded by a four-ring Captain of destroyers, called Armstrong, who, as Senior Officer, assumed command of the operation. Because of his hooked nose he was known affectionately as 'Beaky Armstrong'. He also had a keen nose for U-boats. Captain Armstrong, as Captain of the 19th flotilla was well known and well respected. He had had many years of experience in destroyers and, along the way, he had collected a DSO, a DSC and bar. Thus, the scene was set, with five destroyers, all of whose Asdic sets registered a submerged U-boat, and all of whom were keen to ensure that it never again saw the Fatherland. There was a suspicion that this U-boat was probably *Penelope's* killer, in which case there was a score to be settled. Later intelligence proved this not to be so; *Penelope* was torpedoed by U410, but the fact that we did not know that at this time did not make life any easier for our quarry.

Immediately we arrived on the scene, the Asdic operator reported a clear echo. We ran in at speed and placed a diamond pattern of depth-charges, that is, one each from port and starboard throwers simultaneously, and another from the stern trap. The steel canisters each contained 300lb of explosives and, when they detonated, the ship shuddered. There are thuds under the soles of the feet with each explosion as the steel decking expands and contracts, as a tin can does when pressed. Then the shock waves send a shimmer across the surface of the sea, seconds before the columns of water from each explosion shoots high into the air, to hang momentarily before falling back into a broiling sea. We swung around at speed, retraced our steps and repeated the operation. Then Aldis lamp began to flash.

The message from Captain Armstrong was that the U-boat was known to have been submerged over twenty-four hours. Sooner or later she would have to surface for air, so there was no point in wasting depth-charges. *Laforey* had made large inroads into her supply, as had the other two ships, Obviously the U-boat Captain was carrying out a diving and rising routine which, so far, had paid off. In short, Captain Armstrong would be counselling patience and no more depth-charge attacks were to be made. This left *Hambledon* and *Blencathra* with their supplies intact.

At 1800 hrs we were ordered to action stations. At 1830 hrs the guns' crews went below in relays for a quick supper and at 2000 hrs the whole ship's company was back at action stations. Shortly after, the sun began to decline until it stood on the horizon as a blood-red orb, which gradually sank until it had disappeared, leaving a twilight, followed by darkness. The five ships were now steaming slowly in a large circle, the focal point of which held the U-boat. Five Asdic operators were all homed-in on the underwater target, while the Hunter radar operators each had four blips on their screens. When each screen registered a fifth blip, it would be apparent that the U-boat had surfaced. There was no tension amongst the guns' crews. In fact, as the star shells were being taken out of the ready-use lockers and laid out on the upper deck, it might have been no more than a routine exercise. No one doubted that this underwater marauder would not see daylight, nor surface again once it had been put down. Neither was there any sentiment; the Atlantic packs had shown none in their slaughter of our merchant shipping when they were bloated with odds in their favour. None would be shown here.

Towards midnight the sky sported a few stars, and the moon chose to show its face briefly. But the overcast was low, with an abundance of cloud, and the night could be said to be dark. The sea was moderately calm with no swell strong enough to cause any undue movement of the ship, so from a weather viewpoint the setting was perfect. Before sunset, the Asdic operator had reported underwater noises, consistent with some sort of repairs being carried out to damage, probably caused by the depth-charging.

Subsequent interrogation of the survivors from this U-boat revealed her to be U223. Many years after the event I did some research on her. She was originally commanded by Lieutenant Commander Wachter and operated in the Black Sea and North Atlantic. Her record of sinkings and attempted sinkings are as follows:

1943
2 February. Torpedoed the US Army Transport *Dorchester*;
23 February. Finished off two ships torpedoed by another U-boat – U628.

She then transfers to the Mediterranean:

2 October. Sank a ship of 5,000 tons off the Algerian coast.
December. Off the Algerian coast, she missed her targets on 4, 7, 8 and 9 December.
11 December. Torpedoed the British frigate *Cuckmere* but did not sink her. (*Cuckmere* survived the war.)
1944 Change of command. Her present Commanding Officer is Lieutenant Gerlack.
25 January. Off Anzio. Attacked a British corvette without success.

29 January. Fired torpedo at, but missed, a destroyer.
30 January. Missed a landing craft and two tank landing ships.

U223 had achieved only a small measure of success. When she came into commission, the fat days enjoyed by the packs between 1940 and 1942 were over.

Before nightfall, Captain Armstrong signaled to all ships, '*Hambledon* will illuminate when enemy surfaces.' This was a wise precaution because there was no point in all ships firing star shell then, perhaps, in the melee, each ship leaving further illumination to someone else. The position was clear – there was to be one illuminator. At approximately 0100 hrs the Hunter radar operator reported a pirate echo at Green 90. This brought the guns' crews into instant action, with all guns swinging round onto the bearing. 'Alarm green 90, star shell spread commence – commence – commence!'

In seconds, the star shell flares were hanging in the air and, beneath them lay the U-boat, glistening in the light like a huge black cigar. She had surfaced broadside-on to us at a range of approximately 1,500 yds, although bow to stern – that is, travelling in opposite directions. Unless her gun were manned, she presented to us as a non-belligerent target. I placed the horizontal wire of the sight half-way up the conning tower, while Brown placed his vertical wire down the leading edge.

When I yelled, 'Layer target!' Brown pressed the trigger for ranging shots. The gun barked four times and our shells could be seen bursting in the sea on the far side. A slight depression then again, 'Layer target!' and we were plastering the conning tower. I depressed to just above the waterline and Brown – taking the cue – swung to right and left as we raked the hull from stem to stern; then, slight elevation, and we raked the upper deck to preclude the manning of the gun. The after 4 inch gun maintained a steady spread of star shell and seldom less than four flares were hanging over the target throughout the action. The forward 4 inch twins fired repeated salvoes of semi-armour-piercing shells; the forward pom-pom's single stream of dull red tracer was homing-in at an angle from ours, and amidst all the racket could be heard the yammering of the starboard Oerlikon, spitting out its 20mm shells, whose tracer glowed a brilliant white and which hurtled to the target like lethal flying pencils.

Only one gun in the ship remained inactive – the port Oerlikon's arc of fire was obstructed by the foremast and the funnel. The destroyer opposite *Hambledon* on the U-boat's port side was pouring in similar salvoes, while the other three completing the encirclement were all doing likewise. The enemy was trapped in a murderous, merciless crossfire against an adversary bent on paying off old scores – some of several years' standing – and one is left to imagine the horrific inferno that met the crew members as they emerged from the conning tower hatch.

Suddenly a rocket was fired which all ships took to be a surrender signal; there had been no attempt to man the gun, and fire from the five destroyers began to ease off. Then, to our amazement, the U-boat was bathed in brilliant light as one ship switched on her searchlight. The whitish-purple beam was reflected back from the water onto the illuminator and revealed her to be the *Laforey*. What immediately followed highlighted the result of switching the searchlight on, and what could only be seen as the sheer fighting spirit of the Captain and crew of the U-boat.

U223 had been submerged almost thirty hours. Her listening apparatus would tell her of the number of hunting craft above her. She had been repeatedly depth-charged at the commencement of the action, probably damaged, then left to sweat it out until her air would be dank and foul. When she surfaced there seems to have been no mad scramble to evacuate. She would probably come first to periscope depth and it is possible her Captain would see a destroyer broadside-on to his bows and the edge of the light from star shell flares. If he did not, then he would get that information immediately the searchlight was switched on. I believe he would have had little or no conning to do. *Laforey* was so positioned that all that was required was for the order to be given for three torpedoes to be released from the bow tubes straight up the searchlight's beam, which also means that the torpedomen must have been at their stations.

What of *Laforey*? Since *Hambledon* kept up a constant spread of star shells, there was no reason whatsoever for searchlights to be used. If they were, *Laforey*, in her vulnerable position, should have been the last ship to have attempted to use one. *Hambledon* (had she had one) could have done so with impunity, as could her opposite number on the U-boat's port side. I can only guess, therefore, that *Laforey* believed that the U-boat (because of the hammering she had taken), was too badly crippled to retaliate, and had illuminated her by searchlight to administer the coup de grâce. As the torpedoes exploded, there was a blinding flash from *Laforey* and her searchlight went out.

Immediately, firing from the other four ships recommenced, rose to full fury, and at that point figures could be seen spilling out of the conning tower. Her hull must have already been pierced in the initial attack and now, in very short time, she was settling by the stern until her bows came high in the air and she vanished. *Laforey* went down by the bows shortly after. The action had lasted about ten minutes when the last star shell flare went out, leaving complete blackness and an eerie quiet.

The four remaining destroyers now began a rescue operation of survivors. In the area where the U-boat had gone down, tiny red lights were seen at sea level. These we knew to be the small battery-powered lamps worn clipped to the lifebelt, since we ourselves had them. Whistles were also being blown and there were repeated cries of, '*Hilfe!*' (help) from the German survivors. As we drew near, the scramble nets were unfurled and I waited to get my first glimpse of the enemy. A German sailor struck out towards us with a strong crawl stroke. He seized the net, swarmed up it and stood dripping and bewildered on the upper deck. Shortly after, a batch of eight joined him, and they were all conducted aft below decks. At this point the Captain decided that his first duty lay with *Laforey* survivors, so we steamed on to the area where she had gone down.

I read an account of this action from a *Laforey* survivor thirteen years later, who was rescued at 0600 hrs that morning by *Tumult*. He writes, 'It seemed that our destroyers had shoved off without us, but I remembered only too well that we had done the same thing on previous occasions ourselves.' The writer's timing and the ships involved did not agree with my records so I wrote to him pointing out several discrepancies. He replied, admitting I could well be right since his diaries went down with his ship.

Tumult picked him up five hours after *Laforey* was sunk. I can also testify that *Hambledon* had left German survivors in the water expressly to find *Laforey* survivors, and that we steamed in circles slowly for some considerable time to do so. *Tumult* and *Blencathra* were already on the spot when we arrived and had picked up all that were to be found. Despite that, we still continued the search, without success, and only when we were satisfied that the rescue work was completed did we return to find German survivors.

We rescued approximately fourteen Germans and *Blencathra* a smaller number. Neither the Captain of the *Laforey* nor the Captain of U223 survived. Survivors from *Laforey* totaled sixty-five, and 181 of her company perished. One of the survivors, in a letter to a newspaper in 1961, described how, 'a great number managed to get away but either the boilers or two depth-charges left onboard blew up, killing a lot of chaps.'

Two of our prisoners died before we reached Naples and were sewn up in canvas shrouds. At approximately 1100 hrs we were west of the Isle of Capri and the bodies were committed to the deep from the starboard side amidships – not the quarterdeck. I do not recall any prayers being said. Two bare-foot German Officers, each swathed in a blanket, toga fashion, were brought on deck to witness the ceremony. These two German sailors were given a picturesque burial spot in the shelter of the cliffs on the south-western corner of Capri. As the bodies fell with a splash into the blue waters, their Officers sprang to attention and gave the Nazi salute.

At noon we entered Naples harbour from where we had answered the call twenty-six hours previously. During the afternoon we received the following signal:

'From: Flag Officer, Western Italy. To: *Hambledon*
The destruction of U223 this morning was a magnificent example of skillful and determined hunting, and reflects great credit on all who took part. I feel sure you will mourn with me the loss of *Laforey*, the leader of the attack, at the moment of victory'.

From her arrival on the scene to her being torpedoed, *Laforey* had held the U-boat by Asdic for over seventeen hours. It is possible she joined the two other destroyers who were escorting the convoy, then signaled for reinforcements in the shape of *Hambledon* and *Blencathra*. That it was skillful and determined hunting was certainly true but, with the unnecessary loss of *Laforey*, it was something of a pyrrhic victory.

The U-boat was a hated species among British sailors. They viewed any action against enemy surface ships as being a 'clean' fight in which the best side won, and they were only too aware that the Germans would give little quarter. After *Rodney* had poured salvo after salvo into a doomed and crippled *Bismarck*, *Rodney's* Captain had said, 'I can't say I enjoyed this part of the business much, but didn't see what else I could do.'

His remark came because *Bismarck* had stubbornly refused to strike her battle flag. Any sailor could understand these sentiments, as we all admired the German fighting spirit. No-one saw U-boats in that light. Germany had instigated unrestricted U-boat warfare in the First War and had resumed it immediately at the start of the Second. Our own submarine activity, therefore, was seen as enforced retaliation against what the Germans had chosen to do, and all sailors had long memories of the U-boat Atlantic pack activity, which claimed so much shipping and so many lives. U-boats were seen as a pestilence, which had to be stamped out if we were to survive, and sentiment had no place in the matter. Having acquired this outlook during the war, it was long after the cessation of hostilities before I could rid myself of it, and bring myself to acknowledge and admire the fighting spirit shown by the Captain and crew of U223.

Depth-charging destroyers were a regular feature of wartime newsreels and magazines. It was commonly assumed that, once a U-boat had been detected, a few depth-charges would either sink it or force it to the surface to be destroyed by gunfire. The chances of a kill as quickly as that, however, were few. One has only to read Lothar-Günther Buchheim's excellent book on U-boat warfare, 'Das Boot', to get a German perspective. Buchheim himself had served in U-boats. Destroyer and U-boat Captains often spent hour after hour playing cat and mouse, each trying to read the mind of the other, and each trying to predict the other's moves. The truth was that to sink a U-boat, a depth charge had to explode within twenty-five feet of its pressure hull and, as the U-boat had the freedom of three-dimensional movement, this was by no means an easy thing to accomplish. The hedgehog depth charge thrower, which came late in the war, fired banks of rocket-propelled smaller charges from the fo'c'sle to give a much wider spread. But even the hedgehog did not solve the problem. The escorts – destroyers, sloops, corvettes, frigates and trawlers – had to learn endless patience and tenacity, and even then, they were not automatically rewarded with a kill.

The Asdic dome emitted a narrow sound beam in a series of pulses which produced an echo (the 'ping') from any underwater object. It had a range of 3,000 yards and produced an accurate range and bearing. The transmitter could, however, be rendered inaccurate by differing density layers in the sea, particularly in deep Arctic waters. Our escorts in the Murmansk convoys were often bedeviled by these conditions.

Whilst travelling on the surface, the U-boat was a diesel-driven vessel. Submerged, it reverted to being a mobile diving bell which could travel at seven knots for a limited period on its battery-driven engines. It was in the capacity of a diving bell that the U-boat sought to escape destruction, by alternately diving and rising or, where possible, lying doggo on the bottom, beyond the reach of depth-charge explosions. The average maximum setting for our depth-charges up to early 1943 was only 550 feet, and U-boats were capable of submerging to twice that depth. Consequently, U-boat killing was not as easy as many imagined. It was always dangerous.

Chapter 19

Hambledonians Afloat

Less than a month after the new CO joined the ship, we were at Anzio and he had to endure the bad weather and endless patrolling no less than we did. Although I have no proof of it, I believe it would be he who decided that something should be done to raise morale. The point was we were not getting sufficient shore leave to break the monotony and it was all work and no play. I believe also that he would ask the nineteen-year-old Midshipman if he had any ideas, then charge him to set something in motion.

The Midshipman and a Sub-Lieutenant shared a sleeping cabin in the workshop flat, which meant they had to go through the after seamen's mess deck to reach it. Occasionally the 'Middie' would stop in the mess for a chat and, in his comings and goings, must have been amused by the mimicry and quips from the comedians. In March 1944, he drew me aside and asked me if I thought it possible to make use of the talent by getting together a small concert party. Immediately I queried lack of space to perform and lack of props. He said we wouldn't need either; the show could be broadcast from the WT room to all parts of the ship, and all that was needed were written sketches.

I sounded out half a dozen of the boys whom I thought had the most talent, including, of course, Chipeau, who became the star performer. Then I went to work on the sketches and produced them for typing in the ship's office. Since we could read from a script, few rehearsals were required, and, within two weeks of the idea being mooted, we were ready to perform. The ship's best artist drew some cartoon posters and gave them the heading 'Hambledonians Afloat' and, after suitable publicity, the concert party met in the WT room and made the broadcast. We had no idea how it would go. The first sketch was a bit stilted until the members got the idea of coming in on cue and, since I had placed the best sketches later in the programme (with the best one last of all), the early fluffs were forgotten. Similarly, the lads gained confidence as the better material came up and, much to our surprise, it all went with a bang and was received with great enthusiasm. Naturally, nothing succeeds like success, and repeat performances were requested.

I had cast myself as a Robb Wilton-type trawler Skipper, dithering and bumbling his way through a fight with a surfaced U-boat and exchanging shots with his Holman projector. The following day, the Middie said, 'I thought the Captain was going to have an accident at your Robb Wilton sketch. He thought it was the funniest thing he had heard in years.'

We had onboard a very talented jazz pianist, who could sit at a piano and have everyone tapping their feet within seconds. It seemed a pity that such talent was going to waste, so a second-hand piano was purchased in Naples, installed in the wardroom and trundled into the WT room for broadcasting sessions. So now we could have musical items in our concerts and listeners in the various messes could join in the singing.

The next item on the agenda was a ship's magazine. Requests went around the ship for contributions and these came in in a steady stream. I wrote a poem extolling the ship, which I thought was good at the time. Looking at it today, it is so banal and lacking in everything that goes towards making a good poem, that it makes me squirm with embarrassment. Yet the boys did not think so, and the editor thought fit to publish it. The magazine was called *Potmess* (the naval term for stew) and, in the first foreword by the Captain, he said he hoped it would not die a natural death.

When all the material had been sorted and edited, it was typed on stencils, and I went ashore in Naples with the Midshipman, where we ran off the material on a Gestetner, and collated and stapled together about sixty copies. This, too, went down well, and for the next edition I wrote an article called 'The First Lieutenant's Orders'. It was pretty scurrilous – not against the First Lieutenant – but against those who use his name – and I doubted it would be acceptable. Nevertheless, the editor (a Sub-Lieutenant) acting on the maxim 'publish and be damned' included it. When it appeared, the cartoonist had done a sketch of me standing before the Captain as a defaulter and saying cheekily 'Shall get a bowler hat, Sir?'

Unlike our two previous COs, Captain Toone had a well-developed sense of humour and thoroughly enjoyed all the material, both oral and written. In fact, the more scurrilous it was, the more he seemed to enjoy it. In retrospect, it is obvious that there must have been a good rapport between leaders and led, otherwise some of the articles and poems would not have been acceptable. It was never a question of tilting at authority as much as the pricking of pomposity and proving that even naval discipline has its humorous side if one cared to look for it.

Eventually it was decided that we should have a try at a stage show even if it meant putting it on for two nights so that everyone could see it. Little writing was required for this. I merely had to produce a scenario and the rest would be ad libbing. It was to be pure burlesque and the ingenuity of the cast quite surprised me. Sailors are noted for their skills with needle and thread, and the most amazing costumes were fashioned – including wigs for the 'females'. During the first show, the audience comprised all the Officers, with as many ratings as could be accommodated. The second show was an all-rating audience and was more hilarious than the first, since the cast felt more able to let their hair down. By then everyone had seen it and we were thinking of dismantling the props and dispensing with the costumes, when the Midshipman informed me that the Captain had decided to invite guests onboard to see the show the following Sunday evening.

Irving Berlin was touring the war zones with his musical *This is the Army*, and it was showing in the San Carlo Theatre in Naples. The invited guests were Irving Berlin himself and several of his production and administrative staff. I was somewhat sceptical about a sailors' amateur burlesque, with no written dialogue, having any entertainment value for professionals, but it was a 'Royal Command' and, if it flopped – so be it. Chairs were brought down from the wardroom, to be filled by all our own Officers, American Army Officers and – bang in the centre – the man we had all known by name since our childhood. I need have had no qualms; the boys rose to the occasion, and the show was a riot from start to finish,

I had no part in the show. After I had cobbled it together, I took charge of the props, helped the cast to dress and made a few suggestions for changes and so forth. But I was dubbed producer and, much to my horror, when the final laughter had died down and Irving Berlin's PRO had made a short speech of thanks, there was a shout for the producer to reply. I had never made a speech in my life and this was the very last thing I had expected. I hoped that, if I did not appear, the shouting would cease but, of course, it continued and grew in volume. When I finally confronted the audience I was so petrified that my head began to wobble. Fortunately, immediately behind me was a pipe running horizontally through the mess deck, and I jammed the back of my head against it.

I then said the only thing I could think of through my befuddled brain, 'Thank you for doing us the honour. I hope that our show will not prove so popular that the audience-figures will begin to drop in another show, which we hear is being staged in the San Carlo Theatre.' And that was all I said. The Officers of both nations guffawed, Irving Berlin put back his head and roared with laughter, and the sailors hooted and whistled. Pandemonium reigned for so long I was able to make a discreet exit.

When everyone had departed and the stage had been dismantled, we were slinging our hammocks ready to turn in, when the duty Bos'n's Mate came into the mess to tell me my presence was required in the wardroom. There I was introduced by the Captain to Irving Berlin, who said, 'Great show, son! You should be in show business.' It was a courteous pat on the back from a man who had seen sailors entertaining themselves and had entered the spirit of the thing.

Turning to his PRO (a smartly dressed Warrant Officer called Ben Washer) he said, 'Ben, see all these boys in the cast have a drink and give them tickets to our show, and when they come along, give them the best seats in the house.' So, I rounded up the cast for drinks (who all asked for beer and had to be content with gin) and finished up the evening sitting on the edge of the Officers' bath being entertained by Warrant Officer Ben Washer.

It was three weeks before we were able to make use of our tickets, and when we did, we were conducted to the front row of the stalls. As I write this, Irving Berlin is celebrating his hundred and first birthday so, at that time, he would have been fifty-four years of age – just about the time he wrote 'I'm Dreaming of a White Christmas'. There was a drama critic present at our show, and the following was printed in *Potmess* Magazine:

'In one respect, *The Trial of Aggie Weston* staged in the aftermess deck of *Hambledon* on 12 March resembled that well known drama *The Trial of Mary Dugan*, but there the similarity ended! The indictment of Aggie for stowing away on board *Hambledon* and importuning members of the ship's company, provided a riot in burlesque.

From the moment Judge Shoofly Davies, resplendent in rope-stranded wig and tin-lid chain of office, climbed the boxes to his judicial seat, the fun was fast and furious. The accused, veiled of face but exposed of limb, had guilt written all over her and, as most of her was visible, and she persisted in making incriminating asides to the witnesses, the verdict was never in doubt. Judge Davies in fact did not bother to call upon the defending attorney for his final speech but told the jury what verdict they should bring in, and after they had done so, donned the black cap, pronounced sentence, and leaned over in obvious enjoyment to watch it carried out in court.

The moral of the play appears to be that stowaways should keep stowed away, because if they 'expose' themselves, they are for it. Later there were individual turns and community singing. A jolly good get-together. More please!'

Six months after I left the ship, I was given the privilege of seeing my personal file. It is record of a rating's conduct, character, and general efficiency, with a note on any outstanding contribution he has made in his ship or shore establishment. The final entry for *Hambledon* read, 'He has proved a decided asset to this ship's company in amateur theatricals.'

I felt that that was not my most important contribution to the war at sea. Nevertheless, it was the nearest I ever got to being mentioned in dispatches! The Accommodation Officer in Pembroke noticed it and invited me to join the barrack concert party, but since it was an invitation not an order, I declined it, principally because I had no desire to stay in the barracks one day longer than necessary.

Chapter 20

Normandy

When I returned from leave on 19 May the ship was in dry dock which, fortunately, was flooded the following day. When in dry dock, for obvious reasons, the ship's toilet and bathroom facilities cannot be used, neither can 'gash' (rubbish) be thrown overboard. Consequently, all refuse has to be carried ashore, and all toileting and ablutions carried out in dockside facilities, so there is much trekking to and fro over the gangway.

We went down river to Sheerness for a degaussing test, then ammunitioned ship, which took a whole day. On 25 May we went to sea with *Mendip* and *Blencathra* to carry out a four-inch, high-angle practice shoot. We finally left Sheerness at 2000 hrs on 27 May and anchored off the Isle of Wight at 0600 hrs the following morning. For the next week we carried out E-boat patrol off the south coast and, during that time, I managed two runs ashore on the Isle of Wight. The weather was hot and sunny and I enjoyed long walks between Yarmouth, Totland and Alum Bay.

While I had been on leave, people were asking me where the invasion was likely to be, as though I had some inside information. I assumed a landing would be made in France but where on the French coast I knew no more than anyone else. That a cross-Channel invasion was afoot was obvious by the amount of shipping in the area and, on 2 June, tank-landing craft (LCTs) were being loaded in Portsmouth harbour. By the forenoon of 5 June, the slower-moving LCTs and the LCIs (infantry craft) were getting under way until, by night fall, the mass of shipping which had been lying at anchor was noticeably thinned-out. At 2200 hrs we hauled in our anchor and were under way.

With the clocks at double British Summer Time, night was just falling, but it was still light enough to see the size of the armada as we overhauled ship after ship. An hour after we left Portsmouth, the news was broken to us that we were to support a landing to be made in Normandy by the British and Canadian 2nd Army under Montgomery. The distance to the coast off Aromanches was approximately 120 miles, which meant that at 10 knots convoy speed we should arrive at 0930 hrs on D-day, 6 June. There were no incidents during the night but, even in the dark, we were conscious of being surrounded by a huge mass of shipping. Wherever I looked through binoculars, there were ships on every bearing to the horizon.

When dawn came the sight was almost unbelievable, a solid phalanx of ships of every description, seemingly as thick as the traffic in Piccadilly. After Sicily we had expected it; but none of us was quite prepared for the sheer size of it. I felt certain that, no matter what fortifications the Germans had prepared, nothing eventually was going to stop a force like this. It had to be on any reckoning, irresistible and indomitable. There was, too, a feeling of safety in numbers. If German aircraft broke through, which of the hundreds of ships in our area alone were going to be unlucky enough to be hit? Their targets were so prolific they would be spoilt for choice.

Before dawn broke, we could hear gunfire and, as we neared the beachhead at 0930 hrs, bombarding by battleships, cruisers and destroyers was already taking place. The old warrior *Warspite* was there, repaired and back in action, loosing off her 15 inch salvoes. The LSTs were close up to the beach unloading, and all manner of small landing craft were shuttling past us full of men, tanks, guns and lorries. Every conceivable type of purpose-made landing craft and barge could be seen at different times during the day; craft for tanks, assault, flame-throwing, rocket firing, obstruction clearance, anti-aircraft (Landing Craft Flak), emergency repairs and hospital craft for taking off the wounded. Then, there were the amphibious craft, the jeeps and DUKWs (amphibious transport) and (something we had not seen in Sicily) amphibious tanks. Three landings were made from three beaches in the British sector but we knew the Americans were making two further ones to the west. There was far more shipping involved than we could see.

The Americans met more resistance than the British and their landing area was more difficult to negotiate. For our part, we could see no resistance at all; material was pouring ashore and there seemed to be a never-ending stream of infantry craft ferrying in troops. The Luftwaffe did not appear overhead and there was an abundance of allied fighter cover. We had been told during the night that all Allied planes would be painted with white stripes around their wings and fuselages and the only aircraft we saw all day were so marked. It was at Normandy on D-day that I saw my first Mustang fighter come hurtling across the sky and wondered if the Spitfire was now a slow-coach.

During the afternoon we attempted to take in tow a waterlogged assault craft. We got a wire secured to it but had to slip it off quickly because it began to sink. By 1700 hrs, unloaded ships had formed up into a convoy and we were designated as one of the escorts. No less than 221 escorting craft were in use at Normandy – a mixture of destroyers, frigates, corvettes, sloops and trawlers. As we got under way and out into the Channel, the shipping now consisted of fully-laden ships coming in from all over the south coast, with the empty ones making the return journey. They literally ran into thousands, which was why so many escorts were needed.

Although all the German capital ships had been sunk or immobilized there was still the danger from U-boats and E-boats from Le Havre and Cherbourg. We arrived in Plymouth early next morning and tied up to a buoy adjacent to Saltash bridge. The convoy we had escorted dispersed as it drew near the south coast, ships making their way to different ports for re-loading. In the afternoon I was watch ashore and it seemed peculiar to be walking around in Devonport eighteen hours after leaving the Normandy beachhead.

The following afternoon, we escorted the battleship *Nelson* for two hours, then left her to escort a fast assault ship, which already had an escort of four sloops. Shortly after taking up position, one of the sloops had an Asdic contact and fired her 'Hedgehog'. Hedgehogs were banks of rocket-launched small depth-charges, fired ahead of the ship from the fo'c'sle. We also picked up an echo and fired a diamond pattern. However, we did not stay hanging around but hared off after the assault ship, leaving two sloops to continue the Asdic sweep.

In the small hours of next morning, the long convoy we had joined was attacked by a pack of eight E-boats, and two LSTs were torpedoed, one of which burned fiercely. We fired star shells into where we assumed the attack had come, and our assumptions proved correct; but the E-boats laid a smoke screen before attacking through it and retreated behind it after launching their torpedoes.

At 0900 hrs, we dropped anchor in the American sector and remained there all day. Bombarding was taking place by heavy American naval units, and during the night enemy aircraft attacked the shore rather than shipping in the harbour. The following night, we went on E-boat patrol with the sloop *Hind* and frigate *Broxbourne* and for the next few days we alternated between patrolling during the night and convoying during the day. There was much E-boat activity during the hours of darkness, with groups of between five and ten trying hard to break through the escort to get at the convoy. Reports were coming to us from other escorts and star shells were seen on different bearings. We even had an aircraft reporting having seen a pack of nineteen, but the convoys to and from the beachhead were well protected to the extent that the E-boats were later to try almost do-or-die tactics. The U-boats were also trying hard to get through the escort screen.

On 14 June we left Plymouth at 1930 hrs to escort a large convoy with *Hind*, *Broxbourne* and *Magpie*, the latter commanded by the Duke of Edinburgh post-war. At 2300 hrs, *Hind* had an Asdic contact and began depth-charging. We also picked up a contact and dropped several patterns, losing contact shortly after. *Hind* reported diesel oil on the surface and took samples, and though both ships continued sweeping till 0300 hrs, there was no further contact and we rejoined the convoy, arriving off the beachhead at 1130 hrs. This convoying from the south coast to Normandy was to continue for several more weeks and in that time, we saw the Mulberry Harbour being constructed. We had seen the concrete caissons being towed out soon after D-Day and as we went back and forth, we could see the jetty getting longer and longer until finally it was in use with ships berthed alongside it.

Mines dropped by aircraft at night continued to be a menace. On 18 June, we arrived off the beachhead at 1000 hrs and by 1030 hrs we were sent full speed to find an infantry assault ship which had struck a mine on her way back in convoy. We found her under tow during the afternoon and escorted her to Portsmouth. Mines became such a menace that we had to resume our East Coast practice of clearing lower deck and battening down through areas known to have been mined. On 2 July, a large liner we had escorted in to the beaches struck a mine on the way back and sank at 1800 hrs.

On 4 July, one of our charges was *Ulster Monarch*, the ship that had been bombed off Cape Bon. In the same convoy the following day, a mine-sweeping trawler, about a mile astern of us, struck a mine and blew up. I was watching her steaming serenely along when there was a terrific explosion, a cloud of smoke, and she had disappeared in less than a minute, leaving four survivors. The shock of the explosion touched off another mine uncomfortably close on our port side, so once more we cleared lower deck and battened down, and the convoy was diverted. The infantry assault ships had been ordered to do likewise and their upper decks were lined with soldiers who were, no doubt, feeling apprehensive.

We escorted the convoy to the beachhead, arriving at 1600 hrs. At 1700 hrs we were on our way back with another convoy, which was formed up in line ahead to lessen the danger from mines. To no avail; at 2030 hrs, when just clear of the anchorage, an American merchantman struck yet another mine. There was no visible damage but she had a definite list astern when we left her, with three escorts standing by. Later we heard three enemy aircraft had been shot down by AA fire the previous night, while in the act of mine-laying.

That same night we received a signal from *Brissenden* who had a U-boat contact in a position twenty-two miles from us. Later came another signal, 'Am still attacking, nearly expended charges.' We fully expected being called to take over, but there must have been other escorts in closer proximity. The convoying and patrolling went on, with escorts determined to keep the convoys clear of marauders.

One little incident cheered us up enormously when leaving Plymouth to meet a convoy off Portsmouth. During the evening of 7 July, just outside Plymouth, we met a Tribal class destroyer coming in. Naturally all binoculars were on her pennant numbers and the lookout reported her as F51. Immediately she was recognized as *Ashanti* and, as we drew abreast of her, there was John Barnes on the bridge, doing a very un-officer-like thing. In his excitement at seeing *Hambledon* for the first time since relinquishing command of her, he was jumping up and down, waving his cap around his head in circles. We could see the gold braid on its peak – the 'scrambled eggs' he had acquired after leaving us. John Barnes would of course, have heard of *Hambledon s* role in the Italian Fleet's surrender and would, no doubt, be intrigued. *Ashanti* herself had done sterling work escorting Russian convoys, and we were all more than surprised to see her off the south coast. It was only later that we learned she had recently had a running fight, in company with the Polish destroyer *Piorun*, against seven German minesweepers.

The ships were sighted between the Channel Islands and the Brittany coast and *Ashanti* and *Piorun* gave chase, opening fire at 3,000 yards, with the enemy scattering, seeking shelter under the Jersey coastal batteries. The outcome was three ships sunk, one in difficulties and probably sunk and, of the remaining three, two were stopped and burning fiercely when *Ashanti* and *Piorun* withdrew. So, John Barnes had given a good account of himself in several ways since assuming command of *Ashanti*.

We had heard of the V1 flying-bombs falling on London. The first one arrived on 15 June – but we had never actually seen one until 15 July. We were returning from Aromanches and I had the middle watch (midnight to 0400 hrs). It appeared as a bright star in the distant sky and seemed to approach very slowly, getting brighter as it drew nearer. I followed its course through binoculars and could make out no shape – only a flame like a blow-lamp. As it drew nearer its speed seemed to increase; the noise it made sounded like a deep-toned, two-stroke engine. There were two, the second following quickly after the first, and both were travelling in the direction of Southampton. AA fire on the coast brought one down, and we saw it explode in mid-air as it crossed the coastline. The second was illuminated by searchlight as it flew inland, and seemed to explode on the ground. We had seen our first 'doodlebug.'

At 0930 hrs that morning we arrived in Plymouth and I was a Captain's requestman, having made up my mind at last to do something about promotion. My request to take a higher gunnery course was granted, which meant I could be released when a replacement arrived onboard. This happened sooner than I expected. We commenced a boiler clean on 19 July, and the ship's company was given six days' leave. Two days after my arrival back from leave, my relief turned up, and I left *Hambledon* on 28 July, after having served in her for three years and two months,

The way had been open for me to take a higher gunnery course any time after becoming an Able Seaman (AB) in November 1941, certainly in May 1943, before we left for the Med. But I have never for an instant regretted hanging on for our eleven months with the Mediterranean Fleet. In July 1944, however, it was obvious to us all that the Navy's war in the west was as good as over. It had been fought since the day war was declared when the signal went round the fleet, 'Winston is back.' Now our armies were well established ashore, and the fight was going to be all military, with RAF support.

Like everyone else, I assumed the Navy's war would switch to the Far East, and I could not see *Hambledon* going there. In short, I felt she had had her day, and the rest would be routine so, I'm almost ashamed to say, I abandoned her. I did set foot aboard her twice more, once when she came into Chatham dockyard in 1945 and again when she visited Cuxhaven in 1946. The fact was, I had seen all the Officers change entirely and outstayed most of the original ship's company, so I had few qualms about leaving. Six days after I left, one of our 16th Flotilla Hunts, the *Quorn*, was sunk off Normandy by an explosive motor boat.

In the plethora of books and endless debates about the Normandy invasion, there has been much speculation as to what might have been, such as enemy troops and Panzer divisions being held back against an expected landing across the Straits of Dover and Hitler's misguided strategies, which culminated in high command quarrels between Von Runstedt and Rommel, the Germans' difficulty in getting reinforcements through by road and rail due to allied air strafing; all of which seems to be begging the question. Normandy was a classic piece of planning by all three arms of the allied forces which was a resounding success. Naturally, in planning of this scale, mistakes were made and things did go wrong, but the fact remains that the armies were put ashore and stayed ashore, and it was the beginning of the end. The enemy must have known so when the dawn of 6 June revealed the tremendous size of the armada standing off the Normandy beaches.

The course of the fighting after 6 June fell almost entirely on upon the German Army. No enemy capital ships were left in service, and the Luftwaffe in the west was a spent force. The only two problems facing the Navy after D-day were U-boats and mines. The latter did cause much ship damage and sinkings, but far too many ships were involved for mining activity seriously to hamper the flow of material. As for the U-boats, eighteen of the forty-three deployed off Normandy had been sunk within a month of D-day and, by the end of August 1944, Admiral Doenitz had decided that overall losses were no longer acceptable.

All the operating flotillas were, therefore, recalled and U-boat warfare discontinued. The loss of life of U-boat crews was greater, pro rata, than any other arm of service of all the Second War's combatant forces. Considering that over 5,000 ships and craft of various types were involved at Normandy, losses were relatively few. The allied navies had deployed 138 bombarding warships, 287 minesweepers, 495 light craft and 441 auxiliaries. In addition, the 221 convoy escorts of destroyers, corvettes, sloops and Asdic trawlers thrown around the endless convoys had effectively screened them from the marauding U-boats and E-boats to the point where no sustained penetration had been possible. The World, hopefully, will never see an invasion of that magnitude again, and I feel privileged to have been fortunate enough to have seen it and to have played a small part in it.

Although I did not realize it at the time, my sea war was over when I left *Hambledon*. Even had I gone back to sea after completing the training I was going ashore to do, it would only have been for seven months before the dropping of the two atomic bombs on Japan ended the war. I have recalled what life was like on a destroyer in wartime – the discomfort, the living conditions, the comradeship, the action. I realize that I have said little about my feelings and emotions regarding the loss of life, and while under attack.

There were times when the loss of life of my fellow-countrymen upset me emotionally to the point of making me almost physically sick, putting me off my food and depressing me for long periods after the event. Yet I could never shrink from what I saw as having to be done, and conditioned myself into seeing enemy aircraft and war vessels as infernal machines which had to be destroyed, and men as unfortunate to be involved with them. The self-preservation instinct was also, of course, involved, in that if you did not destroy the enemy, he would destroy you. Another strong emotion was retaliation. On seeing the loss of life of one's own countrymen in other ships lost to enemy action, one tended to wish to seek retribution almost as an act of keeping faith. I think it is also a fact that involvement in fighting becomes, after a time, a way of life. It is deplorable but true, that the only difference between one way of life and another is the degree of risk involved. All of us had been switched from doing one thing to doing another, and what was at first perhaps unpleasant and unpalatable eventually became a natural lifestyle.

And, if to be fearless is to be a hero, then I was no hero, because there were times when I was very frightened. One of the largest convoys ever sent to Russia was continuously bombed for four days, and many ships were sunk. There was a *Reuter*'s correspondent onboard the cruiser *Scylla*, flagship of Rear Admiral R.L. Burnett. When it was all over the Admiral said to the journalist, 'Well, Reuter, were you frightened?' He replied, 'Yes, very, sometimes'. 'So was I.' said the Admiral, 'and anyone who says he wasn't is a bloody fool.'

The infernal jangling of the action stations alarm bell stopped me dead in my tracks for the split second before the adrenaline began to flow, to send me scurrying to action stations with a pounding heart. The self-preservation instinct is so strong that the fearless must needs have some sort of death-wish which is not present in the vast majority.

As a gunnery rating, I was always very conscious of my part in the ship's defence. This had been instilled in the gunnery school in various ways, including getting it across poetically. The following is from memory; at this distance in time it may not be word-perfect, but it is very near the mark:

> 'If you can keep your head in heat of action,
> And calmly ply the principles you know.
> If cannon, shell and bomb prove no distraction,
> Because your mind is bent upon the foe.
> If you can match the battle's fateful minute,
> With stout heart and a well-directed gun,
> The victory is yours, you're bound to win it,
> And which is more, you'll save your ship, my son.'

There was a verse preceding it which I cannot now recall, but corny as it seems, the ditty (appearing in a booklet on eye-shooting, together with cartoons) had its effect on me. It left me in no doubt about my responsibility and I feel sure that gave me grace under pressure to come to terms with fear and subdue it. I could pin-point the occasions where – like the proverbial cat – I had used up at least six of my nine lives. So, I came ashore hugging the remaining three to my breast, to be taken to a Far-East war that did not materialize.

E-boat chasing could be thrilling and exciting, and we became so skilled at it – plus the fact that it was fast and furious while it lasted – that the fear element was swamped by elation. Asdic sweeping could be a monotonous soul-destroying business, which only came alive when a 'ping' was reported.

And as no-one expects to be torpedoed (it is always other ships that are unlucky – never yourselves), the fear element is reduced to a nagging anxiety, up to the point when the torpedo strikes.

Air attack was frightening from start to finish. Psychologically, the aircraft has the advantage if only because of its speed and the fact that he is the instigating attacker, whereas you are fighting-off his attack. Even today, the screaming of RAF fighters, (coming as they do from nowhere, without warning, and hurtling past) sets my heart racing, and there is a vivid recall of events even though they happened nearly half a century ago.

I was fortunate in getting a ship which proved to have a charmed life. *Hambledon* was not a super fleet destroyer. Compared with destroyers such as the Lightnings, the Tribals and the J and K classes, the Hunts were lacking speed and firepower. But they were attractive ships and had an aura about them all their own. Many writers of war time memoirs seem inevitably to refer to them as the 'little' Hunts, and it is a term of affection. They were hard-hitting as well as hard-worked, and their presence was always welcome in any convoy.

When several of the Hunts were sold to foreign navies after the war, I imagine *Hambledon* would not have been a saleable proposition. Apart from the mine damage she had sustained, she had put in an inordinate amount of sea time, and had suffered too many bumps and near misses to be attractive to buyer. In a way I am pleased about that; pleased that only British sailors trod her decks. Most of the Hunts that were not sold were scrapped in the late 1950s. *Hambledon* was scrapped on the Tyne in 1957 and perhaps that was fitting in that she was built there. Today, there are Hunt class minesweepers and I suppose the class will always be perpetuated in some form or other, if only because the fox hunt is so thoroughly English.

Among the many other ships that were eventually scrapped was *Warspite*, arguably the most successful of the last war's battleships, certainly the best known. When she was sold for scrap in 1947 she broke her tow on the way to the breaker's yard and was wrecked off Mount's Bay. It was almost as though she considered herself worthy of something better than the ignominy of the scrap dealers blow torch; and of course she was. What a pity she could not have been preserved as a floating museum, an example of one of the last of the big ships as the cruiser *Belfast* has been preserved.

The 16th Flotilla played a commendable role in the war and had its share of travail. Of its nine destroyers, *Hambledon, Cotswold* and *Quorn* all suffered mine damage and *Quorn* was eventually sunk off Normandy. *Makay, Whitshed* and *Worcester* (with the two Sheerness destroyers) were the only warships to face the German fleet in its Channel dash, during which *Worcester* earned all our admiration. Later, *Makay, Worcester* and *Windsor* all acted as escorts to Russian convoys. Then *Hambledon* went to the Med and stole all the headlines from under the noses of the Med fleet. All this was in addition to the flotilla's everyday task of playing its part in getting the east coast convoys through. Yet there was nothing really outstanding in all this. Other flotillas had the same experiences, and some suffered worse casualties. Naturally, every man would tend to view his flotilla as being better than any other and that made for esprit de corps. But in his heart of hearts, he knew that any other flotilla would, if the need arose, show the same fortitude and equal, if not surpass, his own.

On What Evidence?

Making the Case in Medical Decision-Making

ROBYN BLUHM
MARK TONELLI

OXFORD
UNIVERSITY PRESS

Oxford University Press is a department of the University of Oxford.
It furthers the University's objective of excellence in research, scholarship,
and education by publishing worldwide. Oxford is a registered trade mark of
Oxford University Press in the UK and in certain other countries.

Published in the United States of America by Oxford University Press
198 Madison Avenue, New York, NY 10016, United States of America.

© Oxford University Press 2025

All rights reserved. No part of this publication may be reproduced, stored in a retrieval system,
transmitted, used for text and data mining, or used for training artificial intelligence, in any form or
by any means, without the prior permission in writing of Oxford University Press, or as expressly
permitted by law, by license or under terms agreed with the appropriate reprographics rights
organization. Inquiries concerning reproduction outside the scope of the above should be sent to
the Rights Department, Oxford University Press, at the address above.

You must not circulate this work in any other form
and you must impose this same condition on any acquirer.

CIP data is on file at the Library of Congress.

ISBN 9780197503836

DOI: 10.1093/9780197503867.001.0001

Printed by Marquis Book Printing, Canada

The manufacturer's authorized representative in the EU for product safety is
Oxford University Press España S.A. of Parque Empresarial San Fernando de Henares,
Avenida de Castilla, 2 – 28830 Madrid (www.oup.es/en or product.safety@oup.com).
OUP España S.A. also acts as importer into Spain of products made by the manufacturer.

Contents

Introduction	1
1. A Brief History of Medical Knowledge	8
2. Evidence-based Medicine	31
3. Knowledge of Mechanism and Pathophysiologic Reasoning	59
4. Experiential Knowledge	85
5. Patient Values	112
6. Case-based Reasoning	137
References	161
Index	170

Introduction

Dr. Lee's first appointment of the afternoon looked to be challenging. Mr. Jackson was a frequent visitor to the general medicine outpatient clinic, primarily because he was not feeling better. His problem list was extensive, a litany of the most common chronic maladies afflicting Americans of a certain age: Type II diabetes, hypertension, hyperlipidemia, coronary artery disease (CAD), congestive heart failure (CHF), chronic obstructive pulmonary disease (COPD), and a chronic pain syndrome. And his presenting complaint was always the same; he simply felt bad. Bad, for Mr. Jackson, meant some combination of fatigue, malaise, dyspnea, and pain. Mr. Jackson felt unable to do the things that he wanted to do; he was not living the life he wanted to live. Trying to deal appropriately with Mr. Jackson's medical issues always took time, meaning that the rest of the afternoon's visits would end up starting late. On top of that, Dr. Lee had a medical student shadowing her today, meaning she would have to explain her clinical reasoning.

Dr. Lee was committed to practicing evidence-based medicine (EBM). This obligation required that she apply the best available evidence, meaning the results of rigorous clinical research, to decisions around the treatment of her patients. For Mr. Jackson, living up to this commitment was particularly difficult. The number of research studies and clinical practice guidelines that might reasonably apply to Mr. Jackson was staggering and often conflicting. Guidelines for COPD were developed using research subjects who did not have CAD, and vice versa. Moreover, treating his hypertension and hyperlipidemia might decrease his risk of cardiovascular complications in the long term, but did nothing to make him feel better in the short term. In fact, the medications for these diagnoses appeared to make him feel worse. Attempts by Dr. Lee and her colleagues to adhere to practice guidelines meant that Mr. Jackson was now prescribed over a dozen different medications. Some, like an oral beta-blocker for his heart failure and an inhaled beta-agonist for his COPD, appeared to work in direct opposition to one another. The medical student would almost certainly ask about that.

While multi-morbidity like Mr. Jackson's is not at all uncommon in clinical practice, the combinations and interplay between diseases have proven to be particularly challenging for clinical researchers. And despite Dr. Lee's well-intentioned attempts to apply the knowledge gained from clinical research to Mr. Jackson's care, that approach was failing. Mr. Jackson was, in fact, back in the clinic with the same complaints, feeling too weak, tired, and short of breath to even take care of himself, much less to get out to work in his garden, to visit friends and family, to travel.

Dr. Lee knew that being an evidence-based practitioner did not mean that she should be slavishly devoted to following clinical practice guidelines, to practicing "cookbook" medicine. EBM allowed and even encouraged her to integrate her individual clinical expertise with the best available results of clinical research in order to make decisions for particular patients. But, practically, how was she supposed to do that? Her clinical expertise in large part derived from her experience taking care of patients, yet she had learned early on that primary clinical experience was an unreliable guide. In medical school and residency, she had learned how to carefully and critically evaluate research methodologies and statistical analyses, but no one had ever really taught her anything about integrating her clinical expertise into her practice. And if she could not articulate how she was reasoning, her medical student would be no wiser either. For Mr. Jackson to have any chance of improving, she knew that she would need to bring more knowledge to bear than that derived from clinical research. She would need to rely on her personal experience, her understanding of pathophysiology, and, perhaps most importantly, on a more intimate understanding of Mr. Jackson himself.

Dr. Lee, like every physician in virtually every clinical scenario, was facing the "integration problem." The integration problem stems from the widely acknowledged fact that the results of clinical research, even of the highest quality, can never be prescriptive regarding the care of individual patients. Providing the best care for Mr. Jackson required augmenting the knowledge provided by clinical research with other kinds of knowledge, and maybe even acknowledging that clinical research might not be the "best" guide at all. While a practical problem for clinicians, the challenges posed by integration are, at their heart, philosophical in nature. Solving this integration problem requires, at a minimum, understanding of how clinicians gain and demonstrate expertise, what kinds of medical knowledge can legitimately be brought to bear in practice, and how knowledge of individual patients should be obtained and considered in clinical decision making. Dr. Lee, in striving to provide the best care for Mr. Jackson and her other patients, needed to better understand how to optimally utilize all of her medical knowledge. A clearer understanding of the process of clinical judgment would also make her a better teacher, both for her students and for her patients.

Tackling the integration problem requires analyzing the problem philosophically. Matters related to knowledge—to its production, value, and proper use—fall under the philosophical subject area of epistemology. And while clinicians will not typically have formal training in epistemology, anyone engaged in the evidence-based medicine movement, as promoter, teacher, or practitioner, has assumed and adopted certain epistemic claims. EBM assesses, ranks, and orders medical knowledge and provides a basic framework for clinicians attempting to apply that knowledge. The EBM movement represents, at its core, a school of medical epistemology. The integration problem represents an epistemic complication of EBM, although the fundamental issues regarding the relative value of different kinds of medical knowledge have been part of medicine since its inception. Disagreements regarding the reliability and value of various kinds of medical knowledge also provided the impetus for the development of EBM. Incorporating the work of clinicians and philosophers of medicine, both supportive and critical of EBM, this book examines that history, analyzes the assumptions and conflicts still ongoing, and offers a potential solution for the integration problem.

We begin, in Chapter 1, with a brief historical overview that introduces the various kinds of knowledge relevant to medicine and explains when and how they became important to clinical practice. We suggest that medicine, prior to the late 20th century, has gone through three "epistemological eras," dominated respectively by medical theory, by clinical observations, and by laboratory research. With the start of each new era, we see similar patterns of devaluing (rightly or for ill) the knowledge that characterizes the older era, and of a spectrum of responses to new knowledge from uncritical adoption through to a refusal to adopt new ideas and practices. It takes time for the actual value of a new approach in medicine to be determined.

Chapter 2 introduces a fourth epistemological era—our current era of evidence-based medicine. The chapter starts with a discussion of the development, evolution, and persistent challenges of EBM. We will examine the early and sustained criticisms raised by clinicians and philosophers, the responses of proponents of EBM, and the development of EBM into its current form. We look at the kinds of clinical research preferentially valued by EBM. These study designs, derived from epidemiology, aim to identify factors that affect an outcome of interest in a large population, whether that factor is a therapeutic intervention or an environmental, biological, or demographic factor. Given our focus in this book on treatment decisions, we mainly discuss the randomized controlled trial (RCT), which aims to evaluate the efficacy of an intervention. These studies are designed to look for a statistical association between an intervention and a specific outcome of interest, with the discovery of such an association viewed as a necessary condition of a more meaningful claim, an attempt to determine causality.

Central to this chapter will be the observation that, while it has evolved in response to criticism, EBM still has not solved the "integration problem." That is, while EBM arguably provides a useful framework for assessing the quality of clinical research and an approach to answering general clinical questions, it does not yet provide comprehensive guidance for practicing clinicians treating individual patients. EBM currently instructs clinicians to integrate the results of their appraisal of the evidence with their clinical expertise without providing any instructions or framework for doing so. The dominance of EBM in medicine and the "hierarchy of evidence" actually prevent the integration problem from being taken as seriously as it should. In order to help address the integration problem, Chapters 3 to 5 look closely at various additional kinds of medical knowledge, focusing in particular on their value in clinical decision making. These include knowledge of physiological mechanisms (Chapter 3), direct clinical experience (Chapter 4), and knowledge of patients' values (Chapter 5).

The insistence of EBM that clinical research provides the "best" evidence in medicine has led to the devaluing of mechanistic reasoning and experiential knowledge in all aspects of medicine. We will examine and expound upon the continued value of these two kinds of general medical knowledge for clinical decision making. In contrast with population-level clinical research, research on mechanisms (Chapter 3) examines *how* a factor of interest produces an outcome. These studies are often conducted in animals, though human research that focuses on elucidating physiological understanding rather than on clinical outcomes may also be considered mechanistic research. Research on physiological mechanisms provides clinicians with a pathophysiologic understanding of health, disease, and illness, an understanding that is relevant to clinical judgment.

Both epidemiological and physiological knowledge are founded primarily upon scientific investigations. By contrast, clinicians develop a wealth of experiential knowledge gained through hands-on training and clinical practice, which we discuss in Chapter 4. This knowledge provides clinicians with a rich set of source cases and underlies the expertise that EBM proponents note is necessary for integrating knowledge gained from epidemiologic research. Although there is a robust scientific literature on the development of clinical experience, it focuses almost entirely on diagnostic reasoning and so does not tell us much about how to integrate different kinds of knowledge in making treatment decisions. A small, recent set of papers that extends this research to what the authors call "management reasoning," which, along with theories of expertise, helps define the contribution of primary experience to therapeutic decision making.

In Chapter 5, we focus on the importance of knowledge of particular patients in order to make clinical decisions that benefit those individuals. Within the EBM framework, the most important thing to know about an individual patient is whether they would have been included in a specific clinical trial or meet the basic criteria for guideline application. As EBM advanced, it has acknowledged that the goals and values of individual patients needed to be taken into consideration, but as with other aspects of the integration problem, EBM itself has little to say regarding how that should take place.

Looking beyond EBM in both medicine and philosophy of medicine, several alternative approaches have been proposed that provide a broader, more humanistic context for clinical practice. What these frameworks share is the belief that understanding the patient as a person, rather than just understanding their physical state or their relationship to inclusion/exclusion criteria of clinical trials, is central to medical practice. This understanding goes beyond simply incorporating an individual's preferences and goals into clinical decision making. In Chapter 5, we survey these different approaches to incorporating patients' values, experience, and perspectives in clinical decision-making. We argue that, while they raise important issues with regard to the limits of a purely biomedical model, none of them is able to solve the integration problem. Each of these approaches focuses on understanding a patient's values and circumstances but stops short of showing how this understanding informs clinical judgment.

As part of Chapter 5, we briefly examine a number of different conceptual models and methods, including decision analysis and values-based practice, that have been proposed to describe the kind of judgment physicians use in making clinical decisions. These face the challenge, realized or not, of balancing the perceived strengths and validity of knowledge gained from scientific methods with the necessity of incorporating experiential knowledge and knowledge of particulars to arrive at an individualized clinical judgment. We agree with the general approach of trying to utilize the totality of knowledge regardless of kind. This epistemic pluralism is central to optimal clinical practice and is a necessary condition of any attempt to solve the integration problem. We argue, however, that none of the conceptual models discussed have been able to provide clinicians with a coherent and workable model of clinical decision making.

In Chapter 6, we propose a solution to the integration problem in the form of case-based reasoning. A case-based approach provides the clinician with an explicit model that aids in making specific clinical decisions, a framework that will resonate with practitioners as it values their background knowledge and experience. Case examples, including Mr. Jackson's, provide an opportunity to see how case-based reasoning helps reach decisions that fit with the considered judgment of clinicians, even when, at times, appearing to run counter to choices mandated by simple reliance on the results of clinical research. We conclude by summarizing the rationale supporting an explicit and original case-based framework that provides a solution to the integration problem.

While this book necessarily employs some philosophical terminology and methods of argumentation, it does not presume the reader has a background in philosophy. While we believe the arguments contained here will survive critical philosophical scrutiny, the book is written for clinicians, those people for whom the integration problem is real and immediate. This book is for people like Dr. Lee, who want only to provide the best care for individual patients, care that serves those patients, not simply complies with external mandates. And this book is for medical educators, those searching for a way to explain and teach sound clinical judgment, preventing the next generation of clinicians from relying upon "cookbook" medicine. Over the last two decades, the work of philosophers of medicine has advanced our understanding of clinical medicine, but that work has had little impact on clinical practice. While we do not endorse the Galenic ideal that all physicians ought to be philosophers (nor that philosophers become physicians), we believe that a basic understanding of epistemology will allow clinicians to more effectively use all that they know for the benefit of their patients. We believe that bringing some philosophy of medicine into the practice of medicine will benefit clinicians, educators, students of medicine, and patients alike.

1
A Brief History of Medical Knowledge

Even as Dr. Lee enters the examination room, her assessment of Mr. Jackson has begun. He looks tired and defeated. She will start with some open-ended questions, listening carefully to his symptoms, searching for recognizable patterns. She will listen to his heart and his lungs, look at his ankles and hands. She will review his laboratory testing and a recent chest X-ray done during an emergency room visit. She will try to make sense, medical sense, of what she hears and sees. All the while, she will be making clinical decisions, regarding what to ask next, what to advise and recommend. Fundamentally, she will do what clinicians have done since the dawn of clinical medicine, combining skilled observation and reasoning in an attempt to benefit her patient. But Dr. Lee will be working with new tools and tests, as well as an expansive base of medical knowledge and reams of information unavailable to her predecessors. The very kinds of medical knowledge and reasoning she will use have also developed and evolved over time. While her clinical practice rests upon a long history, she will be operating with a set of epistemic assumptions that is relatively new.

In modern medical practice, there is a basic template for what happens when someone gets sick and seeks medical help. They present to a clinician (physician, advanced practice provider, nurse, therapist) who listens to them describe their symptoms, asks clarifying questions, and does a physical examination. Additional tools may be used to measure physiological characteristics that cannot be directly observed with accuracy, like temperature, blood pressure, and oxygen saturation, augmenting the physical exam. Depending on the symptoms and the information gleaned from the physical exam, additional laboratory, radiographic, or functional testing may be pursued. In the current era, the patient will be informed of any proposed diagnostic or therapeutic interventions and, at a minimum, will have the opportunity to consent to or decline them. In more complex situations, the clinician may discuss with the patient the different courses of action available at a given point in the process of diagnosis and treatment and then work with the patient to help them choose the course that is best for them. In this era of EBM, decisions, particularly regarding treatment, will typically be informed by the results of clinical research that examines the efficacy and safety of those interventions.

Throughout this process, the clinician seeks and obtains the information they need to best care for the patient. The specific information required will change depending on the nature of the patient's problem, but this basic scenario characterizes, with few exceptions, modern clinical medicine.

It has not always been this way. While obtaining a history and doing some sort of physical assessment goes back to the beginning of clinical medicine, the information, both general and specific to individual patients, that clinicians require to make medical decisions has changed significantly over time. By this, we don't simply mean that—because we know so much more about the causes of disease and their pathophysiology, and because we have many more and better treatment options available than we used to have—contemporary doctors need to know more than previous generations of physicians. Although this is true, it vastly oversimplifies the changes that have occurred in what *counts* as medical knowledge and in our understanding of why different kinds of knowledge are important.

Our purpose in this chapter is to introduce some recurring questions and debates that are central to our understanding of how medical knowledge is derived and used. In philosophical terms, questions about how clinicians acquire and employ knowledge are ultimately questions about medical epistemology, or theory of knowledge. Although we introduce them through a historical approach, these epistemic issues have been enduring and remain highly relevant to current practice. We first introduce two central tensions in medical epistemology: (1) Between rationalist versus empiricist approaches to medical knowledge, and (2) between knowledge of general scientific claims and knowledge of individual patients. We then present a brief historical overview of three different eras of medical epistemology, demonstrating how these tensions played out at different times. In these different eras, different kinds of medical knowledge (theory, clinical observation, laboratory research) have been emphasized. Each of these eras had a particular way of understanding the relationship between rationalism and empiricism, and each had its own view on the question of how general knowledge should be used to treat the individual patient. Seeing how these kinds of knowledge have been understood to contribute to medical practice will be essential to our analysis of what contemporary clinicians need to know and how they should utilize that knowledge.

Rationalism and empiricism

The first distinction that we will introduce is that between rationalism and empiricism. In philosophy, "rationalism" and "empiricism" refer to two opposing views on the source of knowledge: Rationalism is the view that all knowledge ultimately comes from theoretical reasoning, while empiricism sees knowledge as fundamentally deriving from experience. Within medicine, these basic definitions hold, but both the concepts and the relationship between them are more complicated.

Since the beginnings of Western clinical medicine in ancient Greece, medical thinking has incorporated both rationalist and empiricist commitments. Throughout medical history, various schools of medicine, at times in competition with one another, have adopted more rational or more empiricist frameworks. At times, one of the views has been dominant in medical thinking. The Oxford English Dictionary, for instance, notes the historical medical definition of "empiric" as a "quack," attesting to the dominance of rationalism in European medicine in the 17th–18th centuries. Yet thinking of the tension between the two ideas in terms of something like a switch, shifting from one extreme to the other, is a bit too simple. Medical thought has generally incorporated some aspects of both rationalism and empiricism.

Moreover, the meaning of the two terms has not been constant. Both "rationalism" and "empiricism" have meant different things at different times—and even at the same time—and these shifts in meaning also affect how the relationship between the two concepts has been understood. For example, to say that something is rational means simply that it is "grounded in good reasons" or "reasonable," so that something that is not rational is irrational, meaning unsupported by good evidence and reasoning. Oddly, as we will show, some forms of rationalism have been quite irrational in this sense. At other times, the term is used to refer to detailed explanations of *how* a phenomenon (e.g., a disease or a response to a treatment) comes to occur. This second use contrasts with the idea that empiricism is concerned only with *what* happens, or *whether* a phenomenon occurs. On these definitions, someone strongly committed to empiricism might believe that what matters is that a diagnostic test predicts a patient's clinical state, or that a treatment improves this condition; knowing the biological explanation for why they do so is unimportant. But for others, that is not enough.

"Empiricism" has perhaps even a more convoluted and confusing series of meanings within medicine. In current medical usage, treating a condition "empirically" typically implies treating without knowing much about the underlying condition (e.g., empiric antibiotics for a fever) and the phrase implies doing the best thing possible under these less-than-optimal circumstances. The sense that this approach is second best also reflects the historical use of "empiric" as a term denigrating health care providers who were not physicians and lacked a physician's theoretical knowledge. Contrast that with the demand for "empirical evidence" expressed by those embracing evidence-based medicine to get a sense of just how confused this language has become. The notion of "empirical evidence" more closely adheres to the philosophical sense of the term, as evidence based on careful observation. Here, will strive to use "empirical" and "rational" in their more formal, philosophical senses.

General knowledge and knowledge of individuals

The second distinction we will trace is the relationship between general knowledge and knowledge of particulars. This epistemic distinction and the challenges arising from it also trace back to classical Greek philosophy. In medicine, the relationship is between knowledge of general causal claims, for example, about how a disease tends to present in a patient, or about the effectiveness of a treatment in a group of patients, and specific knowledge of an individual patient. The first kind of knowledge currently comes mainly from scientific research, both basic and clinical, though physicians also develop knowledge of generalities over time through their own clinical experience. The second kind of knowledge is gleaned from directly interacting with an individual patient. A central theme of this book is that a clinician needs to be able to use both kinds of knowledge effectively. The results of biomedical research, whether from clinical or other epidemiological studies or from laboratory research, are only useful for clinicians when placed in the context of caring for an individual patient. Conversely, clinical interactions with patients, while personal, are shaped by scientific knowledge, including both epidemiological and physiological research, but also by studies that examine aspects of the clinical encounter, including history taking, techniques of physical examination, communication skills, or that aim to better understand patients' experiences and their values.

Scientific research, whether done in the laboratory or the clinic, allows us to make general claims about, for example, the causes of symptoms and the pathophysiology of disease; the average prognosis of a patient with a particular disease; and whether a treatment is effective for that disease. We describe these as "general" causal claims for several reasons. First, they do not apply in all cases. Saying that the average life expectancy of someone with abdominal mesothelioma is eight months is compatible with some rare patients living for twenty years beyond the time of diagnosis (Gould, 2013). Nor does the fact that a medication lowered blood pressure on average across a study population guarantee that it will have any effect on the blood pressure of a particular patient. Second, they are oversimplifications. Saying that smoking causes lung cancer ignores all of the other factors that are necessary for lung cancer to develop, even though we know quite a bit about mutagenesis, DNA repair, etc. Despite these caveats, it is clear that this kind of general knowledge is valuable and that a solid understanding of science is important for medical practice.

In addition to general scientific knowledge, however, physicians need knowledge of individual patients. There are many different kinds of knowledge relevant here, including how the patient resembles, and differs from, other patients the physician has known with a similar clinical presentation or diagnosis; the patient's clinical condition at a particular time; the patient's circumstances (e.g., social, familial, financial); and their goals and values for treatment, their health, and their life.

As will become clear, the relationship between general knowledge and knowledge of individuals is also not simply a matter of applying the former in the care of individual patients. Although the relationship between general knowledge and knowledge of particular patients has been understood differently at different times, and there is disagreement about the extent to which general knowledge can tell us about individuals, general knowledge is never in itself prescriptive; it does not straightforwardly dictate clinical decision-making.

A brief history of medical knowledge

One way to help clarify what doctors need to know is to look at the history of how certain kinds of knowledge came to be seen as important to medical practice. The question of what doctors need to know has not always been answered in the same way. This is, of course, partly because as science developed, new disciplines, such as physiology, bacteriology, and epidemiology, emerged and became relevant to medicine. But it is also because views have changed regarding what medical knowledge should include—even the scientific knowledge we now see as being obviously relevant to medical practice was not always recognized as being important, and, in many cases, a lot of additional work was and is necessary to *make* a discovery clinically useful.

In this section, we provide a brief overview of three eras of medical epistemology. (A fourth era, our current era, will be covered in the next chapter.) Each of these three eras was characterized by a different kind of knowledge that served as the paradigm of what doctors needed to know. For each era, we begin by outlining the dominant approach to medical epistemology, as it was developed in Europe, and then show how it was imported to and adapted in the United States, affecting practices of diagnosis and treatment, and also medical education. Because of the way that the development of medical knowledge and practice in America draws from various European models, focusing on the American context provides an especially clear illustration of the main epistemological contributions of the three eras.

Rationalist theory and empiricist practice

The first era of medical epistemology that we will discuss was characterized by an emphasis on rationalist theorizing. Although historically the tension between this kind of rationalism and an opposing empiricism reaches back to ancient Greece, we will begin our discussion of these two opposing tendencies somewhat later, in the 17th to the early 19th centuries. During this era, there was a striking distinction between the two approaches that clearly illustrates both the differences between them and the criticisms raised against each. At this time, throughout much of Europe, there was a sharp distinction between physicians, who tended to be members of the upper middle classes and who therefore received a classical education, and a variety of other medical practitioners, including surgeons, bonesetters, and midwives, who were members of the lower classes and who learned their trade through apprenticeships.

Physicians of this time were quintessential rationalists: They learned a great deal of theory about the nature of disease and about its causes, which informed their choice of treatments. Until the 18th century, medical theory consisted largely of variations of and elaborations on Greek medical thought. The dominant doctrine of the humors stated that there were four "rational fluids" in the body: Blood, yellow bile, black bile, and phlegm. These four humors corresponded to the four elements that made up the primal matter of the universe: Air, fire, earth, and water. The relative balance of the four humors within each person influenced their appearance, their personality, and the kinds of disease to which they were most susceptible. Health, in the Hippocratic tradition, occurred when the four humors occurred in the appropriate balance, or equilibrium, for that individual; disease occurred when this equilibrium was disturbed, whether by an environmental cause or by an individual's diet or activity. The patient's symptoms, together with knowledge of their circumstances and constitution, allowed the physician to identify the particular kind of humoral imbalance the patient suffered from. "Essentially, there was one disease state, a humoral derangement or 'distemper,' but as many variants of it existed as there were patients, for the symptoms of disease depended on the individual's humoral constitution" (Reiser 1978, p. 8).

This belief in the importance of an individual's constitution also influenced attitudes toward treatment. During most of the 17th and 18th centuries, treatment was governed by what came to be called the principle of therapeutic specificity. "Treatment was to be sensitively gauged not to a disease entity but to such distinctive features of the patient as age, gender, ethnicity, socioeconomic position and moral status, and to attributes of place like climate, topography, and population density." (Warner 1997a, p. 58).[1]

Over time, new theories of disease were developed that moved away from humoral explanations of health and disease to argue that disease was ultimately caused by, depending on the theoretical system, problems with the nerves, the blood vessels, or another part of the body. These newer systems, however, were very conservative in that they retained the ideas that health was a state of balance, that disease involved some sort of imbalance, and that an individual's unique constitution and circumstances determined the specific kind of imbalance from which they suffered. The result of these

---

[1] The principle of specificity also provides another illustration of the many competing uses of the terms "rationalist" and "empiricist." Empiricism was used in a negative sense to talk about mechanical, rote treatment practice and the lack of judicious decision-making. But the lack of judgment could stem from either having no theoretical understanding of medicine (e.g., in the case of non-physician practitioners) or from having too strong an allegiance to a particular rationalist theory.

new and competing theoretical developments was a proliferation of rather baroque medical systems that owed very little to either clinical or scientific observations (as we understand both of those things today) and much to philosophical speculation. In their textbook, *Philosophy of Medicine*, Wulff et al. describe this rationalist tendency as "speculative realism" in order to emphasize the fact that theorizing occurred in the armchair, rather than in the clinic or the lab (1990, p. 33). Although at the time, these theories were considered the pinnacle of medical knowledge, with medical education consisting almost entirely of learning these theories through reading and lectures, the medicine of this era now seems to us to be both quaint and outright dangerous. Perhaps as a lingering effect of medicine's rationalist history, contemporary physicians are often skeptical of what they see as theorizing, instead stressing the importance of well-established facts as a guide for medical practice. Although, as we shall see, there can be a lot of theory involved in establishing facts, the emphasis on observable facts reflects the empiricist aspects of medicine.

As with rationalism, empiricism has a number of different meanings and connotations. As we have noted, during the 17th and 18th centuries, empiricism was associated with second-class medicine—the kind of practice learned on the job and involving physical interactions with patients—without any theoretical understanding.[2] Surgery was an empirical practice, distinct from the practice of medicine. Several other apprentice-trained practitioners specialized in a particular technique or area of medicine, such as midwifery, bonesetting, or the removal of bladder stones or cataracts. Such medical trades were considered empirical because they were taught through hands-on experience and because they were based on some practical assessment of the outcome of an intervention, rather than on a theoretical rationale for the treatment.

The strongly rationalist character of medicine during this era had clear implications for medical diagnosis and treatment. Two points are especially important to note. First, physicians learned the information they required for diagnosis primarily by hearing their patients report on their symptoms.

---

[2] The possession of a large body of basic medical knowledge still separates medical professionals from other jobs in health care fields, including technicians and various categories of medical assistants, but it is also the case that some things that doctors used to need to know have also become the responsibility of other professions or occupations (e.g., compounding medicines, using diagnostic tools like a microscope). Moreover, although all contemporary jobs in health care require significant practical training, akin to an apprenticeship, they also require some scientific knowledge acquired in the classroom.

They did not conduct a thorough physical examination of their patients; physical examination was limited to what they could directly observe, generally without touching, of their fully clothed patient. Diseases were understood to essentially *be* their symptoms, in contrast with our current view that symptoms are clues about an underlying disease that causes those symptoms. Because of this, a patient's reports of their symptoms and their individual circumstances told the physician most everything he needed to know to diagnose the patient and to determine the appropriate treatment for them. In fact, it was not uncommon for physicians to diagnose and to suggest treatment for their patients through the mail, based solely on the patient's or a family member's description of the patient's state.

Moving away from the details of the elaborate medical theories of this time period, Charles Rosenberg emphasizes the importance of an underlying basic understanding of the nature of the body and of disease, which was shared by both doctors and patients. "The body was seen, metaphorically, as a system of dynamic interactions with its environment. Health or disease resulted from a cumulative interaction between [an individual's] constitutional endowment and environmental circumstance" (Rosenberg, 1979, p. 5). The dynamic nature of the body meant that it was also a system of "intake and outgo" (p. 6). Disease manifested in visible signs—vomiting, sweating, diarrhea—as the body attempted to return to equilibrium. Drawing again from Greek medicine, doctors of this period tended to believe that the body could often heal itself, but that medical intervention could aid the healing powers of nature (*vis medicatrix naturae*) by promoting these visible signs of healing. Treatments of this period, which included mineral substances such as mercury or arsenic, botanical remedies, and, most notoriously, bloodletting using leeches or a lancet, were therefore expected to produce "visible and predictable physiological effects" (p. 8). If they did, both physician and patient believed that the treatment worked, though Rosenberg also notes that the recovery of the patient, when it occurred, was more likely the result of the fact that most diseases were self-limited.

We began this section by contrasting rationalism and empiricism, and associating each epistemological approach with, at least during this period in Europe, different categories of health care providers. Physicians were the better-educated group, specifically in terms of their knowledge of rationalist medical theories. They also had higher social status than the various groups of apprentice-trained practitioners, who took an empiricist approach to their work. In America, however, there was less of a difference between physicians and other health care providers. Throughout the colonial era, and even into the 19th century, the lack of opportunities for university education meant that most physicians also learned through apprenticeships—though a small number of elite students did travel to Europe, initially to Edinburgh and London, to study medicine at a university.

Apprenticeships varied greatly in quality; there were no standardized expectations for what a physician should be able to do, and no examinations to ensure that they could do it. The apprenticeship period did have a generally accepted structure, however. During the first year, an apprenticeship involved "reading medicine with the doctor"—that is, reading classic books of medical theory—as well as helping with office calls and with compounding medicines. In the second phase, the apprentice would begin "riding with the doctor" to make house calls and to assist with any surgical procedures (Rothstein, 1972, p. 85). This rough structure is still reflected in the division of medical education into preclinical and clinical work, though both phases have undergone vast changes.

In the late 18th and early 19th centuries, medical training began to change. Local medical societies formed that aimed to develop medicine as a profession, and coming to an agreement regarding what a physician needed to know was central to this goal. One strategy for meeting this aim was the setting of standards for apprenticeships. In addition, medical schools began to open in the United States, mainly in the Northeast. Although the division between university-educated physicians and various groups of health care providers without such an education was not as sharp as it had been in England, there were still important differences *among* physicians, specifically between the highly educated elite, who mostly lived and practiced in East Coast cities, and physicians who had only apprenticeship experience. The historian John Duffy suggests, however, that because the apprenticeship system "emphasized common sense and sound practical experience," it might have better prepared aspiring physicians for clinical practice than did medical schools, whose graduates "were far better versed in the subtle philosophical distinctions between various theories than in clinical medicine" (Duffy, 1993, p. 39).

Despite the strong rationalist influence on medical education in "elite" medical schools, Rothstein suggests that the majority of physicians were not generally interested in the theory underlying the application of a therapy, just in whether it *worked* (Rothstein, 1992, pp. 21–22). As formal medical education began to develop in the United States, physicians tended to retain this strong orientation toward practice. More generally, the professional identity of American physicians tended to center on the practice of medicine, rather than the possession of a body of uniquely medical knowledge; physicians were defined in terms of what they *did*, rather than what they *knew*. This focus on practice shaped both their treatment practices and their reception of new developments in medical knowledge as the 19th century progressed.

With regard to treatment, American physicians came to reject the idea that the body could naturally heal itself, in favor of so-called "heroic" therapies. Although earlier physicians accepted the Hippocratic belief in the healing power of nature, American physicians increasingly believed that intervention in the course of disease was absolutely necessary. Benjamin Rush, who is considered to be the father of heroic therapy, warned against doing too little for one's patients: "Always treat nature in a sick room as you would a noisy dog or cat[;] drive her out at the door and lock it upon her" (quoted in Warner, 1997a, p. 18). Large doses of medicine were therefore used to dramatic effect; purging and bleeding became emblematic of "real" medical practice. Heroic medicine came to distinguish "regular" physicians from botanical healers, homeopaths, and other medical "sects" that offered a gentler approach to healing (Rothstein, 1992). Rothstein argues that it is these differences in therapeutic practice, rather than in medical theory, that distinguished among different kinds of medical practitioners during this period.[3] This tendency toward action rather than reflection may continue to characterize contemporary American medical practice (Stegenga, 2017).

Despite this practical orientation, medical education in the first American medical schools resembled European models in that it consisted largely of lectures on medical theory, anatomy, and materia medica (therapeutics), rather than in practical experience. Students at this time were required to attend two years of medical school, but the academic year was only four months long, and the second year was a repeat of the first. In addition, there was very little opportunity for hands-on medical training. As we will see, the second and third eras in medical epistemology developed because (mostly) university-educated, "elite" physicians traveled to Europe

---

[3] This interpretation fits with the idea that it was the actual practice of medicine that made someone a physician.

to gain the clinical experience their home environment and university education could not provide. They then brought these new ideas back to the United States, and because they often took leadership positions in medical education, they had an influence on the medical profession that was out of proportion to their fairly small numbers.

Clinical observation and medical empiricism

The first wave of European travel by elite American medical students began in the 1830s, and at this time, their destination was Paris. Although formal medical education was developing in the United States during the early 19th century, opportunities for gaining clinical experience were still limited. By contrast, the organization of the hospital system in Paris allowed students access to a much larger number and a greater variety of patients than they would be able to see at home. While they were there, the visiting Americans were also influenced by the French approach to medicine, which stressed careful observation, both in the clinic and at the autopsy table. From an epistemological perspective, French medicine was beginning to replace rationalist explanations of disease with empirical observation of patients and correlation of their signs and symptoms with anatomical changes observed at autopsy. Opportunities for this kind of clinicopathological correlation were unfortunately common, as progress in pathology and diagnosis were not matched by improvements in the ability to treat disease, and because patients who entered the hospital were often severely ill, with little hope of recovery.

In addition to the opportunities afforded by the sheer number of patients in Parisian hospitals, French physicians had been developing new techniques of observation that fostered the development of an empiricist approach to medicine. In the clinic, progress in observation included new approaches to physical examination, particularly the techniques of inspection, palpitation, auscultation, and percussion that remain central to physical examination today (Bynum, 1994, p. 33). New instruments to aid clinical observation were also being developed by French clinicians; most influential among these was the stethoscope, invented in 1816.

Although the visiting American medical students and young physicians spent much of their time acquiring clinical experience with living patients, their Paris education also included exposure to autopsies, often of patients they had observed in the clinic before their death.[4] This practice, formalized by Giovanni Morgagni in Padua in the previous century, allowed students to correlate clinical signs and symptoms with specific "morbid appearances" of the body and its parts. Some of these changes were observable at the level of gross anatomy, while other changes were more subtle and affected specific tissues within an organ, rather than the entire organ. Early scientists focusing on tissue changes were sometimes "naked eye anatomists" (Bynum, 1994, p. 32). As technological advances improved the quality of microscopes, however, their use became more common. This allowed improved distinction among diseases—for example, microcopy could allow the anatomist to distinguish between malignant and benign tumors and to recognize cases in which cancer spread from a primary site to other kinds of tissue (Reiser, 1978, p. 77).

For both "naked eye" anatomy and clinical microscopy, observing properly required learning both the techniques of clinical examination and how to interpret the different visual and auditory signs—to distinguish among them and to recognize them as indicating a particular disease. It also involved learning to distinguish between normal and pathological tissues (and among different kinds of pathology). For some students, this also involved learning the techniques of microscopy, including both how to prepare specimens and how to use the microscope properly. As Reiser notes, "[t]o become a first-rate observer required a knowledge of optics, chemistry, and anatomy, accompanied by dexterity in manipulating the instrument, and time to educate the eye and to become acquainted with the illusions inherent in the best magnifying instruments. The microscope per se could not confer the power of observation upon the unlearned" (Reiser, 1978, p. 80). In a very real sense, an experienced clinician or microscopist sees something different than a novice when they (e.g.) see a rash as pityriasis versicolor, or a slide on a sample as taken from a cancerous liver. Importantly, expanding observation in this sense was focused on developing knowledge of the particular; this new medical gaze was directed at individual patients.

In addition to developing skills in clinical observation, members of the Paris Clinical School also applied a more basic empirical skill, long a part of science and commerce, to medicine: counting. With large numbers of

---

[4] In addition to attending large lectures by physicians at the various Parisian hospitals, visiting students also participated in private tutorials, either individually or with a small group of other American students. These tutorials were important given the difficulty that many American students had in understanding the larger lectures, which were given in French (Warner, 1998).

patients in institutional settings, physicians could keep careful track of the number of persons who presented with certain symptoms or diseases, as well as the outcomes in these groups (Shryock, 1961). Quantification in clinical medicine went from vague and often unsupported (e.g., "many patients improve") to more precise and documented (e.g., "90 of 100 patients improved"). In our modern parlance, clinical observation moved from being "unsystematic" to "systematic." This leap in quantification, accompanied by the recognition that patients might improve due to, or in spite of, therapeutic interventions, meant that quantifying outcomes in untreated patients was also warranted. An 1835 study by Pierre Louis is often described as a precursor of contemporary clinical research methods. Louis compared the outcomes of 100 patients with pneumonia who were treated with bloodletting to a group of patients who were not bled, raising skepticism regarding the value of that traditional intervention. This ability and willingness of physicians in the Paris Clinical School to keep careful track of patients and their outcomes laid the foundations for the development of the clinical epidemiology that dominates our last half century of medical epistemology.

This move toward quantification across groups, or populations, of patients created a new kind of medical knowledge. While grounded in observation rather than theory, and hence empirical, aggregated information was generally gathered by multiple individuals and could be shared with other physicians who had never been involved in the care of these patients. This new type of empirical knowledge, created by systematic observation and its reporting, is indirect—contrasting with the direct and personal experiential knowledge that clinicians gain from their own clinical practice.[5] The relative importance of quantification and basic statistical analysis to the practice of clinical medicine was controversial from the outset. It was debated both at a meeting of the French Academy the same year that Louis announced his findings and at the Paris Academy of Medicine two years later (Shryock, 1961; Matthews, 1995). Early criticisms of this approach included skepticism about extrapolating from averages and the risk of no longer seeing patients as individuals, arguments that have also been levied at the EBM movement over the last three decades. While EBM declared itself a new paradigm for the practice and teaching of medicine (EBM Working Group, 1992), the roots of the movement and recognition of its limitations were over 100 years old. Much of what we deal with in this book centers on the

---

[5] We will say much more about knowledge obtained from clinical experience in Chapter 4.

ongoing debate regarding the relative value and practical utilization of this kind of processed empirical medical knowledge.

We draw two important lessons from the influence of the Paris Clinical School. First, although it represents the development of a new medical empiricism, it also demonstrates the mutual interdependence of empiricism and rationalism in medicine. This is because interpreting the meaning of clinical observations, or observations through a microscope, requires some theory that justifies discriminating between patients or samples that are considered normal and those that are abnormal. In some cases, discriminating between two things and assigning each to the appropriate category is straightforward: It's easy to tell the difference between a liver and a brain, even without specialized training. In other cases, discrimination requires more practice: Histology students need to learn to differentiate between liver tissue and brain tissue. In still other cases, determining whether a particular sample of liver tissue is normal or is in the early stages of cancer requires not just practice, but a great deal of educated judgment. Moreover, this judgement involves understanding an increasingly detailed theory of the differences between the two categories, to help make the distinction of whether the two samples belong in different categories. For all three kinds of cases, explaining *why* the particular judgement was made requires some understanding of what makes the items in the two categories different, though the complexity of what needs to be understood is different in each of the cases. All of this means that the question of whether the two observations are of different kinds of things (an empiricist question) is not always completely separable from the question of *why* they differ (a rationalist question).

Second, the shift to a strongly empiricist approach to medicine also shows that medicine is not just a matter of knowing, but also of *doing*. Previous generations of physicians knew how to fit a patient's description of their symptoms into their preferred medical theory, but increasingly throughout the 19th century physicians had to acquire important information about their patients through hands-on experience. Examining patients required physicians to use their senses (with, and without, the aid of new devices). Just as Parisian students using a microscope for diagnosis required not only the ability to distinguish between the two classes of tissues, but also the ability to prepare the specimens and to use the microscope properly,[6] physicians had to learn the new clinical techniques required to properly examine patients.

---

[6] This is another example where contemporary physicians no longer need to know how to do these things (except, perhaps, during training), as this knowledge has been outsourced to laboratory technicians and/or to specialists.

Developing these clinical skills was not easy. Consider the example of auscultation: When the stethoscope was developed, Laennec provided detailed and careful descriptions of the sounds heard through a stethoscope and what they meant, making it much easier to learn to use this instrument. But these were not the only challenges in learning new techniques; as Reiser notes, the new technology was still met with resistance, for several reasons: "some physicians were reluctant to abandon [older] techniques that had cost them so many hours to learn; others recognized in themselves certain physical limitations such as poor hearing, or harbored the vague fear of being unable to master the new technique" (1978, p. 32). In retrospect, we can see that the physical examination provides crucial information to physicians, but Reiser emphasizes that, from about 1819 to 1850, its usefulness was hotly debated (p. 29).

Overall, this expanded empiricism led to a greater understanding of disease, including the ability to connect particular groups of symptoms with anatomical signs. Unfortunately, this new diagnostic knowledge did not give rise to corresponding progress in therapy. American students frequently commented in letters home on both their discomfort with their inability to do anything for their patients and their dismay at what they perceived as French physicians' lack of concern about this problem (Warner, 1998). There was also a deeper epistemological problem. The French diagnostic approach emphasized consistent correlations between symptoms and anatomical lesions and tended to lump similar patients into groups. But virtually all physicians of that period were still committed to the principle of therapeutic specificity. It was therefore commonly accepted that treatment had to be carefully calibrated to an individual's unique constitution and circumstances. The view that individual patients were just one example of a more universal set of symptoms, pathology, or disease ran directly counter to the entrenched view that therapy relied on a deep understanding of the individual patient and their circumstances, and a physician's expert judgement of what was required (Warner, 1997a, p. 59). This epistemic tension continues to this day.

In summary, during this era of medical knowledge, the traditional, rationalistic understanding of disease, dating back to Hippocratic theory, was challenged by a new empiricist approach to medicine. Parisian empiricism was grounded in careful observation at the bedside and at autopsy, and the attempt to correlate patients' symptoms with anatomical lesions. It also expanded the target of observation to groups of similar patients, both in an attempt to understand prognosis and treatment effects, but also to produce some kind of more general knowledge. This shift took some time, as physicians had to learn, and to accept as useful, new techniques of examination, new ways of thinking about diagnosis, and information generated from the observation of large groups of patients. Moreover, American physicians were troubled by the lack of progress in therapeutics, especially because both they and their patients were coming to doubt the value of heroic approaches to treatment. It would still be several decades before major treatment advances started to become available.

Laboratory research and physiologic rationale

Although by the mid-19th century, there were increasing opportunities in the U.S. for clinical training, the number of places available was still significantly smaller than the number of students who wanted to fill them. This meant that American medical students and recent graduates continued to travel to Europe to gain clinical experience. Starting in about the 1850s, however, they began increasingly to travel to German-speaking countries, and within a couple of decades, Germany had replaced France as the most popular destination for medical education. As was the case with students who went to France, students who travelled to Germany were motivated primarily by the opportunity to observe patients and to learn clinical skills at the bedside, but once they arrived and began work, they were influenced by aspects of German research and clinical practice that they had not entirely foreseen. Germany was at that time in the forefront of laboratory research, and a small but significant number of students immersed themselves in laboratory work, subsequently bringing home this new approach to American medical education and, eventually, to clinical practice. In the clinical context, one major influence of German practice was the increasing acceptability of specialization in a particular area of medicine.

By the middle of the century, Germany became the primary center for the development of the discipline of physiology, which had grown out of, but was gradually becoming distinct from, both anatomy and chemistry. Work in anatomy, as we saw in the context of Parisian medical science, encompassed both gross anatomy and microscopy, and led to a better understanding of both normal and pathological structure. Research in chemistry initially focused on the intake of food, oxygen, and water, and the analysis of substances (e.g., urea, carbon dioxide, water, and salts) that were excreted or exhaled. In this early research, only inputs and outputs were observed directly, but scientists were able to draw inferences about the chemical processes that occurred within the body, processes that were not observed directly (Bynum, 1994, p. 96).

Over time, physiological research was further refined, as new experimental methods, techniques, and instruments were developed. The kymograph, invented by Carl Ludwig in the 1840s, was the paradigm of these new "instruments of precision." It was created to measure blood pressure and provide a visual representation by translating it to a paper record. By the 1860s, the kymograph was used extensively by physiologists, who also adapted it to measure other physiological processes. This "graphic method" of doing physiology did not open the black box, but it gave scientists new information about what was happening inside it, and about the processes that linked the observed inputs and outputs.

This kind of research was rationalist in its aims, attempting to explain *how* the observed outputs were generated, rather than, as empiricism would do, show simply *that* these outputs were generated consistently in the presence of particular inputs. But this was no longer the speculative theorizing that characterized medical rationalism in previous centuries. Explanations of the observations made in the lab were the product of careful scientific experiments. As Merrilee Borrell notes, "[t]he introduction of recording techniques allowed investigators to separate and measure transient physiological events. Graphic registration of processes such as muscle contraction and nerve conduction gave researchers insight into phenomena inaccessible merely by the dissecting knife" (Borrell, 1987, p. 293). Moreover, this new rationalism incorporated the insights of the previous era of clinical empiricism by emphasizing the importance of careful observation. The new scientific instruments, like those used in the clinic, were "designed to extend the senses and enhance the investigator's powers of discrimination" (Borell, 1987, p. 293).

As physiology continued to develop, it began to replace anatomy as the central medical science. Toward the end of the 19th century, an increasing number of leading physicians and educators, many trained in Germany, began calling for a greater alignment between physiology and pathology. Pathology was still primarily an anatomical science, and it was believed that a functional understanding of disease was only possible if pathology became an experimental, rather than an observational science (Maulitz,

1987, p. 209). This change also included a shift in the conception of what it *meant* for medicine to be scientific. Whereas Parisian empiricism understood scientific inquiry to rest on careful observation of individuals or groups of patients, experimental research—which moved beyond observation to intervention—was now viewed as the right way to do medical science. Moreover, proponents of the new experimental methods were optimistic that this research would have important clinical implications. Just as chemistry and physics had discovered laws of nature governing the inanimate world, physiology would discover universal laws of biology, which in turn would serve as the foundations of clinical medicine.

Even though no such universal laws had been discovered yet, the belief that they were there to be found began to change the way physicians thought about both disease and therapy. Traditionally, disease was understood as an imbalance affecting the whole person, and symptoms were believed to be the body's attempt to restore that balance. Traditional medical treatments, on this view, represented external attempts to restore balance, often by causing the same physiological symptoms as the disease. With the development of physiology, however, disease came to be understood in terms of specific, measurable parameters such as temperature and heart rate (Warner, 1997b). These parameters had a normal value (or range of values), and in cases where an individual had, for example, an abnormally high temperature, they were considered to have a disease. Although they might also be experiencing visible symptoms of fever, such as rigors or being warm to the touch, these symptoms were now considered merely indicators of the true, underlying, and increasingly measurable pathology. Theory, now based upon careful experimentation, allowed for more "scientific" rationalism to take hold amongst physicians, who could reason about the pathophysiological mechanism underlying a patient's presentation.

For some physicians, optimism about the contributions of laboratory science to medicine extended to therapeutics. As physiological processes came to be better understood, physicians began to believe that therapies could be developed that would target these processes. This belief in "rational therapeutics" was, at least in the late 1800s, based largely on faith rather than direct experimental evidence. Several new drugs were developed during this time and came to be widely used, and these were thought to be simply the first of a coming wave of new treatments. Moreover, just as the understanding of disease changed from the symptomatic state of the whole person to a set of abnormal, and quantifiable, physiological characteristics, the goal of treatment came to be seen as restoring those quantifiable parameters to a normal state (in the modern parlance: "treating the numbers") instead of restoring balance to the individual.

This change, however, was controversial because it required physicians to give up the principle of specificity, which had previously guided treatment. Recall that this principle said that, because the manifestation of disease in an individual was unique, treatment had to be carefully tailored to that individual and their circumstances. Because of the large number of individual characteristics that influenced an individual's response to a treatment, "there could be no fixed, universally applicable rules in therapeutic practice" (Warner, 1997b, p. 92). This focus on the individual, therefore, as Warner puts it, placed therapeutic knowledge in a different epistemological category than knowledge of basic biology. And, given the extent to which medicine was identified with therapeutic practice during this period, it meant that, fundamentally, medical knowledge was understood to consist in sound therapeutic judgment, rather than mastery of biological facts. Similarly, physicians who were committed to the empiricist emphasis on clinical observation continued to argue that such careful observation was the only way to understand "the individual peculiarities of the sick patient" (Warner, 1991, p. 463). Still, gradually, physicians shifted their focus from an individual and their symptoms to more universal physiological processes. Reflecting this shift, Steven Stowe documents the way that published case reports have changed from narratives that "almost always spoke of patients' bodies and biographies, seeking a way to combine them in the name of healing" (Stowe, 1996, p. 163) to their current form, in which "specialized, calibrated, and often highly quantified language drains the patient's suffering from the case" (p. 165). Warner suggests that this transformation was largely accomplished by the 1880s (1997b, p. 95).

Starting in the late 1890s and continuing into the early 20th century, new treatments like salvarsan and diphtheria antitoxin would become "potent symbol[s] of the therapeutic fruitfulness of basic laboratory science" (Warner, 1992, p. 138). The growing success of laboratory research in explaining disease and informing therapy was also reflected in changes in medical education and medical practice in the United States. Increasingly, medical thought in the United States was shifting from the empiricism adopted from the Paris Clinical School to a greater acceptance of the importance of rationalist investigations of physiological processes for clinical practice. This was another way in which the influence of German medicine was manifested in the United States, as German medical students had long been required to pass an examination that required significant knowledge of physiology. The famous Flexner Report on the state of medical education, published in 1910, was the culmination of efforts by physician-educators committed to the importance of physiology to reform the curriculum of medical schools (Flexner, 1910).

The claim that advances in the laboratory had important implications for clinical practice received some of its plausibility from the connection American visitors to Germany drew between the "instruments of precision" used in laboratory experiments and the diagnostic instruments becoming more common in the clinic. Although the stethoscope had been widely used since the 1850s, new tools for making observations in the clinic were being developed and gradually (and not without controversy) being incorporated into clinical practice. The ophthalmoscope and the laryngoscope were developed in the 1850s and came into common use over the next two decades. The ophthalmoscope, in particular, had a great impact on clinical practice because it revealed several different and complex eye diseases, resulting in the development of ophthalmology as a specialty (Reiser, 1978, p. 50).

The clear benefits of these tools also inspired the development of other instruments to measure patients' pulse, blood pressure, and lung capacity.[7] As with the microscopes used by the previous generation, early versions of these instruments required users to undergo specialized training. By the early 20th century, the number of instruments and tests that required specialized knowledge to use resulted in increased specialization in clinical practice.

The trend toward specialization also required a change in the attitude of the medical profession. Previous generations had associated specialization in a particular area of medicine or technique with non-physicians such as midwives or bonesetters. To many physicians, "specializing in one disease was tantamount to admitting that you could do nothing else and were thus ill-educated or not properly educated at all" (Bynum, 1994, p. 192). At the same time, and somewhat inconsistently, physicians who worked in a specialty area were viewed as putting themselves above their peers by claiming knowledge others did not possess, "and this went contrary to notions of medical equality" (ibid.).

---

[7] Similarly, it was around this time that diagnostic tests were first developed for the analysis of blood and urine (Reiser, 1978, p. 136).

In fact, specialists *did* have knowledge that physicians who were not in their area of specialization lacked. We have already emphasized the training required to use the new diagnostic instruments and interpret their meaning. In addition, physiological research meant that the amount of knowledge available regarding particular organs and systems was increasing. Moreover, a specialist had greater clinical experience with patients who had a particular kind of health problem than a general practitioner could hope to acquire. All of these factors likely influenced the increasing acceptability of specialization (Weisz, 2005).

More generally, by the late 19th and early 20th century, medical science was flourishing. Laboratory research had led to greater understanding of normal and abnormal physiology, which informed the development of diagnostic tools and was beginning to lead to new treatments. Both the speculative rationalism and the clinical empiricism of earlier eras had been largely supplanted by a new, experimentally grounded rationalist view of medical knowledge. This also had implications for the question of how scientific knowledge was related to knowledge of the individual, both in theory (as shown by the increasing optimism that researchers would lead to universal laws guiding diagnosis and therapy), and in practice (as physicians shifted to controlling physiological processes rather than understanding and managing a patient's unique symptoms).

Summary

This brief history of medical epistemology notes the sources of many of the features of clinical practice that characterize the scenario we described at the beginning of the chapter, highlighting the recurring patterns and debates that occur each time a new approach to medicine, or a new technique or therapy, is introduced.

First, scientific discoveries do not simply or obviously translate into the clinic, for a variety of reasons. New ideas take hold only when physicians are not fully committed to older ways of thinking and practicing. Enthusiastic proponents of new ideas face critics who are reluctant to accept them, so that novel approaches can elicit both unwarranted optimism and inflexible rejection. Most clinicians, though, likely fall somewhere in the middle of these new extremes, willing to adopt new techniques, instruments, therapies, and ideas they find useful in clinical practice.

Second, when new ideas and tools are introduced, they do not necessarily replace older ones or resolve all lingering questions. The techniques and habits of careful observation developed during the era of French influence continued to be important as laboratory research took a central role in developing medical knowledge. And even though newer research led to more "objective" indicators of disease, the success of a therapy that targets these indicators is still measured in large part by the extent to which they improve patients' symptoms.

Third, the two recurring tensions we introduced early in the chapter continue to influence medical research and practice. Broadly speaking, we can understand an empiricist approach to medical knowledge to focus on establishing *whether*, and under what circumstances, a phenomenon occurs, and a rationalist approach to focus on understanding *how* it occurs. At different times, these questions have been answered in different ways, and the relative importance of the two questions—both in establishing general medical knowledge and in the practice of an individual physician—remains very much up for debate. Disagreements continue, we shall see, about what scientific studies can offer the practicing clinician who aims to provide the best care possible for an individual patient.

Our brief history of medicine has brought us to the late 19th century, by which time the historian William Bynum has claimed that medical knowledge and practice much more closely resembled the medicine of the late 20th century (during which he was writing) than it did the medicine of the beginning of the 1800s. Bynum's book, however, was published in 1994 and so does not discuss the major shift in medical knowledge that characterizes our current epistemological era. Evidence-based medicine, introduced in the early 1990s, now dominates medical epistemology. We turn to this fourth era in the next chapter, where we will see that all of the epistemological issues we have introduced in this chapter arise yet again when we ask how the results of clinical trials should inform clinical decision-making.

2
Evidence-based Medicine

Dr. Lee considers herself an evidence-based medicine practitioner. She remembers the introduction of EBM during her residency training. Her attending physicians would ask her why she wanted to order a particular test or start a certain therapy, expecting that the answer would be based on a clinical research study with which she was familiar. The attending physicians seemed to know all of the relevant studies in their respective specialties, perhaps because only a small number of studies existed at that time. She attended journal clubs where new clinical research reports were analyzed and discussed, learning the tools necessary to perform such analyses herself. More often than not, such reports, even those published in top medical journals, were found lacking in one way or another. At the end of discussion, someone would invariably ask, "How will this change your practice?" That question always made the link between research seem a bit nebulous.

Still, Dr. Lee tried to keep up with the literature relevant to her primary care practice, often utilizing systematic reviews. She relied heavily on clinical practice guidelines. Her practice monitored "evidence based" metrics and she prided herself on achieving those goals. When she taught the medical students who rotated in her clinic she always tried to justify her medical decisions by referencing evidence—a study, a meta-analysis, or systematic review. Of course, she was an evidence-based practitioner; what was the alternative?

In the previous chapter, we surveyed three epistemological eras in medicine. We are now in a fourth era, that of evidence-based medicine (EBM). Like the two preceding eras, EBM was made possible by new developments in the sciences. The main science that underlies EBM is epidemiology, which builds on the kind of "clinical counting" first developed by the Paris Clinical School, utilizing newer methods in experimental design and analysis to look at clinical outcomes in populations of patients. Epidemiology itself generally focuses on identifying statistical connections between various risk factors, including demographic, biological, and environmental factors, and the probability of developing a disease. Clinical trials extend epidemiological methods to the assessment of treatment outcomes, that is, to the question of whether an intervention makes a statistically significant difference to patient outcomes at a population level.

Since its introduction in the early 1990s, evidence-based medicine has come to dominate discussions of medical knowledge. In this chapter, we briefly describe the origins and development of EBM, and introduce and assess some related developments in medicine and medical research. We then discuss several criticisms of EBM levied by both clinicians and philosophers. With this background established, we turn to the question of what EBM does well and what it largely fails to do. Specifically, the major achievements of EBM have been to draw attention to the importance of clinical research for medical practice, to contribute to improvements in the quality of this research and its reporting, and to promote the teaching of skills needed to critically appraise clinical studies. These are important contributions that should be lauded. At the same time, however, the dominance of EBM has focused the conversation on the quality of clinical research and largely ignored the question of how to *use* it in clinical practice. For the most part, EBM's advice on this second issue is that clinicians should, after identifying and assessing relevant clinical research sources, integrate this evidence with their knowledge of the patient's unique biology and values. It does not, however, explain how to do this and, as a result, EBM has created a new epistemic challenge, which we are calling the "integration problem."

Defining evidence-based medicine

While EBM formally arrived in the early 1990s, advanced by "The Evidence-Based Medicine Working Group" comprised of clinicians at McMaster University in Canada (EBM Working Group, 1992), many of EBM's core assumptions, assertions, and axioms were rooted in earlier work in clinical epidemiology. Packaging those concepts and approaches under a single, well-conceived brand led to wide acceptance and early uptake. Centers for, and courses in, EBM have been developed throughout the world, with the term being used to describe not just the work of the original EBM Working Group, but also a number of similar efforts that aim to ensure that clinical practice is informed by the results of clinical trials. The framework and methods of evidence-based practice have been adopted in other healthcare disciplines (e.g., evidence-based nursing, evidence-based physiotherapy) and beyond (e.g., evidence-based education, evidence-based librarianship). The term "evidence-based" is also frequently used in a loose sense, as a term of approval to show that a claim is well-founded or a course of action well-grounded. This latter usage makes clear both the influence of EBM and the rhetorical appeal of the chosen terminology.

Originally, EBM was developed within the specialty of internal medicine to reflect a specific set of problems observed by academic clinicians working in a tertiary health care setting and medical school. One of these problems was that therapeutic innovations were slow to be adopted in the clinic. Studies showed that the length of time a physician had been in practice was a good predictor of their preferred treatments: Rather than keeping up with the literature and adopting newer therapies as they were shown to be effective, physicians often continued to do as they had been taught in medical school and residency. And even in medical school, physicians might not be learning about the newest or best-supported therapies. During the 1970s and early 1980s, it became apparent that clinical practice varied geographically; clinicians in one area were likely to use one treatment while clinicians in a different location used another for what seemed to be the same condition. This variation implied that practice patterns were being shaped by either ignorance of the relevant clinical research or something other than knowledge of the most effective treatment.

Such problems motivated EBM's overarching goal: To promote the use of current "best evidence" in clinical practice. EBM has pursued this goal through two primary means, which we will show are actually in tension with each other. One approach is to teach medical students and clinicians how to find and critically appraise research relevant to their practice, instead of relying on local custom or authority. This aspect of EBM is anti-authoritarian; it aims to give physicians the tools they need to use current best research evidence in their own clinical practice. The second means of achieving EBM's overarching goal is the development of "digested and summarized" resources to save busy clinicians the burden of finding and appraising research studies for themselves. That is, it aims to establish an authority regarding best evidence and, thereby, best practice.

The first of these means of promoting the use of research evidence in clinical practice is depicted in a 1992 article, published by the EBM Working Group in *JAMA*, that introduced EBM to the medical community. In the first of two vignettes, a resident is asked by a patient who has just experienced a first seizure about his risk of recurrence. She turns to the senior resident and the attending and relays their answers to her patient. In the second vignette, instead of relying on these local authorities, she goes to the library and finds and reads the relevant studies. She identifies one that includes patients similar to hers, and—after determining that the study's quality is sufficient to inform practice—reports the study findings to her patient. The *JAMA* article is also clear that the patient in the second scenario is more satisfied with the answer to his questions, in addition to having been given a more precise and reliable, because evidence-based, answer.[1]

A second, related aspect of critical appraisal is to articulate clear standards for good, and for clinically relevant, research. We will return below to the question of which characteristics make a particular clinical study good; here we focus on the issue of clinical applicability. As noted above, EBM grew out of the discipline of clinical epidemiology, which used the population-level methods of epidemiological studies to investigate outcomes in the clinic. These methods were held to provide better evidence than two older sources of clinical knowledge, laboratory research, and direct clinical experience. One of these, laboratory studies that aimed to describe physiological processes at work in health and disease were criticized, in part, because they are generally conducted in animals, and not clearly applicable to humans. In addition, physiological processes proved to be both complex and, generally, incompletely understood. Treatments developed based on physiological knowledge were not always effective in actual practice and were sometimes even dangerous. In addition, clinical trials that measure physiological characteristics instead of clinically important outcomes, such as heart attack or death, present additional challenges. It's not always clear that these physiological characteristics, or "surrogate endpoints" accurately predict clinical outcomes. We will say more about these issues in the next chapter.

The second kind of knowledge downgraded by EBM derives from clinical experience, which was viewed as providing only weak evidence to guide clinical practice. This was because any single clinician sees only a small number of patients with a given condition, and it's not clear that their patients will be representative of the larger group, or that there are enough of them to allow for knowledge gained in treating them to be extrapolated beyond that group. In addition, vague appeals to "clinical expertise" and "expert opinion" were

---

[1] It is interesting that these vignettes depict a search for evidence related to prognosis, given EBM's primary emphasis on studies related to treatment.

not to be considered a firm foundation for practice. Systematic study of clinical decisions and their outcomes was required to establish the evidential validity of these claims, but such studies were only rarely available.

Thus, EBM values clinical research—studies using epidemiological methods to examine outcomes in populations—over laboratory research (and the general knowledge derived from it) and over clinical experience. It also makes distinctions *within* the realm of epidemiological studies examining outcomes in patient populations. All of these considerations are reflected in the "hierarchy of evidence," which ranks research methods according to the strength of the evidence that they are thought to provide. The hierarchy of evidence has been central to EBM since its inception and has been described as one of the two central contributions of EBM to medicine (Montori and Guyatt, 2008). In fact, many different hierarchies of evidence have been advanced, some related to treatment, to prognosis, and to diagnosis. However, as we have noted, much of EBM's influence concerns related to therapies, and the hierarchy below is representative of the basic structure of hierarchies of evidence for treatment studies:

- Systematic reviews of randomized trials
- Single randomized trial
- Systematic review of observational studies
- Single observational study
- Physiologic studies
- Unsystematic clinical observations.

We have already discussed the placement of studies using epidemiological methods over those focusing on laboratory measures and over clinical experience (including case studies or case series reports). In this hierarchy, population-level studies occupy the top four levels.[2] Within those four levels, studies that randomly assign participants to a treatment or a control group are ranked more highly than those that compare groups, but don't randomly assign study participants to a group. In addition to distinguishing between randomized and nonrandomized studies, the hierarchy assumes that more

---

[2] The first edition of the *Users' Guides* placed N-of-1 studies at the top of the hierarchy. These are randomized, controlled trials conducted with a single patient, the results of which are used to inform that patient's care (Guyatt and Rennie, 2001). Because these trials are possible only in fairly limited circumstances, including when the patient and physician have the time and resources to conduct one, and because the results are not intended to be generalizable to other patients, most versions of the hierarchy do not include these studies.

evidence is better, so that systematic reviews and meta-analyses, which provide an assessment of the overall results of a number of studies—rank higher on the hierarchy of evidence than a single study.

Generally, the first stage in the critical appraisal of a study is to determine the level of the hierarchy of evidence on which the study belongs. In some earlier publications, the developers of EBM advised only looking at evidence from the highest levels of the hierarchy (when evidence from multiple levels was available); for example, if a literature search identified both randomized and nonrandomized studies, it would be sufficient to focus only on the former (Straus et al., 2005, p. 118). That advice does not tend to appear in later EBM textbooks, though whether a study is properly randomized remains an important—perhaps the most important, given that randomized studies are still at the top of the hierarchy—feature of a study.

Once the "level" of evidence has been determined, a reader can go on to look at other markers of study quality. These include, for a study looking at treatment outcomes: Whether the treatment and control groups were similar, in terms of their demographic and clinical characteristics, at the beginning of the study and whether (as patients in both groups dropped out of the study) they remained that way; how well the allocation of patients to the treatment or the control group was concealed from study personnel and the patients themselves; whether the trial ran to completion or was stopped early; and how complete the follow-up for the trial was (Guyatt et al., 2015, p. 61).

In addition, by drawing attention to the quality of clinical research, EBM and related developments aimed to improve the quality of research itself, or at least the quality of its reporting. This improvement was necessary to enable the kind of critical appraisal just described. The CONSORT statement (standing for "Consolidated Standards of Reporting Trials") was first developed in the 1990s to articulate minimum standards for published clinical trials. It aimed to facilitate transparency and aid readers in assessing the quality of the trial's methods and the reliability of its results (Begg et al., 1996). Since then, the standards have been refined and tools have been developed to help ensure that published trials meet them (https://www.consort-statement.org/).

So far, we have seen that EBM aims to give physicians the skills they need to find and critically appraise the research literature. Recall the resident in the 1992 vignette practicing according to EBM's "Way of the Future" by going to the library to find research studies relevant to her patient's situation.

In reality, however, it has turned out to be difficult for physicians to practice medicine this way. EBM has recognized this, and over the years has been increasingly focused on a second way to achieve the overarching goal of ensuring that clinical practice is based on current best evidence. This is to provide resources that have already done the work of critical appraisal *for* physicians, summarizing or otherwise "prepackaging" study results.

This second way of promoting evidence-based practice is in tension with the first, and represents a compromise between the ideal of evidence-practice as involving direct engagement of physicians with the research literature and the realities imposed by physicians' time for, and interest in, this engagement. Even back in the days before the launch of EBM, the McMaster group recognized that the sheer volume of research published made achieving "The Way of the Future" challenging. In 1986, members of what became the EBM Working Group published a series of articles in the journal *Annals of Internal Medicine*. The first of these offered three broad tips. Two tips acknowledged the difficulties in keeping up with the amount of research being published, advising physicians to focus on papers that are directly relevant to their practice and to begin an article by quickly screening the methods section of these papers to eliminate any papers that were not of high quality. (Note that this second piece of advice reflects EBM's first goal—to promote skills in critical appraisal of the research literature.) The third piece of advice was that physicians should give priority to reading original articles that reported planned investigations, "because only these articles provide sufficient details to assess the relevance, validity, and clinical application of new knowledge" (Haynes et al., 1986, p. 149). They further advise against the tempting practice of skimming just the titles and abstracts of original papers and relying mainly on review articles for up-to-date information. One reason for this is that only journal articles reporting original research give a description of study methods, knowledge of which is necessary "to determine whether the results of the study are likely to be valid, whether they apply to the types of patients the reader sees, and if they do, exactly how to apply them" (p. 151). There is no substitute, the article seems to suggest, for getting down into the weeds of individual studies and doing the work of determining their quality and their relevance to clinical practice.

Yet, over time, EBM and related initiatives have increasingly focused on the production and assessment of summaries of research that aim to *substitute* for engagement with the primary literature. Quite early in the development of EBM, people realized that the goal of keeping up with the published literature was unrealistic. In 1996, Sackett et al. calculated that in order to keep up with publications in general medicine journals, a physician would have to read approximately 19 articles per day—an impossible task given the estimated one hour per week available for reviewing studies (Sackett et al., 1996). In 2000, Guyatt et al. published a paper that distinguishes between "evidence-based practitioners" and "evidence users." The former group can (and presumably do) find and critically assess primary literature related to clinical problems. The latter, while still expected to have some critical appraisal skills, generally rely on the secondary literature, including practice guidelines, and pre-appraised sources of evidence provided by various groups (Guyatt et al., 2000).

Guyatt et al. may be making a virtue of necessity here. They note that their own experience as medical educators indicated that many residents in their program were not interested in "attaining an advanced level" of skills in critical appraisal (p. 954). They also cite a study surveying British general practitioners that shows a similar attitude among practicing physicians. Participants in this study said that they did use evidence summaries and practice guidelines, but they rejected the idea that learning critical appraisal skills was the best way to practice evidence-based medicine (McColl et al., 1998). Secondly, Guyatt et al. acknowledged that even those who *would* like to become evidence-based practitioners face a shortage of time to review the literature, echoing the paper by Sackett et al.

Their solution to these problems is increased reliance on secondary sources of evidence, which they call "evidence-based resources." These resources are both time saving and more acceptable to people who would prefer to be "evidence users" than to do their own critical appraisal. Guyatt et al. describe these secondary resources as providing "immediately applicable conclusions" (a claim we will discuss further below) and suggest that "providing more comprehensive and more easily accessible pre-appraised resources is a second strategy for ensuring evidence-based care" (2000, p. 955).

In response to these realities, EBM has increasingly focused on teaching the skills required for using (and, to a lesser extent, assessing) these summarized and "pre-packaged" sources of evidence. To some extent, an appeal to summarized evidence already exists in the hierarchy in the form of systematic reviews and meta-analyses. Recall that these are studies that review and amalgamate studies on a particular intervention, generally after screening them for a certain level of methodological quality. Meta-analyses, in particular, are thought to provide a more precise estimate of the true effect of a therapy by statistically combining the result of multiple studies. While the results of any single RCT may deviate from the true effect, averaging the results of multiple studies is said to remove random "noise" from the estimate, providing a clearer signal.

Building on the original hierarchy, however, members of the EBM working group have developed the "6S" approach.[3] On the 6S hierarchy, individual studies (ones that have already been pre-appraised as meeting an acceptable quality level) are the *lowest* level. Above are synopses of individual studies published in "evidence-based abstraction journals," which are described as having three advantages over the studies themselves: Readers can be assured that the study summarized is of high quality and clinical relevance; the summary is brief; and there is the "added value" of a commentary on the study. The next two levels up the hierarchy are syntheses (systematic reviews) and synopses of syntheses (also published in "evidence-based abstraction journals"). The second highest level of evidence in the 6S approach is summaries, which include regularly updated clinical pathways or textbooks.

Finally, the top level of evidence is occupied by computerized decision-support systems. Such a system, which "integrates and concisely summarises all relevant and important research evidence about a clinical problem, is updated as new research evidence becomes available, and automatically links (through an electronic medical record) a specific patient's circumstances to the relevant information" (DiCenso et al., 2009, pp. 99–100). Although relatively few of these systems exist, when they do, "you need not go further down the model" (p. 99).[4]

In addition to the resources developed by members of the EBM Working Group, other groups have similarly attempted to provide high-quality evidence summaries to practicing physicians who want to be "evidence users." One of the most influential of these groups is the Cochrane Collaboration, which focuses on the production of systematic reviews and meta-analyses. In its early days, there was a close relationship between the two projects, especially because one of the founders of the Cochrane Collaboration, Murray Enkin, was at McMaster University with members of the EBM Working

---

[3] Here, too, there has been development over time: The "Ss" approach began with a 4S model (Haynes, 2001) and then moved to a 5S and finally a 6S approach.

[4] Like the N-of-1 clinical trials that top the original hierarchy of evidence, computerized decision support systems aim to provide evidence specific to an individual patient.

Group (Daly, 2005). The Cochrane Collaboration started as a joint project between Enkin and Ian Chalmers (in the UK), which aimed to provide a database of clinical trials related to their shared specialty of obstetrics. It soon grew into an international volunteer effort to collect and synthesize studies on numerous areas of practice. Today, the Cochrane Collaboration has published over 7500 systematic reviews, in its online repository, the Cochrane Library (Cochrane Collaboration, n.d.). As EBM has shifted more and more to providing summarized and simplified evidence, it has come to have more in common with the Cochrane Collaboration.

Another, similar, effort has involved the translation of clinical trial evidence into practice guidelines. Although a movement toward developing clinical guidelines predates EBM by several decades (see Weisz et al. 2007), the rise of EBM also influenced the way that guideline developers draw on the available evidence. The Institute of Medicine describes guidelines as providing "recommendations intended to optimize patient care that are informed by a systematic review of evidence and an assessment of the benefits and harms of alternative care options" (Institute of Medicine 2011, p. 4). And, coming full circle, there are now evidence-based approaches to assessing clinical practice guidelines (AGREE Collaboration, 2003).

Given the emphasis on "predigested" and summarized accounts of clinical trials, it seems like the objective of encouraging the use of clinical trial evidence in practice has won out over the objective of cultivating critical appraisal skills. It is still an open question, however, whether this use of evidence summaries is similar to older examples of handing off part of clinical work to others who become experts in that work: We don't tend to see it as a problem that doctors no longer compound their own medicine, or that they send biopsy samples to pathologists for analysis. But there may be negative epistemological consequences to contracting out engagement with the original research because the details that are lost in the process of summarizing studies can be of significant clinical relevance. Replacing the authority of clinical experts with the authority of methodologists does not guarantee clinical success. Critics have argued that clinical trials and population-level evidence are not always directly relevant to clinical practice and are never determinative. Such arguments assert that evidence-based medicine itself does not serve as a sufficient guide to clinical decision-making, or even that it is a poor and misleading guide.

As EBM became better known, it increasingly began to attract criticism. Some of this criticism aimed to defend "traditional" medical decision-making, including the importance of an individual physician's clinical expertise. Some of these traditionalists worried that EBM's approach amounted to "cookbook medicine" that promised results to anyone who simply followed the "recipe" provided by the evidence. Some critics also emphasized the political implications of such practice patterns, suggesting that EBM took professional authority out of the hands of clinicians, putting statisticians and health economists in charge of clinical care, while still leaving clinicians responsible for patient outcomes (Charlton and Miles, 1998). A third variation on this criticism argued that medicine was, fundamentally, an art—one that EBM approaches could not replace. These criticisms all reacted negatively to the very idea of EBM.

Other criticisms came from those who endorsed the basic goals of EBM, but worried about the details of the specific methods used. These critics recognized the importance of good clinical research evidence for clinical practice but believed that EBM had too narrow a view of what counted as good evidence (and, in particular, too strong a reliance on RCTs), or that it overestimated the direct clinical applicability of that evidence. Major points of criticism include the emphasis placed on randomization as a major marker of study quality, and the problems in extrapolating from the results of a study to estimate a treatment's effect in a population not represented in the study, or in an individual patient. In the next two sections, we address each of those criticisms.[5]

Randomization and allocation concealment

As we showed earlier in introducing the hierarchy of evidence, randomized trials either rank unequivocally above nonrandomized studies, or, on a few versions of the hierarchy, get a significant automatic "boost" in quality rating, so that unless they have other significant shortcomings in their design or execution, the default position is that they rate much higher than a nonrandomized trial. In the GRADE system, for example, the rationale for privileging randomization as a design feature are that (1) randomization

---

[5] In the next chapter, where we discuss the importance of knowledge of physiological mechanisms, we will address an additional criticism of EBM: The placement of "physiologic studies" near the bottom of the hierarchy of evidence.

of participants to study groups facilitates allocation concealment ("blinding"), which is seen as necessary to avoid bias in assessing outcomes, and (2) randomization is held to be the best way to balance potential confounding factors (whether known or unknown) between the experimental and the control groups (Guyatt et al., 2008).

Critics have addressed both these claims. With regard to the first, John Worrall (2002) has acknowledged that randomization does facilitate allocation concealment, but he emphasizes that it is not the only way to achieve this goal. Having one person or group of people assign participants to groups and provide them with the experimental or control intervention and another person or group assess the study outcomes also prevents bias in outcome assessment based on knowledge of which intervention a study participant is receiving. In fact, something like this division of labor already happens, as somebody must prepare the packages of study drugs given to participants, and they will know the contents of the packages, but remain uninvolved in outcome assessment.

It is also important to note that it is impossible to conceal group allocation for some kinds of interventions: Surgeons and psychotherapists cannot remain unaware of the treatment they are providing. In these trials, methods other than allocation concealment must be used to avoid bias in outcome assessment. For instance, the National Emphysema Treatment Trial (NETT) evaluated lung volume reduction surgery for patients with severe emphysema. (NETT Research Group, 1999) There was no attempt at concealment; participants, surgeons, radiologists, and pulmonologists all knew who had been operated on and who had not.[6] The study clearly identified a limited phenotype of emphysema patients who had a reasonable chance of benefitting from the operation. The fact that such trials can produce important and clinically useful information should serve as a reminder that allocation concealment/blinding may be neither a necessary nor preferred feature of a study design.

In many cases, to be clear, allocation concealment does serve important purposes. In particular, study participants who are aware of the group to which they are assigned are likely to be biased in their report of relevant outcomes, such as side effects, or experience of improved or worsened symptoms. For example, if they know that they are in the placebo group in a trial,

---

[6] While there have been surgical trials in the past that involved "sham" surgery, putting persons at risk with no chance of benefit is, thankfully, now considered unethical.

they may believe that they are not benefiting from an intervention, regardless of how they are actually feeling, while if they are in the experimental arm or an active control group, they may overestimate their treatment response. Yet even this argument for allocation concealment is limited, as it is not clear that subjects blinded to allocation will always yield more clinically relevant information. Concealment of treatment from subjects may actually detract from the clinical applicability of study results in several ways. In actual clinical practice, people who receive the intervention will know what treatment they are using. Assuming they will respond in a similar fashion to those enrolled in a study who did not know what they were receiving is problematic.

More generally, randomization and allocation concealment are designed to help get at the *direct* effects of intervention, yet many *indirect* effects, such as a clinician's confidence and a patient's trust, will also impact the likelihood of treatment success in the clinical realm. Consider a trial looking at whether green tea can reduce blood pressure in people with hypertension. One cannot reasonably blind subjects from their allocation group if tea is to be consumed in its usual fashion; subjects will know if they are drinking tea on a regular basis. A focus on demonstrating direct effects might lead researchers to develop a pill containing extract of green tea, thereby allowing the provision of a placebo to the control group, concealing allocation. But taking a pill is not the same thing as enjoying a cup of tea in the mid-afternoon. The indirect effects of taking a break from work, putting the kettle on, sitting down with a warm drink, perhaps talking with one's colleagues or family, may combine to affect blood pressure in a way different than green tea extract. The ultimate success or failure of any medical intervention will result from the combined direct and indirect effects. Certainly, there are reasons to want to distinguish between the two, but in clinical practice the distinction is much less important. Patients, and many clinicians, are less interested in whether people are benefiting from a particular intervention due to direct or indirect effects than the fact that they *are* benefiting.

If concealment from subjects is not absolutely necessary to a study's outcome being valid, it would seem most appropriate to avoid it. Instead, patient reports can be incorporated into the study as an outcome to be analyzed, rather than solely taken at face value. That is, it is important to study patient satisfaction with a treatment and reports of its effects when studying the effects of an intervention, and if these reports will be influenced in practice by patients' knowledge of the intervention they are using, then it is probably best to design a trial that mimics this feature of practice. In summary, random allocation is not strictly necessary for allocation concealment, though it can be an effective way of achieving this aim. Nor is allocation concealment always necessary, or even desirable, to demonstrate the clinical value of a particular intervention.

The second reason that EBM gives for its emphasis on the importance of randomization, that it is the best way to balance potential confounding factors across the treatment and the control group, has come in for even stronger criticism. As with the discussion of allocation concealment, there is a legitimate worry underlying EBM's claims. It is important that, with the exception of receiving the experimental or the control intervention, the groups in the study are similar to each other with regard to demographic and clinical characteristics. This is because if the groups are similar, it makes it more likely that any observed outcome differences between the groups are due to the intervention being tested. But if, for example, one group (on average) has a worse prognosis than the other, it is harder to interpret the study results. For instance, if the sicker group receives the experimental therapy and it turns out there are no observed outcome differences between the groups, it's not clear whether the drug is ineffective or whether it caused an improvement (on average) in the experimental group that brought their outcome to the point of similarity with the control group.

In addition to illness severity, age, or the existence of comorbid conditions—all of which are known potential influences on the effect of virtually any medical intervention—there may also be unknown differences between the groups that influence the effects of the study intervention. The claim in favor of randomized over nonrandomized studies is that randomization is the best way to ensure that both known and unknown confounders are balanced between the study groups. But this is not the case in theory, and often does not work in practice. With regard to known confounders, the most effective way to guarantee balance is to deliberately construct the two groups to ensure equal numbers of, say, participants in different age groups and with different levels of illness severity and, perhaps, men and women. Better yet, groups can be constructed with equal numbers of people with particular combinations of these factors (e.g., severely ill young women, moderately ill older men). This strategy does not, of course, deal with unknown confounders—characteristics that affect patient outcomes but that are not known to do so. Researchers can, at least, account for all factors that might possibly do so (whether or not they actually do) and match the groups for all of them. Clearly, this strategy is not always feasible, though it is often possible to balance the groups with regard to the most likely confounders. In studies where one potential confounder is known to have a strong impact on the outcome measured, stratification for that confounder prior to a randomization step is often performed in order to ensure the groups are not mismatched for such a crucial variable. This is done because, in practice, randomization alone does not always result in balanced confounders. Since published reports of studies generally list clinical and demographic information regarding the study groups (classically, in Table 1 of the paper), it is quite common to see that the groups differ with regard to one or more potentially important factors. In these situations, the failure of randomization to achieve balance across confounders is not viewed as a fatal flaw for the study—which raises the question of why randomization was thought to be necessary in the first place.

In summary, the two main arguments in favor of randomization are that it can be used to facilitate allocation concealment and that it represents a reasonable attempt at balancing cofounding variables across the treatment and the control groups. Nobody denies that random allocation is a useful tool, but its importance is overstated. Particularly in the early days of EBM, it was viewed as a *necessary* feature for a high-quality study, and, as we have noted, some EBM textbooks advised *only* looking at randomized studies when both randomized and nonrandomized trials existed. But elevating this particular characteristic of a study above all other important methodological features makes it less likely that people will think critically about, e.g., whether random allocation *has* succeeded in balancing known confounders, and how to interpret the study results when it has not, or when a good quality nonrandomized study should be rated as providing better evidence than a poor quality nonrandomized one. More recently, claims about the importance of randomization have been softened, but it still occupies a higher default level in the hierarchy of evidence and so has an outsized role in determinations of study quality.

Internal versus external validity

Another important area of philosophical criticism of EBM, touched on above, relates to the fact that study conditions are not the same as the conditions under which an intervention will be used in practice. Showing that an intervention produces an effect in a clinical trial, then, does not mean that it will work in the real world. This is the issue of the relationship between the internal validity of a study and its external validity. Internal validity is related to a study's ability to detect a difference in outcomes between the experimental and the control groups in the context of the clinical trial. It is increased by avoiding methodological errors introduced, for example, by confounding. By contrast, external validity focuses on the generalizability of a study's results beyond the trial to the broader context in which clinicians may want to utilize the intervention tested in the study. For example, it may be important to know whether the results of a clinical trial would be similar in a population of patients not represented in the original study—one that consists of patients who, say, are significantly older than those in the trial, or who are taking additional medications that would have excluded them from participating in the trial.

An ineliminable tension exists between these two kinds of validity. The previous section discussed the requirement that in a clinical trial, the treatment and the control groups should have, on average, similar demographic and clinical characteristics. If they do, it strengthens the inference from an observed outcome difference between the two groups to the claim that the intervention being tested in the study is the cause of this observed difference. Something analogous holds *within* the experimental and the control groups: The more similar the individuals in each group are to each other, the "cleaner" the assessment of the effects of the study medication and the less variable their outcomes are likely to be. This means that the "signal" (the average effect of the intervention) is less likely to be obscured by the "noise" of variable outcomes among participants in a group. Age is a good characteristic for illustrating this point. Many clinical trials restrict participation to relatively young individuals. One reason for this is that young people do not manifest the varied physiological changes associated with age that may influence drug metabolism or increase untoward side effects. Another reason is that older people are more likely than younger ones to have multiple health conditions and to be taking medications other than the drug being tested. Given these characteristics, it is reasonably likely that we can expect older individuals to respond differently to the study drug than younger, healthier trial participants. This extra variability is treated as noise when the outcomes in the experimental and control groups are compared; it is thought to obscure the signal of the "real" difference made by the experimental intervention.

Ensuring that participants in a trial, whether in the treatment or the control group, are similar to each other is a way of increasing the *internal* validity of a trial; that is, of designing a trial in such a way that any difference detected between the treatment and the control group can be confidently attributed to the intervention being tested, rather than to other variables that might influence patient outcomes. The cost of this relative precision, however, is that the participants in the trial do not resemble the broader population of patients who might be treated with the study drug (assuming the trial shows that the drug is efficacious) in clinical practice. In other words, trials with high internal validity tend to have low external validity. Another way of designing trials is to enroll a wider variety of patients and, more generally, to create a study protocol that more closely resembles the way that the interventions will actually be used. Studies designed in this way are often called "pragmatic" trials. The problem with this approach is that it results in noisier data—more variability in outcomes and more features that might be responsible for the observed differences in outcomes between the experimental and control groups, making it harder to determine the direct effect of the intervention. To return to the example in the previous paragraph, the results observed in a study that does include both older and younger participants do not actually tell us much about the effect of the drug in either group, but reflect an average outcome that is likely somewhere between the effects that would be observed in each group taken separately.

The problem of external validity arises because there is a tendency among clinical researchers to design trials with high internal validity. The results of these trials cannot always be readily extrapolated to a patient group or an individual patient who differs from the study group in what may be clinically relevant ways. (In philosophy and statistics, this is known as the reference-class problem.) For clinicians, this problem is frequently made manifest as the challenge of determining which, if any, clinical research results are most pertinent to a particular patient. When individual patients differ in significant ways from subjects in a clinical trial, it is not clear that these patients should be expected to have similar outcomes to those observed in the context of the trial. In addition, as noted above in the discussion on allocation concealment, the relative weight of direct and indirect effects of an intervention will be different between a research study and clinical practice, further challenging claims of generalizability, so that even well-matched patients may not be expected to respond as the subjects in the study did.

For clinicians, there are clearly reasons to favor pragmatic trials: Many patients and many clinical decisions are not represented in clinical trials designed to maximize internal validity, which makes extrapolation from trial results particularly fraught. But pragmatic trials also face problems: First, as explained above, variability in outcomes within the trial groups makes it difficult to obtain a precise estimate of the direct effect of an intervention. With regard to this problem, increasing the sample size of the trial will usually allow a more precise estimate; however, this will also increase the time required to run the trial and the cost of the study. Therefore, pragmatic trials are not always feasible. Second, and relatedly, the results of pragmatic trials are still averages, so while this estimate of the effects of a treatment may be based on a wider variety of patients and clinical settings, we still may not know the specific effects of differing characteristics on outcomes—whether a procedure performed in a clinician's office will have similar outcomes to when it was performed in the tertiary care setting of the clinical trial, or whether older patients really do have different treatment outcomes than younger ones. One suggested solution to this second problem is to conduct subgroup analyses—that is, to analyze outcomes separately in different groups of interest. But there is a downside here, as well. Analyzing smaller subgroups means losing the ability to detect an effect because of the smaller size of the group. There is also an increased probability that a false positive result will occur by chance when numerous subgroup analyses are conducted. Simply put, all methodological choices in trial design have downsides.

Extrapolation of trial results to individual patients

Our discussion of clinical trial design and the tension between internal and external validity shows that there will always be uncertainty associated with using the results of a clinical trial, or trials, to make decisions about the best treatment for an individual patient. This is true whether or not a patient is similar, in terms of their demographic and clinical characteristics, to the patients in a relevant clinical trial(s). The problem of how to make good treatment decisions for an individual patient is the central focus of this book, and we will examine it from different perspectives throughout the subsequent chapters. Here, we return briefly to the historical trajectory we presented in the previous chapter, to ask how epidemiological research on outcomes in populations came to replace laboratory research as the preeminent kind of medical knowledge. In doing so, we situate EBM in terms of the two tensions—between rationalism and empiricism and between general scientific knowledge and knowledge of individual patients—that have persisted throughout different epidemiological eras in medicine.

Because of the current centrality of randomized controlled trials to medicine, it is easiest to see the importance of knowing about outcomes in groups of patients in contemporary terms: It seems obvious that we need to do studies that compare groups of patients who have a characteristic of interest with a group of similar patients who do not. For example, to know whether a particular genetic variant significantly increased the risk of a disease, we would compare patients with that variant to those who lack it, and see whether the disease is more common in the former group. To see whether a medical intervention is an effective treatment for a disease, we would compare a marker of disease severity in patients who received that treatment and patients who did not.

These studies are clearly an important source of knowledge for physicians, and use methods that are of relatively recent origin. But we can also identify a number of other ways that doctors have tried to understand outcomes in groups of patients. Even though Hippocratic medicine focused on the individual patient, emphasizing the importance of knowing the patient over that of knowing the disease, it also sorted patients into categories that were thought both to determine the nature of the patient and their ailment (their natural state of balance, as well as the specific kind of humoral imbalance from which they suffered), and to suggest the kind of treatment that would best help restore them to health. The influence of this kind of thinking continued, as we saw in the discussion of the principle of specificity, though the list of different factors that influence a patient's health was expanded beyond their natural constitution to include environmental factors, such as whether they lived in an urban or a rural area, and the climate of their nation or region; lifestyle factors, such as diet, activity level, and occupation; and other factors such as sex, race, and social class. All of these were considered to be relevant to putting the patient in the appropriate category, together with others who had similar health risks and responsiveness to treatment. We also described, in the previous chapter, the numerical method pioneered in 19th-century Paris by Louis, applying then-novel statistical approaches to patient outcomes.

Sorting patients according to their characteristics, regardless of the particular methods of sorting and of comparing across groups, can only lead to probabilistic conclusions. With few exceptions, both antecedent factors and interventions that increase or decrease the probability of an outcome do not guarantee it. At one time, these probabilities were expressed descriptively, in terms of observations that an outcome was more, or less, likely in a particular group or set of circumstances. As the numerical theory of probability was developed and numerical statistics were kept, these descriptions became more precise (think about Louis' numerical method). The development of inferential statistics in the early 20th century enabled the development of contemporary methods in epidemiology and in the clinical trials that borrowed from epidemiology (Susser, 1985; Marks, 1997).

The probabilistic nature of knowledge of outcomes also illustrates both of the tensions we focus on in this chapter. First, the probabilities reported in these studies are general causal claims referring to outcomes in groups, and they do not translate straightforwardly to individuals. We might be able to say fairly confidently (within the limits of statistical confidence intervals) that a treatment is effective in 80% of a population, but it's not obvious what this means for a specific individual. It doesn't make sense to say that an 80% success rate in a population means a treatment will be 80% successful in an individual from that population. We *can* talk about probabilities of 80% in an individual, but this involves a different interpretation of probability and therefore makes different claims about what success means. In a trial of a treatment in a given population, 80% success means that (on average) 80% of people experience improvement or recovery (depending on the specific outcome being measured). Additionally, and with regard to an individual, we might mean that if they are treated repeatedly with the same intervention, they will experience the desired outcome 80% of the time, or that we are 80% confident that they will recover with treatment. These three claims reflect a frequentist, a propensity, and a subjective interpretation of probability, respectively, and the meaning of the 80% figure is not the same in any of these interpretations; we cannot infer any of the individual-level statements from the statement about the population.

The randomized controlled trial *can* provide an estimate of the effect of an intervention in a population. Yet few interventions benefit every member of population, and, as noted above, there will always be a question as to whether a specific patient sufficiently resembles the study subjects making up a particular population. So, while reliance on RCTs may increase our certainty of how often a particular outcome occurs in a population of patients, from a clinical perspective it just shifts the uncertainty to the question of whether the trial results apply to a particular patient and whether they will be one of those to respond positively. It's certainly useful to know that one intervention is effective in about 80% of patients, while a second intervention is effective in only about 30%. But those two statistics do not allow a clinician to determine whether their patient is in the 80%, the 30%, both, or neither. Nor do they say anything about whether that patient is at risk of an adverse event if treated with one or the other of those interventions. To put this point a bit differently, even the best evidence for the effectiveness of an intervention *in general* does not eliminate uncertainty for any clinician or patient *in particular*.

The general/individual tension is also related to the way that the empiricism/rationalism tension manifests in population-level research. Recall that we defined empiricism as being concerned with knowledge gained through experience, and as focusing on *whether* there is a connection between two things, rather than on *how* they are connected. Population-level research is empiricist in that it can tell us whether the probability of an outcome is greater when a certain factor is present than when it is not, but it can't tell us how the treatment and the outcome are related. In the case of a treatment, a clinical trial cannot tell us how the intervention works, in patients for whom it does work, and why it doesn't work to produce the desired outcome in other patients. Granted, by the time a potential therapy is tested in a clinical trial, researchers generally know a fair amount about its mechanism of action; drugs, in particular, are not selected to be tested in clinical trials unless there is a significant amount of preclinical, and early-phase clinical, research that suggests they have clinical promise. But that does not mean that scientists know a great deal about how they affect the body—physiological mechanisms are typically complex and, often, very little is known about why a drug that works in 80% of the population works for them, but not for the other 20%. We will say more about this problem—and some ways of dealing with it—in later chapters; for now, we just note that understanding outcome variability in a population requires a more rationalist approach than clinical trials alone provide.

Moving beyond clinical trials: Two examples

We have argued in this chapter that, no matter how useful clinical trials are, they do not provide evidence that can, on its own, guide clinical decision-making. We close with two examples that show the need to consider the results of clinical research in the context of other information, and explicate the kind of additional information that is needed. The first shows that a clinical study may be useful only for a specific population, and not generalizable to other groups of patients. The second example shows that even highly relevant information cannot simply be "applied" to the care of an individual patient.

The applicability of study results to clinical practice is not just a problem for RCTs of therapeutic interventions. Jack Hirsh, an early proponent of clinical epidemiology at McMaster University, has described a similar problem with regard to the interpretation of diagnostic tests. Impedance plethysmography has high sensitivity and specificity for symptomatic patients with venous thrombosis. Hirsh argues that researchers have a tendency to view the properties of a diagnostic test as invariant—that is, to assume that its sensitivity (the proportion of people with a disease that have a positive test) and specificity (the proportion of people without a disease who have a negative test) are the same in all populations. But when Hirsh and his colleagues began to use impedance plethysmography for screening *asymptomatic* patients, their assumption that the test would have the same specificity and sensitivity for these asymptomatic patients that it had in patients with symptoms of venous thrombosis turned out to be incorrect.

The explanation for the difference in the test properties between the two groups shows both the limitations and the importance of EBM's focus on clinical epidemiological research. First, an understanding of pathophysiology was needed to show why the results of earlier research showing the accuracy of the test in diagnosing symptomatic patients could not be extrapolated to a different clinical group. Asymptomatic patients might still have dangerous blood clots, but they are smaller than those found in patients who were exhibiting symptoms, and so they were not detected by the test. Clinical experience also turned out to play a role in identifying good candidates for the screening test. Among patients with atypical leg pain referred to Hirsh's thrombosis clinic, an initial clinical assessment divided patients into high- and low-risk groups. This initial clinical assessment was largely correct:

Follow-up testing showed that 88% of patients assigned to the high-risk group had thrombosis, compared with only 5% of patients in the low-risk group. As Hirsh describes it: "So we have come full circle in the diagnosis of venous thrombosis. Clinical diagnosis was considered to be unreliable, but people doing the studies—including us—failed to include two important items in the clinical testing. These are the risk factors for venous thrombosis and a probability of another disease. When we add these two items to the symptoms and signs, we are much better than we thought" (Daly, 2005, p. 107). This example shows that different kinds of evidence (physiological and experiential), which are associated with different levels of the hierarchy of evidence, were necessary for knowing how to interpret the test, and even whether and when to use it at all.

At the same time, this example also demonstrates the importance of some insights of the EBM approach. First, Hirsh notes that initially they had uncritically accepted the results of studies that showed similarly high sensitivity of screening impedance plethysmograph. However, those studies were not well-conducted, as they did not blind clinicians to the result of the "gold standard" venography to which the test was being compared, which influenced their assessment of the impedance plethysmography results. Later, better quality, studies found impedance plethysmography to have poor sensitivity. Second, establishing the utility of impedance plethysmography for screening also required systematic investigation both to examine the accuracy of clinical diagnosis and to recognize the different biological characteristics of symptomatic and asymptomatic thrombi and to understand how this influenced the results of the two diagnostic tests. The first point speaks to EBM's focus on the importance of critical appraisal. The second point is consistent with EBM's view that unsystematic clinical experience is a relatively poor source of evidence, but it shows that systematic study of clinical decision-making provides important evidence.

Our second example shows that clinical trial research, on its own, is an insufficient guide for clinical practice. Here, we use a hypothetical example to contrast a "straightforward application" approach, suggested by a literal understanding of EBM, with a more complex and nuanced approach to decision-making. Consider a patient, Harley, who has recently experienced a myocardial infarction. This is a condition for which there is a large amount of relevant clinical research, which shows that there are treatments with clear clinical benefit at the population level. But how should a clinician use this knowledge to treat Harley?

From a philosophical standpoint, EBM appears to encourage or even require clinicians to reason deductively, that is, to proceed from the general to the specific. Here again, EBM claims that knowledge derived from well-designed clinical research provides the best kind of general knowledge for clinical practice. Such knowledge will essentially serve as premises for a kind of logical reasoning, one that can take an almost syllogistic form. For instance, we might note (as UpToDate does) that for patients with myocardial infarction, prompt beta-blocker therapy reduces early mortality and lowers the risk of death long term. This particular claim is based on high-quality evidence derived from multiple clinical trials. Using this evidence-based claim as a premise, our clinical observation that Harley has recently experienced a myocardial infarction would seem to lead directly to the conclusion that Harley should be started on a beta-blocker. This basic clinical reasoning assumes a syllogistic form, along these lines:

> Beta-blockade lowers the risk of death after myocardial infarction.
> Harley has had a myocardial infarction.
> Therefore, Harley should be started on a beta-blocker.

We have chosen an initial premise that is well-supported by clinical research evidence for this example, so such reasoning may appear, on its face, quite sound. But clinicians will, of course, recognize that the conclusion that Harley should be started on a beta blocker is drawn much too quickly. There are contraindications to the use of beta-blockers, which would suggest the conclusion would need some sort of qualifier, along the lines of "if there are no medical contraindications."

In addition, a closer examination of the first premise reveals other limitations of this simplistic version of evidence-based deductive reasoning. First, there is a value component to the first premise and the conclusion that may go unrecognized without careful consideration. Specifically, there is an implicit assumption that lowering the risk of death, both in general and for Harley, is a good to be aimed toward. Such is the case for all medical endpoints toward which clinicians aim; they are seen as positive, beneficial, and good. But this value component cannot be simply taken at face value, and needs to be examined both in general and with regard to the specific patient. Outcome measures of many clinical trials, for example increase in bone density, are in and of themselves valueless. Such surrogate endpoints are assigned value based upon assertions that they are inextricably linked to something that clinicians and patients alike care about, like avoiding hip fractures. More importantly, individual patients may not value an outcome, even one that is assumed to be beneficial by clinicians. Harley may not value a chance at living longer if her quality of life is already at or below an acceptable minimum for her. Not infrequently, patients with advanced malignancy will choose to forego burdensome "salvage" chemotherapy despite evidence that it may provide some marginal survival benefit. We will devote much more consideration to the experiences, goals, and values of patients in Chapter 5. For now, we just point out the necessarily value-laden aspect of any medical decision, no matter how logical it might appear.

Another feature limiting the deductive model of medical decision-making is that premises derived from clinical research are never universal; thus, they are inherently fallible premises. For instance, the premise above, that "beta-blockade lowers the risk of death after myocardial infarction" is not the same as the premise "all patients who have had a myocardial infarction will live longer if they receive beta-blockade." Clinical research evidence, as our examination earlier predicts, can generally only tell us that more subjects benefited from an intervention than were harmed by it, with an understanding that many more may not have been affected either way. The premise "some post-myocardial infarction patients live longer with beta-blockade, some do not, and a few may live less long" makes the conclusion that Harley should receive a beta-blocker logically less compelling.

In one sense, the shortcomings of the deductive approach are obvious, and in fact thoughtful proponents of EBM have never claimed that evidence from clinical research should *replace* clinical experience and knowledge of pathophysiology and of patients' values. But we are left again with a problem that we identified at the beginning of the chapter. In the absence of an explanation of how to integrate these distinct kinds of considerations, it's understandable that critics of EBM have accused it of promoting the kind of deductive reasoning we criticize here. After all, the hierarchy of evidence does clearly place clinical trials above other kinds of knowledge, and even the metaphor of a "base" implies that evidence from clinical research is fundamental to clinical practice, more so than other things that doctors need to know.

Thankfully, there are more ways to reason, in life and in clinical medicine, than by deduction alone. Diagnosis, in particular, often involves a form of abductive reasoning, attempting to discover the best explanation for a set of observations, such as signs, symptoms, and laboratory/imaging studies. Reasoning by analogy, basing conclusions on finding similarities between at least two different systems or exemplars, including patients, is also fundamental to human cognition and can be particularly valuable under a variety of circumstances. Later, we will argue that one variety of analogic reasoning, case-based reasoning, is widely applicable and offers multiple advantages in clinical medicine.

A final note regarding the elephant in the room

So far, we have discussed EBM and evidence from clinical trials without examining some of the underlying features involved in the design, funding, aggregation, and dissemination of clinical research. Jonathan Fuller, a physician and philosopher, has helped elucidate the importance of such meta-research, investigations into these features of the contemporary medical research complex, such as funding and publication bias. Fuller argues that the meta-evidence, produced by meta-research, should be used in considering the clinical research evidence purporting the value of diagnostic and therapeutic interventions (Fuller, 2018). That is, we cannot critically assess the report of a clinical trial without incorporating what we know about the context of how such studies come to be financed, performed, and published in the first place. For the most part, understanding meta-evidence should lead us to be more skeptical of the value of published evidence.

Perhaps the best and most relevant example of the value of this approach lies in examining the results of studies as they relate to the goals of funders, particularly pharmaceutical companies. We have considered bias in the statistical sense, when the results of a trial deviate systematically from the "true" effects of an intervention. As an example, this kind of bias occurs when there are differences between the experimental and control group with regard to a potential confounder, such as age, which can sometimes happen even with random allocation of study participants to groups. But bias can sometimes be deliberately built into a study by funders who want their product to perform well.

Meta-research studies have shown that clinical trials sponsored by pharmaceutical companies are more likely to favor the sponsor's drug than trials with other funding sources. This is not due to outright fraud or to sloppy science; on balance studies funded by pharmaceutical companies are technically very well designed. That is, they meet the criteria for good study design, set by efforts like the CONSORT statement. But they are also designed to maximize the chances of the funder getting the desired results. Richard Smith, the former editor of *BMJ*, has discussed a number of ways that a trial can be designed so that it is biased in favor of the sponsor's drug. These include testing the drug against a comparator already known to be inferior, testing it against too low a dose of the comparator (which will then look ineffective), or too high a dose (so that it causes more side effects than it would if used properly), or measuring multiple endpoints and only publishing the ones that favor the drug (Smith, 2005).

Which potential interventions get studied in the first place depends, particularly in the United States, on the funding entity standing to profit from positive results. Performing a large, high-quality RCT is expensive. While some countries with a national health care system fund research that may lead to cost savings, pharmaceutical sponsors of RCTs almost invariably fund studies of interventions that will increase the cost of care.

The developers of EBM were also well aware of the potential effects of the pharmaceutical industry on clinical decision-making (see, e.g., Sackett and Oxman, 2003). Moreover, at around the same time as the development of EBM, there was a general increase in awareness of these problems—and creative (albeit only moderately successful) means were developed to deal with this kind of bias. For example, the International Council of Medical Journal Editors (ICMJE) established a set of guidelines for manuscripts submitted to medical journals to ensure that published reports of trials were clear and thorough. To avoid problems like selective publishing of results, clinical trial registries were developed that made trial protocols readily available, and journal editors were encouraged to confirm that trial reports submitted for publication had followed the original protocol.

Yet despite these efforts, many of these meta-concerns appear to have only grown in importance. Both EBM "insiders" and philosophers continue to draw attention to publication bias and the continuing influence of industry on the trustworthiness of available evidence. Trish Greenhalgh and colleagues in the EBM Renaissance Group, for example, have specifically called out conflicts of interest and lax oversight by publishers, as well as the tendency of unimaginative research design to produce evidence of low value to clinicians, as undermining the entire mission of EBM. (Greenhalgh et al., 2014).

Summary

In this chapter, we have focused on our current epistemological era, which is dominated by EBM. We traced the history of EBM and how it has changed over time, introducing two epistemological criticisms of EBM, both of which relate to the emphasis on RCTs as the best source of evidence. First, there are multiple aspects of the methods and execution of a clinical trial that contribute to the quality of its results; however, EBM has elevated randomization above these other features. Critics have argued that this is not warranted. Second, the hierarchy of evidence is of little use in helping clinicians to extrapolate from the results of a clinical trial to an individual patient, or to groups of patients who do not resemble the average patient in the trial. In presenting these criticisms, we have aimed to do justice to the important contributions of EBM, while also being clear about its limitations. EBM has focused almost entirely on the application of the results of clinical research to medical decision-making. We will now examine, in detail, the other kinds of knowledge that clinicians possess and must utilize in order to benefit individual patients.

3
Knowledge of Mechanism and Pathophysiologic Reasoning

During her medical school training, Dr. Lee spent a full two years learning physiology, pathophysiology, and the basic science said to underlie health and disease. At the time, she remembers wondering how relevant such knowledge would be to the actual practice of medicine. Much of what she learned during those years never seemed to be necessary in caring for patients. Still, she often found herself thinking about her patients in terms of causes and effects. What were the likely physiologic conditions that were resulting in her patient's symptoms? How might a treatment change those conditions? Her patients typically wanted explanations for their symptoms and her treatment recommendations. Those explanations typically involved a discussion of anatomy, physiology, or pharmacology. She always found herself wanting to understand how a new medication worked, not simply that a clinical trial showed that it did. And when things did not work as expected, she searched for an understanding of why they had not.

Western medicine has a long tradition of reasoning about biological mechanisms when making clinical assessments and decisions. As we described in Chapter 1, for much of the past two millennia, basing clinical practice on a theory of health and disease has distinguished physicians from "lesser" practitioners, including barbers and surgeons, who were considered empirics for their practical training and their reliance on personal observation. Physicians, over the centuries, have held a large number of different theories upon which to give orders and make recommendations. Those who endorsed a humoral mechanism of disease, for instance, focused their therapeutic efforts on re-establishing *eucrasia*, a balance of the humors associated with well-being.

Recognition of the limitations of such reasoning, particularly when it rests upon overly simplistic or even frankly erroneous understandings of physiology, has led to skepticism regarding the value of knowledge of physiological mechanisms for medical practice. Yet anyone who believes that the mechanistic reasoning has been banished from clinical medicine need look no further than the recent focus on the "cytokine storm" purported to kill those with COVID-19; the ideas underlying the humoral theory of disease remain a fixture in medicine, although now there are many more "humors," with names like IL-6 and tumor necrosis factor. Treatments were advanced to restore balance between pro- and anti-inflammatory proteins; the search for *eucrasia* persists.

Contemporary appeals to mechanism, however, have moved far beyond the speculative theories of an earlier epistemological era. Ongoing work in the biological sciences has markedly improved our understanding of the genetic, molecular, chemical, and physiological underpinnings of health and disease. Establishing the components of biological mechanisms and explaining how they function to produce an output, as well as how they can fail to do so, is a scientific pursuit that is both empirical and experimental. Contemporary medical knowledge of mechanisms derives from an understanding, rooted in the basic sciences and human physiology, of how the human organism is put together, including why and how it can fail to function well. Yet it is also true that our understanding of important mechanisms of disease remains incomplete, which leads to justifiable caution in using knowledge of mechanisms in clinical reasoning.

Acknowledging the fallibility of mechanistic reasoning, however, does not eliminate its value for clinical medicine.[1] Knowledge of pathophysiology and reasoning about how pathophysiology is related to a patient's clinical status remain central to medical education and to clinical practice, and rightly so. The knowledge that physicians generally acquire in the pre-clinical years of training, in physiology, pathophysiology, pharmacology, and so on, is largely knowledge of mechanisms. Moreover, they will come to *use* this knowledge in a variety of different ways in their clinical reasoning.

In this chapter, we aim to clarify the different roles that knowledge of physiological mechanisms plays in clinical practice and how this knowledge is justified. We begin with a brief summary of what evidence-based medicine (EBM) says about the place of biological mechanisms, and why evidence from studies that examine these mechanisms ranks low on the hierarchy of evidence. We suggest that this stance is often oversimplified, in part because

---

[1] Moreover, as we have seen in the previous chapter, knowledge from clinical research also remains fallible, at times inconsistent, and prone to over-extrapolation.

the proponents of EBM do not say much about this issue, but also because, more generally, EBM lacks a detailed account of what physiological mechanisms are and why they are important to medicine. We then turn to work in philosophy of science and philosophy of medicine to provide such an account. With this theoretical background in place, we describe several ways in which clinicians rely upon mechanistic reasoning in practice and how these uses are justified on the basis of both the EBM and the philosophical discussions.

Evidence-based medicine and physiological mechanisms

In July 2020, half a year into the coronavirus pandemic, *BMJ* published a letter to the editor that suggested using mast cell stabilizers to treat COVID-19. The author noted that lung damage associated with the infection was caused by cytokine release from mast cells, briefly describing the process of mast cell activation and the resulting symptoms (Myers, 2020). She then pointed out that mast cell stabilizers and mediator blockers are used to treat conditions with similar respiratory symptoms and concluded by naming several mast cell stabilizers that could be trialed, whether as an individual therapy or in some combination, at an early stage of infection in patients with moderate symptoms or on admission to the hospital, to see whether these interventions affect the subsequent course of disease.

This short letter illustrates several ways in which careful reasoning about physiological mechanisms occurs in medicine: It identifies the cause of a set of symptoms and details the underlying physiological mechanism; it draws comparisons with other conditions that have similar symptoms and pathophysiology; and it describes how specific interventions used to treat these other conditions might plausibly alter clinical outcomes in a new one.

At some points in the history of medicine, this kind of physiological reasoning would have been enough to lead clinicians to adopt a therapy. Now, however, physicians would be rightly skeptical of recommendations based only on a physiological hypothesis—note that the recommendation in this letter is to conduct research on these potentially useful interventions, not to rush them into practice. This example is therefore consistent with EBM's general assessment (described in Chapter 2) regarding reasoning about mechanisms, which is that studies examining physiological mechanisms provide only weak evidence that a therapy is effective. Such studies, therefore, are placed near the bottom of the evidence hierarchy.

In support of this low ranking, proponents of EBM claim that clinical trials provide better evidence regarding treatment effectiveness than do studies based on claims about the physiological mechanism of the intervention. Often, the argument for this claim takes the form of examples of cases in which a therapy that had been adopted on the basis of physiological knowledge proved, when an randomized controlled trial (RCT) was conducted, to be ineffective or even harmful (Howick, 2011; Guyatt et al., 2015). In a frequently cited example, pharmacologic suppression of arrhythmias after myocardial infarction resulted in an increased rate of sudden death. While it seemed physiologically reasonable to try to decrease the incidence of arrhythmias in order to decrease deaths due to arrhythmias, things turned out to be a bit more complicated. This kind of example underlies EBM's position that only a study that examines treatment outcomes in large numbers of patients and compares those outcomes with those found in a control group can provide strong evidence of effectiveness. Our intuition that a mechanistic argument was not a sufficient justification for using mast cell stabilizers to treat COVID-19 also turned out to be correct.

But EBM has more to say about our knowledge of biological mechanisms, and about when and how this knowledge should be used in clinical research and clinical practice. In addition to the question of whether (and when) evidence from studies on biological mechanisms can justify claims about the effectiveness of a therapy, EBM's brief discussion of mechanisms is relevant to two additional questions: First, whether knowledge of biological mechanisms can be used to extrapolate from the results of clinical trials to the care of an individual patient, and, second, when and how physiological measurements (so-called surrogate outcomes) should be used as proxies for, or predictors of, clinically important events.

With regard to both of these additional questions, EBM recognizes an important role for knowledge of physiological mechanisms. Knowledge of a patient's biological characteristics is often listed as one of the important factors that must be integrated with the results of clinical research in caring for that individual patient. Here, EBM explicitly acknowledges a role for physiological knowledge, saying that understanding pathophysiology can allow a clinician "to better judge whether the results [of a trial] are applicable to the patient at hand" (EBM Working Group, 1992, p. 2421). Similarly, a key resource on how to practice EBM, *The Users' Guides to the*

Medical Literature, acknowledges that a patient's biological characteristics should "sometimes lead us to hesitate" to apply the results of a study (Guyatt et al., 2015, p. 237). For example, patients who have comorbid conditions and/or who are elderly may not respond the same way as the average trial participant.

By contrast, EBM is wary of clinical research that examines so-called surrogate endpoints. Many clinical trials measure clinically important outcomes such as deaths, heart attacks, or days in the hospital. But other researchers may also (or instead) choose to measure physiological characteristics, such as blood pressure or cholesterol levels, that are supposed to predict these clinical outcomes. That is, they are surrogates or substitutes for clinical outcomes. Researchers may choose to measure these characteristics because changes to the surrogate outcomes occur in the short term, and it is not feasible to conduct a trial that lasts long enough to provide an adequate assessment of the intervention's effects on clinically important outcomes. EBM is not against *all* use of surrogate endpoints. Rather, it cautions against using them when they have not been adequately demonstrated to predict clinical outcomes, which requires establishing that the physiological characteristic being measured is part of the mechanism that leads to the clinical outcome of interest.[2]

Overall, however, we do not believe EBM presents a well-developed account of when clinical claims based upon mechanisms, in general, are justified. To begin to develop such an account, we next turn to work in the philosophy of science.

Philosophy of mechanisms

Understanding of physiological mechanisms is generated from a combination of sources that may include a wide variety of basic, animal, and human investigations (Baetu, 2016). The use of knowledge of mechanisms in medicine, however, does not necessarily depend upon detailed knowledge of these individual experiments. Medical texts distill this research, providing an overview of what is known about these mechanisms, often glossing over

---

[2] This is a particular concern because pharmaceutical companies may conduct trials focusing on surrogate endpoints that may not have any real clinical importance. Research in Alzheimer's disease that focuses on reduction in amyloid is one such example.

a lot of complexity that is evident only when the original studies are examined. This means that, although a clinician may cite a particular clinical trial in support of a clinical claim, only rarely would they refer to a particular laboratory study. Clinicians use a broader understanding of mechanisms to reason to conclusions regarding patient care. Reliance on such reasoning to warrant a clinical claim may be called the "pathophysiologic rationale" for that clinical conclusion (Tonelli and Williamson, 2020).

At the same time, the kinds of epistemological questions we address in this book require a more detailed account of what a mechanism is and how it works—or when and how it can fail to work. In the past few decades, philosophers of science have turned their attention to the wide variety of methods that scientists use to investigate biological mechanisms and to the ways that the results of numerous experiments are brought together to provide explanations of what these mechanisms do. There is now a vast philosophical literature on mechanisms, only a small portion of which has been taken up in work in the philosophy of medicine.[3] Multiple definitions of mechanism are given in the literature, which tend to agree in their main features; we will use the one that philosophers of medicine have tended to draw on:

> A mechanism for a phenomenon consists of entities and activities organized in such a way that they are responsible for the phenomenon.
> (Illari and Williamson, 2012, p. 120)

An example may help to make this definition less abstract. A mechanism that explains a physiological phenomenon, such as synaptic transmission, includes reference to the entities that are components of that mechanism, such as cell membranes, receptors, synaptic vesicles, and neurotransmitters, and to activities—what those components do. For example, we might provide the following mechanistic explanation for synaptic transmission: "the vesicles fuse with the membrane of the presynaptic neuron and release neurotransmitters, which bind with receptors on the postsynaptic neuron." It is also important to recognize that mechanisms can be studied at a number of different levels. Synaptic transition is a phenomenon that involves subcellular and molecular entities and their activities, which has implications for understanding the activity of cells and neural circuits, which in turn explain behavioral phenomena. In the laboratory, scientists

---

[3] We do not aim to do justice to the larger literature here. For an overview, see Craver and Darden (2013) or Craver and Tabery (2023).

will often intervene on a mechanism to see how it works. This might involve, for example, changing an input to the mechanism, or altering the structure of one of the entities that is part of the mechanism, to see how its function changes, and how the phenomenon produced via the mechanism is altered. Experiments involving genetic mutations are an example of this approach that is relevant, albeit in a complex way, to medicine.

This laboratory-based alteration of a mechanism's component is similar to what occurs in the body in many diseases: Alteration in a component of a mechanism changes its function, and thus changes the overall functioning of the mechanism. To continue with our example of synaptic transmission, Parkinson's disease involves the loss of dopaminergic neurons, leading to alterations in brain function that result in the disease's characteristic motor symptoms. Similarly, we can understand the effects of a therapeutic intervention as an input into a physiological mechanism—one that aims to alter the functioning of that mechanism to produce a desired outcome. The symptoms of Parkinson's disease, for example, can be mitigated using drugs that provide the dopamine that the brain is no longer able to make, thus restoring some of the activity of mechanisms that rely on dopamine to function.

This brief sketch of the nature of physiological mechanisms also suggests ways that physicians think about mechanisms in their clinical practice. Their goal in diagnosis is to explain the specific phenomenon of their patient's symptoms, with reference to what they know about the various mechanisms that might be giving rise to those symptoms. Often, this is done with the help of tools (physical exams, patient history, laboratory tests) that provide clues about the underlying mechanisms. In the context of making treatment decisions, however, we have already seen that there is reason to doubt that identifying a biological mechanism linking an intervention with a clinical outcome is enough. In part, this is because much of our knowledge of mechanisms comes from laboratory research, which uses carefully controlled conditions and skillful experimental manipulation to identify the entities that comprise a mechanism and to elucidate the role that each entity plays in bringing about the phenomenon of interest. But outside of the laboratory, there is more variability in what a mechanism does and how its functioning can be influenced by a variety of different inputs and by interactions with other mechanisms. This means that a laboratory study (or a number of such studies) that demonstrates that a mechanism functions in a certain way cannot show that it will function the same way outside of the lab, where factors that can be controlled for in the laboratory setting can influence the mechanism. Much depends, then, on how stable the functioning of a mechanism is across different environmental contexts. Given this point, we can think of clinical research as providing evidence regarding how consistently a mechanism operates. If a clinical trial shows that a treatment causes a clinically relevant outcome in a relatively large percentage of patients, we can infer that the mechanism linking the treatment and the outcome is quite stable.

Knowledge of mechanisms or knowledge from clinical trials?

With this point in mind, we can return to the question of whether knowledge of a physiological mechanism provides sufficient evidence of effectiveness to justify using a particular therapy, drawing on a disagreement between the philosophers Jeremy Howick and Holly Andersen. Responding to EBM's placement of evidence from studies examining physiological mechanisms at the bottom of the hierarchy of evidence, Howick argues that, in some rare cases, reasoning about mechanisms can provide sufficient evidence of treatment effectiveness, so that a clinical trial is unnecessary.[4] He identifies a set of conditions that must be met in order for what he calls "mechanistic reasoning" to be "high quality": (1) Knowledge of the relevant mechanism(s) must be complete, in that there are no obvious gaps in our understanding of the physiological mechanisms that link the intervention to the outcome(s) of interest; (2) we need to recognize and take into account the probabilistic nature of mechanisms' operation, as even mechanisms that we understand very well do not lead to exactly the same outcomes in all cases; and (3) we must also account for the complexity of mechanisms, including the ways in which a mechanism of interest may interact with other mechanisms, for example, as in the case of side effects of therapy (Howick, 2011, p. 144). In the admittedly rare situations in which all of these criteria are met, knowing the mechanism underlying the effects of a therapy provides sufficient knowledge that the intervention is effective and safe; a clinical trial is not required. Howick gives the example of the use of radiotherapy to shrink goiter, which he says does satisfy these criteria. Clinicians are likely to come up with multiple examples by reflecting on practice,

---

[4] Although Howick is generally sympathetic to EBM, in his discussion of the role of mechanisms, he provides only a "qualified defense" of the hierarchy's approach of devaluing mechanisms (Howick, 2011).

for instance ligation of a bleeding artery or careful positioning of patients undergoing prolonged anesthesia for surgical procedures.

Andersen, by contrast, doubts that there *are* any such cases; that is, she says the conditions Howick describes are unlikely to ever occur. She emphasizes how unlikely it is that our knowledge of mechanisms is complete, and also notes that, even in cases where our best understanding indicates two mechanisms may appear to be independent, they may actually interact (Andersen, 2012, p. 995). For example, she describes a case in which infants receiving immunizations were given prophylactic paracetamol (acetaminophen) to prevent fever, based on the reasonable belief that the mechanism of action of the drug and the immune response were separate. In fact, the mechanisms turned out not to be completely separate, and the vaccines were less effective in infants who were given paracetamol. On balance, then, Andersen argues that EBM's position, that knowledge of mechanisms is not sufficient to justify using a therapy in clinical practice, is generally correct.

If we look more closely at the examples Howick and Andersen have given in this section, it's clear that there is an important difference between them. Howick's example of radiotherapy for goiter, as well as our examples of ligating arteries and of positioning a patient during anesthesia, refer to mechanisms at a different level of analysis than Andersen's example of paracetamol and immunization. Specifically, the examples that support the claim that knowledge of mechanisms is sufficient to support an intervention are at the level of gross anatomy, while Andersen's pharmaceutical intervention affects subcellular mechanisms. Higher-level mechanisms, we suggest, are both easier to study and more likely to be robust in different environments, including from patient to patient, than lower-level mechanisms. We will return to this point later in the chapter.

Knowledge of mechanisms and knowledge from clinical trials

So far, we have been influenced in our discussion of the relationship between knowledge of physiological mechanisms and knowledge from clinical research by the hierarchy of evidence. In placing these kinds of knowledge at different levels of the hierarchy, EBM sets us up to ask whether knowledge of a physiological mechanism linking a treatment and a clinical outcome is ever sufficient (i.e., without additional evidence from clinical trials) to show that a treatment will be effective. But this question draws our attention away from an important fact: We need *both* knowledge of physiological mechanisms and epidemiological knowledge to establish that the treatment is effective. In this section, we draw on clinical reasoning and on the philosophy of medicine to illustrate the interdependence of the two kinds of evidence.

In describing EBM's devaluation of evidence from studies of physiological mechanisms, we noted that this view is commonly justified using cases in which physiological studies initially suggested a link between a treatment and an outcome, but the connection was not supported when a clinical trial was conducted. For example, one of the founders of EBM claims: "Millions of dollars' worth of bench research that appeared to show a reduction in atherosclerosis-related oxidative stress with vitamin E therapy was recently tested in an RCT that asked the vital question: Does the vitamin E therapy endorsed by this research really help prevent heart disease? The answer was a resounding 'No.'" (Sackett, 1999, p. 1414). But these cases should also remind us that there needs to be a significant amount of evidence regarding physiological mechanisms before a clinical trial is even conducted: Every trial that *does* confirm an association between a treatment and an outcome is based on a great deal of physiological research. Think again about the *BMJ* letter about mast cell stabilizers, which recommends conducting a clinical trial to test the suggested therapies for COVID-19. The author suggests half a dozen potential interventions with similar potential effects on mast cells, which could be tried singly or in combination. But in what combination(s)? At what dose? For how long? And what kind of effect would count as successful treatment? In short, many more decisions need to be made when conducting a clinical trial than simply identifying a promising compound. Knowledge of mechanisms is important both for making these choices in the first place and for assessing the success or failure of a clinical trial once it is completed.

Like researchers, clinicians approach claims about treatment effectiveness with evidence of physiological mechanisms in mind. A great deal of pre-clinical medical education emphasizes the importance of understanding biological information and processes. Even in an era of evidence-based medicine, the scientific training and biological knowledge of clinicians predispose them to think of causes in mechanistic, rather than probabilistic, terms. In addition to insisting upon statistical demonstration of effect, clinicians want to know why and how a treatment works.

One way in which physicians draw on knowledge of physiological mechanisms is by assessing the results of a clinical trial. Although published reports of clinical trials primarily provide statistical evidence that an intervention has a particular effect on an outcome, practicing clinicians will recognize the ongoing importance of evidence related to the physiological mechanism of action of the intervention as they assess individual reports of clinical research. This knowledge is particularly important in clinical trial reports dealing with a novel intervention.[5]

The first thing to note is that, even though their main purpose is to provide evidence that the intervention makes a statistically significant difference to the outcome(s) being measured, reports of clinical research nearly always include a description of the mechanism of action of the drug or device being studied in the trial. Doing so establishes a biologically plausible explanation of how the drug or device is thought to affect the outcome(s) being measured in the study. For instance, a clinical trial of baricitinib for SARS-CoV-2 infection begins with a description of its biochemical inhibitory effects on "multiple cytokines and biomarkers responsible for COVID-19 pathophysiology" (Marconi et al., 2021). There is no requirement that a study submitted for publication contain such a discussion, as there is, for example, to describe the process of randomization or the statistical analyses used. Yet these discussions are ubiquitous in reports of clinical studies, which suggests that they do serve some important purpose for readers. One possible reason for including them is that describing the mechanism of action explains why researchers chose to perform the study, given the amount of time, effort, and money required to undertake the research.

Another reason is that this kind of description of the mechanism of action of an intervention is intended to influence and/or to aid clinicians reading the paper (Tonelli and Williamson, 2020). There are at least two ways in which this influence might work in the case of studies finding that a new treatment, or an older treatment being tested for a new indication, is effective. First, describing a mechanism that suggests that the treatment is likely to be effective provides background knowledge for the reader; it puts the study into a broader context and gives the reader information they will need to interpret the study's results. More specifically, seeing that there are plausible reasons to hypothesize that the drug or device will have the intended

---

[5] In this section and the following, we are building on arguments first presented in Tonelli and Williamson (2020).

outcome(s) gives the reader some preliminary reason to accept the study's findings. Regardless of the strength of the actual statistical findings of a study, a clinician is more likely to accept those results if they have a strong prior belief that the treatment is likely to work (Rubenfeld, 2001).

To see this, consider a case where there is *no* likely mechanism underlying an effect observed in the study. Ultra-high dilution homeopathic remedies are biologically implausible for at least two reasons. First, they are based on the "principle of similars," which says that a substance that causes symptoms in healthy people can cure those symptoms in people with a disease. No strong scientific evidence supports that this is the case. Second, making such homeopathic remedies involves diluting the substance in a series of stages, so that by the time the process is complete there is likely to be less than a single molecule of the original substance in the remedy. From a biological perspective, it is highly implausible that such homeopathic remedies will have a therapeutic effect. Neither the principle of similars nor the practice of using ultra-high dilution remedies is based on a plausible biologic mechanism that would explain how the homeopathic remedy can improve the condition it is intended to treat.

Despite the lack of a generally accepted mechanism of action for these remedies, a number of clinical trials have tested homeopathic remedies against placebo (or sometimes against allopathic treatments), and there are enough such trials that meta-analyses have also been conducted.[6] Early studies of homeopathic remedies actually supported that homeopathy was more effective than placebo for a variety of conditions. Despite this clinical trial evidence, the implausibility of homeopathy's mechanism of action meant that few people were willing to accept the results of the studies. Critics of homeopathy later pointed out that these trials were of low methodological quality and argued that this, rather than the direct effects of homeopathic remedies, explained their positive results. Similarly, the use of copper bracelets for rheumatic symptoms or topical crystal application for pain relief so lack in biological plausibility that even poorly controlled and underpowered negative studies are considered definitive for rejecting them as legitimate therapies. Those who did accept the results of these trials, and, in fact, those who still argue that there is good evidence for homeopathic

---

[6] Published reports of biologically implausible treatments are rare in mainstream medical journals, in large part because it's highly unlikely that such implausible treatments will be the focus of a clinical trial. In the rare cases where such studies are performed, they are often undertaken with the goal of debunking a popular or traditional remedy.

remedies, were already sympathetic toward homeopathic medicine; their estimate of the probability of claims that the remedy worked was already fairly high.

Most readers of a positive study of the effects of homeopathy or a negative study of crystals or copper jewelry will begin reading these reports believing that there was a very low probability that these treatments are effective. This kind of preexisting belief is called a "prior probability" (often shortened to just "prior")—it represents the confidence that the reader of a clinical trial has in the hypothesis being tested *before* they examine the evidence provided by the trial. A mathematical formula known as Bayes' theorem accounts for both the prior probability of a claim or hypothesis and the strength of the evidence presented in support of that claim to calculate the extent to which new evidence should increase our belief that the claim is true. The result of the calculation is called the posterior probability. Because the posterior probability takes into account both the strength of the study evidence and the prior probability that the claim is true, presenting the same evidence to someone with a low prior (that is, they think the claim is very unlikely to be true) and to someone with a high prior (that is, they think the claim is likely to be true) will still lead to different assessments of how likely the claim is to be true.[7]

How does this relate to the practice of providing background knowledge about mechanisms in a report of a clinical study? We can now see this part of a report of a trial as an attempt to influence a reader's prior probability that the intervention is effective. The background knowledge provided, if it is convincing to the clinician, will raise their assessment of the probability that the intervention tested in the study is effective, which will make the statistical evidence of effectiveness provided in the study more compelling. That is, a clinician who has a strong prior belief based upon mechanistic reasoning that the treatment should work will be more likely to accept that the statistical results really do indicate that the treatment affects the outcomes measured in the study.[8]

---

[7] With enough evidence accumulated in favor of a hypothesis, the initial differences between individuals' priors have less and less effect on the posterior probability.

[8] Note that this explanation might just seem like we are saying that clinicians will just be convinced by what they already believe to be true (and there is some reason to worry about this, as studies examining confirmation bias show us). But it is completely rational to assess new evidence in light of what we already know. Think again about the homeopathy example. Or conversely, if a well-established, effective treatment performs poorly in one study, we would be much more likely to decide that the study results were incorrect than to ignore the large amount of preexisting evidence of effectiveness.

In addition to providing a foundation for clinical trial research, and for interpreting the results of these studies, knowledge of physiological mechanisms can also serve as direct evidence for the claim that the intervention is effective. In terms of Bayes' theorem, here information about mechanisms is used as *part of* the evidence for a claim, rather than as background information we bring to the assessment of new evidence. This use of information about mechanisms is in line with both the basic science training of clinicians and with the position of many philosophers of science. In addition to simply increasing a prior probability that there is a mechanism linking a treatment and an outcome, evidence of a mechanism can serve to rule out other possible explanations for a statistical connection between them.

For example, if evidence from a large, well-done RCT of a new drug shows a reduction in Hgb A1C in the treatment group, this alone cannot show that the drug causes this reduction. Without a plausible physiological explanation, we cannot rule out the possibility that the drug simply interferes with the Hgb A1C assay. We need at least some plausible explanation of a mechanism of action of the drug before we conclude that it effectively decreases blood sugar in diabetics. If a study indicates that there is a strong statistical association between a treatment and a clinical outcome, despite the biological implausibility of a connection, scientists will likely begin to search for a mechanism that explains the statistical finding (Tonelli and Williamson, 2020).

This kind of search does not always result in the discovery of a biologically plausible mechanism. Tonelli and Williamson (2020) cite the example of a randomized trial examining the use of recombinant human activated protein C (drotrecogin alfa) to treat sepsis (Bernard et al., 2001). Whereas, as we described above, clinical trials generally begin with a review of the physiological literature that outlines the mechanism of action of the treatment, this study provided an extended discussion of several possible mechanisms of action for the drug. Tonelli and Williamson note that "the assertion of biological plausibility in this case required tremendous effort, relying heavily upon speculation and emphasizing effects upon parts of the sepsis cascade not generally seen as crucial to outcome, [which] meant that it was not particularly compelling to many clinicians" (p. 117). They suggest that this weak evidence for a mechanism explaining the drug's effects "likely contributed to slow uptake of the drug after approval in the US" (p. 117). Moreover, the drug was later withdrawn from the market, as subsequent clinical trials showed that it had little clinical benefit—a further demonstration that evidence of mechanisms should play an important role in both the decision to conduct and the interpretation of a clinical trial.

Philosophers of medicine have argued convincingly that in the health sciences, both evidence of mechanism and evidence of a statistical connection are normally necessary to make a claim regarding causality. Federica Russo and Jon Williamson and their colleagues have developed an account of causality that incorporates evidence from both studies of physiological mechanisms and knowledge from population-level clinical trials. They begin with the "uncontroversial" claim "that the health sciences look for causes, namely for causes of disease, and for effective treatments" (Russo and Williamson, 2007, p. 157). They then argue that knowledge of causation has two components that are both necessary to support general causal claims, developing what they call the Russo–Williamson thesis (RWT). A paper that applies RWT to questions about EBM presents the thesis as follows:

> In order to establish that A is a cause of B in medicine one normally needs to establish two things. First, that A and B are suitably correlated—typically that A and B are probabilistically dependent, conditional on B's other known causes. Second, that there is some underlying mechanism linking A and B that can account for the difference that A makes to B.
> (Clarke et al., 2014, p. 343)

During medical training, if not sooner, clinicians learn that causation cannot be determined by statistical correlation alone. The RWT asserts that *evidence of a mechanism* linking A and B is necessary in order to establish causality. Such evidence also increases confidence that a causal relationship is relevant to practice, because, they suggest, if we can single out a stable, plausible mechanism, that mechanism is likely to occur in a range of individuals, making the causal relation stable over a variety of populations. If no mechanism is found, it may be because the correlation is spurious, or particular to a specific sample population, or to a specific set of circumstances (Russo and Williamson, 2007, p. 158; Clarke et al., 2014, pp. 343–4).

In addition to evidence of a mechanism, *evidence of statistical dependence* of B on A is necessary because that is the kind of evidence that tells us the extent to which A actually makes a difference to B. Recall that physiological mechanisms exist in a complex environment that affects how they function, and they interact with other mechanisms. Therefore, the existence of a mechanism linking A with B does not guarantee that the occurrence of A will actually cause B to occur. Statistical evidence that A *does* lead to B, in some probabilistic sense, shows that the purported cause actually does make a difference, at least at a population level, to the effect (Russo and Williamson, 2007, p. 159).

In summary, RWT says that research on physiological processes is the best way to show that there is a mechanism linking A and B and clinical research is the best way to show that the presence of A really does make a difference to whether B occurs. These two kinds of evidence have different strengths, so that clinical trials provide better evidence of correlation and physiological research provides better evidence of mechanisms.[9] Using the two together, they say, "produces much stronger overall evidence of efficacy than would either type of evidence on its own" (Parkkinen et al., 2018, p. 93).

Although clinicians may be somewhat removed from philosophical debates regarding causality, this dual requirement of both of these kinds of evidence has a rich tradition in modern medicine, going back at least fifty years to Bradford Hill's exposition of the features that support a judgment of causality beyond mere recognition of an association between two variables. Indeed, biological plausibility was one of Hill's nine proposed types of evidentiary support for determining causation (Hill, 1965). Clinicians may seek, and even demand, mechanistic evidence before believing that a statistical difference alone demonstrates that a study treatment caused the observed outcomes. RWT provides an account of how evidence of mechanisms and clinical trial evidence work together to establish a causal relationship between a treatment and a clinical outcome.

When is mechanism-based extrapolation justified?

Even when a clinician is convinced that there is good evidence to show that a treatment is effective *in general*, the question remains of whether it will be effective for the particular patient in front of them. As the integration problem makes clear, the application of the results of clinical research to the care of individual patients is not straightforward. This is another case in which knowledge of mechanisms can be helpful—though again,

---

[9] In addition, Russo and Williams note that physiological research on mechanisms provides *some* evidence that A makes a difference to B, while a statistical relationship between A and B provides *some* evidence of a mechanism linking the two.

the details of how and when knowledge of mechanisms can aid clinical decision-making are important.

In this section, we examine possible roles of mechanisms and mechanistic reasoning to help provide a broader epistemological context for clinical decision-making. In line with EBM's own recommendations, a number of clinicians and philosophers (including one of us) have argued for using knowledge of physiological mechanisms to determine whether the results of a clinical trial apply to a particular patient (Tonelli, 2006; Andersen, 2012; Tonelli and Williamson, 2020). That is, utilizing pathophysiologic reasoning is one method to help overcome the integration problem. Others (including one of us) have raised concerns about mechanistic reasoning playing this role (Bluhm, 2013; Howick et al., 2013).

In the previous section, we talked about the role of mechanisms in establishing general causal claims (of the sort that "A causes B"). But even when there is good evidence that this claim is (in general) true, it is not true in every case, or in every context. Recall the reasoning behind the inclusion and exclusion criteria in a clinical trial. A primary rationale for excluding some groups (e.g., older adults, people with comorbid conditions) from clinical trials is that there is some reason to think that treatment A will not (as reliably) cause outcome B in these groups. The patient characteristics used to set inclusion and exclusion criteria for a study are chosen precisely *because* they are characteristics that might reasonably be thought to affect the results of the trial; that is, they might influence how much the intervention being tested can affect the outcomes being measured in the study. For example, patients with more severe disease may not respond as well to the dose of a drug being used in the study, or patients who are taking other medications might experience side effects due to drug interactions. So there often will be a good reason to think that a particular patient, one who did not meet the inclusion criteria, will respond differently to the intervention than those who were enrolled in the clinical trial. This leads to the question of whether the results of a clinical trial can be extrapolated to groups of patients not represented in that trial or, in other words, of whether the trial has high external validity.

A second challenge in extrapolating from clinical trials lies in the heterogeneity of even a carefully selected cohort. Clinical trials generally report the average outcome for the participants who received the study intervention. But not all, or even most, patients in such an RCT will have benefited from the intervention, and of those who do benefit, not all benefit equally. Since the trial reports average results, it is quite possible that in a study where the experimental drug is statistically significantly better than the comparator, some patients do much better than the average, while others do not improve, and still others get worse or experience significant side effects. Therefore, even a patient who would have met the criteria for participation in the trial is not certain to benefit from a drug that, on average, produced a positive effect in a clinical trial.

This feature of clinical trials is acknowledged and incorporated into the concept of the Number Needed to Treat (NNT). The NNT (and the related Number Needed to Screen) quantifies how many individuals will have to undergo an intervention in order for one of them to benefit. For instance, studies suggest that twenty-seven COVID-19 patients need to be treated with the drug tocilizumab in order to prevent one death (Afra et al., 2021). This means that well over 90% of patients treated with this potent immunosuppressive drug will not benefit from it. Some of them will even be harmed, developing infectious complications they would have otherwise avoided. This, too, can be quantified, though the Number Needed to Harm is rarely calculated from RCTs. (In addition, RCTs are not typically designed to quantify risk.) Since the NNT for the majority of medications or other medical interventions is higher than 2, and typically much higher, the majority of patients started on most treatments are unlikely to benefit from them. This reality tends to be minimized in the promulgation of clinical practice guidelines and in clinical practice; it is very rarely communicated to patients.

Recall from the beginning of the chapter that EBM does address the issue of extrapolating the results of clinical trials to different patient populations or to individual patients. With regard to the question of whether a trial's results apply to groups of patients, the challenges are downplayed. The *Users' Guides* does acknowledge that a patient's biological characteristics should "sometimes lead us to hesitate" to apply the results of a study (Guyatt et al., 2015, p. 237). However, it also suggests that instead of "rigidly applying a study's *inclusion* and *exclusion criteria*," clinicians should ask themselves "… whether there is some compelling reason why the results do not apply to the patient. You usually will not find a compelling reason, in which case you can generalize the results to your patient with confidence" (italics in the original, p. 68). This imperative, it should be noted, is not based on any evidence. Given our discussion in the preceding paragraph, this suggestion seems overly optimistic.

Regardless of how often there is reason to doubt the applicability of a trial result to an individual patient, however, when there *is* such a reason, EBM recognizes a role for knowledge of physiological mechanisms in extrapolating trial results, saying that "[u]nderstanding the underlying pathophysiology allows the clinician to better judge whether the results are applicable to the patient at hand ..." (EBM Working Group, 1992, p. 2421). Philosophical discussions of this claim have tried to assess whether and under what circumstances this is the case. Howick and colleagues have argued that using mechanistic reasoning for generalizing (or not) trial results to an individual patient is always risky (Howick et al., 2013). For one thing, our knowledge of the relevant mechanisms is usually incomplete; we rarely have the kind of "high quality" knowledge of mechanisms required to make these predictions. Moreover, because the operation of a mechanism is sensitive to the environment in which it operates, and to the operation of other mechanisms with which it interacts, even having a fairly clear understanding of the physiological mechanism linking a treatment and an outcome may not be enough to ground predictions about how the mechanism will actually operate in different circumstances. Howick et al. also argue that our knowledge of mechanisms is obtained in highly controlled laboratory systems and it may not generalize to different circumstances; like RCTs, claims about mechanisms may have problems with external validity. They conclude that, given these problems, we may simply "have to learn to live with a much higher degree of uncertainty and skepticism about the effects of many medical interventions" (Howick et al., 2013, p. 288). All this, Howick and colleagues argue, makes mechanistic reasoning too fallible to be relied upon.

Contra Howick, both Holly Andersen (2012) and Brendan Clarke et al. (2013, 2014) consider cases in which there is evidence of a difference in the operation of a physiological mechanism that can be used to identify groups of patients who are more, or less, likely to show the desired outcomes when treated with the intervention studied in a trial. This second approach appears promising. It is less concerned with elucidating the details of mechanisms' operation, focusing instead on cases in which even limited, incomplete knowledge of mechanisms can help to determine whether a treatment will work for a specific patient. Basically, any given patient has a number of characteristics—demographic, clinical, or physiological—that may be relevant to predicting how she will respond to a treatment. The challenge is to identify and assess the relevance of these characteristics.

In the case of physiological characteristics, some knowledge of the underlying mechanism can help with this identification.

Andersen offers an example of how knowledge of physiological mechanisms may help guide treatment decisions in the case of a patient who has both breast cancer and type II diabetes. Although there is evidence available regarding the treatment of both conditions separately, "there are not sufficient studies available to distill out EBM recommendations for patients with both a specific type of breast cancer and who are on a particular regimen for type II diabetes" (p. 997). In the absence of such evidence, clinicians must use their knowledge of physiology to predict whether the patient's diabetes, or the medications she takes to control it, might affect her response to the therapies recommended for breast cancer. "Between two potential breast cancer treatments, one might be more effective, but also involve a chemical pathway that a practitioner recognizes as involved in some of the problematic symptoms of type II diabetes" (ibid.). Recognizing the potential for the "better" therapy to lead to problems for this patient may lead a physician to recommend the alternative, purportedly less effective therapy. Note that detailed knowledge of *how* the treatment might affect the patient's diabetes is not necessary in this case. The physician needs to know only that there is an important part in the mechanism that indicates the potential for the drug to influence a mechanism related to the disease.[10]

Yet although this case illustrates a role for knowledge of mechanisms in generalizing from the results of RCTs to the care of a particular patient, it is also important to recognize that it depicts unusual circumstances. As Bluhm (2013) has pointed out, in Andersen's example, there is both a choice of reasonably effective therapies and good evidence for avoiding the one that would normally be the top choice. There is no reason to think that this is the case in most situations where it is questionable whether an individual patient will respond well to a therapy that has been shown to be efficacious in clinical trials. Andersen herself acknowledges that this kind of reasoning about mechanisms is not very satisfactory, but says that "there is no better alternative at this stage" (Anderson, 2012, p. 997). Thus, Andersen, like Howick et al., ends up somewhat skeptical that knowledge of mechanisms can be of great help in generalizing from the results of clinical trials.

By contrast, Clarke et al. are optimistic, saying: "evidence of mechanisms is of great help in establishing whether and to what extent causal

---

[10] Understanding a crucial part of an otherwise complex and poorly understood mechanism can also lead to a successful intervention, for instance, targeted treatments for various mutations causing cystic fibrosis (see Solomon, 2015).

claims are valid externally," that is, when "exporting the results or methods of one study to a different population or setting" (2014, p. 346).[11] Like Andersen, they illustrate their claim using an example. The UK's National Institutes of Clinical Excellence (NICE) introduced new treatment guidelines for hypertension in 2011 that make different recommendations for treating different racial/ethnic groups and age groups. According to Clarke et al., "[t]his recommendation was based on RCTs that had been designed to test the efficacy of different treatments in these ethnic groups. In turn, these trials were based upon the plentiful evidence suggesting the operation of different pro-hypertensive mechanisms operating in different ethnic groups" (p. 347).

Crucially, though, this example differs from Andersen's; while the clinician in Andersen's example must proceed with therapy in the absence of relevant RCT evidence, Clarke et al. provide a scenario in which they say that evidence *does* exist in support of targeting treatment decisions to different subgroups. (The analogous scenario for Andersen's example would be one in which a trial had been conducted that included patients with both breast cancer and type II diabetes, and looked for evidence that they had different treatment outcomes than breast cancer patients without diabetes.) This difference undercuts their optimism about the utility of mechanisms in the kind of clinical situation considered by Howick and by Andersen, in which there is no directly relevant evidence.

Ultimately, there's no simple answer to when knowledge of mechanisms can help determine whether the results of a clinical trial apply to an individual patient. While there are certainly cases in which knowledge of mechanisms can aid clinical decision-making (e.g., Andersen, 2012; Tonelli and Williamson, 2020), there are also cases in which using this kind of reasoning is unreliable (e.g., Howick et al., 2013). But these dueling examples do very little to help practicing clinicians know ahead of time whether the situation they are in falls into the first or the second of these categories.

Our discussion in this section shows that knowledge of physiological mechanisms is fallible, but this just puts it on the same footing as knowledge from clinical research studies (Ioannidis, 2005; Ioannidis, 2011). Neither kind of knowledge provides a completely reliable base for clinicians, which may explain why, in practice, clinicians rely on both (Tonelli and Williamson, 2020). As we will explore in more detail in the discussion

---

[11] They later make essentially the same argument in discussing the extrapolation of study results to individuals.

of case-based reasoning, clinicians will need to continue to bring knowledge of difference-making studies as well as pathophysiologic understanding into clinical decisions for individual patients. Basic science and clinical research, mechanistic understanding and evidence-based medicine, should not be viewed as antagonistic, each claiming superiority over the other, but rather as complementary epistemic tools that can be used, in iterative fashion, both to get at causes and to advance the care of individual patients.

Assessing the effects of therapeutic interventions

In the preceding sections, we described the ways that knowledge of mechanisms can inform an initial treatment decision. Similarly, knowledge of mechanisms is important for assessing whether the chosen therapy is having the desired effects in a particular patient. The timing of this kind of re-evaluation will differ depending on the clinical setting and on the intervention—for an acutely and severely ill patient in an intensive care setting, re-evaluation may occur within minutes or hours of initiating the therapy. For more chronic illnesses, it may not occur for days or even months after initiating therapy. Many medications take some time to reach full effectiveness, so re-evaluating too soon may not give a good picture of how a patient will respond.

Population-level, clinical research does not generally give the kind of information needed for evaluating an intervention longitudinally. As we have repeatedly emphasized, even when an intervention is shown to be effective in a sample of patients, not all patients in that sample do benefit. In addition, the methodological decisions made when conducting a clinical trial may not match the way that the treatment will be used in the clinic. A trial will follow a protocol, which may be very inflexible; it typically lasts for only a relatively short time (compared with how long a patient may take the treatment); and it will measure only a few predetermined endpoints. In a clinical setting, things are quite different: Clinicians can change treatments depending on the needs and response of the patient; endpoints not measured in the trial may be important; and patients may take a medication for a much longer time than the study covered—for years or even decades. Moreover, a patient's response to a medication may change over time. Knowledge of mechanisms is important in assessing whether a chosen therapeutic intervention is—or is not—having the desired effects in a particular case. This is true no matter how effective the intervention has been shown to be in clinical trials.

In cases of acute, critical illness, physiologic endpoints are often an important indication of the effects of a treatment, and clinicians will monitor them closely to determine whether the treatment appears to be on track to deliver the desired outcome. This use of physiological measures as intermediate markers of likely treatment success shares similar advantages and disadvantages to the use of surrogate endpoints in clinical research. According to the *Users' Guides*, a surrogate endpoint is a laboratory or physiological measure associated with an outcome that is clinically important—that is, one that directly measures "how a patient feels, functions, or survives" (2015, p. 273). These may include measurements of physiological variables, or of subclinical indicators of disease, for example, blood pressure as a surrogate endpoint for stroke, or degree of atherosclerosis as a predictor of myocardial infarction or coronary death (ibid.). In general, EBM stresses that what patients and physicians want to know from clinical trials is the effect of a therapy on "patient-important outcomes such as stroke, myocardial infarction, *health-related quality of life* (HRQL), and death" (italics in the original, p. 272). However, because assessing these clinical outcomes may require large samples and/or long follow-up periods, physiological measures may be used instead.

The problem, however, is that surrogate endpoints are not always accurate predictors of the patient-important outcomes for which they are used as stand-ins. The *Users' Guides* notes that "[t]o allow trustworthy inferences about what matters to patients ... the marker not only has to be statistically correlated with the relevant patient-important outcomes, but also must capture, to the greatest extent possible, the net effect of the intervention on these outcomes" (p. 273).

In clinical practice, the use of such physiologic measurements and reasoning serves as opportunities to assess whether a treatment strategy is becoming more, or less, likely to result in the desired outcome. Physiologic responses are not typically the goal of therapy, but they can be strong indicators of the clinical endpoints that are actually the ultimate goal, providing important information for the re-evaluation of initial treatment choices.

Consider the case of mechanical ventilation in acute respiratory distress syndrome (ARDS). There is strong evidence from clinical research that using a low (versus higher) tidal volume is correlated with lower ICU mortality. Furthermore, human and animal studies also support this connection by providing a mechanistic explanation of this correlation. But some patients do not tolerate low tidal volumes well, perhaps becoming dyssynchronous with the ventilator or developing profound hypoxemia or acid-base disturbances. In these cases, reasoning about the mechanisms linking tidal volume with the relevant cardiac and respiratory clinical outcomes can justify small increases in the tidal volume delivered. Evidence from clinical trials does not clearly demonstrate any increase in the risk of mortality due to ARDS with such changes, whereas maintaining the initial tidal volume would appear to significantly increase the patient's short-term risk of death. The decision to increase tidal volume can be justified in such cases on the basis of knowledge of physiological mechanisms. In general, intensive care is an area of medicine where, despite being informed by the results of clinical research, mechanistic reasoning plays a large role in patient care (Tonelli et al., 2012).

Although intensive care provides some particularly dramatic illustrations of the importance of knowledge of physiological mechanisms in assessing treatment effects, this kind of reasoning is ubiquitous in medicine. In cases where a patient is responding as predicted to a therapy, clinicians are justified in concluding that they have identified the mechanism(s) responsible for the patient's presenting signs and symptoms and that they have successfully intervened in the relevant mechanism(s)—that is, that their diagnosis was correct and their treatment plan looks to be effective. But when the patient is *not* responding as expected, physicians must use their knowledge of mechanism to change either their diagnosis (some other mechanism of disease is at work) or their treatment (unanticipated mechanisms are influencing the effects of a therapy). For example, a patient diagnosed with acute pneumonia who is being treated with antibiotics according to evidence-based guidelines, but who is not improving after several days of treatment, may not actually have pneumonia, but some mimic. Or the pneumonia may not be caused by the typical pathogens that informed the guidelines. In this case, her clinician can use their knowledge of other relevant disease mechanisms, plus the patient's physiologic trajectory, to arrive at a new diagnosis or treatment plan.

Knowledge of physiological mechanisms is also crucially important in the management of chronic diseases where physiological measurements provide important information required to prevent complications of the disease, for example, diabetes or hypertension. The surrogate endpoints that reflect these physiological measurements may not cause immediate suffering to patients—neither an elevated HgA1C nor moderately high blood pressure makes someone feel unwell—but they are predictors of future problems that will arise if the physiological condition is not treated. Clinicians use this information to determine whether the current treatment should be continued, augmented with other therapies, or abandoned in favor of another therapeutic regimen.

Here again, knowledge of physiological mechanisms provides important information that population-level studies and trials generally cannot. Trials typically provide initial guidance in choosing a treatment that is, on average, effective in managing the patient's condition. But if the initial treatment does not reduce *this* patient's blood pressure, knowing that high blood pressure is part of the causal mechanisms of a disorder suggests that a different intervention is needed to reduce their risk of future complications.

Evaluating the effect of a therapy is, of course, most crucial when the therapy is not working as expected. When the desired therapeutic outcome(s) are being achieved, this provides some evidence that both the initial diagnosis and the choice of treatment were correct. If the therapy is not effective, the clinician will reconsider the initial treatment choice, and/or the initial diagnosis. In both of these situations, the clinician may revisit the patient's signs and symptoms and order more tests to assess their physiological state. A change in treatment is warranted when there is evidence that an unanticipated mechanism either reduces the effectiveness of the initial therapy, or has led the patient to experience side effects. In the case of a new diagnosis, the clinician has essentially decided that the mechanism(s) causing the patient's symptoms were not correctly identified in the first place.

Ultimately, good reasoning about physiological mechanisms in assessing therapeutic outcomes depends on the selection of appropriate physiological characteristics to measure. These are ones that, like surrogate outcomes in clinical research, are known to be part of the causal pathway linking the therapy to the clinical outcome, are consistent across patients, and are close to the targeted endpoint (Aronson, 2005).

Summary

In this chapter, we have argued that in both medical research and clinical practice, knowledge of physiological mechanisms plays a crucial role. Currently, medical epistemology is dominated by EBM, which focuses on the role of clinical research, particularly RCTs, in guiding treatment decisions. EBM does, however, recognize that knowledge of physiological mechanisms plays a role, albeit a limited one, in clinical reasoning. We have aimed to keep the insights offered by EBM, but also to do justice to the crucial role of physiological knowledge in guiding clinical practice. The argument here does not require that pathophysiologic reasoning be certain and infallible, or that it replace population-level studies. Certainly, as our collective understanding of the mechanisms underlying health and disease continues to improve, mechanistic reasoning in clinical medicine becomes more valuable and reliable. We suggest that in the best-case scenario, the two kinds of evidence work together, and when they do, clinicians are justified in having increased confidence in their decision. And we caution that when they are discordant, one approach does not always win out over the other.

4
Experiential Knowledge

Dr. Lee has been practicing general internal medicine for almost thirty years, developing a wealth of personal experience. It seems that experience is what allows her to quickly assess her patients, getting a sense of the acuity of their illness and making rapid determinations of the most likely diagnoses. She has learned to ask the best questions and to listen carefully to what patients are saying, always on the lookout for clues to a diagnosis or treatment plan. While she has certainly developed a certain clinical style, she is able to adapt her approach with individual patients based upon their needs. Her past mistakes have taught her things and her successes provide a foundation of confidence. While she knows this vast experience has made her a better doctor, she struggles with how much to rely upon it day-to-day. Particularly when working with the medical students who rotate through her practice, she avoids reliance on experience alone when explaining a diagnostic or therapeutic decision. She finds herself thinking that experience is at best inadequate and at worst untrustworthy as grounds for any medical decision.

Personal clinical experience, the understanding accrued when a clinician cares for individual patients, represents one of the more contentious sources of knowledge for the epistemology of medical practice. Direct experience is an essential component of clinical training, and there is no disagreement that the knowledge and skills gained from such experience are a necessary element of competent medical practice. The training of physicians requires that much more time be spent in supervised clinical settings than in classrooms or laboratories. But the experiential knowledge derived from direct clinical experience is also routinely devalued, particularly within EBM, as a source of clinically relevant knowledge, and often dismissed as "unsystematic" and "anecdotal" when relied upon in practice.

To some extent, this seeming inconsistency relates to the fact that "clinical experience" is used to describe several different, though not entirely distinct, things. First, "clinical experience" can be used to refer to the kinds of skills that medical, nursing, and therapy students start to acquire when they undergo the practical part of their training, and that they continue to develop throughout their careers as clinicians. Here, clinical experience describes the knowledge required for such activities as history taking, conducting a physical examination, and reading the results of tests and lab reports and relating them to the patient's presentation. It also includes, as we will see, the development of a (somewhat difficult to describe) way of interpreting and reacting to a patient's immediate clinical state. This sense of the term refers to a kind of practical knowledge, of a sort often described in terms of "knowing how," rather than "knowing that."

Second, personal "clinical experience" can be used to refer to a source or kind of evidence, which may be used to justify or support a particular clinical assessment or decision. On this understanding of the term, the question is whether, or when, a clinician can legitimately appeal to their own direct and specific experience as evidence in support of a clinical judgement. In this use of the term, a particular claim can be expressed as "knowledge that," though in at least some cases, it may be hard to put what is known into words. Related to this use of "clinical experience," there is the question of the strength of the evidence provided by the *collective* judgment of a medical community. This question addresses the role of what is often called "expert opinion."

Whereas expert opinion, since it is communicated to the rest of the medical community, is clearly a kind of "knowledge that," appeals to individual clinical experience may or may not be clearly articulated. We take this to mean that "knowing how" and "knowing that" may not always be completely distinct, in ways that we will explore throughout this chapter. Our conclusion will be that what brings these two ways of understanding clinical experience together is a third way in which the term is used. This third use of the term "clinical experience" is used to characterize the *way* in which a clinician does the various tasks involved in caring for a patient; here it marks the distinction between an experienced clinician—one who has attained a certain level of expertise—and someone who has not yet attained this level of expertise.

We begin this chapter with a discussion of what EBM says about clinical experience, drawing on an analysis by the philosopher Sarah Wieten. We will next address the question of when clinical experience can be evidence. That is, what justifies using clinical experience as explicit "knowledge that," as evidence for a clinical decision. We then turn to the question of how clinical expertise should be understood, by introducing three approaches to answering this question. First, the philosophy of medicine literature aims to describe the nature of knowledge in medical practice. Next, the nursing researcher Patricia Benner has used the Dreyfus model of expertise to characterize the development of expertise in nursing. Finally, a body of experimental research on clinical reasoning, which is informed by work in cognitive psychology, studies how reasoning changes as medical students develop into expert practitioners. We conclude that while all of these areas of research reveal important aspects of clinical expertise, they are each insufficient to characterize all aspects of clinical reasoning. Because of this, they do not provide a solution to the integration problem.

EBM on clinical experience and expertise

As with knowledge of physiological mechanisms, EBM places clinical experience low on the hierarchy of evidence. At the same time, however, it identifies clinical experience as a crucial part of clinical practice. In chapter 2, we discussed the placement of evidence gained through clinical experience at the bottom of the hierarchy of evidence. Recall that the major problem identified with this source of knowledge was that an individual clinician has experience of only a fairly small number of patients, as compared with the number of patients required (e.g., in a clinical trial) to detect a statistically significant effect of a treatment. But in addition to this point, there are two other problems that EBM identifies with using clinical experience as evidence in support of a decision. One of these is the "unsystematic" nature of the observations made by clinicians in the course of their practice. In a clinical trial, the research protocol ensures that any observations made of patient outcomes are prespecified and thus reflect features that the trial designers agree in advance are likely to be clinically important, and that all observations are carefully and consistently recorded. In an individual physician's practice, by contrast, they may notice things that are somewhat random or idiosyncratic, with striking but unusual events taking on more significance than would be warranted by existing knowledge and by statistical analysis. Second, EBM was developed in part in response to worries that the views of established medical "experts" had too much influence on medicine, with the result that even younger clinicians were failing to adopt newer, evidence-based practices. Recall here the "way of the past," in the *JAMA* 1992 article, which saw a resident appealing to her clinical mentors, rather than to the relevant literature, to solve a clinical problem (Evidence-Based Medicine Working Group, 1992). Reliance on clinical expertise was seen as the last refuge of medical scoundrels.[1]

Sarah Wieten (2018a) has argued that the *JAMA* article's criticism of expert opinion articulates only one of several ways that EBM has characterized clinical experience, or clinical expertise, and its role in medical decision-making.[2] In the earliest days of EBM, clinical expertise was viewed as a dubious epistemic justification of authoritarian clinical experts, those whose defense of a particular clinical judgment relied upon one's (often vast) direct clinical experience. This downgrading of expertise continued as more sophisticated evidence ranking systems were developed. In particular, Wieten notes, the GRADE system classifies reports of expert opinion, alongside case reports, as low-quality evidence.

At the same time, GRADE acknowledges that expertise is essential in some respects, in particular to interpret all evidence (whether of high or low quality). In Wieten's terms, this acknowledgement means that expertise plays a crucial role "external to" the evidence being considered, as opposed to being an (internal) part of the evidence itself. The 1996 paper by Sackett and colleagues, which we also introduced in Chapter 2, similarly articulates an external role for clinical expertise, distinguishing it from research evidence. According to this paper:

> The practice of evidence-based medicine means integrating individual clinical expertise with the best available external clinical evidence from systematic research. By individual clinical expertise we mean the proficiency and judgment that individual clinicians acquire through clinical experience and clinical practice. (Sackett et al., 1996, p. 71)[3]

Expertise, in this sense, does not itself represent a kind of clinical evidence, but rather the ability to process medical information in a particular way. Specifically, the expertise physicians gain "through clinical experience

---

[1] Methodological expertise, on the other hand, was to be highly prized; the paper, as we discussed in chapter 2, described the ability to find and assess clinical research reports as "the way of the future" for medicine.

[2] Wieten uses the terms "experience" and "expertise" interchangeably, defining expertise as "knowledge gained by subjects in the course of clinical interactions, in contrast with knowledge gained from sources such as journal articles reporting on the findings of RCTs, meta-analyses and systematic reviews or explicit medical education" (2018a, p. 1). We will say more about the relationship between clinical experience and expertise later in the chapter.

[3] Note that the use of "external" in this quotation to describe evidence from clinical research is not the same as Wieten's use of the term.

and clinical practice is reflected in many ways, but especially in more effective and efficient diagnosis and in the more thoughtful identification and compassionate use of patients' predicaments, rights, and preferences in making clinical decisions about their care" (Sackett et al., 1996, p. 4; quoted in Wieten, 2018a, p. 3). As Wieten points out, "[e]xpertise on this account is about efficient reasoning skills for diagnosis, and proper application of evidence to individual patients' needs and values" (p. 3).

The 1996 paper, however, leaves important questions about the role of clinical expertise unaddressed. For one thing, it is described as something distinct that must be integrated with research evidence and patient values. But, again, there is no discussion of how this is to be done, leaving us with the integration problem that motivates this book. For another, it raises the question of just what clinical expertise *is*. Does expertise describe a fund of knowledge that can be tapped in making clinical decisions, that is, evidence in and of itself? Or does it describe a process, akin to the notion of clinical acumen, that clinicians rely upon for diagnostic assessment and therapeutic decision making? The reference to "proficiency and judgment" suggests that latter; however, it seems clear that physicians acquire new knowledge, in addition to judgment, as they gain clinical experience. We will return to this issue in the last section of the chapter.

Both of these questions are addressed by a third model of expertise that Wieten identifies in the EBM literature. This model comes from a paper by Haynes et al. (2002). In this model, the role of expertise is clearly shifted to the task of integration, as opposed to something to be integrated with other factors that inform clinical decision-making. Here, what is to be integrated also changes from the 1996 article: The kinds of information that go into clinical decision-making are presented as "patient preferences and actions," "research evidence," and "clinical state and circumstances." "Clinical expertise" is a fourth component of the model that encompasses the other three. Yet here, again, there is no discussion of how to integrate these different kinds of things. The implication appears to be that this is something the physician already knows; as clinical expertise is described as including "the general basic skills of clinical practice as well as the experience of the individual practitioner" (Haynes et al., 2002, p. A1-2; quoted in Wieten 2018a, p. 4).

In summary, Wieten's analysis shows that "clinical expertise" is used in at least three ways in the EBM literature: To describe a low-quality source of evidence (especially when it is others' clinical experience that is being used as evidence for a decision); to identify an ostensibly non-evidentiary source of knowledge that is distinct from "external" research evidence; and to refer to the ability to integrate various kinds of information when making clinical decisions.[4] In our view, it really *is* hard to separate the different contributions of clinical experience to the practice of medicine, though we think that the best way to begin to do so is to separate the questions of whether and how clinical experience can provide evidence in support of a clinical decision and of what expert clinical reasoning looks like. In the rest of the chapter, we try to do justice to both the "internal," evidentiary role of the kind of experiential knowledge acquired through clinical practice, and the ways in which the development of greater clinical experience has been shown to influence clinical reasoning. With regard to the second topic, we will argue that the available work does help to shed light on important aspects of clinical reasoning, but it ultimately fails to solve the integration problem.

Experience as evidence

One important question about the role of clinical experience is the extent to which it can serve as evidence in support of clinical decisions; specific experiences might generate knowledge that can be appealed to in individual clinical decisions. For instance, a patient presenting with an unusual combination of symptoms might evoke a memory of a similar case, seen years ago, that serves to guide a diagnostic and treatment plan. This is the most straightforward kind of case-based reasoning, an approach to medical decision-making we will have much more to say about in the book's final chapter. While this process will be familiar to clinicians, it also represents the use of "anecdotal" and "unsystematic" experience cautioned against by EBM.

Here, it is worth distinguishing between two claims that might be made about the role for and value of such experiential knowledge in medicine. First, past experience might be a source of knowledge for an individual clinician in making decisions about the care of the patient in front of them, as in our example in the previous paragraph. This kind of situation, although it considers similarities between the past and the current patient, does not amount to making a general claim about the best diagnostic and treatment plan for all patients with those characteristics. Instead, it might simply be one

---

[4] It is also used in a fourth way: To refer to the ability to exercise judgment in interpreting evidence. Presumably this is the kind of experience gained through developing the critical appraisal skills taught by EBM. We have covered this kind of knowledge in Chapter 2 and won't say more about it here.

factor that is integrated with the results of clinical research and the patient's values, in order to decide the best course of action for that patient.

Making such a general claim, that such past clinical experience is relevant to *all* future patients, is the second way of thinking about the role and value of experiential knowledge, which is that the experience of an individual clinician provides evidence, in general, for clinical decision-making. In one reading of EBM's prescriptions, it is only in this second role that experiential knowledge is problematic. Recall that EBM says that clinicians need to integrate clinical research evidence with other factors, including their own clinical expertise, in making decisions about the care of an individual patient. But in this second role, clinical experience ranks extremely low on the hierarchy of evidence.

One reason for downplaying the value of this knowledge is the relatively limited experience of any given clinician. Even someone who has treated many patients over the course of their career has still seen only a fairly small sample of patients. (Compare the case of a clinician who has seen a dozen patients with the particular combination of symptoms we mentioned with the sample sizes required for a contemporary clinical trial.) A second reason EBM downplays individual clinical experience is that it is unsystematic. Clinicians treat the individual patient in front of them, in all their complexity and idiosyncrasy. As we described earlier, however, clinical trials treat this complexity as noise that obscures the "real" (average) effects of an intervention, by balancing potentially confounding factors across the treatment and the control groups. They are therefore held to be a better source of evidence for general claims about average patients or a population of patients. In short, the criticism is that clinical experience is too limited and too variable to be an adequate source of general knowledge.

While it is true, in some sense, that knowledge gained through experience is subjective and unique to an individual knower, this is not the full story. Devora Shapiro (2012) argues that *experience* and *experiential knowledge* are not the same thing and she explains what is required in order for experience to become experiential knowledge[5]:

What is required for one's experience to take the form of experiential knowledge is a particular sort of understanding. This understanding is derived from (1) the experience of x, (2) the individual's reflection on x,

---

[5] Tonelli and Shapiro (2020) build on this theory of experiential knowledge to elucidate the role of experiential knowledge in clinical decision-making. We draw on their discussion throughout the rest of the chapter.

and (3) the connection of her experience of *x* to other, *relevantly* similar experiences of her own and, at times, of others' experiences. (p. 70)

In clinical medicine, the requirement of reflection is echoed in the idea of mindful practice. Pat Croskerry, for example, has emphasized the importance of developing metacognitive skills, in particular to overcome well-documented biases in our thinking patterns (Croskerry, 2013). But reflection is also required in order for physicians to share their experiential knowledge with others. In fact, mentorship is central to medical education and requires that teachers reflect on a clinical experience in order to explain its importance to students. This mentorship allows students to benefit from the experiential knowledge of professionals. Reflection also requires students to develop the ability to consider their own clinical experiences, and these skills are fostered when students are asked to explain their own reasoning for a patient care decision.

Shapiro also emphasizes the importance of connecting an experience to relevantly similar experiences—both one's own and others'. The practices by which medical knowledge is shared within the community allow physicians to make these connections. For example, case reports are an important way of sharing an individual clinician's experience of caring for an individual patient, describing a patient's presentation and the course of their illness in a way that makes the knowledge gained from the case accessible to other physicians.

Shapiro's discussion of experiential knowledge makes it clear that, although experience is personal, experiential knowledge can be social, shared by the community. Making experience explicit means that it can not only be shared but also be assessed. Similarly, experienced knowers who share a background and training can accept or challenge a claim to experiential knowledge, and on the basis of these interactions, an initial claim might be revised (Longino, 2002; Shapiro, 2012). For instance, a medical student who observes three patients with lupus presenting with a malar rash and concludes that such a rash is always present in the disease will need to be corrected, typically by a more senior clinician. Such a rash occurs in about half of patients with lupus.

Experiential knowledge, then, can be made explicit, communicated, and used as evidence for clinical decisions. Individual experiential knowledge, derived from experience with particular patients and particular clinical situations, will be most useful for clinicians in making decision for particular individuals, rather than in establishing general rules; EBM is right that general claims are best supported by research that includes large numbers of patients. Experiential knowledge gives clinicians a rich set of cases to compare to the patient at hand and makes possible their ability to discern crucial differences between those with similar presentations or the same disease. It can also help clinicians determine when randomized trials or clinical practice guidelines do not apply to a particular patient, something that guidelines themselves cannot do (Greenhalgh, 2018).

The fact that experiential knowledge can be made explicit and be assessed by others means that EBM's devaluation of experiential knowledge as "unsystematic" and "anecdotal" is not completely accurate or fair. It is true that a clinician could simply use a claim about their clinical experience to justify a decision or a course of action and could do so in a way that forecloses any further discussion. But that is a caricature of the way that experiential knowledge usually functions in medicine. Moreover, the fact that the experiential knowledge of clinicians can be made explicit and assessed makes it similar to knowledge derived from clinical research and from our understanding of physiological mechanism. It allows experiential knowledge to be assessed and weighed as a part of the "evidence base" available to guide clinical decision-making. Recall that the GRADE framework, for example, acknowledges that judgment is always required to evaluate claims of knowledge, whether they come from a clinical trial, a laboratory study of physiological mechanisms, or a clinician's experience with patients.

So far, we have focused on knowledge based on the clinical experience of an individual clinician, though we have emphasized that even this individual experience can be assessed by the standards of the professional community. Yet some clinicians' experience is, and should be, accorded more weight than others', specifically when they have a great deal of direct experience related to a particular class of patients, typically with a specific disease. Knowledge gained from this focused clinical experience, when made explicit and presented to others with less experience, represents "expert opinion." Such opinions are often valued by other practitioners, not only on a one-to-one basis between colleagues, but also in a more formal way: Expert opinion can make valuable contributions to various formal processes that codify disease-specific knowledge, providing recommendations by a community of experts in a given area.

This, however, is precisely the kind of expert knowledge that EBM places low on the hierarchy of evidence. But as Tonelli (1999) notes, for EBM to allow individual clinical experience to play a crucial role in evidence-based practice, but deny a similarly crucial role for expert opinion, is inconsistent. "The expert's experiential knowledge is not fundamentally different in kind compared with that possessed by the individual, but would be expected to be a richer and more complete version, given the expert's exposure to a larger number of patients of a certain type" (1999, p. 1191).

Nor is this kind of expert opinion merely anecdotal, derived from individual and unsystematic clinical experience. Experts, in addition to being individuals with their own clinical expertise, are also part of a community of experts with regard to a particular area of practice. As such, their expertise may also include understanding of a specialized area of pathophysiology and knowledge of the results of clinical research, as well as their own (and often their community's) primary clinical experience. This expertise contributes to the production of consensus conference reports (Solomon, 2015) and clinical guidelines. This kind of knowledge therefore is not merely a poor substitute for the kind of clinical research evidence privileged by EBM. Rather, the deliberation and adjudication of such evidence by the relevant experts means that these guidelines and reports might well provide *better* guidance than the original trials themselves, as the guidelines then account for the kinds of information needed to determine the relevance of a trial for clinical practice.

In summary, both an individual physician's experiential knowledge and the experience of their professional community can provide valuable evidence in support of a clinical decision. In this capacity, clinical experience leads to knowledge that can be articulated and shared with others, and that can be offered as evidence or justification for a clinical decision. Philosophers often refer to this kind of knowledge as propositional knowledge, or "knowledge that." Direct clinical experience also provides clinicians with a "knowing how" to practice medicine. In the next section, we introduce the concept of clinical expertise by describing how philosophers of medicine have thought about "knowing how" in clinical practice. We then turn to two areas of empirical research on the development of clinical expertise, which show how expert performance emerges as clinicians gain greater experience. Ultimately, however, we will argue that neither of these approaches can fully explain how physicians reason. In the last chapter of the book, we will argue for a case-based approach to clinical reasoning that encompasses the insights drawn from these two areas of research on expertise and fills in the gaps that they leave.

Clinical experience and "knowledge how"

Within clinical medicine, primary experience includes—and arises from—the day-to-day activities of clinicians. Interviewing and examining patients, reading and interpreting radiographs and laboratory tests, making recommendations, and monitoring treatment effects are examples of such activities, which are essential to the practice of medicine. The experience of clinical practice is, in this sense, the experience of particulars. While illnesses and diseases can be understood in a general, disembodied sense (for example, a myocardial infarction represents injury of cardiac muscle due to impairment of blood supply), they are not experienced in a general way. A clinician does not encounter a myocardial infarction, but rather a person with particular symptoms of chest pain and shortness of breath, with a constellation of physical exam findings, and a tell-tale combination of diagnostic test results that indicate injury to his heart. Clinical knowledge is gained case by case, converting patient stories to narratives that can be communicated to other clinicians on rounds or in teaching conferences. Individual patients are the textual material generating experiential knowledge.

As clinicians gain experience, knowledge of particulars coalesces and aggregates, becoming the foundation of the practical wisdom from which clinical expertise emerges. Like other forms of inductively generated knowledge in the sciences, medicine and clinical practice rely on the identification of relevant features in the phenomena under evaluation, and require experienced knowers to observe, review, and discriminate based on expertise. At the same time, clinical experience builds on a foundation of preclinical knowledge. By the time they begin seeing patients in earnest, medical students have undertaken significant classroom study, learning anatomy, physiology, and other pre-clinical topics. This knowledge is necessary, but not sufficient for clinical practice. After all, a medical librarian, with access to any written and recorded clinical research evidence desired, still lacks the knowledge required to make a clinical judgment; the medical librarian lacks the hands-on clinical training and experience with patients that provides adequate grounds for the expertise of a competent clinician. While clinicians need to incorporate other kinds of medical knowledge into clinical decision making, primary experience, and the knowledge it makes possible, is indispensable.

There has been extensive discussion in the philosophy of medicine of the role of experiential knowledge as the basis for clinical expertise, understood as *knowing how* (Fantl, 2017) to practice medicine, as distinct from being aware of the contents of a research paper or a clinical practice guideline (Wieringa and Greenhalgh, 2015). Different authors have characterized this knowledge in different terms; in addition to "knowing how," authors have characterized and defended this central notion of clinical practice as "phronesis," "practical wisdom," and "tacit knowledge." We will not take a stance here as to which of these related ideas offers the best description of the skills and knowledge needed to practice medicine but instead will pull together some of the themes that characterize this aspect of experiential knowledge. First, it is by its nature *practical* knowledge; it enables a physician to do things. This point is reflected in the idea of knowing how. Second, Braude's (2012) discussion of phronesis emphasizes knowledge of particulars, of what to do for *this* particular patient in *these* particular circumstances—though Braude also emphasizes that this knowledge of particulars also requires general medical knowledge. In addition, Henry (2006) emphasizes the importance of tacit knowledge in gaining information about individual patients—both their physical and their psychological characteristics. Braude, again, describes the intuitive wisdom needed to know how to use general knowledge in practice, and when and if such knowledge applies to the individual patient. Finally, Polanyi, who has written extensively about tacit knowledge, emphasizes that this kind of knowledge grows and develops over time, as experience is gained, but that such knowledge never results in certainty (1962).

While these philosophical descriptions converge on a set of characteristics describing the "knowing how" of medical practice, they do not fully explain how this knowledge is acquired or how it relates to the various sources of "knowing that" possessed by physicians. For this, we now turn to two different literatures that have investigated the development of expert performance. We begin with a discussion of the Dreyfus model of expertise, as developed in a clinical context by Patricia Benner, and then turn to an overview of the empirical research on clinical decision-making and the development of clinical reasoning skills in medical students.

The Dreyfus model of expertise

One influential model of expertise has been developed by the brothers Hubert and Stuart Dreyfus (Dreyfus and Dreyfus, 1986) and applied to the clinical sphere by the nursing scholar Patricia Benner (Benner, 2000). The

Dreyfus model helps us to see what is involved in the development of the kind of tacit knowledge identified by philosophers of medicine, and how this knowledge works in clinical practice. Yet, as we will show, this characterization of expertise is incomplete, as it does not account for the important role of explicit and deliberate decision-making in expert clinical practice.

The Dreyfus model of expertise claims that, across domains of knowledge, learners move through five stages of development: Novice, advanced beginner, competent, proficient, and expert. Benner has used this model to characterize the development of nursing expertise. She interviewed nurses at various career stages and in various areas of practice about specific events they experienced at work and how they handled them. Consistent with the Dreyfus model, Benner argues that as practitioners move from level to level, three aspects of their performance change. First, there is a shift from relying on abstract principles (such as textbook descriptions) to using "past concrete experiences as paradigms" (Benner, 2000, p. 13). Second, the practitioner's perception of a clinical situation changes, so that "the situation is seen less and less as a compilation of equally relevant bits, and more and more as a complete whole on which only certain parts are relevant" (p. 13). Finally, the third characteristic of expert performance involves a shift from being a detached observer of a situation to being an involved performer, fully immersed in the situation. This shift also occurs in the development of expertise in other skills, such as riding a bicycle or learning a second language: In the beginning, performance is governed, and taught, by rules. At this stage, "performance is halting and rigid, and one must pay attention to explicit instruction" (p. 37). As the skill develops, however, the practitioner no longer needs to consult the explicit rules of performance and there is evidence that they are not actually relying on those rules. Rather "with experience and mastery, the skill is transformed. And this change brings about improvement in the performance" (p. 38).

Benner emphasizes that the transition to skilled performance does not mean that the principles and rules are simply abandoned. Explicit analysis is needed when, for example, a clinician faces a situation for which previous experience has not adequately prepared them, or when "the expert [initially] gets a wrong grasp of the situation and then finds that events and behaviors are not occurring as expected" (Benner, p. 34), or, we add, when there are multiple ways of understanding a situation and an explicit analysis is needed in order to determine which of these ways is best.

At the same time, however, both Benner's study of nursing expertise and the Dreyfus model itself emphasize tacit knowledge over the explicit application of rules. As the Dreyfuses describe their view: "Human understanding [is] a skill akin to knowing how to find one's way about in the world, rather than knowing a lot of facts and rules for relating them. Our basic understanding [is] thus a *knowing how* rather than a *knowing that*" (Dreyfus and Dreyfus, 1986, p. 4). One major motivation for their work was to show that then-current research in artificial intelligence failed to model human cognition accurately, because computers necessarily relied on "facts and rules" programmed to connect input with a desired output.[6] The Dreyfus model of expertise was intended to describe how human beings, although starting from a similar basis, progress beyond this reliance on explicit instruction to acquire the ability for expert performance in a variety of areas. Their view that explicit knowledge of facts is insufficient for explaining human intelligence and their emphasis on tacit knowledge reflects the philosophy of medicine literature on clinical reasoning.

Although artificial intelligence has changed dramatically since the Dreyfus model was first developed, it is worth looking in a bit more detail at their argument. It turns out that their approach has important similarities with the empirical research on clinical reasoning that we will turn to in the next section. More specifically, the Dreyfus model emphasizes that human intelligence relies on a large amount of tacit knowledge about any number of scenarios we encounter in daily life. Cognitive scientists working in artificial intelligence used the concept of a "script" to describe this knowledge. The most commonly discussed example here is the "restaurant script," which contains our knowledge related to waiting to be seated, looking at a menu, ordering a meal, etc. The script represents a kind of prototypical restaurant experience, but is also flexible enough to incorporate variations, such as restaurants where patrons seat themselves, menus written on chalkboards (or accessed on a phone via a QR code), etc. AI researchers originally thought that they could program scripts that included rich enough information to allow computers to simulate human behavior accurately, but that assumption proved to be wrong. Dreyfus and Dreyfus argued that this failure shows that humans' expert performance (whether in day-to-day life or in a specialized area of knowledge) is not simply a matter of following rules. They describe the phenomenon of expert performance as "skilled coping," as opposed to the application of rules.

---

[6] More recent developments in AI do not rely on explicitly programmed rules, but there is no reason to think that they are a better model of human cognition.

We think, however, that the Dreyfus model is best used for characterizing situations in which an individual's tacit knowledge enables them to cope with a problem without needing to make their reasoning explicit. This kind of performance has the three characteristics that Benner described. To put this point slightly differently, on the Dreyfus model, the term "expert" is used to describe a kind of *performance* that is only achievable by individuals with a certain level of ability. But it is a mistake to shift from recognizing this kind of expert performance to believing that everything an expert *person* does has these qualities. The Dreyfuses' argument that experts rely on tacit knowledge takes on a different tone when we remember that their goal was to describe what human beings, and not computers, can do. Similarly, we started this section by saying that having access to all of the information in the medical literature does not equip one to practice medicine. Rules and propositional knowledge are far from sufficient. But this content knowledge does make an important contribution to practice: Doctors need both the kind of intuitive skill described by the Dreyfus model and the content knowledge acquired through years of study to solve clinical problems. And sometimes, even experts need to engage in explicit problem solving, which is a distinct form of thinking from skilled coping.

In the next section, we turn to the empirical literature that examines physicians' clinical reasoning, which does address the relationship between at least some kinds of explicit problem solving and clinical expertise. As with the Dreyfus model and Benner's work, a major aim of this research is to describe how clinicians develop expertise skills—how they progress from having only classroom knowledge when they begin their clinical training, to engaging in expert practice. At the same time, however, it does investigate clinicians' reasoning processes and may therefore be a promising approach to understanding how clinicians integrate different kinds of information in making a decision. We will show, however, that it does not give a robust enough account of clinical reasoning to address the integration problem.

The cognitive psychology of clinical decision-making

Over the past few decades, researchers motivated largely by a desire to improve medical education have studied clinical decision-making by physicians and medical students. Informed by work in cognitive psychology, they aim to explain the differences between the cognitive processes used by relative novices and those deployed by expert clinicians. As with the philosophy of medicine literature on tacit knowledge, these researchers have developed a number of accounts of these processes, sometimes using different terms to refer to similar concepts and phenomena. For the most part, these studies have examined diagnostic reasoning, though more recently there has been increased interest in examining how doctors reason about treatment decisions, as well. We will not attempt to provide an exhaustive review and analysis of this area of research but will identify some major themes and trends.

Recent reviews of this literature have described different approaches taken by researchers and changes in the way that diagnostic reasoning has been characterized. As the field has developed, it has gone through phases of focusing mainly on either the process of reasoning or on the importance of the specific content (that is, the medical knowledge) required. Now it is generally accepted that theories need to consider both process and content knowledge.

Early work focused on reasoning skills, primarily viewing diagnosis in terms of hypothesis generation and deductive reasoning. On this model, a clinician begins by considering a variety of potential diagnoses, and then both eliminates some of these possibilities and revises their assessment of the probability of others, as additional evidence in support of specific hypotheses accumulates. Using this hypothetico-deductive approach, for example, when seeing a patient with chest pain, the physician begins by considering a number of potential causes, such as a myocardial infarction, an aortic dissection, a pulmonary embolism, or heartburn. They then acquire the information needed to start crossing diagnoses off this initial list.

Researchers quickly realized that this model was insufficient to explain expert doctors' reasoning. Medical students do seem to develop an explicit differential diagnosis and use what Geoffrey Norman calls "processed knowledge": The external, recorded information that is available in textbooks, articles, and other established reference sources. Experienced clinicians, on the other hand, depend directly upon their experience (Norman, 2005). Nor does hypothetico-deductive reasoning adequately characterize the different roles that medical knowledge plays in novice versus expert reasoning. This is in part because hypothetico-deductive reasoning is a domain-general process that can apply in multiple different areas, regardless of what is being reasoned about. In the case of diagnosis, however, it became apparent that a significant amount of domain-specific knowledge was required in order to explain findings that (contrary to what would have been predicted by the early model) experienced doctors did not generate more diagnostic hypotheses than novices. Rather, they came up with *better* ones; clinical experience informs the rapid development of an initial (and sometimes a final) diagnosis. For example, an experienced dermatologist will generally arrive at a diagnosis within seconds of seeing a skin lesion and a veteran general practitioner often reaches a presumptive diagnosis only a few minutes after hearing a chief complaint. Focusing on the nature of this domain-specific knowledge and on how it was accessed helped to explain the ways in which diagnostic reasoning skills developed as medical students gained clinical expertise. Developing expertise in diagnostic reasoning requires extensive experience with patients who have the same kind of illness, as well as of patients with a range of different illnesses (Norman and Brooks, 1997).

Although research on the structure of diagnostic knowledge is complex, and different groups have offered different theories and models to explain it, it is clear now that one major difference between novice and expert diagnosticians is the amount and variety of knowledge that they can draw on as needed (reviewed in Norman, 2005; see also Yazdani and Abardeh, 2019). But there is also evidence for differences in the way that students' and experts' diagnostic knowledge is structured and used. Schmidt and colleagues have extensively studied how diagnostic knowledge changes with clinical experience. They have found that early in their clinical rotations, students have a store of biomedical knowledge, acquired in the classroom, that they use to analyze a case. (Note that this is consistent with their using a hypothetico-deductive reasoning process.) At an intermediate level, they recall a greater amount of relevant biomedical knowledge when describing how they reason about a diagnostic problem. But when they become experts, they actually refer to *fewer* biomedical facts in the diagnostic process. (Schmidt and Boshuizen, 1993). These authors suggest that, with increased clinical experience, experts have developed "encapsulated knowledge." This encapsulated knowledge is expressed by higher-level concepts or simple causal models that incorporate a number of more basic facts (Schmidt and Rikers, 2007). For example, the concept of sepsis might be offered by an expert as an explanation of a patient's presentation, while a relative novice would explain the same presentation with reference to a means of exposure to, and subsequent infection with, gram-negative bacteria; to the resulting immunological response and how it leads to the patient's signs and symptoms; to the release of endotoxins by the bacteria and the resulting vasodilation and blood pressure drop, etc. (ibid., p. 1135). The expert's concept of sepsis encapsulates these details, which need not be enumerated, but which remain available to the clinician, who can "unpack" the higher-level concept in situations where the details are needed in order to reason about the case.

A second fruitful line of research looks at the development of illness scripts, which (like the Dreyfus model) builds on script theory in cognitive psychology. Recall that scripts were first hypothesized by cognitive scientists working in the field of artificial intelligence as a way of describing the kind of context-sensitive background knowledge we all possess regarding a wide variety of everyday scenarios, and explaining why it was so difficult to program computers with the knowledge required to simulate our behavior in these ordinary settings. Similarly, the concept of an illness script was developed as a way of explaining how physicians' knowledge of pathophysiology, clinical signs and symptoms, and initial probabilities of various illnesses is stored together (Barrows and Feltovich, 1987; Custers, 2015).

The theory claims that illness scripts are "activated" when a physician sees a patient whose condition resembles a stored script. These scripts have "slots" that correspond to important aspects of the illness, in much the same way that the classic restaurant script has slots corresponding to looking at a menu, placing an order, etc. In the original paper on illness scripts, Feltovich and Barrows (1984) say that a script has three main features: Enabling conditions (situations in which a diagnosis is likely to occur); fault (the biological malfunction causing the illness); and consequences (signs and symptoms that occur because of the biological malfunction (reviewed in Custers, 2015). For each slot, the most likely variation of the attribute is the default value, which can be replaced if the particular case does not have this variation. Some authors describe the version of the script that includes default values for all attributes as providing a prototype for the illness, a term also borrowed from cognitive psychology (Bordage and Zacks, 1984). This default version of an illness script corresponds with a typical case of that illness, held in the mind of clinicians.

Script theory can help to explain the differences in reasoning between novice and expert clinicians. As we have noted, novices appeal to textbook information in their diagnostic reasoning. This information corresponds to the prototypical version of an illness. By contrast, expert clinicians reason from scripts that incorporate a rich body of knowledge, including the experiential knowledge of that individual physician. These scripts also allow for more efficient reasoning, because the knowledge that is contained in the script is encapsulated. In addition (and echoing the characterization of expert performance on the Dreyfus model), the expert can simply *see* which aspects of the script are most relevant in the particular case being considered, as well as when a patient presentation does not fit with a script or standard pattern (Engebretson et al., 2016). These scripts, since they use encapsulated knowledge, contain relatively little explicit biomedical knowledge, but they include a great deal of information about enabling conditions. They therefore allow the doctor to provisionally rule out "whole categories of disease" and focus on the most probable diagnoses (Schmidt and Rikers, 2007, p. 1135).

In some cases, a patient presentation does fit a standard pattern very closely. For instance, a primary care physician hearing a patient complaining of fever, dry cough, and body aches during the winter will quickly find herself invoking a script of uncomplicated viral infection, perhaps influenza, or (now) COVID-19. When the case at hand is a typical case, an experienced clinician can simply *see* that a patient's presentation matches an illness script. But this apparent simplicity masks the expertise involved in such seeing and the vast store of information that supports this expertise.

Empirical research shows that, as on the Dreyfus model, medical students begin by carefully and explicitly applying information that they have learned, but with increasing experience they come to perceive and to act on a patient's clinical presentation in a whole new way. This process has been observed not only in experimental studies of reasoning about hypothetical cases, but also in studies examining actual practice. There is ample evidence that expert clinicians can quickly and accurately assess a patient's clinical state, whether in general practice (Stolper et al., 2010), in an emergency setting (Wiswell et al., 2013), or in the intensive care unit (Radtke et al., 2017). When a patient presents with an acute complaint, experienced physicians tend to start by making a judgment, which they do quickly and accurately, about the severity of illness. In the context of intensive care, for example, a senior member of the ICU team is often sent to "eyeball" a decompensating patient in another part of the hospital, in order to determine whether, and how quickly, they should be moved to the ICU. This skill is taught to less experienced physicians, with direct oversight from mentors, but the task is entrusted only to experienced clinicians.

This judgment, like the activation of the initial diagnostic scripts described earlier in the chapter, occurs automatically and within seconds. There is also evidence that experienced physicians perform at least as well as quantitative tools that have been developed to predict patient outcomes, including mortality in critically ill patients (Knaus et al., 1995; Sinuff et al., 2006). These "gut feelings" develop and remain highly accurate, even when the only information available to the clinician comes from a video record, rather than from direct interaction with a patient (Sibbald et al., 2017).

Acquiring expertise in clinical reasoning involves the development of expert intuition, which to a large extent replaces the explicit appeal to propositional knowledge observed in novices. But at the same time, propositional knowledge must play a role in clinical reasoning. In an article reviewing the state of research on clinical reasoning, Geoff Norman suggests that "[f]or straightforward and frequently encountered problems, similarity-based reasoning is undoubtedly effective and efficient" (2005, p. 425). By contrast for rare and complex problems, "the expert is able to marshal an extensive array of scientific and experiential knowledge" (2005, p. 425). For example, a physician may recognize that a patient presentation does not exactly match a specific illness script, but it might not be immediately clear which of the multiple other scripts available to a physician best matches the patient's signs and symptoms. In other cases, as in our example of a patient with a viral infection, their presentation differs from the most likely script in some important ways. In the case of a patient who appears at first to exhibit the signs and symptoms of influenza, but also has profound shortness of breath and low oxygen saturation, the experienced physician will quickly recognize that these deviations from the pattern "uncomplicated influenza" mean that they now require a quite different diagnosis and treatment.

These more complex situations are sometimes described as requiring analytic reasoning, as compared with the non-analytic reasoning that occurs when similarities are recognized. But these situations are under-researched, as is the question of what factors prompt the transition between non-analytic and analytic reasoning. One relevant paper by Mamede et al. suggests that a combined, analytic and non-analytic approach is optimal, and has shown that one situation that triggers a shift from a non-analytic to an analytic approach is a case that is ambiguous. That is, the patient presentation "corresponds to the typical pattern of a disease but also includes features consistent with alternative diagnoses" (Mamede et al., 2007, p. 1186).

This interplay between non-analytical and analytical reasoning is, however, reflected in a third subarea of empirical research on clinical decision-making, which draws on the extensive literature on dual-process theories. On these accounts, fast, automatic cognitive responses (so-called Type I processes) can sometimes be replaced by a deliberate reasoning (Type II) process. Much of this body of research, both in the context of medical diagnosis and more generally, has been concerned with biases in human reasoning that result in the inappropriate deployment of Type I processes (or, rather, the failure to use Type II reasoning when it is required). This focus on biased reasoning leads researchers to advocate for more reflective and deliberate reasoning in order to avoid such biases (see, e.g., Croskerry, 2013). But this focus on biases, while important, downplays the fact that very often, non-analytic reasoning works, and works quite well. Nor do dual-process approaches to clinical reasoning have much to say about when to switch between the two reasoning strategies. (One exception here is the study we mentioned by Mamede et al.) In summary, perhaps the major contribution of dual-process theories is to remind us that tacit knowledge alone is not sufficient to explain all clinical reasoning.

There is another important limitation of the empirical research literature that we have described in this section. Specifically, it has focused almost entirely on diagnostic reasoning, and, more narrowly, on the initial judgment made by clinicians of the most likely diagnosis for a case that is described to them in terms of the patient's initial presentation. Similarly, in the context of medical education, educators draw lessons from the cognitive literature to support and guide students as they develop their diagnostic reasoning skills. So here, too, clinical reasoning has often meant only diagnostic reasoning. Only recently has there been an interest in looking at the cognitive science of therapeutic reasoning. We will turn to this topic in the next section and will show that, to the extent that it is influenced by the research on diagnosis, it remains limited in what it can tell us about analytic reasoning.

Therapeutic reasoning

We acknowledge Norman's worries about the current tendency to disparage experiential knowledge in medicine, but we believe that it is generally accepted that significant clinical experience is required for effective and efficient diagnosis, and the empirical research on diagnosis has shed some light on how clinical experience affects the cognitive processes involved in diagnostic reasoning. In the case of therapeutic decision-making, however, there is both less research and less agreement about the role that experience plays. This is, in part, a consequence of worries that physicians might not be using the "correct" or "best" therapy available for treating a given condition, perhaps because they rely on older interventions that are less effective than newer ones, or more generally fail to keep up to date on best therapeutic practices. But this worry, although not entirely unjustified, oversimplifies therapeutic decision-making, seeming to reduce it to the selection of the correct therapeutic agent. The reality is that therapeutic decision-making is much more complex than that, and clinical experience plays a crucial role in treatment decisions.

Experiential knowledge informs a number of treatment decisions, including initial triage, the selection and sequencing of diagnostic tests and therapeutic interventions, and the location where care is given. For instance, once a diagnosis of pneumonia is made, clinicians must assess the severity of the infection, taking into account the underlying conditions in the patient, in order to make therapeutic decisions. Are there concerns for atypical or opportunistic organisms? Should sputum cultures be collected, bronchoscopy be considered? Does the patient need to be hospitalized, perhaps admitted to the ICU? Much more goes into the therapeutic decision-making than the choice of antibiotics based upon an evidence-based guideline.

Treatment decisions must represent individualized care. Clinical experience guides physicians in developing a therapeutic relationship with a patient (Cassell, 2013). This relationship informs decisions about how and when to rely on indirect effects for therapeutic outcomes, which may include placebo effects, expressions of the clinician's confidence, the amount of time spent with a patient, and strategies for fostering a patient's agency. All of these can lead to better outcomes in some circumstances (Sullivan, 1993).[7] The kind of experiential knowledge that clinicians rely on in deploying these strategies takes time and experience to develop.

Treatment isn't finished when a therapy has been selected. Experiential knowledge is also crucial in assessing the effects of a treatment. Together with a clinician's knowledge of pathophysiology, clinical experience helps

---

[7] Note, too, that these factors are not measured in most randomized trials. Instead, trials tend to be designed in such a way as to eliminate or control for their effects. Which means clinicians come to understand these effects largely through experience.

physicians to decide whether a patient is responding as expected to an intervention. For example, a patient with a presumed acute bacterial infection will likely be treated with an appropriate antibiotic, and patients with such infections generally respond quickly to these treatments. But if the patient does not respond as expected, the experienced physician will soon recognize this and will rethink both the original diagnosis (e.g., consider non-infectious etiologies) and the treatment decision (e.g., anti-inflammatories in lieu of antibiotics).

Finally, many therapeutic choices are centered not on the choice of a particular medication, but on whether to treat at all. Many of the disorders that occupy a primary care clinician's day, such as hypertension, hyperglycemia, hypercholesterolemia, or osteopenia, do not affect the day-to-day experiences of patients but rather are risk factors for other disorders. Deciding to start treatment of one of these risk factors may be influenced by clinical practice guidelines, but does not necessarily follow from them. Starting a medication, with the associated costs, burdens, side-effects, and potential drug interactions, in order to lessen the risk of an outcome that may already be unlikely, regardless of "best" evidence, still requires careful consideration, likely improved by clinical experience. Remember from the discussion of the Number Needed to Treat, most patients started on medications for chronic processes that raise the risk of other disorders will never benefit from the treatment.

All of this puts the question of the choice of "best" therapy in a much different context than simply selecting a treatment from a list of available options. Yet, as we have noted, therapeutic reasoning is understudied compared with diagnostic reasoning. Much of the literature on therapeutic reasoning is prescriptive (no pun intended) in that it focuses on how physicians *should* reason—for example, discussions of decision trees, of using clinical practice guidelines, and of the extent to which physicians' actual prescribing practice habits reflect "best practice." By contrast, most research on diagnostic reasoning attempts to understand how physicians *do* reason. It aims to characterize the cognitive processes underlying this activity, how these processes change as clinicians gain greater experience, and the factors that influence diagnostic accuracy.

The relationship between diagnosis and therapeutic decision-making, in its simplest form, is considered to be sequential: A physician makes a diagnosis and then determines the appropriate therapy for the patient. This is often an oversimplification: There is evidence that physicians consider therapeutic decisions in tandem with their diagnostic reasoning, and in some cases they may begin treating the patient before a definitive diagnosis is reached. The existing literature on diagnostic reasoning may inadvertently reinforce the notion that diagnostic and therapeutic reasoning are separate and sequential, because the experimental tasks used in many studies tend to involve presenting physicians (or students) with a case description (generally one with a presumed correct answer) and examining how they arrive at a diagnosis, not allowing for a more iterative process. Unlike the actual practice of diagnosis, these studies generally do not allow the physician to ask the patient follow-up questions or to order diagnostic tests that will provide additional information, or even to use trials of different therapeutic interventions to aid in diagnosis.

In reality, moving between diagnostic and therapeutic reasoning requires what David Cook and colleagues call "management reasoning." These authors distinguish between simply reaching a diagnosis (as it has been studied by researchers), which they describe as a process of classification, and management reasoning, which they define as "the process of making decisions about patient management, including choices about treatment, follow-up visits, further testing, and allocation of limited resources" (Cook et al., 2018, p. 2267). They identify several differences between these two kinds of reasoning, including the fact that management decisions need to integrate the values and preferences of patients (and other stakeholders) and to be responsive to constraints, such as availability of local resources, as well as the need for management plans to be fluid and to include the flexibility needed for "ongoing monitoring and frequent adjustments" (p. 2267). From an epistemic perspective, then, management decisions must incorporate context-specific knowledge of both the patient and the system one is working within as well as relying on both experiential and pathophysiologic knowledge.

Empirical work by this research group has led them to further characterize the process of management reasoning using methods similar to those used in studies of diagnostic reasoning—research participants are presented with a case and asked to explain what they would do and how they made their decision. Based on their studies, they identify some further similarities and differences between management reasoning and reasoning about diagnostic classification (Cook et al., 2022). One important similarity between the two types of reasoning is that, for both, it is important to predict and to communicate to patients potential future events, including disease prognosis, and the appropriate next steps in care. Another is the need for physicians to have significant illness-specific knowledge. Unlike diagnostic (classificatory) reasoning, however, management reasoning also requires (1) a knowledge of the systems that provide healthcare and (2) a trusting relationship between physician and patient. This second requirement also facilitates a third requirement, which is that, in management, the physician must play a role as a teacher and motivator for the patient.

The initial call for more research on management reasoning (Cook et al., 2018) has led another group of researchers to suggest that there might be management scripts, akin to the illness scripts said to be used by physicians in diagnosis (Parsons et al., 2020). They say that management scripts, like illness scripts, "are rooted in pathophysiologic and clinical medical knowledge, much of which is shared by most clinicians within a given specialty" (p. 1180). They are also, however, idiosyncratic, in that they are based on the clinician's own past learning and experience.

Like illness scripts, management scripts are said to be evoked during a patient encounter, and to consist of important features of the clinical decision(s) or clinical problem(s). Once the appropriate script is selected, "slots" or variables in the script can be filled in with information that is relevant to the specific patient or context. For the management script, these slots "might include the severity or urgency of diagnosis, comorbid conditions, current medications, allergies, patient preferences, logistic constraints etc." (Cook et al., 2022 p. 203). They have found that the scripts used by physicians tend to be largely predetermined, unless unexpected occurrences or information arise, and that "[t]he best scripts seem to be grounded in a general framework and then tailored to both the specific illness and the patient" (Cook et al., 2022, p. 200).

We also suspect that there are no separate illness and management scripts: That like the original script hypothesis by cognitive scientists, physicians' scripts contain information both about how to understand a situation and what to do about it. We will say more about this in the chapter on case-based reasoning, where we will argue that scripts in clinical medicine can be seen as case fragments, snippets of cases that contain core information necessary for the practice of medicine. Cases, and the scripts that derive from them, are the repositories of clinical knowledge necessary for diagnosis, prognosis, and treatment decisions alike.

We welcome the expansion of research on physicians' reasoning to the realm of management and we agree that script theory provides a useful theoretical approach. However, in our view, scripts are limited in that they do not say much about the *reasoning* in clinical reasoning. Recall that illness scripts are automatically invoked when a physician meets a patient, and that the scripts of expert physicians contain a large amount of tacit knowledge. This means that they are best suited to elucidate non-analytic reasoning of the kind that the Dreyfus model says occurs in expert performance. But this is only part of the story. Focusing on management reasoning makes it clear that theories of clinical reasoning must also account for the explicit weighing of alternative; that is, for the kind of analytic reasoning that occurs when a script that is automatically invoked is not sufficient to solve a clinical problem. Attending to these situations will allow us to address a number of questions unanswered by script theory, such as how physicians decide which of the multiple scripts initially evoked by some clinical situations should be selected to guide further reasoning, how the slots in a script are filled in when the default value does not fit the patient's presentation or needs, and when to "unpack" encapsulated knowledge to consider explicitly the detailed knowledge it contains.

Summary

In this chapter, we have discussed the nature of clinical experience and its role in medical decision-making. We have shown that individual clinical experience can be articulated in a way that allows it to serve as evidence for a clinical decision, and that the collective knowledge of expert members of a medical community can also provide valuable evidence to inform clinical decisions. This means that clinicians are not only allowed but should be *encouraged* to incorporate primary experience into clinical decisions.

In addition to providing a source of evidence for decisions, clinical experience changes *how* physicians make decisions. This is the point emphasized by philosophical discussions of tacit knowledge and by the Dreyfus model of expertise. A large body of research examines how clinical experience functions in diagnostic (classificatory) reasoning, which is compatible with theories of tacit knowledge and expertise. What is missing, however, and what is especially important as the literature expands to consider management reasoning, is an account that can not only incorporate automatic, tacit responses but also offer a framework for understanding explicit, analytic reasoning, and that can address the lingering questions we posed in the previous paragraph. Most important for our purposes in this book, although the concept of management scripts does promise to broaden the empirical literature on clinical reasoning, like the work on illness scripts in diagnostic classification, the failure to address these questions means that it does not solve the integration problem. We will, in the final chapter, present an alternative, case-based approach to clinical reasoning that allows these questions to be addressed. But first, we will turn to the crucial issue of how clinicians take into account the experiences, goals, and values of individual patients as a part of every clinical decision. Understanding not only the importance of this process, as EBM acknowledges, but also how to actually make it happen, is central to resolving the integration problem.

5
Patient Values

Dr. Lee reviews Mr. Jackson's clinical information. His BMI remains high, in the mid-30s, where it has been for years. His blood pressure is still mildly elevated, despite treatment with two anti-hypertensives. His Hgb A1C remains above target. "Down to a couple of cigarettes a day," he responds to a query about his smoking. He has been down to a couple of cigarettes a day for as long as Dr. Lee has known him.

He reports that his shortness of breath with exertion is no different from the past, despite the addition of several inhaled medications over the last year. He admits that he does not always use these medications, or others, as consistently as they are prescribed. "Just too many of them," he notes. The co-pays are also high for several of his medications, so they do not always get filled on time. He is trying to eat better, but he is often too tired to shop and cook, so he reverts to processed and fast food.

Rather than focusing on specific symptoms and laboratory testing, as she has done in the past, Dr. Lee shifts her inquiries. She knows that he is a widower who lives alone, but learns that he participates in the care of 3 grandchildren who live nearby. He has also been very active in his church, getting joy from the social interactions he has there. He is more limited by generalized malaise and fatigue than by his shortness of breath or chronic pain. As she begins to inquire about what he is hoping to gain from treatment of his medical conditions, he becomes more engaged in the conversation. Not surprisingly, his goals have nothing to do with his blood pressure or Hgb A1C. He wants to have the energy to be a part of the lives of his grandchildren and keep up his work with the church. "I am not trying to live forever, I just want to be able to live for what time I have left, you know?" He has tremendous respect for medicine in general and for Dr. Lee in particular. "I know you can't fix everything that is wrong with me," he tells her, "but I know you are trying to help me."

No matter how good the scientific evidence available to guide a clinical decision, it cannot be the sole determinant of the right course of action for a patient; the patient's experience, preferences, and values also need to be considered and integrated with other factors that inform clinical decision-making. In some cases the patient may simply not want the therapy that the evidence shows is most likely to be successful for them, where "successful" means achieving treatment outcomes, such as a reduction in symptoms or lowering the risk of complications, generally thought to be desirable. Beyond that, however, what counts as success always depends on the patient. The relationship between evidence and values gets complicated. In this section, we provide an overview of the literature on several questions related to patient values: Which values are relevant? What roles can (and should) these values play? How can a clinician learn about patients' values? How should this information be incorporated into decision-making?

In addressing these questions, we start by using as a framework a classic paper by Ezekiel Emanuel and Linda Emanuel (1992) that presents different models of the physician-patient relationship.[1] Each model has a different approach to incorporating values into clinical decision-making. Structuring our overview in terms of these models allows us both to consider different possible answers to these questions and to show that the best answers to them are different in different clinical contexts. After providing an overview of these different ways of thinking about the role values play in clinical decision-making, we introduce two currently influential ways of incorporating patient values into decisions: Decision-theoretic approaches and values-based practice (VBP). Both of these approaches can be useful, but each also has limitations. In the final section, we draw on work in philosophy of medicine on the nature of health and illness to discuss the factors at play in complicated cases where values conflict or change over the course of a patient's illness. We then briefly discuss different ways of learning what patients' values are, closing the chapter with a brief summary of patient values as a topic of medical knowledge.

First, however, it is important to clarify what is meant by talking of patient values. At the risk of sounding overly simple, values are things that are important to us. We will take a broad view, acknowledging that a variety of kinds of values can influence health care choices. Probably the first thing that comes to mind when we think about values and health care is cases in

---

[1] While this description centers on physician-patient relationships, it is relevant to the interactions between many non-physician providers and patients as well.

which a patient's religious or ethical values influence the treatment options that they are willing to consider. For example, a patient's strong belief that human life, in the sense of personhood, begins at conception would be expected to influence their choice of how to respond to a prenatal test that indicates a high probability of a serious genetic disorder. Religious beliefs are also often invoked in decisions regarding how long to continue with life-sustaining treatment in a terminal illness (Clarfield et al., 2003). These are the kinds of situations frequently discussed in introductory bioethics courses.

Another way of thinking about the values relevant to health care is through the question, "What do you value in life?" In response to this question, people often talk about family and friends, work, or hobbies. They may also talk about their physical experiences of health and illness, and about how better managing symptoms could help them engage in valued activities, or about independence, and their ability to choose for themselves. We will say more about these kinds of values later in the chapter; for now, we will just note that the goals of many health care interventions center on promoting patients' abilities to pursue the things they value.

Finally, values are reflected in the weighing of risks and benefits associated with a treatment, including the desire for control of some symptoms rather than others, and tolerance for the risk of particular clinical outcomes or side effects. For example, some people with advanced cancer will desire pain control, even if it diminishes their ability to engage with family members, while others are willing to tolerate more pain in order to be present with family. In some cases, a treatment has a number of risks that make it unacceptable to some patients, but for other patients, the benefits of the therapy outweigh these risks. For instance, the marginal increase in risk for blood clots and endometrial cancer associated with hormone replacement therapy may be perfectly acceptable for some women whose quality of life has been profoundly impacted by severe post-menopausal symptoms.

We also want to distinguish between values and preferences. We use the term "preferences" to refer to choices among different possible courses of action related to treatment or to diagnostic tests. Preferences often reflect underlying values, and at times may be determined by them, but they are worth discussing separately because they are more easily incorporated into decision-making than are patient values themselves. Why this is the case will become clearer in the next two sections.

What roles might patient values play in clinical decision-making?

Over the past several decades, it has become increasingly accepted by healthcare providers and by society as a whole that patients should be involved in making decisions about their own care, to the point that it is easy to forget that this has not always been the case. Traditional medical practice has been characterized as being paternalistic: The doctor is like a wise father figure who knows what is best for his patient and makes decisions accordingly. This decision-making process might involve providing the patient with information about the planned therapy, but it was also seen as acceptable to provide only selected information to the patient that would encourage them to agree with the doctor's plan (Freedman, 1975; Emanuel and Emanuel, 1992). Similarly, diagnoses, especially of cancer, as well as a poor prognosis were often withheld from patients, justified to avoid hopelessness. This practice of benevolent lying was even written into the American Medical Association's first Code of Ethics (Sokol D., 2006). According to Emanuel and Emanuel, the ethical justification for the paternalistic model was based on the idea that there were objective, health-related values shared by both doctor and patient. To put their point slightly differently, the paternalistic model assumed that both the physician and the patient wanted the same thing—for the patient to be restored to health—and it was the physician who had the expertise required to make that happen. Since the physician understood both the medical knowledge and the relevant values, there was little need for him to consult the patient in his decision-making.

These days, we know that we can't take for granted that there are shared and objective health-related values. Legal and ethical consensus has been reached that patients have the right to have information about their health, their treatment options, and the possible outcomes of these different treatment options, explained to them: Neither medical knowledge nor clinical decision-making "belongs" solely to the physician. Because of this, Emanuel and Emanuel suggest that the *paternalistic* model is only acceptable in emergency situations, when there is no time to get informed consent before starting a treatment. We would add to this point, however, that in cases where it is clear that the physician and the patient desire the same outcomes, the patient may choose to cede much of the decision-making to their physician. Often, these situations involve either routine clinical decisions; prescription of antibiotics for strep throat, for example, does not generally require a discussion of patient values—or, at the other end of the clinical spectrum, care for acute and critical illness, where it is agreed that the goal of care is to see the patient through the medical crisis. (To be clear, we are distinguishing between informed consent, which should be obtained in any but the most dire emergencies, and the explicit discussion of patient values, which may or may not be necessary.) These situations do not constitute paternalism, as long as the patient has agreed to let the physician make decisions on their behalf and retains the right to change their mind in that regard. Note that both the initial delegation of decisions to the physician and any subsequent change of mind reflect what the patient values, specifically, the extent to which the patient values being involved in decisions about their care. In between these extremes, discussion of a patient's values and how they relate to different possible courses of action becomes necessary, with the amount of discussion varying in different clinical circumstances and relationships.

Moving beyond paternalism, values can influence clinical decision-making in a variety of ways. In the simplest kind of case, they can serve to rule out—or to rule in—an available course of action. Imagine a situation in which several, roughly equally effective, therapies are available and have been discussed with a patient. They may prefer one of these options because they know someone who takes the same medication and is happy with the results; they value the familiarity of the intervention. Or consider a case in which it is reasonable to consider treating a condition (e.g., some forms of chronic low back pain) using lifestyle changes, a pharmacological therapy, or a surgical intervention. The patient may be reluctant to consider surgery, effectively removing it from the list of choices. Here, there is not so much *integration* of patient values as a preference-based *selection* among the available options.

Things get more complicated when there are significant differences in the likely effectiveness or risks of the different options available. Here, the patient and clinician must consider the patient's preferences both with regard to the interventions themselves and to the risks and benefits of each option. To return to the case of the patient whose friend had had success with a therapy, if there is good reason to think that this medication will not be as safe or effective for this patient, perhaps because of the potential for an interaction with another drug they are taking, then despite their initial preference, they will likely end up changing their mind in favor of a different option. Preferences can also change as patients acquire more information or come to have experience of the other treatments available; surgery may again become a viable option for the patient with low back pain if neither lifestyle modifications nor medication leads to the desired clinical improvement or their symptoms worsen significantly.

The examples we have given here reflect what Emanuel and Emanuel (1992) call the *informative* model of the physician-patient relationship. In this model, the physician is a technical expert who diagnoses the patient and presents them with the available therapeutic options. The patient, who best knows their own values, considers the options and expresses a preference for one treatment over others. In this scenario, the clinician takes little to no responsibility for the actual decision, outsourcing treatment choice to the patient. In fact, the physician's professional input is limited to the listing of reasonable medical alternatives. (This can be referred to pejoratively as the "vending machine" model of medical care.) The examples, then, really represent the exercise of treatment preferences, rather than incorporation of patient values into a medical decision. Preferences, being fairly simple expressions of opinion, tend to be easier to incorporate into decision-making than values. However, as we have discussed above, values, particularly ethical or religious values, can also rule in or rule out certain treatment options. The informative model provides a useful characterization of these scenarios, as well.

Admittedly, the examples provided thus far are straightforward, in that they do not present complex choices for either the patient or the clinician. Certainly, there are cases in which patients' preferences might present more difficulties, such as when a patient prefers an ineffective treatment (e.g., herbal remedies for cancer, ivermectin for COVID-19) or refuses a clearly effective one (e.g., antibiotics for bacterial meningitis). But typically, even in these cases, the patient and the clinician share a general treatment goal—improvement in the patient's condition—even though they may disagree about the best way to achieve this goal.

More complicated are cases in which the goals of therapy are in question or are a point of disagreement. Some of these cases have a straightforwardly accepted solution, when, for example, they involve a competent patient who decides to refuse a treatment, even one considered standard of care. A classic example is the right of a Jehovah's Witness to refuse a life-saving blood transfusion on religious grounds. While this decision on the part of the patient may be hard for the physician to accept, assuming they do not share the patient's religious beliefs, they are legally and ethically obligated to respect the decision.

Another situation in which a patient may also refuse potentially life-prolonging therapy occurs when they no longer feel that it is worth the burden caused by the treatment itself (e.g., another course of chemotherapy for a patient with advanced pancreatic cancer). In these cases, like the Jehovah's Witness, the patient has a clear knowledge of their own values and an understanding of the outcomes associated with both accepting and refusing therapy and has made their decision based upon their knowledge and values. The main difference between this case and those like the Jehovah's Witness's refusal of a blood transfusion is that a physician may be more likely to share, or at least to feel comfortable accepting, the values that underlie the patient's decision. But in both cases, the patient is making the decision based on their values and can articulate both the decision and the reasoning to their physician.

In other cases, however, a patient may not know what they value or how to prioritize among competing values. Moreover, in the case of chronic or progressive conditions, patients' values might change over time. A patient who is first diagnosed with a significant, life-changing illness may not yet understand what the effects of their diagnosis will be, what it is like to live with, for example, diabetes or a progressive neurological disorder. These kinds of cases do not fit the informative model of the physician-patient relationship. Emanuel and Emanuel have proposed two models that allow for dealing with complex or conflicting patient values. In the *interpretive* model, a physician presents a patient with the relevant medical information about their condition and the available treatment options, in the same way as in the informative model, but also goes beyond simply informing the patient, because the physician also helps the patient to clarify their values and how those values might affect treatment goals and choices. The fourth model, the *deliberative* model, adds a final dimension to the conversation: In addition to discussing the patient's values, the physician also makes a treatment recommendation that reflects their own values as an advocate for the patient's health. This model recognizes that, despite the value that we place on patients' right to make their own decisions, many people *want* their physician to make a treatment recommendation. While on this model, the final decision remains in the hands of the patient, their doctor's advice may be an important factor in their decision process. The deliberative model of the physician-patient relationship embraces a notion of shared decision-making, about which we will have more to say later.

The deliberative model also gives us a template for dealing with cases such as the ones we mentioned above, in which a patient wants to refuse an effective treatment, or to use an ineffective one, despite valuing improved health as the goal of their clinical care. As an advocate for health, the physician can emphasize the goals shared with the patient to guide them to a specific therapeutic recommendation and can strive to understand the patient's reasons for expressing a choice that might seem to be at odds with their stated health-related values. This engagement, even when it takes the form of persuasion, is legitimate, rather than a return to paternalism, if the physician's goal is to help the patient to make decisions that accord with their values, rather than to argue that the patient should decide in ways that are contrary to their values (Brock and Wartman, 1990). However, having this kind of conversation requires that the physician is able to understand the patient's values and how they should inform the choices among treatment options. We will suggest in the last section of the chapter that what is required is for the physician to understand the patient well enough to be able to answer that patient's question: "What would you do, if you were me?" (Tonelli and Sullivan, 2019).

In summary, in this section we have used Emanuel and Emanuel's four models of the physician-patient relationship to outline different roles that patients' preferences and values might play in making treatment decisions. In the next two sections, we survey two approaches, decision analysis and values-based practice, that have been proposed for understanding and eliciting patients' values and using those values to make treatment decisions. Although both of these approaches go well beyond the informative model, because patients do not simply select among the available treatment options, we will show that they both share the informative model's assumption that patients know, or can easily come to know, their own values and preferences.

Decision analysis and the quantification of values

Decision analysis is a quantitative procedure that allows clinicians to calculate the relative desirability of different treatment options associated with a clinical decision, based on (1) the probability of each possible outcome of the treatments and (2) the value that the patient places on that outcome, expressed as a utility. Utilities reflect patient preferences for different outcomes, but are not quite the same. Preferences can be ranked (which outcome is most/least desirable, and where the other outcomes fall relative to these extremes); utilities go further than simply ranking outcomes, as they assign a numerical value to these preferences and arrange them on a ratio scale to reflect the relative strength of the preferences. Combining utilities and probabilities gives the expected utility for each possible outcome. Decision theorists generally say that a rational decision-maker should choose the option with the highest expected utility.

Proponents of EBM have done some work to develop decision theory as a way of incorporating patient values into clinical decision-making. There are several reasons for this: First, the quantitative nature of patient utilities makes it easy to combine with the probabilistic evidence obtained from clinical trials. Second, it is consistent with the general ethos of EBM; the first order of business is to obtain the best available evidence, and then in a subsequent step, an individual patient's utilities are calculated and a decision is made. This does not require challenging or even considering the relevance of the evidence provided by clinical trials, though, as we will show, some accounts of decision analysis take a more nuanced approach to calculating the probability of the various outcomes of interest.

To show how decision analysis is meant to work, we borrow a simple example from Sox et al. (2007) of a 46-year-old laborer with back pain and foot drop due to a herniated disc. The decision to be made is between surgery (a laminectomy) or injection of an enzyme, papain, that dissolves the herniated disc. To determine which of these procedures has the highest expected utility, the clinician would list the various possible outcomes of each of the two treatments and the probability of each outcome, then work with the patient to calculate the expected utility for each decision. In this example, there are two possible immediate outcomes from surgery: It may result in the patient's death (highly unlikely) or in their survival. Survival will be associated with one of several subsequent possible outcomes: Recovery, continued back pain, or continued back pain and foot drop, each with a specifiable probability. Papain injection has the same three possible outcomes that can occur in the patient has survived surgery, though the probability of each outcome is different for each of the two treatment options. Once the probabilities of each possible outcome (of each possible decision) have been determined, utilities are assigned to each outcome through a process of asking patients to identify their preferences among different outcomes when the probability of each outcome is varied.

The major strength of decision analytic approaches to clinical decision-making is not, in our view, their quantitative nature, though some find a quantitative approach preferable, but rather the fact that they require making explicit the various choices available, the different possible outcomes of each choice and their probability, and the value that a patient places on each of these outcomes. Viewing an exercise in decision analysis as a tool, rather than as a failproof algorithm that determines the right course of action, draws our attention to several places at which judgments are necessary: (1) Specifying the outcomes; (2) assessing their probability; (3) assigning utilities to the outcomes; and (4) assessing the results of the analysis.

With regard to the first of these judgment points, although some outcomes are easy to specify, such as death or stroke, others may be more complicated. To return to the back pain example above, the original example includes "continued back pain" as a possible outcome of both surgery and treatment with papain. But from the patient's perspective, it may be worth splitting up that outcome into "no difference in pain after treatment" and "substantial alleviation of pain after treatment." Of course, splitting outcomes like this means that separate probabilities need to be specified for each outcome, which brings us to the second area in which judgments must be made. Probabilities for each outcome may be based on different sources: At the simplest, the probability of an outcome can be drawn from the results of a clinical trial or meta-analysis. But this strategy depends on there being studies that measure the outcomes that are relevant to a given patient. In the example of pain after surgery, the available studies may not distinguish between the two possible categories ("no difference in pain" and "substantial alleviation of pain"). More generally, this approach has all the limitations seen in our earlier discussion of "applying" the results of clinical research in practice: The probability that a specific patient will benefit from an intervention, or will experience a particular side effect, may not be the same as it is for the average patient in the trial. If there is reason to suspect this is the case, a clinician may decide to increase or decrease the probability estimate found in the clinical literature when constructing a decision tree with that patient. In the terms we used in Chapter 2, this involves interpreting the probability given in the trial as a subjective assessment of the probability that the current patient will experience the outcome. In this way,

Kassirer et al. (2009, p. 33) suggest that the probability of an outcome, as reported in the clinical trial, serves as an "anchor point" or benchmark that can be increased or decreased using the physician's best judgment about how the patients' own situation and characteristics affect the probability of the outcome.

As Sox et al. recognize, decision analysis works better with some outcomes than with others. In particular, it works well with outcomes that are easily assessed (e.g., death, stroke, continued pain) and quantifiable (e.g., life expectancy, as compared with the average for people of the patient's age). Things are more complicated when the relevant outcomes have to do with the patient's ability to function, to engage in activities that make their life worth living. There are operational definitions for some aspects of functioning, such as mobility, and questionnaires that measure various aspects of functioning, including perceived health, physical activity, and social activities, but the extent to which these measurements capture the (average) experience of patients who undergo a treatment is unclear. Moreover, leaving aside the adequacy of these measures, information about such outcomes is often unavailable, as clinical studies do not tend to report functional status (Sox et al., 2007, p. 196), and even when they do so, the information only covers the relatively short period of the trial and follow-up. Similarly, if the most relevant trials do not measure (all of) the outcomes represented in the decision tree being constructed by the clinician and patient, a subjective assessment may also be needed: If a trial of back surgery outcomes measures only "moderate improvement" and "full recovery," but the patient will only consider surgery if there is a possibility of significant improvement, an estimate of the probability of the outcome may be selected that is intermediate between the two probabilities reported in the trial.

The fact that judgment is required in assigning utilities to the various outcomes being considered is quite clear, though we shall show later in the chapter that in practice doing so may not be straightforward. What may be less clear is how this relates to the fourth place where a decision analysis requires judgment—assessing the results of the analysis. Decision theorists make an explicitly normative claim: A rational decision-maker *should* choose the option with the highest expected utility, but it may be that after conducting the analysis, the patient balks at choosing that outcome. In this case, the best next step is not to assume that the patient is being irrational, but to revisit the patient's utilities for each outcome, their views on the different treatment options, or both. It may be that, upon revisiting their preferences, the patient actually prefers a different outcome, one that is more likely with a different treatment choice.

Alternatively, the patient's feelings about the treatment itself (e.g., surgery) may need to be explored. Emotions routinely lead us to make decisions that otherwise do not appear to be rational, at least according to decision analysis. Fear, in particular, can lead patients to reject a high utility option that is associated with significant risk. Exploring the emotions underlying a decision, rather than assuming that emotional concerns need to be discounted, can be useful for patients and physicians alike.

Finally, it is important to again acknowledge the difference between preferences and values mentioned at the beginning of this chapter. Decision analysis focuses solely on the former, with a general assumption that these preferences follow necessarily from values. And many preferences do stem from underlying values. But values may also run counter to preferences, such that individual patients may reject options that otherwise seem to maximize the chance of their preferred outcome. Valuing bodily integrity may preclude surgical options that have a higher utility than more conservative approaches. Not wanting to burden loved ones or not having adequate social support may preclude an intervention that necessitates prolonged recovery or significant caregiver effort even when it offers the highest likelihood of achieving a preferred outcome. Choosing according to one's values is rational. And in cases where a patient's values are in conflict, it is truly difficult.

In summary, decision analysis can be a useful tool for discussing preferences with patients and integrating those into treatment decisions. But it works best when both the probabilities of the outcomes and the utilities assigned to them are clear, and when the outcomes are fairly simple and easy for a patient to envision. Like the informative model, decision-theoretic approaches assume that a patient knows (or can readily discover using the standard gamble method) the relative value of the different possible outcomes.

Values-based practice

Another well-developed approach to incorporating patient values into clinical decision-making is values-based practice (VBP). VBP positions itself as a partner to EBM that is "complementary to and supports evidence-based approaches" (Fulford, 2008, p. 12); it aims to provide for the assessment of values what EBM provides for the assessment of research evidence. Parallel to EBM's steps of acquiring and assessing evidence, VBP suggests that clinicians should, as part of the clinical encounter, elicit a patient's values and then consider them in light of the values of other people involved in their health care, including both health care providers from various disciplines and family members. On the VBP model, it is up to the physician (or sometimes to another provider who is working with the patient, for example, when the decision to be made is about access to programs or services, rather than relating to a medical therapy) to manage values, especially in cases of value conflict. VBP emphasizes that both the values of patients and the values of providers are important, and it cautions against the extremes of both a consumerist model—on which the patient is always right—and a traditional paternalistic approach—on which patients simply follow the doctor's orders. Rather, VBP "starts from a premise of mutual respect and relies on a robust process to support balanced decision-making in the particular circumstances" (Fulford et al., 2012, p. 6).

Because of the wide range of values it considers, the scope of VBP is wider than our concerns in this chapter: Examples discussed in a central VBP textbook include cases in which a teenaged patient with mild acne requests a clinically inappropriate treatment with potentially dangerous side effects, and one of a patient who refuses to give up smoking despite having COPD. By contrast, we have narrowed our discussion to the role of patient values in selecting among available treatment options, to reflect our focus in this book on the nature of clinical decision-making. Moreover, where VBP does address cases in which a clinician and patient are deciding among different treatment options, it emphasizes cases in which their values are in conflict. This focus is importantly different from that of integrating patient values into clinical decision-making. As we discussed in the first section of this chapter, there are cases in which a patient's values are different from the physician's, and in some cases these differences influence the process of deciding on the best treatment. While we acknowledge the importance of recognizing that clinicians bring their values into the clinical encounter, we disagree with VBP's assumption that what is required in these circumstances is "balancing" these different values.

Sarah Wieten's analysis of VBP makes clear some of the other assumptions that the method makes about patient values: First, it relies on a sharp distinction between facts or evidence, on the one hand, and values, on the other

(Wieten, 2018b, p. 9). In this, it resembles Emanuel and Emanuel's informative model. This assumption allows VBP to carve out its own territory without coming into conflict with EBM. But, as we have pointed out above, thinking about patient values separately from thinking about evidence is not going to help in cases where the best existing evidence is not relevant to what matters most to a patient. In fact, when VBP discusses a case like this, in which a patient in her 40's is diagnosed with breast cancer and wants to pursue breast-conserving surgery, rather than a mastectomy, the book does not provide a resolution to the case, choosing instead to use their depiction of the "opening moves" (Fulford et al., 2012, p. 112) in the conversation between the patient and her surgeon to illustrate the importance of mutual respect to VBP.

Leaving this case unresolved is, in fact, a very unusual move in the literature on VBP, which brings us to another point raised by Wieten: The examples given to illustrate VBP do not illustrate situations involving "strong or intractable clashes of values" and "a mutually beneficial agreement is always reached" (Wieten, 2018b, p. 9).[2] Moreover, this agreement is reached without any significant change in the various parties' values. Instead, a foundation of mutual respect and willingness to communicate allows the physician to resolve the existing conflicts. Even in cases where a patient's values do appear to change over time, VBP views this as a matter of uncovering their true values, rather than of the values themselves actually changing (ibid.) This assumption sits oddly with VBP's definition of values as "preferences, needs, hopes [and] expectations" (Fulford, 2008; quoted in Wieten, 2018b, p. 9), as those are exactly the sort of things that one might expect serious illness to change. In the next section, we address this issue in greater detail.

In summary, VBP calls attention to the importance of being able to make values, both the patient's and clinician's, explicit in clinician decision-making. But it also draws a distinction between values and "factual" medical evidence, insisting that parallel analyses are undertaken, which of course means that conflicting conclusions can be reached when a patient's values cause them to want something that is not what the "best evidence" suggests they should want. This represents a false dichotomy, one that needs to be

---

[2] Even in the breast cancer case, it is implied that the case is not an instance of failure to manage values appropriately. The book simply "[did] not have space" to follow the case to its resolution (Fulford et al., 2012, p. 110).

rejected. The "best" decision for an individual patient will be one that incorporates both the relevant medical knowledge and the relevant values into a single analysis. We will discuss this in much more detail in the final chapter of the book. We also take the position that the clinician's role is to elucidate and incorporate the patient's values into the decision at hand, rather than to "balance" them with their own. The professional values of clinicians are centered on providing benefit to individuals seeking care, benefit that will be in large part determined by that individual's values. While no clinician is obligated to offer or provide a service that is non-beneficial or highly likely to cause harm simply because it is requested, such requests are rare in medicine and should be met with a careful exploration of the reasons for the request, not an assertion of the primacy of the clinician's values.

Why understanding patients' values is crucial

As we noted in introducing the interpretive and deliberative models, patients may not always be able to readily articulate their own values and to use this knowledge to identify their preferred treatment. Moreover, a patient's values and preferences may change over time in ways that are difficult for them to foresee, or even to recognize right away as these changes are beginning to occur. This is especially common when a patient receives a new and serious diagnosis, or when their health changes dramatically, or when they have a health condition that is progressive or that fluctuates in severity over time. In addition, as patients gain experience in living with a chronic health problem, the way they understand their situation may change. For example, a patient's initial reaction to a new diagnosis may be one of fear and dread, but as they learn what it is like to actually live with the illness, they may realize that it is not as disruptive or difficult as they had feared, or adjust to the disruptions and challenges it presents. This adjustment may lead them to reassess what they value most in life, to re-envision the goals they have for themselves and for their medical treatment.

In this section, we draw on work in philosophy of medicine that addresses the concepts of health and illness to describe some ways that patients' experiences and their health-related values might change over time. We then turn to empirical, qualitative studies to provide some examples of what might be important to patients living with a serious health condition and to identify the kinds of values that can shift over time. In keeping with our focus in this book, we will be mainly concerned with how shifting values can inform treatment decisions made by a patient and their physician, though we also note that, in addition to medical interventions, they might also discuss the possibility of accessing services that provide emotional support, including peer support, or assistance from other health professionals such as occupational therapists, physical therapists, or social workers.

Medical treatments may aim at multiple goals. Four of the most common are the management of symptoms; the prevention of unwanted outcomes (whether due to the disease itself or to a treatment undertaken); the maintenance or restoration of the patient's ability to engage in pursuits that they value; and the maintenance or restoration of a patient's agency. Specific interventions may aim at one or more of these goals. Controlling symptoms, such as chronic pain or dyspnea on exertion, and preventing disabling complications, such as stroke, may be the primary means for higher-level goals, such as allowing individuals to pursue activities they value and actively engage in all aspects of their life.

The philosopher Lennart Nordenfelt (1995; 2007) has defined health precisely in terms of an individual's valued activities. He claims that someone is healthy when, and to the extent that, they are able to achieve their "vital goals," or their most important goals in life. For many of us, these goals include work, social activities, and hobbies. Certainly, illness can affect our ability to do these things, at least with the ease that we're accustomed to. For example, travel may become more difficult if illness limits dietary choices, affects mobility, or causes someone to become tired more quickly than they used to. If seeing new places is a vital goal for someone, then on Nordenfelt's account of health, any condition that prevents them from doing so, or makes it harder for them to do so, makes them less healthy.

Nordenfelt also recognizes that illness can change people's goals. Someone who used to love international travel, or back country camping, might come to appreciate the less strenuous joys of exploring local towns on weekend trips. On Nordenfelt's theory, this person has regained health—not by becoming able to do again the activities they previously valued, but by changing the goals that are important to them. This may seem counterintuitive: If someone still has the same physical challenges, then changing what they value does not seem to make them more healthy. This reaction is based on a common, though mistaken, perception of health and illness as mutually exclusive.

The philosopher and physician Mark Sullivan (2016) notes that, in an era of chronic disease and disability, only a miniscule amount of time patients deal with illness is spent in the company of medical practitioners. The primary role of clinicians, then, is in assisting and advising patients in how to deal with illness, allowing them to define, mitigate, and control the impact on their lives. Agency, over one's illness and one's life, is the closest thing to a primary good toward which medicine should aim. Sullivan describes clinicians not as authorities on things medical, dispensing cures, but as partners for individual patients seeking to live their lives to the fullest extent despite the presence of pain, disability, and physical decline. In accepting their role as centered on the function and agency of patients, clinicians must actively seek to know patients as persons, as individuals, not as exemplars of a particular diagnosis or targets of clinical practice guideline.

In addition to thinking about how to help individuals to achieve goals or maintain agency, it is important to understand what it is *like* to be ill. Phenomenology is a branch of philosophy that focuses on human experience (e.g., of perception or of embodiment) and it has provided useful resources for articulating what it is like to be ill. The phenomenological perspective can be extremely useful for clinicians seeking to care for persons, not simply for patients. Even though we cannot ever experience an illness in the exact way that another does, being able to acknowledge and explore the uniqueness of another's lived experience is essential to partnering with patients. Havi Carel has emphasized the extent to which illness affects everything about our experience: It is "a systematic shift in the way the body experiences, acts, and reacts as a whole" (Carel, 2018, p. 37). This shift affects not only our experience of our body, but also of our relationship with the world, our perceptions of our environment and our ability to interact with it. For example, Carel talks about how, for someone who is no longer able to walk as quickly as she used to, it may be necessary to translate "healthy time," like someone describing a distance as "a ten-minute walk," to reflect their own pace and experiences.

Seeing the connection between the goals of medical care and the phenomenology of illness allows us to revisit the relationship between health and illness. Empirical research on the experiences of people with chronic illness shows how complex this relationship truly is. Many people with chronic health conditions, despite experiencing both significant symptoms and diminished ability to engage in valued activities, rate their health as good. This suggests that being healthy is not simply a matter of the absence of disease, or even of having the symptoms of a disorder well-controlled. There are various ways that people might come to understand their illness and experience the way it influences their life as a whole. For some people, the experience of illness can become meaningful in a way that changes their values in what is viewed as a positive way. Susan Moch (1989) developed the concept of "health within illness" to describe the view that illness can be viewed "as an event that can expand human potential" (p. 23). Others worry that this perspective can become a standard to which patients are held, to learn and to benefit from being ill (Ehrenreich, 2001). Although there are valid worries about seeing illness in so positive a light, the fact is that some patients do come to see it this way and their values should be taken seriously.

For other people (and perhaps even for those who view illness in spiritual terms), coping with illness may involve periods of "ordinariness" or equilibrium, in which the illness has been incorporated into their daily life, alternating with periods of distress (Kralik, 2002; Ambrosio et al., 2015). These cycles may reflect the fluctuation of symptoms, changes in functional status (e.g., loss of the ability to engage in specific activities as a health condition progresses), or changes in an individual's circumstances that affect the resources (financial, emotional, social) they have for dealing with their health condition.

Relatedly, people's understanding of their condition and their relationship to it can change over time. Roddis et al. distinguish between people who "live with" their health condition and those who "live alongside of it" (2016, p. 7). People in the former group view their illness as part of their identity and can integrate it into their daily lives. This kind of integration also contributes to an individual's experience of being healthy despite having a health condition. Similarly, an individual's ability to cope with daily tasks and an overall sense of well-being can lead to a sense of health, even in the face of diagnosed disease (Simon et al., 2005).

The extent to which an individual is, in general, able to integrate their health condition into their lives, to modify their expectations and the activities they value, and to develop ways of coping with changes in their physical experiences and abilities, may all affect their values in ways that influence their treatment goals and preferences. Alternatively, patients may have adapted their lifestyle and environment in ways that contribute to their ability to function day-to-day and no longer view these functional goals as something that medical therapies should help them with. Clinicians who engage with their patients' goals and values will have a better understanding of the aspects of daily function that they would like treatment to improve.

In summary, values have a complex interaction with health and illness. Existing values may determine how profoundly an illness affects an individual. Serious and/or chronic illness can be expected to change a person's goals and values, often in a profound way. We believe it is not enough to simply acknowledge the importance of values for medical decision-making, allowing the patient to incorporate them on their own after medical information is provided by the clinician. Rather, we argue that clinicians bear the responsibility for incorporating the goals and values of patients into medical recommendations and decisions. For that to happen, clinicians must develop expertise not only in the handling of medical knowledge, but also in acquiring knowledge of the individual patient. We turn to this topic in the next section.

Eliciting patients' values

One important question remains to be covered in this chapter: How should physicians elicit patients' preferences and values? If the incorporation of those values and preferences into medical decisions remains, at least in part, the clinician's responsibility and not something that is simply outsourced to the patient, then clinicians must seek to know the patient well enough to arrive at the best treatment choice or recommendation. In many simple cases, in-depth knowledge is not necessary and the assumption that patient preferences will match their values can be expected to hold. Preferences, in general, are fairly easy to elicit, when a clinical question is straightforward (e.g., is this sore throat and fever related to a streptococcal infection?) and goals are clear (e.g., we would like this sore throat to go away and avoid any complications). Often in such cases the patient already has some knowledge of their options through previous experiences of their own, or of a friend or family member, or through looking for information about their condition (Roddis et al., 2016). Finding such information has become much easier, though also potentially more dangerous, with patients' access to the internet and to social media. (See Kukla, 2007, for example, for a discussion of these issues and their impact on the physician-patient relationship.) Even if patients do not have much pre-existing knowledge or experience, and so do not already have an idea of their preferences going into a clinical encounter, simply providing information and answering questions about the available choices will often be enough to enable them to clarify what they want. This is the kind of situation captured in Emanuel and Emanuel's informative mode, and in decision analytic approaches that ask patients to help determine the utility they attached to different treatment options.[3]

Still, many clinical decisions, in both acute and chronic illness, are far from straightforward. Diagnoses are uncertain, treatment options are complex, outcomes are far from guaranteed, and setbacks and complications are common. Earlier, we have examined the different kinds of medical knowledge and reasoning that must be considered and weighed to arrive at clinically sound judgments, but that alone is insufficient to provide individualized care to patients. Without the ability to incorporate knowledge of the patient—knowledge of their experiences, goals, and values—physicians cannot treat patients as persons. For all but the most basic clinical interactions, physicians need skills in communicating with patients to discover or to decide on what course of action is best.

Although we have emphasized, up to this point, discussion between an individual physician and an individual patient, research can be useful in improving and guiding these conversations. In the previous section, we cited some qualitative studies that contributed to understanding patients' experiences with a particular health condition, or of a particular therapy. This literature can be a valuable starting point for understanding a patient's values, in that it aims to elucidate the views and experiences of patients living with a particular health condition or kind of health condition. Yet this literature is insufficient for a variety of reasons. Surveys present complementary information to qualitative research: Whereas qualitative studies provide depth and richness to patients' experiences, surveys give information about how common particular experiences are, or which concerns patients have most frequently. Like clinical trials examining the effects of a treatment on health outcomes, the available qualitative and survey literature may be more or less relevant to an individual patient's situation, but it can provide a valuable place to start. As the developers of VBP note, this kind of research "can help us understand the values that are *likely to be in play* in a given situation," but not which *actually* matter in that situation

---

[3] Although the decision analytic approach may seem to involve more discussion of patient values than is generally found in the informative model, it actually converts preferences, which are rank-ordered, to utilities, which are numerical values. It therefore depends on patients already having a sense of how much they value the different possible outcomes of a treatment.

(Fulford et al., 2012, p. 65). That is, research can supplement, but not replace, conversations with the individual patient.

Another important source of knowledge of which values are likely to be important in a given clinical situation is the physician's past clinical experience. As Quill Kukla (2007) points out, when a patient has recently become ill and received a diagnosis, a physician who has treated many patients with a similar diagnosis will have a better idea of what the patient should expect than the patient herself will have at that time. Importantly, this knowledge is not just of the strictly clinical outcomes that may occur, but also of the potential changes in a patient's emotional and psychological responses to their illness, and of the effects of their health on their daily lives and relationships.

Another way of thinking about patients' values and about communicating with patients is offered by narrative medicine, which was developed with the aim of fostering skills to aid clinicians in better knowing patients. Rita Charon (2006, 2007) calls out the need for clinicians to develop narrative competence, the ability to hear, understand, and respond to the stories patients tell. Exercising these skills leads to affiliation; the "authentic and muscular connections" between clinician and patient (Charon, 2007, p. 1267). Narrative medicine emphasizes a patient's uniqueness, sees the patient as a person, and takes a holistic view of the patient and their circumstances. While narrative approaches are applicable beyond conversations about treatment choices (e.g., they are useful for eliciting information important for diagnosis and for discussing long-term goals of care), the skills they teach in careful listening, seeing from the patient's perspective, and understanding the patient's situation as an ongoing story of their life, are well-suited for helping a patient to understand and articulate their preferences and values and, more broadly, what they hope to gain from therapy. These skills flesh out the interpretive and deliberative models' requirement that the physician help a patient to discover or decide on the values relevant to their choice of treatment.

Katherine Montgomery, even prior to this focus on narrative medicine, has noted that physicians have always dealt in stories, adapting the stories of patients into standard narrative formats to share with other doctors (Montgomery Hunter, 1991). Often this adaptation, this medicalization of the patient's story, strips the story of those personal elements that are not seen as germane to the diagnostic or therapeutic focus of the clinician. Clinicians need only think of the example of the "poor historian," the patient who, in telling their story, offers either too much, too little, or all the wrong kind of information necessary for the clinical task at hand. The stories of illness that patients tell never fit the standard format that is most efficient from a clinical perspective, which the clinician develops and will eventually write into a chart note. That is, the actual narrative practice of clinicians, standardizing the personal stories of patients, generally runs counter to the very goals of narrative medicine. As we will discuss in more detail in the final chapter on case-based reasoning, narrative processing on the part of clinicians is absolutely necessary in making the illness of an individual patient into a case, a process that is itself necessary for medical decision-making. What Charon and colleagues call for in their focus on narrative competence is a much broader understanding on the part of clinicians of the many aspects of the patient's story, of their experience of illness, that are relevant for provision of clinical care. Removing patients' experience, values, and social context from the story of illness may seem expedient, but it ultimately disadvantages patients and clinicians alike. Rather than aiming for "just the facts," clinicians do well to encourage patients to share the context in which an illness is occurring. Assuming to know what the patient expects to gain from the clinical encounter is a poor substitute for asking.

There is also growing recognition in medicine of the extent to which patients' health is shaped by social determinants, and of the ways in which social factors can affect the choices that are realistically available to patients. Training in structural competency aims to increase physicians' understanding of these issues, as well as their ability to navigate them with their patients (Hansen and Metzl, 2019).

Clinicians may balk at the idea of having to have in-depth knowledge of their patients in order to do their job. Obtaining such knowledge seems time consuming in a profession that values efficiency. Certainly, as we have noted, not every clinical situation demands deep knowledge of the patient as a person. But for the care of most patients with severe acute disease or chronic, progressive illness, specific knowledge of context and values will be crucial in order to achieve patient-centered goals.

Tonelli and Sullivan (2019) suggest a practical way for clinicians to judge the depth of patient-specific knowledge needed in a clinical encounter: The clinician must know the patient well enough to be able to answer the patient's question, "What would you do, *if you were me*?" The question, "What would you do, if you were me?" is often not welcomed by clinicians engaged in conversations around care and does not necessarily change their recommendations. (Mendel et al., 2010) The question may suggest that the patient is abdicating responsibility for decision making and raises the specter of paternalism by requiring that the clinician demonstrate that she has an opinion regarding an optimal course of action. Yet the "if you were me" clause in the question demands that clinicians learn and know enough about the experience, goals, and values of an individual patient in order to render a valid substituted judgment, a judgment that matches that of the patient who knows what the physician knows. This avoids paternalism, where the clinician feels she knows what is best, independent of patient input. The approach requires informed empathy for the patient, empathy composed not simply of an emotive component, which might lead clinicians astray (Bloom, 2016), but also of an epistemic component, an attempt to know what the patient knows regarding his illness. Tonelli and Sullivan argue that being able to answer the question, even when it is not asked, is necessary for the clinician to be an active partner of the patient. The answer to the question is not to be limited to a particular treatment choice, but may very well involve significant work, lifestyle, and behavior modifications on the part of the patient. It may also require a re-examination of priorities and previous choices. When the answer the clinician reaches in considering the question is different from the decision communicated by the patient, the default is not to acquiesce to the patient's decision. Rather, this discordance means that one person has the other person wrong, and it is not always clear where the misunderstanding lies. Discordance may mean that the clinician does not understand the patient, but it could also mean the patient does not understand something the clinician is trying to convey. Intractable disagreement should be rare. Within a therapeutic relationship, such discordance is an invitation to a deeper examination of the knowledge, understanding, and values of both parties. (Note that this is different from VBP's way of considering both parties' values, in that the goal here is to do justice to the patient's values, not to "balance" both sets of values.) It is not sufficient to simply respect patient choice; clinicians must truly understand a patient's choice in order to know why it is best for that particular person.

Clinicians interested in practical guidance for incorporating patient goals and values can look to the Patient Priorities Care (PPC) approach developed by Mary Tinetti and colleagues. (https://patientprioritiescare.org/) The PPC process was specifically designed for patients, like Mr. Jackson in the vignette that runs throughout this book, with multiple co-morbidities, often under the care of multiple sub-specialists. Employing clinical practice guidelines in such settings assumes that patients desire whatever outcome has been studied, for example, a reduction in risk of mortality or stroke. Treating such a patient for each disease independently often results in polypharmacy along with the subsequent adverse effects and cross-reactions. Multiple sub-specialty consultants, each focused only on their chosen organ system, tend to create incoherent and burdensome treatment plans aimed at various outcomes that may or may not be at all important to the patient. The PPC model makes no such assumptions, acknowledging that patients may not value these "benefits," particularly if they come with significant burdens and effects on quality of life (Tinetti et al., 2019). To elucidate patient goals, the program teaches communication strategies that facilitate both patient-clinician as well as clinician-clinician interactions. In exploring context and values with patients, clinicians are encouraged to actively demonstrate shared decision making by using phrases such as "Knowing what I know about you, I would suggest…" Such an approach requires the clinician be able to answer the question, "What would you do, if you were me?" in order to make specific and individualized recommendations regarding care, still leaving open the possibility of further deliberation if the recommendation meets with an alternative view.

Summary and conclusion

In a book on medical epistemology this emphasis on what patients know may seem out of place to some. After all, the common notion of the physician-patient relationship has the physician in possession of medical knowledge, knowledge that the patient is seeking to have brought to bear on their condition. Such a relationship is epistemically imbalanced. Patients have knowledge, obtained by direct, lived experience and reflection, that is absolutely necessary to the understanding and amelioration of their illness. From a philosophical perspective, failing to fully acknowledge and incorporate the knowledge of patients into medical decision making represents an epistemic injustice (Kidd and Carel, 2017). From a clinical perspective, it results in care that is not person-centered.

The notion that patient preferences, goals, and values rightly influence medical decision seems to be universal in contemporary medicine. The understanding that these unique features of individual patients represent knowledge is less so. We argue that the context and direct experience of patients represent knowledge that clinicians must actively elucidate and incorporate into clinical decisions. It is not the patient's job to make sure that their goals are targeted and their values are respected; it is the clinician's.

6
Case-based Reasoning

After examining and talking with Mr. Jackson, Dr. Lee reflects upon what she has learned from and about him. She tries to reconcile those specific attributes, experiences, and goals with what she knows from reading clinical research and practice guidelines, from understanding the pathophysiology of his multiple illnesses, and from her years of clinical training and practice. Her goal is to recommend a course of action best for Mr. Jackson, one that will aid him in reaching his goals and maintaining his agency. This requires considering, weighing, and integrating multiple, and sometimes conflicting, grounds for action. She compares Mr. Jackson to other cases, those she has seen, those formed by her understanding of the pathophysiology of disease, and those average cases derived from clinical research. And then, understanding that her choices and recommendations are at best only probably right, she will advise Mr. Jackson.

Clinical medicine is a practice in particulars, requiring decision-making focused on individuals. In earlier chapters, we have looked at the kinds and sources of general medical knowledge, including the results of clinical research, research on and understanding of physiological mechanisms, and direct clinical experience. Each of these has utility in clinical practice and the value of each fluctuates depending upon the clinical situation. In the previous chapter, we emphasized the importance of knowing individual patients, of understanding not only the particulars of their clinical presentation, but also of their experiences, goals, and values. Excellent clinicians must be able to access, weigh, and incorporate general medical knowledge as well as knowledge of the particular patient in order to arrive at the best choices or recommendations for individuals. Up to this point, we have only suggested how this process should proceed, using the concept of integration to emphasize the need to consider all of the different kinds of knowledge relevant to clinical decision-making.

We began this book by pointing out that EBM has an integration problem, and by adding much more than clinical research results to the mix, we may have seemed to only make that problem worse. In this chapter, however, we offer a solution to the integration problem, one that is rooted in case-based reasoning. We start by describing the basic components of case-based reasoning, including construction of a target case and reasoning by analogy between that target case and one or more source cases. Next, we introduce a more detailed model of clinical reasoning that is based on Stephen Toulmin's model of argumentation, which Toulmin and Albert Jonsen incorporated into their account of case-based moral reasoning. While this formal approach may initially seem complex, upon careful consideration we expect clinicians will find case-based reasoning very familiar, describing much of their clinical reasoning and practice.

Case-based reasoning

Clinicians think in cases. They see cases, remember cases, discuss cases, describe cases and write about cases. This focus on the case goes back to the very beginning of medical practice, persisting through millennia. Cases are not only the daily unit of work in medicine, they are also the building blocks of medical knowledge. As we have noted, training for clinical practice depends heavily on direct clinical experience, the seeing of cases. Here we will argue that the best clinical research results and the understanding of mechanisms of disease also work to produce average and idealized cases, respectively, in the minds of clinicians. So, if clinicians spend their days seeing cases and have a fund of medical knowledge based upon cases, it makes sense that they do, and should, also reason in cases.

Case-based reasoning (CBR) has a rich tradition in moral reasoning (Jonsen and Toulmin, 1988), is entrenched in some professions, such as the law, and is also an important approach in the field of artificial intelligence. While clinicians, we believe, think and reason in cases, relatively little attention within medicine has been paid to the structure, skills, and strategies that comprise sound case-based reasoning. We will show that, structurally, reasoning from cases most closely resembles an argument, in which a variety of sometimes conflicting warrants and their backing must be considered in order to arrive at a conclusion that is never certain, but that hopefully represents the best of the available options. Clinicians must develop the skills to access not only the results of clinical research, but also knowledge acquired from accumulated clinical experience, mechanistic understanding, and, crucially, knowledge of and from patients themselves. The strategies of CBR rely heavily on analogic reasoning, the comparison of cases. Deductive and inductive reasoning have limited utility in CBR, which is much more abductive (in diagnosis, where it involves seeking the best explanation) and pragmatic (in therapeutics, where it involves seeking what is most likely to work) in nature. In what follows, we will more carefully examine and explicate these features of CBR, arguing that CBR can provide a rigorous and explicit framework for providing individualized medical care.

Making the case

The general structure of case-based reasoning involves the comparison of a (target) case-at-hand to one or more better-understood (source) cases. Source cases serve as repositories of information and knowledge that may be useful for dealing with the target case.

In clinical medicine, the target case is derived from the individual patient for whom a diagnosis, prognosis, or treatment plan is being sought. While we talk about patients as cases, it is more accurate to say that they are the sources of cases, as creating the case requires a process. Specifically, to make a case, the story the patient tells is edited by the clinician into a medical narrative, combined with results of physical, laboratory, and radiographic examinations, producing a disembodied description recognizable to other clinicians. Medical education trains clinicians to create cases, separating clinically relevant wheat from unhelpful chaff, reformatting information that can be summarized in several minutes even though it may have taken hours to accrue. While Dr. Lee interacts with Mr. Jackson as a person, she also thinks of him as a case of middle-aged man with multiple co-morbidities.

It is important to recognize, however, that the individual patient is a person, not a case. The development of a case is necessary for patients to benefit from the medical system, but it also comes with the risk of losing sight of the patient's individuality. Foucault notes the depersonalization produced by the medical gaze necessary to separate and package the medically relevant aspects of illness from the rest of the individual (Foucault, 1994). In the last chapter, we emphasized the need for clinicians to elucidate and incorporate patient-specific knowledge into medical decisions. Patient-specific features are often crucial to the case. For instance, a history of non-adherence to medical treatments or limited financial resources is a clinically relevant aspect of a case. But other particular features, such as an affinity for classical music or one's college *alma mater*, are less likely to be. Many core aspects of an individual's identity will be left out as their case is made, yet clinicians must remember that, while they reason in cases, they care for people.

After constructing the target case from the medical encounter, clinicians will search for other, similar cases with which to compare that target case. Such source cases can originate from a variety of places. Sources cases derived from a single individual remembered by the clinician, or from a published case report, are straightforward examples. More often, however, there is no single case available to serve as an appropriate source case. In those situations, aggregations of cases obtained by direct experience will produce a "typical" case in the minds of clinicians, a stripped-down and abstract conceptualization of a particular diagnosis or syndrome. For instance, a clinician might hold in her mind a typical case of Type II diabetes in her clinical practice: A sedentary, overweight, middle-aged person with metabolic syndrome. Certainly, she recognizes that this does not describe all of her patients with Type II diabetes but does serve to provide a source case that the patient in front of her may, or may not, closely resemble. And the degree of resemblance, as we shall see, is what matters.

In addition to arising from a physician's own clinical experience, source cases can also be derived from different areas of medical research. Statistical information, like that produced by clinical research, can be most easily utilized by clinicians when it is converted into an "average" case. This approach goes back to the earliest days of statistical medicine. In 1835, the influential Belgian statistician, Adolphe Quetelet noted that the consideration of the "average man" was absolutely necessary in order to assess the health of any particular individual (Caponi, 2013). Perhaps the earliest formulation of the biostatistical theory of disease, the "average man" was defined by statistical analysis and then used as a benchmark to define disease as significant divergence from the average. Over time, the study of specific disorders allowed for moving beyond the average (normal) man to the average pathological case. Developed still further, clinical research, particularly the therapeutic RCT, allowed for the average subject of a clinical trial to become an average case with regard to anticipated course, prognosis, and response to treatment. The average subject of a study is partially defined and thoroughly constrained by the inclusion and exclusion criteria. Similar to Quetelet, clinicians make use of clinical research data by turning the statistical average into a case, an average patient. Philosopher and physician Hillel Braude notes that clinicians necessarily assign an "essentially anthropomorphic structure to statistical reasoning, particularly in its application to clinical reasoning" in order to utilize the results of clinical research in clinical practice (Braude, 2012, p. 147). Clinicians, then, compare the target case before them to the average case(s) reported in clinical studies and trials. Again, it is divergence of the target case from the average case that remains critically important.

Understanding of physiological mechanisms further complements a clinician's pool of source cases by providing "idealized" cases. These cases rely on an in-depth understanding of mechanisms, generally gleaned from a wide survey of the medical sciences, including genetics, pharmacology, and physiology (Schaffner, 1986). We have emphasized in our discussion of physiological mechanisms, in chapter 3, that knowledge of these mechanisms is based on the results of numerous laboratory studies. (This is in contrast to population-level research, where it may be possible to refer to a single clinical trial to construct an average case.) More specifically, idealized cases require the aggregation of interlevel scientific knowledge related to a condition. For example, an idealized case of Type II diabetes will involve understanding of glucose metabolism, insulin resistance, and nutrition science. Since they are primarily derived from the basic sciences, idealized cases tend to serve as sources of pathophysiologic knowledge.

Cases, both target and source, are constructed by clinicians in order to facilitate clinical decision-making. Clinical experts hold in their minds a tremendous number of cases- typical, idealized, and average cases—that they can access when needed. Because the source cases are generally ones in which the best course of action is already determined, they provide a starting point for thinking about what to do in the current situation. Not all source cases are created equal, however. Those where there is strong consensus regarding the quality of the knowledge contained therein can serve as exemplar cases, reliable touchstones for clinicians engaged in clinical decision-making. Other, less clear-cut, cases may be helpful in decision-making, but do not provide a reliable enough guide to serve as exemplars. Even with such exemplars, however, no target case is completely identical to a source case. Clinical decision-making requires a thoughtful comparison, searching for knowledge from source cases that is most relevant to the case at hand and the discounting of knowledge that, upon reflection, is not applicable.

Reasoning by analogy: Comparing cases

Analogical reasoning occupies a central place in CBR, with clinicians drawing analogies between the current, target, case, and one or more relevant source cases. Again, these source cases might be an average case derived from a clinical research study, or an idealized case based upon a mechanistic understanding of disease. The methodology for sound analogic reasoning has been explored by philosophers. For a source case to provide reliable guidance for a particular case, there should be (1) meaningful material similarities between cases, (2) a causal connection present in both cases, and (3) no essential differences between analogs (Hesse, 1966; Bartha, 2016).

These three conditions make clinical sense. Obviously, we want to compare cases with similar presentations or diagnoses to one another. We compare cases of chronic cough to other cases of chronic cough; case of heart failure to other cases of heart failure. The requirement of "meaningful material similarities" is generally straightforward in medicine.

The importance of a causal connection reinforces the relevance of mechanistic understanding for clinical practice. Determining the cause of a particular presentation or malady is generally crucial to making a definitive diagnosis and developing a successful treatment plan. So, as far as possible, clinicians will want to compare cases that reflect identical causes. Patients may present with hypotension, along with its signs and symptoms, for a wide variety of reasons. Getting at the cause of the hypotension, attempting to determine whether it is due to a loss of vascular tone, say, or heart failure, is the first step in determining a treatment strategy that is likely to be effective. Clinicians do best to compare a hypotensive patient with heart failure to other cases of heart failure, not to those with low blood pressure related to sepsis. Knee swelling caused by trauma should not be used as a source case for non-traumatic knee swelling.

Very often, the key to comparing cases in clinical medicine comes down to the "no essential differences" condition, a condition that requires judgment. No list of essential differences can be applied uniformly across cases. Age, sex, particular co-morbidities, medical history, and myriad other personal attributes are relevant to some clinical decisions, but irrelevant to many others. For instance, considering a patient's sex is not relevant to deciding on a treatment for bacterial pneumonia, but is an essential difference when seeking to determine the cause of pain in the lower abdomen. In reasoning by analogy, comparing a particular case to source cases derived from experience, pathophysiologic understanding, and clinical research results, clinicians are often left trying to determine if the patient in front of them differs enough from the cases they are considering to render the knowledge contained in those cases less relevant.

The "no essential differences" condition is often at the center of the integration problem, as well. Clinicians looking to use the results of a therapeutic RCT in making a decision about specific patients often find themselves asking how closely the patient resembles the average subject enrolled in the study. From the perspective of trial design and interpretation, this issue is framed as one of generalizability: Are the study results likely to be relevant to a broader group of persons than those sampled? Generalizability is typically seen as an attribute of the study itself, associated with constraints set by inclusion and exclusion criteria. EBM has emphasized the importance of generalizability, recognizing that not all clinical studies produce clinically relevant knowledge.

From the perspective of the specific patient and clinician, however, generalizability is beside the point. Rather, the question is whether there are essential differences between the patient-at-hand and the average subject of the study. Simply knowing whether the patient met the eligibility criteria of the study or, on the other hand, would have been excluded from enrollment in the study does not determine whether essential differences exist. No patient will be identical to the average subject of a research trial, but are the differences between them enough to undermine the warrants generated from that study?

In determining whether differences between a specific patient and comparison cases are essential, no hard and fast rules or methods apply. But case-based reasoning provides a framework for clinicians, pointing them to specific kinds of knowledge and reasoning that are likely to be relevant for such an assessment. Are there physiologic aspects of the individual's presentation that differ from the typical or average patient? Co-morbidities often fall into this category. Does the clinician's experience with similar cases suggest some reason this patient may respond differently to treatment? Are the patient's goals and values aligned with the assumptions and outcomes of clinical studies, the goals and values of other past patients? Are there contextual barriers or facilitators to consider, such as costs or availability of an intervention?

The expert clinician has developed a sense of how to reason with cases, both for the initial selection of source cases and for recognizing when the source cases do not provide clear guidance for the current situation. In these situations, the clinician must engage in explicit reasoning about what to do when, for example, there is reason to think that there *are* essential differences between the source and target cases. While there is only one target case, generated from the patient-at-hand, there are potentially multiple source cases to which that target case can be compared. At times, those different source cases may suggest different courses of action. In the next section, we look more closely at the pattern of reasoning that occurs in situations where the relationship between the target and the source cases must be explicitly analyzed. Specifically, we argue that Stephen Toulmin's model of argumentation captures this kind of reasoning (Upshur and Colak, 2003; Tonelli, 2006).

Decision-making as argument: Arguing cases

To say that sound clinical reasoning adopts an argumentative format may initially seem foreign, given the connotation of antagonism that is often associated with argument. But making an argument is really about arriving at and defending a claim, bringing evidence to support an assertion. In clinical medicine, these claims typically relate to a diagnosis, a prognosis, or a treatment plan made by a clinician in attempt to benefit a patient. A clinician diagnosing pneumonia claims to know that a patient's presentation stems from a bacterial infection of the lung. When prescribing an antibiotic to treat the pneumonia, the claim is that the specific medication is likely to result in a resolution of symptoms and the avoidance of complications. In telling the patient that they should start feeling better in a few days but will probably take a few weeks to get back to baseline, the clinician claims to be able to predict the course of treated pneumonia with some confidence. Each of these claims is subject to challenge and, if challenged, the clinician would be expected to bring some reasons and evidentiary support to back them up. This is what we mean by saying that clinical reasoning takes an argumentative format.

While there are different models of argumentation, philosopher Stephen Toulmin's has perhaps the most relevance to contemporary medical decision-making. Toulmin developed and refined his model of argumentation in the last century, defending a practical and real-world approach (Toulmin, 1953, 2003). In *The Abuse of Casuistry*, Toulmin and bioethicist Albert Jonsen defend case-based reasoning and use clinical medicine as an obvious example of such reasoning in practice. Jonsen further refined this model specifically for case analyses in bioethics (Jonsen et al., 2022). In this section, we describe the Toulmin model and show that it provides a framework not just for ethical analyses, but for clinical decision-making more broadly. In doing so, we go beyond the examples offered by Jonsen and Toulmin to argue that this approach to clinical reasoning solves the integration problem.

Toulmin lays out what he calls the "pattern" of an argument, identifying six distinct parts to an argument that are, broadly speaking, the same in all argumentative contexts (e.g., medical, legal, philosophical). He begins by distinguishing between the claim that the argument is making—or, in other words, the conclusion of the argument—and the information that the conclusion is supported by or based upon (Toulmin, 2003, p. 90). This information is the data supporting the argument—though many writers who use the Toulmin model of argument use the term "evidence."[1] In order to avoid confusion stemming from EBM's focus on evidence from clinical research, we will use the term "data," but is important to recognize that data here encompasses much more than statistical information or the output of experiments. Data, in our usage, can be any kind of information that provides support for the claim.

Often, the data initially provided in support of a claim are enough to convince a listener to accept the claim. Sometimes, providing additional data is required. For example, a patient's clinical presentation may provide data in support of a diagnostic claim (say, an acute coronary syndrome), but additional data from laboratory tests (say, an EKG and troponin) might be needed for that claim to be supported strongly enough that the clinician is willing to accept and act upon it.

At other times, however, the issue is not *whether* the data support the conclusion, but rather *how* the data provided supports the conclusion. In other words, the connection between the data and the conclusion needs to be made clear. On Toulmin's model, this connection is supplied by warrants, which Toulmin describes as "general, hypothetical statements, which can act as bridges" between the evidence and the conclusion (Toulmin, 2003, p. 91). Another way to think about the difference between data and warrants is that data are pieces of information relevant to a claim, while warrants express general rules or principles that explain why that information is relevant (Toulmin, p. 91).

---

[1] Toulmin himself seems to use the terms "data" and "evidence" interchangeably.

We can illustrate the difference and the relationship between data and warrants with an example from medicine. In the context of diagnosis, an important piece of data is provided by the results of a diagnostic test performed on a patient. The data "the patient's chest X-ray demonstrates lobar consolidation" is evidence for the claim "this patient has pneumonia." However, the warrant expressed by "patients with pneumonia often have lobar consolidation, representing airspace filling, on chest radiographs" is needed to clarify the inferential connection, or to bridge the gap, between the data and the claim. Certainly, this single piece of data and corresponding warrant does not mean, with certainty, that the patient does have pneumonia; medical claims are rarely convincingly demonstrated by appeal to a single warrant.

In many cases, as Toulmin notes, the warrants relevant to our arguments remain implicit—we only explicitly talk about the data and the claim that the data supports. For example, upon hearing that a COVID PCR test is positive one will likely assume that a patient with respiratory symptoms has a COVID infection, making the connection between the data and the claim without needing to be told the warrant; most symptomatic people with a positive COVID PCR have active COVID infection. But in other cases, where the listener does not know the connection expressed in the warrant, or where they doubt that the data support the claim, the warrant can be made explicit.

Consider this variation: Instead of testing positive for COVID, the symptomatic patient has tested negative, and instead of seeking out a PCR test, they have used a home testing kit. Does their negative COVID test support the claim that they do not have COVID? It does, but the support for the claim in this case is not as strong as it was in our first example. One way to explain why this argument is weaker than the first one is to examine the warrant linking this piece of data (the negative home test) and the claim that the patient is COVID negative. This warrant might be "a negative result on a COVID home test indicates that a patient does not have COVID." We know, however, that home tests are less sensitive than PCR tests, so a certain percentage of negative tests are false negatives. The warrant invoked here is relatively weak.

Comparing the strength of the warrants in our two COVID examples lets us introduce two other features Toulmin ascribes to arguments. First, a "qualifier" expresses the strength of the connection that a warrant creates between the data and the claim it supports. In our first example, the qualifier (in italics) indicates that the warrant is very strong: "This symptomatic patient tested positive on a PCR test for COVID, so they *almost certainly* have COVID." By contrast, the weaker support provided by the warrant in our second example can be expressed as follows: "This symptomatic patient tested negative on a home test for COVID, so they *probably* do not have COVID." Again, the negative test does provide some evidence to support the claim that the patient doesn't have COVID, but because the warrant provided in this case is weaker, the qualifier reflects this weaker relationship between the data and the claim.

Second, Toulmin talks about "conditions of rebuttal," which spell out the circumstances in which the warrant *does not* provide the presumed connection between the data and the claim. In our second example, a negative test might be a false negative if, for example, the test was done too early in the course of the infection, or if the sample used for the test was not collected properly. Both of these circumstances, if we know they are the case, lower our confidence that the negative test results supported the claim that the patient did not have COVID. This is because they provide alternative explanations for the negative outcome of the COVID test in this particular case and an explanation in general of the relative weakness of the warrant.

So far, we have talked about how to support claims about a particular patient's condition, using data about them as an individual, and showing that, if necessary, we can make explicit the warrants that provide the connection between the data and claim in a particular case. We have also shown that some warrants provide stronger connections than others, and explained how the strength of the connection between the data and the claim depends on whether potential rebuttal conditions (which mean that the warrant does not apply) occur in this particular case. This brings us to a central component of the Toulmin model, which is the "backing" for a given warrant.

Backing warrants

Establishing the acceptability of a warrant *in general* requires a different kind of information than showing that the warrant applies in a given case. Toulmin refers to this kind of general justification as the "backing" for a warrant, and he emphasizes that different kinds of warrants have different conditions for backing. One important aspect of the Toulmin model is that both the kinds of warrants that are acceptable in supporting a claim and the kinds of knowledge used to provide backing for warrants vary depending on the particular discipline in which a claim is made. That is, the knowledge that can be legitimately relied upon in any argument is field-dependent. An argument regarding a claim in theoretical physics will rest upon warrants that appeal to very different kinds of knowledge than an argument regarding a diagnosis in the clinic. A crucial task for any discipline, then, is identifying the areas of field-specific knowledge that can serve as evidence in support of a claim. Warrants in medicine can also be classified this way: They may be general or particular to the patient. Support for any clinical claim will appeal to one or more warrants, reasons why the diagnosis, prognosis, or treatment plan seems to be appropriate given the data available regarding the patient and their clinical state. In the preceding chapters, we provided detailed discussions of the kinds of knowledge that are relevant to medicine: Knowledge derived from direct experience, from clinical research, and from basic science/mechanistic research. General warrants acceptable in medicine are backed by these kinds of knowledge. Knowledge of the individual patient may provide patient-specific warrants, but also determines the relevance and weight of more general warrants for the particular case.

Many warrants are general in nature. For example, "Shingles manifest as a vesicular eruption in a dermatomal distribution" may be appealed to in trying to reach a diagnosis for an individual presenting with a rash. General warrants, in practice, are the first-line reasons that a clinician will give in defense of a diagnostic ("Bacterial pneumonia presents with acute onset of fever, productive cough and an infiltrate on CXR"), therapeutic ("Antibiotics for bacterial pneumonia should target the most likely pathogens"), or prognostic ("Bacterial pneumonia typically responds rapidly to appropriate antibiotics") claim. In practice, as we have noted, warrants are often left unspoken. In academic medicine, they are the initial responses of both trainees and experienced clinicians who are queried about how they reached a clinical decision. Warrants provide general reasons to support a claim, and choosing the relevant warrants applicable to particular cases is the first step in sound clinical judgment. We might agree with the warrant "Beta-blockers reduce all-cause mortality after a myocardial infarction," but that warrant has no relevance in a case of pulmonary embolism.

Warrants that are relevant to medical reasoning are backed by knowledge that derives from five general topic areas (see Table 6.1). A particular warrant may receive backing from all or only some of these kinds of knowledge.

Table 6.1 Backing for Medical Warrants

General Medical Warrants	
	Clinical research results/compilations
	Mechanistic understanding
	Direct clinical experience
Specific Warrants	
	Patient-specific physiology, experience, and values
	Contextual features

For instance, the warrant that cystic fibrosis transmembrane (CFTR) modulators will improve the function of multiple organ systems in persons with cystic fibrosis can be backed by the direct observation of patients, mechanistic understanding of how intervention at the earliest point in the cystic fibrosis disease pathway will impact downstream events, and by the results of clinical trials. While some might see the last type of backing as sufficient, the other forms of backing provide additional support for the warrant. Backing from all three topic areas greatly increases the likelihood that a general warrant will serve as a solid foundation for diagnostic or treatment decisions.

By contrast, warrants backed by a single kind of medical knowledge, to include clinical research, are more tenuous, both less likely to hold for a particular individual or to remain as legitimate warrants at all. Proponents of EBM have compiled multiple examples where mechanistic reasoning supported therapeutic interventions that were ultimately found to be non-beneficial or even harmful (Howick, 2011, pp.154–157). The use of certain medications to suppress arrhythmias after myocardial infarction, for example, did accomplish that seemingly positive outcome but was associated with a higher overall mortality. Similarly, long-standing practice, based upon experience, generally offers only weak backing when that alone supports a warrant. Continuing to do something just because we have always done it that way is weak backing, particularly when what we are doing makes little mechanistic sense and/or is contradicted by clinical research.

From the perspective of the Toulmin framework, we can understand EBM as being concerned primarily with how strong the backing coming from clinical research is for warrants. First, the hierarchy of evidence amounts to claiming that warrants are strongest when they derive from and are backed by randomized controlled trials or systematic reviews of such trials and progressively weaker when they rely on knowledge obtained from lower levels of the hierarchy. Second, the advice that EBM gives for assessing the quality of an individual study is based on the idea that better quality studies provide better backing for the warrants they support.

While EBM initially focused on the value of the results of clinical research, a consensus has developed that understanding of mechanisms and direct clinical experience still serve as legitimate sources of medical knowledge. These three topic areas, which differ in kind, serve as backing for essentially all general medical warrants invoked by clinicians. The strength of the backing that they provide for any particular warrant is not dependent upon the topic area, but rather on the support it provides for the warrant in that clinical context. Within EBM, the focus on the strength or grade of evidence clearly acknowledges this fact, with multiple, large, randomized controlled trials generally providing stronger backing than single, small, uncontrolled studies. This portion of the EBM hierarchy of evidence, as discussed in chapter 2, dealing solely with kinds of clinical research, is coherent. Similarly, mechanisms that are poorly understood and highly complex typically provide weaker backing than a simple, well-understood mechanism.[2] Appeals to experience are generally stronger when that experience is extensive and even collective, weaker when based upon very limited observations.

The relative weakness of relying on backing provided by clinical trial results tends to be less emphasized. Yet there are multiple examples where even well-done clinical trials of therapeutic interventions, including those convincing enough to lead to regulatory approval, turned out not to hold up under more scrutiny. For instance, drotrecogin alfa (Xigris) was approved by the FDA for severe sepsis on the basis of well-designed randomized controlled trials that demonstrated a reduction in mortality, only to be withdrawn later as ineffective. In *Medical Nihilism*, philosopher Jacob Stegenga argues that our faith in the effectiveness of medical interventions, even (and maybe particularly) those that are backed by published clinical research, should be quite low. Central to Stegenga's (2017) argument is the recognition of the myriad of factors that bias research and reporting in a manner

---

[2] Recognizing this point helps us to see why Jeremy Howick's discussion of "high quality" evidence of mechanisms (discussed in chapter 3) focuses on examples like shrinking goiters using radiotherapy, rather than on pharmaceutical interventions that have multiple effects throughout the body.

that serves to inflate the value of most medical interventions. Clinicians and medical educators are familiar with many of these factors, including p-hacking, publication bias, and industry sponsorship of research. Jonathan Fuller, in looking at the evidence produced by meta-research, the examination of these biasing features of the medical research system, also concludes that our confidence in primary evidence, the reports of clinical research studies, and the hypotheses supported by such research should typically be adjusted downward (Fuller, 2018). Similarly, the epidemiologist John Ioannidis has famously argued that most published research findings are false (Ioannidis, 2005). As such, warrants that rest on clinical research alone, without additional support from mechanistic understanding or direct experience, are weakly backed relative to warrants supported by multiple kinds of medical knowledge.

When warrants upon which clinical decisions are based rest upon backing from a single kind of medical knowledge, a clinician's confidence in them should be relatively low. The same is true when backing is inconsistent, say when clinical experience is not consistent with expectations set by clinical research. On the other hand, when warrants are backed by multiple kinds of medical knowledge, clinician's confidence should be higher. While we used CFTR modulators in cystic fibrosis as an example above, many standard medical therapies, such as diuretics for congestive heart failure and insulin for Type I diabetes mellitus, are backed by medical knowledge from all three domains. Such complete and consistent backing provides confidence that backing from a single domain generally cannot achieve.

In addition to general warrants, there are patient-specific warrants, which are based on data from the specific patient and context, and apply only to that patient and in that context. As a personal and prudential discipline, clinical medicine must be able to incorporate the knowledge gained regarding a particular patient with more general medical knowledge. As we saw in the last two chapters, the knowledge gleaned from patients goes beyond preferences and values to include specific aspects of the patient's presentation, physiology, and experience. These features provide important reasons in support of a clinical claim; they produce warrants backed by very specific aspects of particular persons. And they greatly affect the relevance of even established general warrants to the case at hand. Individuals may not value the same outcomes that were used in clinical research, or their physiology or co-morbidities may suggest that they will not respond in the same fashion as a more typical case. These individual distinctions may serve to make general warrants, even those with excellent backing, less compelling. Patient-specific warrants may run counter to those derived from general medical knowledge, effectively serving as rebuttals. For instance, a primary care clinician might invoke the patient-specific warrant, "Ms. Wilson tends to have significant side-effects to a wide variety of medications" in deciding not to start a new antihypertensive for borderline elevated blood pressure, despite clinical practice guidelines that would support such treatment.

Although we have not discussed this topic area in detail, it is important to note that the clinical context in which care is being provided may also present specific warrants that must be considered in reaching a clinical judgment. Contextual features include a broad array of legal, financial, ethical, and social warrants that may constrain clinical choice. For instance, the patchwork and ever-shifting laws around therapeutic abortion in the United States may provide a warrant, such as "a dilation and curettage is illegal in the setting of a viable pregnancy" that serves as counter to all medical and personal warrants. Less dramatic contextual warrants are common in medical practice. For example, clinical decisions may be affected by warrants related to insurance coverage, the availability of specialized care, and even time of day or the day of the week that various interventions are available.

Thinking in cases

At the beginning of the chapter, we described the basic process of case-based reasoning, in terms of the construction of a target case based on the patient-at-hand and the selection of relevant source cases. Now that we have also outlined Toulmin's model and begun to show how it explains clinical reasoning in medicine, we can bring together these two sections of the chapter to show that, in medicine, cases function to house warrants. More specifically, average cases house warrants obtained from the results of clinical trials; idealized cases house warrants that come from laboratory research on and understanding of physiological mechanisms; and particular past cases or typical cases, which amalgamate or abstract from a number of particular past cases, house warrants from clinical experience. Particular warrants arise from the patient-at-hand and from the context within which care is being provided.

Making this link between cases and warrants allows us to clarify why arguing on the Toulmin model can be (and, in medicine, is) a form of case-based reasoning. Jonsen and Toulmin emphasize that clinical medicine is a form of practical argumentation and, as such "draw[s] on the outcomes of previous experience, carrying over the procedures used to resolve earlier problems and reapplying them in new problematic situations" (Jonsen and Toulmin, 1988, p. 35). The success of this kind of reasoning, however, depends on "how closely the *present* circumstances resemble those of the earlier *precedent* cases" and these similar features between the past and current cases provide warrants that presumptively justify treating the current case in the same way as the last ones (ibid.). Thus, similar cases, ones that are strongly analogous to the current case, provide the strongest warrants for the claim that the current case should be treated like the past one(s).

Recall, too, that in our introduction to case-based reasoning, we said that a clinician can frequently *just see* the analogy between the target case and a relevant source case. Similarly, in introducing the Toulmin model, we said that the warrants that support the inference from data to claim frequently go unexpressed. This is in part because comparing cases facilitates the inference from data (about the current case) to claim (about what should be done in the current case)—in Jonsen and Toulmin's words, the resolution of a previous case "passes sideways" to the new case to allow the resolution of the new situation. The strong analogy between the source case(s) and the target case can be so obvious to the expert clinician that they do not need to spell out their reasoning.

Thus, when the warrants and backing from each of these topic areas support a particular diagnosis, prognosis, or treatment plan, clinical decisions are relatively straightforward. When warrants conflict and/or backing for warrants is weak, however, clinicians must weigh warrants for relevance and strength. In such circumstances, clinicians must compare the case at hand to other cases, those derived from clinical research, mechanistic understanding, and direct experience.

Clinical judgment, then, is the consideration of potential essential differences between an individual patient and similar cases. This is the primary work of medical decision-making. Warrants and backing relevant to a particular case can come from any and all of the field-dependent topic areas of clinical medicine. The clinician cannot rely on any single source of knowledge, but must consider all relevant knowledge and information available.

Fortunately, very often in medicine the warrants and backing relevant to a particular case all support a specific diagnosis, prognosis, or treatment plan. But when they do not, when they conflict, the clinician must adjudicate between them, weighing each to determine what is, only probably, the best diagnostic or treatment strategy.

By thinking in cases, clinicians are encouraged, if not required, to use all of the knowledge available to them in order to arrive at what is only probably the right diagnosis, the most effective treatment strategy, and the most accurate prognosis for the patient in front of them. There is no generic "best evidence" on which to base these conclusions. Rather, clinicians must elucidate and explore all relevant warrants, examine their backing, and, when they conflict, weigh them against one another. The five topic areas that define the field-specific knowledge relevant to clinical medicine serve as framework for this review of the relevant warrants. The clinician combines what she knows about medicine, from clinical research, pathophysiology, and experience, with what she has learned from the patient and from the context in which she practices. Clinicians will compare the patient before them with other patients, real and abstract, looking for similarities, causal connections, and any essential differences. Then, they will reach conclusions that allow them to educate, inform, guide, and assist the individual patient before them.

Making this process explicit is the primary pedagogical method of clinical training in medicine. Trainees are asked to explain how they reached a particular diagnosis or treatment plan; to lay out the warrants and backing used to support their choice. Medical educators model this approach to reasoning as they make explicit the reasons and support that lead them to a particular decision. We have argued that medical education could benefit from more closely examining some of these (particularly challenging) decisions by explicitly requiring an epistemic analysis, clearly identifying the warrants and type of backing being invoked in challenging cases (Tonelli and Bluhm, 2020). When clinicians disagree about a particular case, such a careful examination can be particularly elucidating. With similarly experienced clinicians, rarely do disagreements come down to one knowing something the other does not, but rather to how specific warrants are being weighted or how strong backing is considered to be. Clarifying the source of compelling warrants, whether they are based upon experience, mechanistic reasoning, or the results of clinical research can be extremely helpful in understanding disagreement and in coming to consensus.

Consider the following examples, which illustrate how different kinds of warrants might function:

Case 1: A medical student on his dermatology clerkship evaluates a patient with a new, flat, violaceous skin rash and reports back to the attending dermatologist, "I think he has lichen planus." The attending asks how the student reached this conclusion. "Well," says the student, "I have read that lichen planus typically comes up over a couple of weeks and this looked like the picture of lichen planus in the dermatology atlas I had to buy for this rotation." These warrants, one backed by knowledge of a description of a typical case and the other by very limited visual experience, are relatively weak, meaning the probability and our confidence of a correct diagnosis are likely to be relatively low. When the attending examines the patient, she confirms, "This is lichen planus." The relieved and inquisitive student asks how she reached that conclusion. "This looks like lichen planus," the attending notes, a warrant based upon tacit knowledge gained from decades of direct experience. "Oh, and see these wispy white lines on the plaque? These are Wickham striae, often seen in lichen planus," she says, adding a warrant based on a deep understanding of a typical case. While the clinicians reached the same diagnosis, we have more confidence in the attending's claim, as it is based on warrants with stronger backing.

Case 2: A critical care fellow is having challenges ventilating a young patient with acute respiratory distress syndrome (ARDS) due to COVID-19 infection. The fellow has set the ventilator to deliver a tidal volume of 6 ml/kg of ideal body weight for the patient, but on these settings the patient continually triggers the ventilator for an additional breath with every cycle (breath-stacking), setting off pressure alarms and effectively delivering up to double the tidal volume desired. Despite increased sedative medication and adjustments to ventilator parameters other than tidal volume, this breath-stacking persists. In discussions with the attending intensivist, the fellow notes that there is a strong warrant to use 6 ml/kg tidal volume, as this approach was associated with an overall improvement in survival in ARDS patients in a large, well-done RCT, providing strong backing. The fellow is considering prolonged neuromuscular blockade in order to take away the patient's ability to initiate breaths and, hence, alleviate the possibility of breath-stacking, but notes that this will increase the risk of long-term weakness should the patient survive. The attending increases the tidal volume of the ventilator to 7 ml/kg and the breath-stacking nearly completely resolves. The attending notes that the study cited as backing by the fellow compared 6 ml/kg to 12 ml/kg, with the group receiving 12 ml/kg having a worse survival. The attending makes an argument based on mechanistic reasoning that 7 ml/kg in this patient does not result in any significant physiologic change (beyond being better tolerated) and would not be expected to negatively affect survival. The patient on 7 ml/kg is not essentially different from the average patient in the study who received 6 ml/kg, she argues. In this example, warrants from clinical research and from knowledge of the patient's physiological state appeared to support different approaches. But a closer look at the clinical trial evidence that provided backing for the warrant to use 6 ml/kg tidal volume and an understanding of the mechanisms of lung injury helped adjudicate this conflict.

Case 3: A middle-aged man undergoes an evaluation for abdominal pain, with a stomach mass seen on upper endoscopy returning as gastric carcinoma on biopsy. In discussing treatment options with his physician, he rejects the recommended surgical resection of the tumor. When asked to explain this refusal, he volunteers a belief that the CIA has implanted microfiche in his stomach. He has been pursuing a federal lawsuit based upon this assertion, and surgical resection would remove the evidence he needs to prove his case. Concerned that he is making a decision based on a delusion, the physician requests that the patient be evaluated by a psychiatrist. The evaluation confirms a fixed delusional disorder, which fails to respond to intensive therapy, including an inpatient stay, and pharmacologic intervention. Throughout, as his legal case remains active, the patient refuses surgical resection, even while acknowledging that he likely does have cancer and that the cancer will almost certainly kill him if not resected. His oncologist believes that the patient should be compelled, legally, to undergo resection, but the patient is competent in the eyes of the law. His family and his primary care physician, citing the central importance of his fixed delusion to his life, support the patient's decision. If he refused surgery for religious reasons, they argue by analogy, we would respect his wishes. This personal warrant, regardless of objective veracity, made it clear that compelling surgery, even if it prolonged his life, would do irreparable harm by violating his agency. Note that even though, ultimately, the patient's choice was decisive, the physician still offered him additional kinds of information to consider, in an attempt to change his mind. Even in the face of strongly-held values, other relevant data must be considered and discussed with patients.

This last point is important to emphasize, as it shows that claims made in clinical medicine are always subject to rebuttal. Diagnoses can be questioned, prognoses challenged, and treatment plans debated. Rebuttals may take a number of different forms: They may introduce new warrants for consideration, or cause a physician to question the strength of backing of a particular warrant (as we saw in the second case, above), or the relevance of a warrant to a particular case. Rebuttals may also come in the form of new information, such as diagnostic test or a previously missed piece of history. A skin biopsy, in the first case above, that was more consistent with psoriasis than with lichen planus, would serve as a rebuttal that necessitates a reconsideration, though not necessarily a rejection, of the initial diagnosis. Rebuttals can come from other clinicians, who weigh warrants and see the strength of backing differently. And, as in case 3, rebuttals can come from patients, who may question whether a clinician's decision or recommendation really fits with their experience, goals, and values.

Being open to rebuttal is a hallmark of a mindful clinician. Clinicians are appropriately cautioned to avoid anchoring and early closure, cognitive biases that close them off from consideration of possible rebuttals. Thoughtful proponents of EBM exhort clinicians not to practice "cookbook" medicine, to avoid thinking that clinical practice guidelines dictate care. This requires looking for reasons why the guidelines might not apply to a particular patient, for a rebuttal to the argument that underlies those guidelines. Clinical conclusions, whether diagnostic, therapeutic, or prognostic, are by their very nature only probable, never certain. Being open to rebuttal acknowledges that fact. Epistemic humility is the hallmark of an ethical clinician (Schwab, 2012).

Looking at Mr. Jackson, Dr. Lee decides on a change in strategy. Efforts to comply with clinical practice guidelines for diabetes, hypertension, hyperlipidemia, coronary artery disease, congestive heart failure, and chronic obstructive pulmonary disease have resulted in polypharmacy, a regimen of multiple medications nearly impossible to adhere to. Most are aimed at reducing Mr. Jackson's risk for complications; very few at improving his day-to-day sense of well-being. Dr. Lee knows from experience that drug interactions and negative side effects are common in patients like Mr. Jackson. Her understanding of both the clinical trials and the pathophysiology of his many disorders allows her to recognize that reduction in risk is not the same as provision of benefit. In fact, most of his medications are unlikely to provide any specific benefit to Mr. Jackson. She has seen this all before, in other patients with multiple medical conditions. Having heard Mr. Jackson describe the life he wants to be able to live and his willingness to emphasize quality over quantity, Dr. Lee presents her new strategy to him for consideration. The medical student listens intently.

"I would like to start eliminating several of your medications, as I do not think they are making you feel better. They may very well be making you feel worse, even if they may reduce your risk of some complications. And I would like to concentrate on the issues, including your chronic pain, that are most limiting for you. Are you on board with that approach?"

With an answer in the affirmative, Dr. Lee uses her knowledge, gained from clinical research, pathophysiologic understanding and clinical experience, to identify several medications that offer only marginal risk reduction and are most associated with negative side-effects: A medication that lowers blood pressure a few points but causes fatigue, an inhaler that improves airflow but had not reduced his sense of shortness of breath, a second-line diabetes medication that had reduced his HgB A1C but probably led to a 15 pound weight gain.

"I think we should stop these medications now."

"And to get you back to doing what you want to be doing, I think enrolling in a pulmonary rehabilitation will be helpful. I have put in a referral. And I am going to encourage you again to try and lose some weight. Will be easier on those knees. Will you meet with the dietician again?"

A willing partner, Mr. Jackson agrees to the changes and says he looks forward to doing pulmonary rehabilitation. Dr. Lee turns to the medical student after Mr. Jackson leaves the examination room. Explaining all of her clinical reasoning in this case will not be possible at the moment, as there are other patients waiting. "We are going to come back to this case at the end of the afternoon," she explains, "there is a lot to unpack here."

Summary

Our examination of the complex practice of clinical medicine has utilized methods and insights from the philosophy of medicine in a way that we hope resonates with practitioners and medical educators. The primary tensions in medical knowledge—between rationalism and empiricism, between the general and the particular—have existed for millennia; we have certainly not resolved them here. Our goal has been to improve clinicians' understanding of these tensions, provide a way to navigate them, to assist in the process of clinical decision-making, and to make it easier to teach others. While the impetus for this undertaking came from the recognition of the limitations of the evidence-based medicine movement's description of medical practice, we have strived to avoid critique without offering alternative ways of understanding and incorporating a wide variety of medical knowledge into clinical decision-making. Our focus throughout has been demonstrating the value of the many things that doctors, nurses, and therapists know and suggesting how that knowledge can be brought to bear for the benefit of individual patients.

Knowledge gained from direct clinical experience and from understanding of mechanisms of health and disease remains valuable to clinicians and their patients in an era when the focus has been almost solely on knowledge gained from clinical research. None of these forms of knowledge, alone, is sufficient for the practice of medicine. Clinicians and policy makers alike need to avoid "mistaking a part of medical knowledge for the whole" (Tanenbaum, 1993, p. 1270). We have also emphasized the importance of knowing patients and of using what we know about specific individuals in making clinical decisions. The practice of clinical medicine, unlike the enterprise of clinical research, is personal and prudential. General knowledge, even when well-established and firmly held, can only take clinicians so far. If the goal of medicine remains aimed at the benefit of individual patients (rather than populations), then knowing patients is paramount for practice.

Case-based reasoning provides a framework for making judgments, diagnostic, prognostic, and therapeutic, regarding specific patients and requires an inclusive strategy with regard to medical knowledge. It allows us to move from the "untidy, methodologic pluralism" (Solomon, 2015, p. 225) that characterizes the production of medical knowledge to the embrace of epistemic pluralism in the service of individual patients. Using this framework can help clinicians better understand their own reasoning and better communicate that reasoning to trainees, colleagues, and patients. It may ameliorate the inclination toward an unquestioning reliance on clinical practice guidelines that leads to "cookbook" medicine. In medical education, identifying warrants, examining backing, and addressing rebuttals in an explicit fashion not only provides trainees with a clearer understanding of the reasoning of expert clinicians but can also help clarify the reasons for disagreements amongst these experts. Understanding how others are invoking and weighing various warrants in support of clinical claims goes a long way in understanding the variability in medical practice.

To those who might argue that such an approach is too complicated, too open-ended, to "subjective," we would reply that real danger lurks in pretending that a complex undertaking such as clinical medicine can be simplified and made "objective." Many medical decisions are straightforward, reliant upon exemplar cases and based on strong warrants with backing from clinical research, mechanistic understanding, and direct experience. When decisions are not straightforward, understanding that the knowledge most relevant for clinical decision-making falls under only five topic areas can allow clinicians to fairly quickly make sure they are considering and weighing all the relevant information in a particular case. Being able to make explicit the warrants underlying any clinical decision represents an exercise in mindfulness for individual clinicians, provides the groundwork for examining disagreements among clinicians, and serves as the core teaching tool for clinical training.

In the end, doing best by patients requires clinicians to utilize all of their knowledge in service of the aims of the individuals seeking their care and expertise.

References

Afra K, Chen LYC, Sweet D. 2021. "Tocilizumab for hospitalized patients with COVID-19." *Canadian Medical Association Journal* 193(15): E521.

AGREE Collaboration (2003) "Development and validation of an international appraisal instrument for assessing the quality of clinical practice guidelines: The AGREE project." *British Medical Journal Quality and Safety* 12(1): 18–23.

Ambrosio L, García JMS, Fernández MR, Bravo SA, Ayesa SD DeC, Semsa MEU, Caparrós N, Portillo, MC. 2015. "Living with chronic illness in adults: A concept analysis," *Journal of Clinical Nursing* 24(September 17–18): 2357–2367.

Andersen H. 2012. "Mechanisms: what are they evidence for in evidence-based medicine?" *Journal of Evaluation in Clinical Practice* 18(October 5): 992–999.

Aronson JK. 2005. "Biomarkers and surrogate endpoints." *British Journal of Clinical Pharmacology* 59(May 5): 491–494.

Baetu TM. 2016. "The 'Big Picture': The problem of extrapolation in basic research." *British Journal of Philosophy of Science* 67(December 4): 941–964.

Barrows HS, Feltovich PJ. 1987. "The clinical reasoning process." *Medical Education* 21(2): 86–91.

Bartha P. 2016. "Analogy and analogical reasoning." In *The Stanford Encyclopedia of Philosophy*, edited by EN Zalta. Stanford: Metaphysics Research Lab, Stanford University. https://plato.stanford.edu/entries/reasoning-analogy/

Begg C, Cho M, Eastwood S, Horton R, Moher D, Olkin I, Pitkin R, Rennie D, Schulz KF, Simel D, Stroup DF. 1996. "Improving the quality of reporting of randomized controlled trials. The CONSORT statement." *Journal of the American Medical Association* 276: 637–639.

Benner P. 2000. *From Novice to Expert: Excellence and Power in Clinical Nursing Practice*. Commemorative Edition. Pearson.

Bernard GR, Vincent JL, Laterre PF, LaRosa SP, Dhainaut JF, Lopez-Rodriguez A, Steingrub JS, Garber GE, Helterbrand JD, Ely EW, Fisher Jr, CJ. 2001. "Efficacy and safety of recombinant human activated protein C for severe sepsis." *New England Journal of Medicine* 344(March 10): 699–709.

Bloom P. 2016 *Against Empathy: The Case for Rational Compassion*. New York: Ecco.

Bluhm R. 2013. "Physiological mechanisms and epidemiological research." *Journal of Evaluation in Clinical Practice* 19(June 3): 422–426.

Bordage G, Zacks R. 1984 "The structure of medical knowledge in the memories of medical students and general practitioners: categories and prototypes. *Medical Education* 18(6):406–416.

Borrell M. 1987. "Instruments and an independent physiology: The Harvard physiological laboratory, 1871–1906." In *Physiology in the American Context: 1850–1940*, edited by GL Geison. American Physiological Society. 293–321.

Braude HD. 2012. *Intuition in Medicine: A Philosophical Defense of Clinical Reasoning.* Chicago: The University of Chicago Press.

Brock DW, Wartman SA. 1990. "When competent patients make irrational choices." *New England Journal of Medicine* 322(May 22): 1595–1599.

Bynum WF. 1994. *Science and the Practice of Medicine in the Nineteenth Century.* Cambridge: Cambridge University Press.

Caponi S. 2013. "Quetelet, the average man and medical knowledge." *História, Ciências, Saúde-Manguinhos* 20(July–September 3): 830–847.

Carel H. 2018. *Illness: The Cry of the Flesh.* New York: Routledge, Taylor & Francis Group.

Cassell EJ. 2013. *The Nature of Healing: The Modern Practice of Medicine.* Oxford: Oxford University Press.

Charlton BG, Miles A. 1998. "The rise and fall of EBM." *Quarterly Journal of Medicine* 91(June 5): 371–374.

Charon R. 2006. *Narrative Medicine: Honoring the Stories of Illness.* Oxford: Oxford University Press.

Charon R. 2007. "What to do with stories: the sciences of narrative medicine." *Canadian Family Physician* 53(8): 1265–1267.

Clarfield AM, Gordon M, Markwell H, Alibhai SMH. 2003. "Ethical issues in end-of-life geriatric care: The approach of three monotheistic religions – Judaism, Catholicism, and Islam." *Journal of the American Geriatric Society* 51: 1149–1154.

Clarke B, Gillies D, Illari P, Russo F, Williamson J. 2013. "The evidence that evidence-based medicine omits." *Preventive Medicine* 57(December 6): 745–747.

Clarke B, Gillies D, Ilari P, Russo F, Williamson J. 2014. "Mechanisms and the evidence hierarchy." *Topoi* 33(December 3): 339–360.

Cochrane Collaboration. (n.d.). website:www.cochrane.org

Cochrane Library. https://www.cochranelibrary.com/

Cook DA, Sherbio J, Durning SJ. 2018. "Management reasoning: beyond the diagnosis." *Journal of the American Medical Association* 319(22):2267–2268.

Cook DA, Stephenson CR, Gruppen LD, Durning SJ. 2022. "Management reasoning scripts: qualitative exploration using simulated physician-patient encounters." *Perspectives in Medical Education* 11(4): 196–206.

Craver CF, Darden L. 2013. *In Search of Mechanisms: Discoveries Across the Life Sciences.* University of Chicago Press

Craver C, Tabery J. 2023. "Mechanisms in science." *Stanford Encyclopedia of Philosophy.* (Ed.), E. Zalta. https://plato.stanford.edu/archives/fall2023/entries/science-mechanisms/

Croskerry, P. 2013. "From mindless to mindful practice-cognitive bias and clinical decision making." *The New England Journal of Medicine* 368(June 26): 2445–2448.

Custers, EJFM. 2015. "Thirty years of illness scripts: Theoretical origins and practical applications." *Medical Teacher* 37(May 5): 457–462.

Daly, J. 2005. *Evidence-Based Medicine and the Search for a Science of Clinical Care.* 1st ed. Los Angeles: University of California Press.

DiCenso, A, Bayley L, Haynes RB. 2009. "Accessing pre-appraised evidence: fine-tuning the 5S model into a 6S model." *Evidence-Based Nursing* 12(4): 99–101.

Dreyfus HL, Dreyfus SE. 1986. *Mind over Machine: The Power of Human Intuition and Expertise in the Era of the Computer.* The Free Press: New York.

Duffy J. 1993. *From Humors to Medical Science: A History of American Medicine.* Champaign: University of Illinois Press.

Ehrenreich, B. 2001. "Welcome to Cancerland." *New York: Harper's Magazine* 303(1818) 43–53.

Emanuel EJ, Emanuel LL. 1992. "Four models of the physician-patient relationship." *Journal of the American Medical Association* 267(April 16): 2221–2226.

Engebretsen E, Heggen K, Wieringa S, Greenhalgh T. 2016. "Uncertainty and objectivity in clinical decision making: a clinical case in emergency medicine." *Medicine, Health Care, and Philosophy* 19(December 4): 595–603.

Evidence-Based Medicine Working Group. 1992. "Evidence-based Medicine: A new approach to teaching the practice of medicine" *The Journal of the American Medical Association* 268(November 17): 2420–2425.

Fantl J. 2017. "Knowledge How." In *The Stanford Encyclopedia of Philosophy*, edited by EN Zalta. Stanford: Metaphysics Research Lab, Stanford University.

Feltovich PH, Barrows HS 1984. "Issues of generality in medical problem solving." In Schmidt HG, De Volder ML, (Eds.), *Tutorials in Problem-Based Learning* Van Gorcum. pp. 128–142.

Flexner A. 1910. *Medical education in the United States and Canada. From the Carnegie Foundation for the Advancement of Teaching.* New York City: The Carnegie Foundation for the Advancement of Teaching.

Foucault M. 1994. *The Birth of the Clinic: An Archaeology of Medical Perception.* Trans. Sheridan Smith AM. New York: Vintage.

Freedman B. 1975. "A moral theory of informed consent." *The Hastings Center Report* 5(August 4): 32–29.

Fulford, KWM. 2008 "Values-based practice: A new partner to evidence based practice and a first for psychiatry?" *Mens Sana Monogr.* 6(1):10–21.

Fulford KWM, Peile E and Carroll H. 2012 *Essential Values-Based Practice: Clinical Stories Linking Science with People.* Cambridge: Cambridge University Press.

Fuller J. 2018 "Meta-research evidence for evaluating therapies." *Philosophy of Science* 85(5):767–780.

Gould SJ. 2013. "The median isn't the message." *American Medical Association Journal of Ethics* 15(1):77–81.

Greenhalgh T, Howick J, Maskrey N. 2014. "Evidence based medicine: a movement in crisis." *British Medical Journal* 348:g3725.

Greenhalgh T. 2018. "Of lamp-posts, keys and fabled drunkards: a perspectival tale of 4 guidelines." *Journal of Evaluation in Clinical Practice* 24(October 5): 1132–1138.

Guyatt GH, Rennie D. 2001. *Users' Guide to the Medical Literature: A Manual for Evidence-Based Clinical Practice*, 1st ed. Chicago: American Medical Association Press.

Guyatt GH, Meade MO, Jaeschke RZ, Cook DJ, Haynes RB. 2000. "Practitioners of evidence based care. Not all clinicians need to appraise evidence from scratch but all need some skills." *British Medical Journal* 320(7240):954–5.

Guyatt GH, Oxman AD, Vist GE, Kunz R, Falck-Ytter Y, Alonso-Coello P, Schunemann HJ. 2008. "GRADE: an emerging consensus on rating quality of evidence and strength of recommendations." *The British Medical Journal* 336(7650 April): 924–926.

Guyatt G, Rennie D, Meade MO, Cook DJ. (Eds.), 2015. *Users' guides to the medical literature: a manual for evidence-based clinical practice*, 3rd ed. McGraw-Hill Education.

Hansen H, Metzl JM. (Eds.), 2019. *Structural Competency in Mental Health and Medicine: A Case-Based Approach to Treating the Social Determinants of Health*. New York: Springer.

Haynes RB, McKibbon KA, Fitzgerald D, Guyatt GH, Walker CH, Sackett DL. 1986. "How to keep up with the medical literature: I. Why try to keep up and how to get started." *Annals of Internal Medicine* 105(1): 149–153.

Haynes, RB. 2001. "Of studies, summaries, synopses, and systems: The "4S" evolution of services for finding current best evidence." *American College of Physicians Journal Club* 134: A11-13 (*Evidence Based Medicine* 6: 36–38).

Haynes BR, Deveraux PJ, Guyatt GH. 2002. "Clinical expertise in the era of evidence-based medicine and patient choice." *British Medical Journal Evidence-based Medicine* 7:36–38.

Henry SG. 2006. "Recognizing tacit knowledge in medical epistemology." *Theoretical Medicine and Bioethics* 27(3): 187–213.

Hesse MB. 1966. *Models and Analogies in Science*. Notre Dame: University of Notre Dame Press.

Hill AB. 1965. "The environment and disease: Association or causation?" *Proceedings of the Royal Society of Medicine* 58(May 5): 295–300.

Howick JH. 2011. *The Philosophy of Evidence-Based Medicine*. Chichester, West Sussex: BMJ Books, Wiley-Blackwell.

Howick JH Glasziou P, Aronson JK. 2013. "Problems with using mechanisms to solve the problem of extrapolation." *Theoretical Medicine and Bioethics* 34(July 4): 275–291.

Illari PM, Williamson J. 2012. "What is a mechanism? Thinking about mechanisms across the sciences." *European Journal for Philosophy of Science* 2(September 1): 119–135.

Institute of Medicine (US) Committee on Standards for Developing Trustworthy Clinical Practice Guidelines; Graham R, Mancher M, Miller Wolman D, et al., editors. 2011. *Clinical Practice Guidelines We Can Trust*. Washington (DC): National Academies Press (US). Available from: https://www.ncbi.nlm.nih.gov/books/NBK209539/ doi: 10.17226/13058

Ioannidis JPA. 2005. "Why most published research findings are false." *Public Library of Science Medicine* 2(August 8): e124.

Ioannidis JPA. 2011. "An epidemic of false claims. Competition and conflicts of interest distort too many medical findings." *Scientific American* 304(June 6): 16.

Jonsen AR, Toulmin SE. 1988. *The Abuse of Casuistry: A History of Moral Reasoning*. Berkeley: University of California Press.

Jonsen AR, Siegler M, Winslade WJ. (Eds.), 2022. *Clinical Ethics: A Practical Approach to Ethical Decisions in Clinical Medicine*, 9e. McGraw-Hill Education.

Kassirer J, Wong J, Kopelman R. 2009. *Learning Clinical Reasoning* 2nd Edition. Lippincott Williams & Wilkins

Kidd IJ, Carel H. 2017. "Epistemic injustice and illness" *Journal of Applied Philosophy* 34(February 2): 172–190.

Knaus, WA, Harrell Jr. FE, Lynn J, Goldman L, Phillips RS, Connors Jr. AF, Dawson NV, Fulkerson Jr. WJ, Califf RM, Desbiens N, Layde P, Oye RK, Bellamy PE, Hakim RB, Wagner DP. 1995. "The SUPPORT prognostic model. Objective estimates of survival for seriously ill hospitalized adults. Study to understand prognoses and preferences for outcomes and risks of treatments." *Annals of Internal Medicine* 122(February 3): 191–203.

Kralik D. 2002. "The quest for ordinariness: Transition experienced by midlife women living with chronic illness." *Journal of Advanced Nursing* 39(July 2): 146–154.

Kukla, [Q.]R. 2007. "How do patients know?" *The Hastings Center Report* 37(September–October 5): 27–35.

Longino H. 2002. *The Fate of Knowledge*. Princeton: Princeton University Press.

Mamede S, Schmidt HG, Rikers RMJP, Penaforte JC, Coelho-Filho JM. 2007. "Effects of reflective practice on the accuracy of medical diagnosis." *Medical Education* 41(12):1185–1192.

Marconi VC, Ramanan AV, de Bono S, Kartman CE, Krishnan V, Liao R, Piruzeli MLB, Goldman JD, Alatorre-Alexander J, de Cassia Pellegrini R, Estrada V, Some M, Cardoso, A Chakladar S, Crowe B, Reis P, Zhange X, Adams DH, Ely EW. 2021 "Efficacy and safety of baricitinib for the treatment of hospitalized adults with COVID-19 (COV-BARRIER): A randomized, double-blind, parallel-group, placebo-controlled phase 3 trial." *Lancet Respiratory Medicine* 9(12): 1407–1418.

Marks HM. 1997. *The Progress of Experiment: Science and Therapeutic Reform in the United States 1900–1990*. New York: Cambridge University Press.

Mathews JR. 1995. *Quantification and the Quest for Medical Certainty*. Princeton NJ: Princeton University Press.

Maulitz RC. 1987. "Pathologists, clinicians, and the role of pathophysiology." In *Physiology in the American Context: 1850–1940*, edited by GL Geison. American Physiological Society. 209–236.

McColl A, Smith H, White P, Field J. 1998. "General practitioners' perceptions of the route to evidence-based medicine: A questionnaire." *British Medical Journal* 316: 361–365.

Mendel R, Hamann J, Traut-Mattausch E, Buhner M, Kissling W, Frey D. 2010 "'What would you do if you were me, doctor?': Randomised trial of psychiatrists' personal v. professional perspectives on treatment recommendations." *The British Journal of Psychiatry*. 197(6):441–447.

Moch SD. 1989. "Health within illness: conceptual evolution and practice possibilities." *Advances in Nursing Science* 11(4):23–31

Montgomery Hunter, K. 1991. *Doctors' Stories: The Narrative Structure of Medical Knowledge*. Princeton: Princeton University Press.

Montori VM, Guyatt GH. 2008. "Progress in evidence-based medicine." *Journal of the American Medical Association* 300(October 15): 1814–1816.

Myers B. 2020. "Vaccines, convalescent plasma, and monoclonal antibodies for covid-19. Rapid response. Mast cell stabilisers and covid-19." *British Medical Journal* 370:m2772.

NETT Research Group. 1999. "Rationale and design of the National Emphysema Treatment Trial: a prospective randomized trial of lung volume reduction surgery." Chest 116(6): 1750–1761.

Nordenfelt LY. 1995. *On the Nature of Health: An Action-Theoretic Approach*, 2nd ed. Dordrecht: Kluwer Academic Publishers.

Nordenfelt LY. 2007. "The concepts of health and illness revisited." *Medicine, Health Care and Philosophy* 10(March 1): 5–10.

Norman G. 2005. "Research in clinical reasoning: Past history and current trends." *Medical Education* 39(April 4): 418–427.

Norman GM, Brooks L. 1997 "The non-analytical basis of clinical reasoning." *Advances in Health Sciences Education* 2:173–184.

Parsons AS, Wijesekera TP, Rencic JJ. 2020. "The management script: A practical tool for teaching management reasoning." *Academic Medicine* 95(8):1179–1185.

Parkkinen V, Wallmann C, Wilde M, Clarke B, Illari P, Kelly MP, Norrell C, Russo F, Shaw B, Williamson J. 2018. *Evaluating Evidence of Mechanisms in Medicine: Principles and Procedures*. New York: Springer.

Polanyi M. 1962. *Personal knowledge: Towards a Post-Critical Philosophy*. London: Routledge and Kegan Paul.

Radtke A., Pfister R., Kuhr K., Kochanek M., Michels G. 2017. "Is 'gut feeling' by medical staff better than validated scores in the estimation of mortality in a medial intensive care unit? The prospective FEELING-ON-ICU study." *Journal of Critical Care* 41: 204–208.

Reiser SJ. 1978. *Medicine and the Reign of Technology*. Cambridge: Cambridge University Press.

Roddis JK, Holloway I, Bond C, Galvin KT. 2016. "Living with a long-term condition: understanding well-being for individuals with thrombophilia or Asthma." *International Journal of Qualitative Studies on Health and Well-Being* 11(August): 31530.

Rosenberg CE. 1979. "The therapeutic revolution: Medicine, meaning and social change in nineteenth-century America." In Vogel, MJ and CE Rosenberg (Eds.). *The Therapeutic Revolution: Essays in the Social History of American Medicine*, 1st ed. Philadelphia: University of Pennsylvania Press. pp. 3–25

Rothstein WG. 1972. *American Physicians in the Nineteenth Century: From Sects to Science*, 1st ed. Baltimore: Johns Hopkins University Press.

Rubenfeld, GD. 2001. "Understanding why we agree on the evidence but disagree on the medicine." *Respiratory Care* 46(December 12): 1442–1449.

Russo F, Williamson J. 2007. "Interpreting causality in the health sciences." *International Studies in the Philosophy of Science* 21(August 2): 157–170.

Sackett DL. 1999. "Time to put the Canadian Institutes of Health Research on trial." *Canadian Medical Association Journal* 161(November 11): 1414–1415.

Sackett DL, Rosenberg WM, Gray JA, Haynes RB, Richardson WS. 1996. "Evidence-based medicine: What it is and what it isn't." *The British Medical Journal* 312(7023 January): 71–72.

Sackett DL, Oxman AD. 2003. "HARLOT plc: An amalgamation of the world's two oldest professions." *The British Medical Journal* 327(7429 December): 1442–1445.

Schaffner KF. 1986. "Exemplar reasoning about biological models and diseases: a relation between the philosophy of medicine and philosophy of science." *The Journal of Medicine and Philosophy* 11(February 1): 63–80.

Schmidt HG, Boshuizen HP. 1993 "On the origin of intermediate effects in clinical case recall." *Memory and Cognition* 21(3):338–351.

Schmidt HG, Rikers RMJP. 2007 "How expertise develops in medicine: knowledge encapsulation and illness script formation." *Medical Education* 41(12):1133–1139.

Schwab A. 2012 "Epistemic humility and medical practice: Translating epistemic categories into ethical obligations." *The Journal of Medicine and Philosophy: A Forum for Bioethics and Philosophy of Medicine*, 37(1): 28–48.

Shapiro D. 2012. "'Objectivity' and the arbitration of experiential knowledge." *Social Philosophy Today* 28(January): 67–82.

Shryock RH. 1961. The history of quantification in medical science. *Isis* 52:215–237.

Sibbald M, Sherbino J, Preyra I, Coffin-Simpson T, Norman G, Monteiro S. 2017. "Eyeballing: The use of visual appearance to diagnose 'sick.'" *Medical Education* 51(July 11): 1138–1145.

Simon JG, De Boer JB, Joung IMA, Bosma H, Mackenbach JP. 2005. "How is your health in general? A qualitative study on self-assessed health." *European Journal of Public Health* 15(April 2): 200–208.

Sinuff, T, Adhikari NKJ, Cook DJ, Schünemann HJ, Griffith LE, Rocker G, Walter SD. 2006. "Mortality predictions in the intensive care unit: comparing physicians with scoring systems." *Critical Care Medicine* 34(March 3): 878–885.

Smith R. 2005. "Medical journals are an extension of the marketing arm of pharmaceutical companies." *Public Library of Science Medicine*2(5):e138. doi: 10.1371/journal.pmed.0020138.

Sokol DK. 2006. "How the doctor's nose has shortened over time; a historical overview of the truth-telling debate in the doctor-patient relationship." *Journal of the Royal Society of Medicine* 99:632–636.

Solomon M. 2015. *Making Medical Knowledge*. Oxford: Oxford University Press.

Sox HC, Blatt MA, Higgins MC, Marton KI. 2007. *Medical Decision Making* Philadelphia: American College of Physicians.

Stegenga J. 2017 *Medical Nihilism*. Oxford: Oxford University Press.

Stolper E, Van de Wiel M, Van Royen P, Van Bokhoven M, Van der Weijden T, Dinant GJ. 2011 "Gut feelings as a third track in general practitioners' diagnostic reasoning." *Journal of General Internal Medicine* 26: 197–203.

Straus SE, Richardson WS, Glasziou P, Haynes RB. 2005. *Evidence-Based Medicine: How to Practice and Teach EBM*, 3rd ed. Toronto: Elsevier.

Stowe SM. 1996. "Seeing themselves at work: Physicians and the case narrative in the mid-19th-century American south." *The American Historical Review* 101(1): 41–79.

Sullivan MD. 1993. "Placebo controls and epistemic control in orthodox medicine." *The Journal of Medicine and Philosophy* 18(April 2): 213–231.

Sullivan MD. 2016. *The Patient as Agent of Health and Health Care*. Oxford: Oxford University Press.

Susser M. 1985. "Epidemiology in the United States after World War II: The evolution of technique." *Epidemiologic Reviews* 7(1): 147–177.

Tanenbaum SJ. 1993. "What physicians know." *The New England Journal of Medicine* 329(October): 1268–1271.

Tinetti ME, Naik AD, Dindo L, Costello DM, Esterson J, Geda M, Rosen J, Hernandez-Bigos K, Smith CD, Ouellet GM, Kang G, Lee Y, Blaum C. 2019. "Association of patient priorities-aligned decision-making with patient outcomes and ambulatory health care burden among older adults with multiple chronic conditions: A nonrandomized clinical trial.: *Journal of the American Medical Association Internal Medicine*. 179(12): 1688–1697.

Tonelli MR. 1999 "In defense of expert opinion." *Academic Medicine* 74:1187–1192.

Tonelli MR. 2006. "Integrating evidence into clinical practice: an alternative to evidence-based approaches." *Journal of Evaluation in Clinical Practice* 12(June 3): 248–256.

Tonelli MR, Curtis JR, Guntupalli KK, Rubenfeld GD, Arroliga AC, Brochard L, Douglas IS, Gutterman DD, Hall JR, Kavanagh BP, Mancebo J, Misak CJ, Simpson SQ, Slutsky AS, Suffredini AF, Thompson BT, Ware LB, Wheeler AP and Levy, MM. 2012. "An official multi-society statement: the role of clinical research results in the practice of critical care medicine." *American Journal of Respiratory and Critical Care Medicine* 185:(10)1117–1124.

Tonelli MR, Sullivan, MD. 2019. "Person-centred shared decision making." *Journal of Evaluation in Clinical Practice* 25: 1057–1062.

Tonelli MR, Bluhm R. 2020. "Teaching medical epistemology within an evidence-based curriculum." *Teaching and Learning in Medicine* 33(1): 98–105.

Tonelli MR, Williamson J. 2020. "Mechanisms in clinical practice: Use and justification." *Medicine, Health Care and Philosophy* 23: 115–124.

Tonelli MR, Shapiro D. 2020. "Experiential knowledge in clinical medicine: Use and justification." *Theoretical Medicine and Bioethics* 41(2–3):67–82.

Toulmin S. 1953/2003. *The Uses of Argument*: Updated edition. Cambridge: Cambridge University Press.

Upshur REG, Colak E. 2003. "Argumentation and evidence." *Theoretical Medicine and Bioethics* 24(July 4): 283–299.

Warner JH. 1991. "Ideals of science and their discontents in late nineteenth-century medicine." *Isis* 82(3): 454–478.

Warner JH. 1992. "The fall and rise of professional mystery: Epistemology, authority and the emergence of laboratory medicine in nineteenth-century America." In *The Laboratory Revolution in Medicine*, edited by A Cunningham and P Williams. Cambridge: Cambridge University Press. 110–141.

Warner, JH. 1997a. *The Therapeutic Perspective: Medical Practice, Knowledge, and Identity in America, 1820–1885*, 1st ed. Cambridge: Harvard University Press.

Warner JH 1997b. "From Specificity to Universalism in Medical Therapeutics: Transformation in the 19th-Century United States." In *Sickness and Health in America*:

Readings in the History of Medicine and Public Health, edited by JW Leavitt and R Numbers. 3rd Edition, revised. Madison, WI: University of Wisconsin Press. 87–101

Warner JH. 1998. *Against the Spirit of System: The French Impulse in Nineteenth Century America Medicine*, 1st ed. Princeton NJ: Princeton University Press.

Weisz G. 2005. *Divide and Conquer: A Comparative History of Medical Specialization*, 1st ed. Oxford: Oxford University Press.

Weisz G, Cambrosio A, Keating P, Knaapen L, Schlich T. 2007. "The emergence of clinical practice guidelines." *Millbank Quarterly* 85(4): 691–727.

Wieringa S, Greenhalgh T. 2015. "10 years of mindlines: a systematic review and commentary." *Implementation Science* 10(April): 45.

Wieten S. 2018a "Expertise in evidence-based medicine: a tale of three models." *Philosophy, Ethics and Humanities in Medicine.* 13(1):2

Wieten S. 2018b. "'What the patient wants': An investigation of the methods of ascertaining patient values in evidence-based medicine and values-based practice." *Journal of Evaluation in Clinical Practice* 24(1): 8–12.

Wiswell J, Tsao K, Bellolio MF, Hess EP, Cabrera D. 2013. "'Sick' or 'not-sick': accuracy of System 1 diagnostic reasoning for the prediction of disposition and acuity in patients presenting to an academic ED." *The American Journal of Emergency Medicine* 31(October 10): 1448–1452.

Worrall J. 2002. "What evidence in evidence-based medicine?" *Philosophy of Science* 69(S3 September): S316–S330.

Wulff HR, Pederson SA, Rosenberg R. 1990. *Philosophy of Medicine: An Introduction*, 2nd ed. London: Blackwell Scientific Publications.

Yazdani S, Abardeh MH. 2019 "Five decades of research and theorization on clinical reasoning: a critical review." *Advances in Medical Education* 27(10): 703–716.

Index

For the benefit of digital users, indexed terms that span two pages (e.g., 52–53) may, on occasion, appear on only one of those pages.

Tables are indicated by *t* following the page number.

A
acute respiratory distress syndrome (ARDS), 81–82, 155–156
agency
 CBR and, 156
 clinical experience and, 106
 experiential knowledge and, 106
 medical treatment goal of, 127
 patient values and, 128
 warrants and, 156
allocation concealment (blinding)
 bias addressed by, 42
 criticism of, 42–44
 defense of, 42–43
 definition of, 41–42
 EBM and, 41–45
 generalizability and, 47
 goals of, 42–43
 randomization's relation to, 41–45
analogical reasoning, 55–56, 137–138, 142–144, 153
anatomy
 development of, 18–20, 24–25
 medical education and, 18–19, 95
 "naked eye" form of, 19–20
 physiology as replacing, 25–26
Andersen, Holly, 66–67, 77–79
apprenticeships, 13, 16–17
argumentation, 6–7, 137–138, 144–148, 153
artificial intelligence (AI), 97–98, 102, 138–139

B
balance as basis of health, 13–15, 26, 59
Benner, Patricia, 96–99
bias
 CBR and, 150–151, 157
 clinical experience and, 92
 clinical reasoning and, 105, 157
 confounders and, 44–45, 56
 EBM and, 56–57, 157
 guidelines for addressing, 57
 pharmaceutical-sponsored research and, 56–57
 publication form of, 56–57, 150–151
 randomization and allocation concealment to address, 41–43
blinding. *See* allocation concealment (blinding)
BMJ (British Medical Journal), 56–57, 61, 68
body, the
 disease theories and, 13–14, 18, 26
 as dynamic system, 16
 humor system for, 13–14
 medical knowledge of, 16, 18
 natural healing attributed to, 18
Braude, Hillel, 95–96, 140–141

C
case-based reasoning (CBR)
 agency and, 156
 analogical form of, 142–144, 153
 argumentation in, 144–147, 153
 bias and, 150–151, 157
 case vignette for, 137, 157–158
 causation and, 142
 clinical experience and, 140–141
 clinical judgment as, 153–154
 clinical trials and, 148–149, 150–152
 comparing cases in, 142–144
 construction of cases in, 141
 COVID-19 and, 155–156
 definition of, 138–139
 diagnosis and, 139–140, 142, 144–146, 147–148, 153–155, 157
 EBM and, 143, 145, 149–150, 157
 examples of, 155–157
 experiential knowledge and, 143–144
 generalizability and, 143
 general knowledge and, 159
 idealized cases and, 138, 141–142, 152
 integration problem and, 137–138, 143–145

knowledge and, 141, 154
laboratory research and, 152
limitations of, 139–140
link between cases and warrants in, 152–158
mechanistic understanding of clinical practice and, 142
medical education and, 154
no essential differences condition in, 142–143
overview of, 137–138, 158–160
physiological knowledge and, 141
probability and, 155
RCTs and, 140–141, 149–151, 155–156
rebuttals and, 157
reliable guidance in, 142
source cases in, 139, 140–142, 143–144
steps in, 139–141
structure of, 139
target cases in, 139–141, 152–153
warrants and, 146–158
causation, 73–75, 78–79, 142
CBR. *See* case-based reasoning (CBR)
Clarke, Brendan, 77–79
clinical decision-making
argumentation and, 144–147
clinical experience and, 90, 93
clinical reasoning and, 99–105
cognitive psychology of, 99–105
deductive model of, 54–56
experiential knowledge and, 89, 90–94, 99–105
general knowledge and, 91, 95–96
medical education and, 154
medical knowledge and, 12
narrative and, 132–133
patient values and, 115–124, 130
physiological knowledge and, 74–75, 79
warrants and, 153–154
clinical experience. *See* experiential knowledge
clinical judgment
as case-based reasoning, 153–154
experiential knowledge and, 6, 88
knowledge of particulars and, 6, 95
medical education and, 154
physiological knowledge and, 4–5
rebuttals and, 157
warrants and, 152, 154–157
clinical observation, 19–24, 27
clinical reasoning. *See also* case-based reasoning (CBR)

analogical form of, 55–56, 137–138, 142–144
analytical and non-analytical forms of, 104–105
bias and, 105, 157
clinical decision-making and, 99–105
diagnosis and, 99–101, 102–103, 105–106, 107–109
EBM and, 54–56, 149
empirical research on, 86–87, 98
experiential knowledge and, 89–90, 92, 94, 96, 97–103, 104–110
hypothetico-deductive form of, 100–102
management form of, 108–109
mechanistic form of, 4–5, 59–61, 66–67, 71, 75, 77, 81–82, 149
pathophysiologic form of, 61, 63–64, 75, 79–80, 84
physiological knowledge and, 60, 66–68, 82
script theory and, 109–110
therapeutic forms of, 105–110
warrants and, 148–149
clinical research. *See* clinical trials; evidence-based medicine (EBM); integration problem; randomized controlled trials (RCTs)
clinical trials. *See also* randomized controlled trials (RCTs)
CBR and, 148–149, 150–152
challenges of, 34, 75–76
COVID-19 and, 68–69, 76
databases for, 39–40
EBM's emphasis on, 32–33, 34–36, 39–41, 45–48, 51, 56–57, 150–151
epidemiology and, 31–32
experiential knowledge and, 91
extrapolation from, 41, 47–51, 62, 76
hierarchy of evidence and, 67–68
inclusion/exclusion criteria in, 5, 46, 75
inferential statistics and, 50
knowledge from, 66–74
minimum standards for, 36
moving beyond, 52–56
patient values and, 120, 131–132
physiological knowledge and, 62–63, 66–74, 78, 80–83
pragmatic trials contrasted with, 47–48
reports from, 69–73
warrants and, 149–151
Code of Ethics (AMA), 115
CONSORT statement, 36, 56–57

COVID-19
  ARDS resulting from, 155–156
  CBR and, 155–156
  clinical trials and, 68–69, 76
  experiential knowledge and, 103
  physiological knowledge and, 62
  warrants and, 146–147

D
decision analysis, 119–123
decision-making. *See* clinical decision-making; decision analysis
deductive model of clinical decision-making, 54–56
diagnosis
  abductive reasoning in, 55–56
  CBR and, 139–140, 142, 144–146, 147–148, 153–155, 157
  clinical reasoning and, 99–101, 102–103, 105–106, 107–109
  data and, 146
  EBM and, 52–53, 55–56
  empiricism and, 10, 23
  experiential knowledge and, 88–89, 90–91, 95, 100–109
  hierarchy of evidence and, 35
  instruments for, 28–29
  medical education and, 13, 23, 105
  medical knowledge and, 12, 23, 28
  patient values and, 115, 118–119, 126, 128, 131, 132
  physiological knowledge and, 65–66, 82–83
  rationalism and, 15–16
  script theory and, 109
  tests for, 10, 52–53, 95, 106–108, 114, 146, 157
  warrants and, 146–148
  withholding of, 115
disease theories
  balance as basis of health and, 13–15, 26
  biostatistical theory, 140–141
  body and, 13–14, 18, 26
  humoral theory, 13–15, 49, 59–60
  medical knowledge and, 9, 10–12, 13–16, 23–24, 27
Dreyfus, Hubert, 96–98
Dreyfus, Stuart, 96–98
Dreyfus model of expertise, 96–99

E
EBM. *See* evidence-based medicine (EBM)
EBM Working Group (McMaster University), 32–34, 37, 39–40
education, medical. *See* medical education
Emanuel, Ezekiel and Linda, 113, 115–117, 119
empiricism
  changing understanding of, 10
  class dimensions of, 13–15
  clinical observation and, 19–24, 27
  definition of, 10, 51
  diagnosis and, 10, 23
  EBM and, 48–49, 51
  medical education's emphasis on, 27–28
  medical knowledge and, 10–11, 13, 15–24, 25–29
  Paris Clinical School and, 20–21, 25–28
  quantification as new form of, 21–22
  rationalism's relation to, 10, 13, 22, 25
  surgery associated with, 15
  terminology of, 10–11
epidemiology, 4, 20–21, 31–35, 50, 52–53
epistemology, 3, 6–7, 9, 13, 20–21, 85, 135. *See also* medical epistemology
European models of medical education, 18–19, 23–24
evidence, hierarchy of. *See* hierarchy of evidence
evidence-based medicine (EBM)
  allocation concealment and, 41–45
  bias and, 56–57, 157
  case vignette for, 31, 36–37
  causation and, 73
  CBR and, 143, 145, 149–150, 157
  clinical reasoning and, 54–56, 149
  clinical trials emphasized in, 32–33, 34–36, 39–41, 45–48, 51, 56–57, 150–151
  contributions of, 35
  critical appraisal of studies emphasized in, 34, 36–38, 40, 53
  criticism of, 21–22, 32, 41–48, 41 n.5
  decision analysis and, 120
  deductive model of medical decision-making and, 54–56
  definition of, 32–41
  development of, 21–22, 31–34
  diagnosis and, 52–53, 55–56
  empiricism and, 48–49, 51
  epidemiology as main science underlying, 31–33, 34–35, 50, 52–53

INDEX

experiential knowledge downgraded by, 34–36, 41, 52–53, 85, 87–90
extrapolation of knowledge and, 34–35, 41, 47–51
generalizability emphasized by, 143
goals of, 33, 36–38, 41
hierarchy of evidence and, 35–36, 39, 41–42, 45, 55, 87–88, 91, 93–94, 150
integration problem unsolved by, 3–4, 137
introduction to medical community of, 33–34
laboratory research and, 34–35, 48–49
limitations of, 52–56
medical education and, 32–33, 38
meta-research and, 56–57
moving beyond clinical trials and, 52–56
overview of, 31–32, 58
Paris Clinical School's influence on, 31–32
pharmaceutical industry and, 56–57
physiological knowledge downgraded in, 34, 61–63, 68, 75–78, 81, 91, 93, 94, 150
practice guidelines and, 37–38, 40
probability and, 48, 50–51, 52–53
quality of clinical research promoted by, 36
randomization and, 41–45
rationalism and, 48, 51
research engagement and, 36–39
as school of medical epistemology, 3
specificity principle and, 49
surrogate endpoints and, 34, 54–55
terminology of, 32–33
validity and, 45–48
warrants and, 149–150
"Way of the Future" of, 36–37
"Evidence-Based Medicine Working Group, The" (McMaster University students), 32–34, 37, 39–40
experiential knowledge
agency and, 106
anecdotal and unsystematic forms of, 53, 85, 90
bias and, 92
case vignette for, 85
CBR and, 140–141, 143–144
clinical decision-making and, 89, 90–94, 99–105
clinical judgment and, 6, 88
clinical reasoning and, 89–90, 92, 94, 96, 97–103, 104–110
clinical trials and, 91

cognitive psychology of clinical decision-making and, 99–105
COVID-19 and, 103
definition of, 85–86, 88–89
diagnosis and, 88–89, 90–91, 95, 100–109
Dreyfus model of expertise and, 96–99
EBM's downgrading of, 34–36, 41, 52–53, 85, 87–91, 93–94
experience distinguished from, 91–92
general knowledge and, 11, 91
GRADE system and, 88, 93
hierarchy of evidence and, 87–88, 91, 93–94
information processing and, 88–89
integration problem and, 89–90, 99
intuition and, 104
JAMA article criticizing, 87–88
"knowledge how" and, 95–96
medical education and, 18–20, 24, 99–100, 103
mentorship and, 92
overview of, 85–87, 110–111
patient care and, 90–91, 106
patient values and, 132
phronesis and, 95–96
reflection and, 91–92
script theory and, 102–103, 109–110
sharing of, 92–94
specialization and, 29
unaddressed questions surrounding, 89
warrants and, 147–148
expertise. *See* Dreyfus model of expertise; experiential knowledge
extrapolation of knowledge, 34–35, 41, 47–51, 62, 74–80, 91. *See also* generalizability

F

fallibility, 55, 60, 77, 79–80
Flexner Report (1910), 27–28
French medical education and knowledge, 19, 21–22, 23–24. *See also* Paris Clinical School
Fuller, Jonathan, 56, 150–151

G

generalizability, 45–47, 52, 143. *See also* extrapolation of knowledge
general knowledge
application to individual patients of, 9, 95–96
CBR and, 159
clinical decision-making and, 91, 95–96
EBM and, 54

general knowledge (*Continued*)
  experiential knowledge and, 11, 91
  individual knowledge's relation to, 11–12
German medical education and knowledge, 24–26, 27–28
GRADE system, 41–42, 88, 93
Greek medicine and philosophy, 11, 13–14, 16

H
hierarchy of evidence. *See also* integration problem
  clinical trials and, 67–68
  definition of, 35
  diagnosis and, 35
  EBM and, 35–36, 39, 41–42, 45, 55, 87–88, 91, 93–94, 149–150
  experiential knowledge and, 87–88, 91, 93–94
  limitations of, 58
  physiological knowledge and, 61–62, 66–68
  RCTs prioritized in, 35–36, 41–42, 45, 55, 149–151
  6S approach to, 39
  warrants and, 149–150
Hippocratic tradition, 13–14, 18, 23–24, 49
Howick, Jeremy, 66–67, 77–78, 150 n.2
humoral theory of disease, 13–15, 49, 59–60

I
idealized cases, 138, 141–142, 152
informative model of physician-patient relationship, 117–119, 123, 124–125, 130–131
integration problem. *See also* case-based reasoning (CBR); hierarchy of evidence
  audience for current volume on, 6–7
  case vignette for, 1–2
  CBR and, 137–138, 143–145
  definition of, 2–3
  EBM as unable to solve, 3–4, 137
  experiential knowledge and, 89–90, 99
  generalizability and, 143
  idealized cases, 137–138
  medical knowledge and, 3
  no essential differences condition and, 143
  overview of, 2–3
  philosophy required to address, 2–3
  physiological knowledge and, 74–75
  solving of, 2–3
  structure of current volume on, 3–7

International Council of Medical Journal Editors (ICMJE), 57
intuition, 62, 104, 153

J
JAMA (Journal of the American Medical Association), 33–34, 87–88
Jonsen, Albert, 144–145, 153
judgment. *See* clinical judgment

K
knowledge. *See also* experiential knowledge; general knowledge; medical knowledge; physiological knowledge; warrants
  encapsulated forms of, 101–103, 109–110
  epistemological study of, 3, 6–7, 9, 13, 20–21, 85, 135
  "knowing how" *vs.* "knowing that," 85–86, 94–98
  medical epistemology, 3, 9, 13, 18–19, 29–30
  of particulars, 6, 11–12, 95–96
  philosophical study of, 3, 6–7, 9, 13, 20–21, 85, 135
  probability and, 50
  processed form of, 100–101
  propositional forms of, 94, 99, 104
  tacit form of, 95–100, 105, 109–110
knowledge of mechanisms. *See* physiological knowledge

L
laboratory research
  CBR and, 152
  EBM and, 34–35, 48–49
  medical education and, 27–28
  medical knowledge and, 11, 24–30
  physiological knowledge and, 64–66
Louis, Pierre, 20–22, 49

M
mechanisms, physiological. *See* physiological knowledge
mechanistic reasoning, 4–5, 59–61, 66–67, 71, 75, 77, 81–82, 149
medical decision-making. *See* clinical decision-making
medical education
  anatomy and, 18–19, 95
  CBR and, 154
  clinical decision-making and, 154
  clinical judgment and, 154

INDEX   175

development of, 14–15, 16–19, 27–28
diagnosis and, 13, 23, 105
EBM and, 32–33, 38
empiricism and, 27–28
European models of, 18–19, 23–24
experiential knowledge and, 18–20, 24, 99–100, 103
Flexner Report on, 27–28
laboratory research and, 27–28
limited availability of, 24
medical knowledge and, 16–19, 24, 27–28
mentorship as central to, 92
physiological knowledge and, 60, 63–64, 68, 73
physiology in, 27–28
preclinical and clinical division in, 17
rationalism and, 17–18, 27–28
in US, 17–19, 27–28
warrants and, 154, 159–160
medical epistemology, 3, 9, 13, 18–19, 29–30
medical knowledge
  apprenticeship system and, 16–17
  balance as basis of health and, 13–15, 26
  of the body, 16, 18
  brief history of, 10, 12–29
  clinical decision-making and, 12
  clinical observation and, 19–24
  combined approach required in, 10–11
  diagnosis and, 12, 23, 28
  disease theories and, 9, 10–12, 13–16, 23–24, 27
  empiricism and, 10–11, 13, 15–24, 25–29
  general and individual knowledges in, 11–12, 27
  heroic therapies and, 18, 23–24
  instruments and tools in, 19–20, 23, 25, 28–29
  integration problem and, 3
  medical education and, 16–19, 24, 27–28
  medical gaze and, 20
  medication and, 26–27
  microscopy in, 19–20
  overview of, 8–9, 29–30
  physical examination in, 8–9, 11, 15–16, 19, 23
  physicians distinguished from other practitioners and, 13, 16–17
  quantification resulting in new kind of, 20–22
  rationalism and, 10–11, 13–19, 22, 25–27
  recurring debates on, 29–30
  specialization and, 28–29

speculative realism in, 14–15
stethoscopes and, 23
theory's relation to practice in, 10, 13–19, 22
therapeutic specificity principle and, 14, 23, 27
Medical Nihilism (Stegenga), 150–151
medical training. *See* medical education; medical knowledge
meta-research, 56–57, 150–151
microscopy, 19–20, 24–25, 28

N

narrative medicine, 132–133
National Emphysema Treatment Trial (NETT), 42
National Institutes of Clinical Excellence (NICE) (UK), 78–79
Norman, Geoffrey, 100–101, 104
Number Needed to Treat (NNT), 76, 107

O

observation. *See* clinical observation

P

Paris Clinical School
  clinical counting developed at, 31–32
  clinical observation at, 19–21
  empiricism emphasized at, 20–21, 25–28
  epidemiology's development and, 20–21, 31–32
  lessons from influence of, 22
paternalism, 115–116, 119, 133–134
pathophysiologic reasoning, 61, 63–64, 75, 79–80, 84
patient care, 40, 63–64, 81–82, 90–92
patient values
  agency and, 128
  case vignette for, 112
  change over time in, 118–119, 126–130
  chronic and progressive conditions and, 118–119, 128
  clinical decision-making and, 115–124, 130
  clinical trials and, 120, 131–132
  complicated cases and, 117–118
  decision analysis and, 119–123
  definition of, 113–114
  diagnosis and, 115, 118–119, 126, 128, 131, 132
  eliciting of, 130–135
  empathy for, 133–134
  experiential knowledge and, 132
  health's relationship with, 127–129

patient values (*Continued*)
  limitations of current research on, 131–132
  narrative medicine and, 132–133
  overview of, 112–114, 135–136
  paternalistic model and, 115–116
  Patient Priorities Care (PPC) approach and, 134–135
  phenomenology of illness and, 128–130
  philosophy of medicine and, 126–127
  physician-patient relationship and, 113, 117–119, 126, 130–131, 133–134
  practical guidance for incorporation of, 134–135
  preferences distinguished from, 114, 117, 123
  probability and, 119–122
  quantification of, 119–123
  refusal of treatment and, 117–118
  religious conviction situations and, 117–118
  rights and, 115–116
  significance of, 126–130
  social determinants and, 133
  treatment goals based on, 112–113, 116–117, 118–119, 127–130
  uncertainty about, 118–119
  values-based practice (VBP) and, 123–126, 131–134
pharmaceutical industry, 56–57
philosophy of mechanisms, 63–66
philosophy of medicine
  clinical reasoning in, 97–98
  experiential knowledge in, 95–96
  health and illness concepts in, 126–127
  knowledge in medical practice in, 86–87
  medical incorporation of, 6–7
  patient values in, 113, 126–127
  physiological knowledge in, 64
  tacit knowledge in, 99–100
Philosophy of Medicine (Wulff et al.), 14–15
physician-patient relationship
  common notion of, 135
  deliberative model of, 118–119
  informative model of, 117–119, 123, 124–125, 130–131
  interpretive model of, 118–119
  patient values and, 113, 117–119, 126, 130–131, 133–134
physicians
  apprenticeships for, 16–17
  differences among, 17
  distinguished from other practitioners, 13, 16–17
  education required by, 16–17
  practice emphasized over theory by, 17–18
  rationalism associated with, 13–14, 16–17
physiological knowledge
  assessing effects of therapeutic interventions and, 80–83
  Bayes' theorem and, 71–72
  biological plausibility and, 70–71, 72–74
  case vignette for, 59
  causation and, 73–75, 78–79
  CBR and, 141
  chronic disease and, 83
  clinical decision-making and, 74–75, 79
  clinical judgment and, 4–5
  clinical reasoning and, 60, 66–68, 82
  clinical trials and, 62–63, 66–74, 78, 80–81, 83
  conditions for justified extrapolation and, 74–80
  COVID-19 and, 62
  definition of, 64
  diagnosis and, 65–66, 82–83
  EBM's downgrading of, 34, 61–63, 68, 75–78, 81, 150
  extrapolation of knowledge and, 74–80
  fallibility of knowledge of, 79–80
  hierarchy of evidence and, 61–62, 66–68
  homeopathic remedies and, 70–71
  inclusion and exclusion criteria and, 75–76
  integration problem and, 74–75
  laboratory research and, 64–66
  limitations of, 60–62, 65–66
  medical education and, 60, 63–64, 68, 73
  overview of, 59–61, 84
  pathophysiologic reasoning and, 61, 63–64, 75, 79–80, 84
  philosophy of mechanisms and, 63–66
  principle of similars and, 70
  probability and, 71–72
  randomization and, 69
  RCTs and, 62, 78–79
  surrogate endpoints and, 63, 81–83
physiology, 24–26, 27–29, 59–60. *See also* physiological knowledge
practice guidelines, 37–38, 40, 76, 107, 134–135, 151–152, 157, 159–160
pragmatic trials, 47–48
principle of similars, 70
principle of specificity, 14, 23, 27, 49
probability, 48, 50–51, 52–53, 71–72, 100, 119–122, 155
publication bias, 56–57, 150–151

Q

quantification
- of clinical observation, 20–21
- development and criticism of approaches based on, 21–22
- medical knowledge resulting from, 20–22
- as new form of empiricism, 21–22
- rationalism and, 22
- of values, 119–123

R

randomization
- allocation concealment and, 41–45
- arguments in favor of, 43–45
- bias addressed by, 41–43
- criticism of, 41
- direct and indirect effects and, 43
- EBM's prioritization of, 41–45
- goals of, 43
- physiological knowledge and, 69

randomized controlled trials (RCTs). *See also* clinical trials
- CBR and, 140–141, 149–151, 155–156
- centrality of, 49
- costs associated with, 57
- extrapolation to individual patients of, 48–51
- hierarchy of evidence and, 35–36, 41–42, 45, 55, 149–151
- limitations of, 50–52
- Number Needed to Harm rarely calculated from, 76
- patient sorting and, 50
- pharmaceutical sponsorship of, 57
- physiological knowledge and, 62, 78–79
- probability and, 50–51
- specificity principle and, 49

rationalism
- changing understanding of, 10, 25
- class dimensions of, 13–14
- definition of, 10
- diagnosis and, 15–16
- EBM and, 48, 51
- empiricism's relation to, 10, 13, 22, 25
- medical education and, 17–18, 27–28
- medical knowledge and, 10–11, 13–19, 22, 25–27
- physicians associated with, 13–14, 16–17
- quantification and, 22
- rational therapeutics approach, 26–27
- scientific form of, 26
- speculative form of, 14–15, 25, 29

terminology of, 10
reasoning. *See* clinical reasoning
relationship, physician-patient. *See* physician-patient relationship
research. *See* clinical trials; evidence-based medicine (EBM); integration problem; laboratory research; medical knowledge; pragmatic trials; randomized controlled trials (RCTs)
research engagement, 37–39
Russo-William thesis (RWT), 73–74

S

Sackett, DL, 37–38, 88
script theory, 102–103, 109–110
6S approach, 39
Sox, HC, 120–122
specialization, 24, 28–29
specificity principle, 27, 49
statistics, 50–51, 140–141. *See also* probability
stethoscopes, 19, 23, 28
Sullivan, Mark, 128, 133–134
surrogate endpoints, 34, 54–55, 63, 81–83

T

tacit knowledge, 95–100, 105, 109–110
theories of disease. *See* disease theories
therapeutic specificity principle, 14, 23, 27
Tonelli, MR, 72–73, 91 n.5, 93–94, 133–134
Toulmin, Stephen, 143–148, 152–153. *See also* argumentation
trials. *See* clinical trials

U

United States
- Europe's influence on medical profession in, 13, 18–19
- laboratory research and, 27–28
- medical education in, 17–19, 27–28
- physician and other provider distinction in, 16–18
- research funding in, 57

Users' Guides to Medical Literature, The (Guyatt and Rennie), 35–36 n.2, 62–63, 76, 81

V

validity, 34–35, 37, 45–49, 77
values-based practice (VBP), 123–126, 131–134. *See also* patient values

W

warrants
  agency and, 156
  backing of, 147–152
  case examples of function of, 155–157
  cases as functioning to house, 152–158
  CBR and, 146–158
  clinical context providing, 152
  clinical judgment and, 152, 154–157
  clinical reasoning and, 148–149
  clinical trials and, 149–151
  confidence in, 149, 151
  data's relation to, 146
  diagnosis and, 146–148
  EBM and, 149–150
  experiential knowledge and, 147–148
  general form of, 148, 149t, 151–152
  hierarchy of evidence and, 149–150
  implicit form of, 146, 148, 153
  medical education and, 154, 159–160
  single kind of medical knowledge-backed warrants, 149, 151
  specific form of, 149t, 151–152
  strength of, 146–147, 153
  types of, 149t
Wieten, Sarah, 86–87, 88–90, 124–125
Williamson, Jon, 72–73